Artisans in Europe, 1300–1914

This book is a survey of the history of work in general and of European urban artisans in particular, from the late Middle Ages to the era of industrialization. Unlike traditional histories of work and craftsmen, this book offers a multifaceted understanding of artisan experience situated in the artisans' culture. It treats economic and institutional topics, but also devotes considerable attention to the changing ideologies of work, the role of government regulation in the world of work, the social history of craftspeople, the artisan in rebellion against the various authorities in his world, and the ceremonial and leisure life of artisans. Women, masters, journeymen, apprentices, and nonguild workers all received substantial treatment. The book concludes with a chapter on the nineteenth century, examining the transformation of artisan culture, exploring how and why the early modern craftsman became the industrial wage-worker, mechanic, or shopkeeper of the modern age.

JAMES R. FARR is Professor of History at Purdue University, West Lafayette, Indiana. He is a specialist in French history and the history of work, and has published *Hands of Honour: Artisans and their World in Dijon, 1550–1650* (1988) and *Authority and Sexuality in Burgundy, 1550–1730* (1995).

NEW APPROACHES TO EUROPEAN HISTORY

Series editors
WILLIAM BEIK *Emory University*
T. C. W. BLANNING *Sidney Sussex College, Cambridge*

New Approaches to European History is an important textbook series, which provides concise but authoritative surveys of major themes and problems in European history since the Renaissance. Written at a level and length accessible to advanced school students and undergraduates, each book in the series addresses topics or themes that students of European history encounter daily: the series embraces both some of the more "traditional" subjects of study, and those cultural and social issues to which increasing numbers of school and college courses are devoted. A particular effort is made to consider the wider international implications of the subject under scrutiny.

To aid the student reader scholarly apparatus and annotation is light, but each work has full supplementary bibliographies and notes for further reading: where appropriate chronologies, maps, diagrams, and other illustrative material are also provided.

For a list of titles published in the series, please see end of book.

Artisans in Europe 1300–1914

JAMES R. FARR

Purdue University, West Lafayette, Indiana

CAMBRIDGE
UNIVERSITY PRESS

PUBLISHED BY THE PRESS SYNDICATE OF THE UNIVERSITY OF CAMBRIDGE
The Pitt Building, Trumpington Street, Cambridge, United Kingdom

CAMBRIDGE UNIVERSITY PRESS
The Edinburgh Building, Cambridge, CB2 2RU, UK   www.cup.cam.ac.uk
40 West 20th Street, New York, NY 10011–4211, USA www.cup.org
10 Stamford Road, Oakleigh, Melbourne 3166, Australia
Ruiz de Alarcón 13, 28014 Madrid, Spain

First published 2000

Printed in the United Kingdom at the University Press, Cambridge

Typeset in Plantin 10/12pt   [CE]

A catalogue record for this book is available from the British Library

ISBN 0 521 41888 7 hardback
ISBN 0 521 42934 X paperback

Contents

Figures

Illustrations

Tables

Acknowledgments

Although this book carries my name as the sole author, no work of history stands alone. In the last decade or so there has been an outpouring of publications on Europe's artisans before 1900. Most of this literature centers on the eighteenth and nineteenth centuries, but enough exists on the late medieval and early modern period that a book like this can be written. This was decidedly not the case scarcely fifteen years ago. I am, therefore, first and foremost indebted to the scores of authors who, while I was working on my monograph on Dijon's artisans in the early 1980s, were working silently on the multifaceted artisanal experience in many other European towns and cities. The fruits of their labor I have harvested in this survey, although, of course, I alone bear the responsibility for how I have woven their findings into my own interpretation – reflecting a "new approach," to invoke the title of the series in which this book appears – of the meaning and cultural significance of this collective experience.

I also owe deep debts of gratitude to several scholars who graciously read drafts of the manuscript, sometimes more than once, and who generously offered bibliographic suggestions. Without the criticism and fruitful suggestions of Steve Kaplan, Gail Bossenga, Len Rosenband, Chris Friedrichs, Phil Benedict, and Jim Amelang, this book, whatever its current merits, would have been distinctly inferior. Several institutions have likewise contributed to this project. I warmly thank the American Council of Learned Societies and the Shelby Cullom Davis Center at Princeton University for their generous support.

Finally, I thank my mother, Mary Margaret Farr. She has always carried an almost mystical veneration for the past within her, and no doubt on those family vacations of my youth when historical sites and monuments constantly dotted our itineraries, she instilled in me an appreciation of the connectedness between the present and the past, between the living and the dead.

West Lafayette, Indiana, 1998   JAMES R. FARR

Introduction

This book is about artisans in Europe's cities and towns from the late Middle Ages into the era of industrialization. It is also about modernization which, as we will see, was a process that partly shaped and was shaped by the unfolding history of labor, laborers, and labor relations. On such a large canvas, how does one rough out meaningful generalizations? Historians who make comparisons across vast stretches of time and place tread upon a knife's edge: on one side lurks the trap of endless listings of difference; on the other dwells the danger of underrepresenting the heterogeneity and diversity of the European artisanry by overdetermining similarities. It is difficult to generalize about crafts and craftsmen and craftswomen, for, as we will see, trades in urban society varied greatly from one to another. And yet, amid all of this diversity, we can still make out an outline of a more or less coherent artisan culture that endured for half a millennium.

To speak of artisan culture sets this book apart from most previous histories of craftsmen and craftswomen. In the mid- to late nineteenth century artisans became subjects of historical investigation, and since then three types of writings have emerged. One longs nostalgically for a world that was rapidly disappearing. This romantic vision of artisan life emphasizes the organic and communal nature of the artisan world, and overtly contrasts it with the emergent industrial society which these authors perceive to be plagued by anomie and social fragmentation. These histories are marked by their authors' implicit conviction that the artisanal, preindustrial past was a better world that had fallen victim to the destructive, antisocial forces of industrial capitalism. In these accounts we find the guild as the central institution in artisan life, and a ready assumption that prescription – the dictates of guild statutes and by-laws which so often sought to harmonize the relationships between guild brethren – reflected practice, or the actual behavior of artisans.

From the pens of economic historians also have flowed guild histories, and these, too, generally have accepted prescription as practice; but here, guild regulations against competition, for example, have not been

1

viewed positively as guarantors of societal harmony. Rather they have been taken to task for impeding the emergent free economy of liberal capitalism. The guild as millstone around the neck of economic growth is a theme that has had a near stranglehold on historical writings on guilds for most of the twentieth century.

The third perspective that has distinctly marked artisan histories written since the late nineteenth century is one that, like the nostalgic guild histories, equally emerged from assumptions about the impact of capitalism on traditional social relations. Here, however, the authors intend to account for the history of working-class formation. If the guild histories have tended to focus our attention upon master craftsmen, working-class histories have shifted our scrutiny to journeymen.

Each of these perspectives on artisan history has merit, but it tells only part of the story and, moreover, the explanatory power of each is often sapped by an overdetermined economism that informs its author's assumptions. At worst, such histories are teleological and even tautological, positing capitalism as the natural economy and guild or governmental regulation, therefore, as artificial and somehow unnatural. This liberal fallacy rests upon two questionable assumptions that have weakened guild histories for decades: first, that the existence of government or guild regulations in historical records is evidence for their effectiveness, and second, that regulatory activity in the economy "distorts" it and renders the system within its stultifying grasp "inadequate" to meet the demand that would otherwise be met in a "free," self-regulating economy. To measure economies and the role of guilds within them in this way, however, is ahistorical, misleading, and even tautological, for it assumes without empirical proof that a natural economy (if such existed) would function in an expansionary and developmental mode. This hypothetical system then becomes the measuring stick for actual economies which, like the craft economy of early modern Europe, are then in turn declared inadequate and distorted.

Yet even the working-class or guild histories that avoid such tendentious and circular reasoning often are narrowly informed by economistic assumptions, and so ignore a multiplicity of other logics that went into the construction of artisan culture. Surely an understanding of the artisan experience requires more than examining its economic dimension, important as that was? As Gervase Rosser recently wrote, "Much of the over-simplification of traditional views [of artisans] results from the failure to recognize that an individual simultaneously possessed plural identities . . . The very concept of the 'artisan' in modern historiography has tended to be too unitary and too static." He rightly concludes that "the categories of 19th century discourse have blinkered modern interpretation."[1]

What, then, was an artisan? A deceptively simple question becomes surprisingly complex when we shift away from the traditional frameworks in which this question could be answered toward one informed by cultural analysis. One could respond to this question, as many historians have before, that artisans were members of guilds, or one could offer a production-centered definition, that artisans were skilled people who fashioned artifacts with their hands and tools but without the aid of machinery, the classic handicraftsmen. Yet even according to this definition we must note diversity, since "artisans" can be placed on a spectrum with, at one end, a journeyman working for wages little distinguishable (from our labor-centered perspective though, as we will see, certainly not from the journeyman's perspective) from wage-workers with no connection to the world of journeymen. At the other end of the spectrum we find entrepreneurial artisans no longer working primarily with their hands, spending most of their time wholesaling products or managing their enterprises. These men and women are almost indistinguishable (again from an economistic perspective) from merchants. Indeed, the boundaries at each end of the spectrum were porous, with men and women sliding into and out of what we think of as artisanal activity. In this book we will encounter "artisans" involved in many types of labor and production. As we will see, however, such a definition, important as it is, is only partial.

Karl Marx has been immeasurably influential in how historians have thought about craftsmen in particular and labor history in general. He isolated labor as the quality that makes us truly human, and assumed that economic rationality was essential to the labor process. Marx, for all his historicism, nonetheless "naturalized" labor no less than classical economists like Adam Smith or David Ricardo had before him, making it the foundation of the edifice of culture. Most historians of artisans, Marxist or not, have similarly "essentialized" labor, assuming that this activity defined an artisan's identity.

These traditional institutional and economic frameworks, however, are insufficient to analyze important aspects of the experience of the groups of people – men and women – whom we have labeled "artisans." Not every such person in fact belonged to a guild (few women did in their own right), nor were weavers (as they would be the first to tell us) simply men or women who happened to weave thread, bakers simply men or women who happened to cook bread. To grasp the sense that

[1] Gervase Rosser, "Crafts, guilds and the negotiation of work in the medieval town," *Past and Present* 154 (1997), 8–9.

these men and women had of themselves and that others had of them, requires moving beyond an institutional or productive (even economic) framework toward one that can accommodate both meaning and questions of identity.

To explain how artisans fashioned their identities and shaped their culture, let us consider the matter of status. As we will see, artisans from the late Middle Ages well into the nineteenth century were defined and defined themselves not primarily as producers as their labels may suggest, but rather as members of an *état*, a rank or "degree," a *Stand*. They designated themselves (and were so designated by the authorities) by occupational label not just because this described what they did (it often did not), but rather because it signaled status, for in the old regime status was in part contained through naming and the possession of titles. In the historical context of the hierarchical world of early modern Europe, identity (artisanal, or any other) was formed through erecting and maintaining boundaries between an imagined "us" and "them," and so identity was rooted in, as Peter Sahlins puts it, "a subjective experience of difference."[2] It was, therefore, relational, and contingent upon context. If we think of cultures as "meaningful orders of persons and things,"[3] then we might also recognize that groups of people cohere around shared values and activities. To keep the howling chaos of experience at bay, groups imagine boundaries of their communities in part by locating and defining activities in specified places – homes, workplaces, churches, taverns, and so on – and delimiting who belongs within them. By including or excluding individuals from those places or from performing those activities, they spell out the membership of the group, and so contribute to the ongoing process of shaping a culture. Of course, individuals can and do belong to multiple groups, resulting often but not necessarily in a hierarchical valuation of the various groups by the individuals so engaged.

Work, I would suggest, can best be understood when it is imbedded in cultural relations of which it was only a part, however important. Again, to quote Rosser:

work . . . so far from being a mere function of socio-economic relations, was a varied, complex and evolving process, negotiated between individuals, which itself contributed significantly to the formation of ideas about society as a whole. Social structure, far from being a given, is the constantly renewed and revised product of human agency, however much that agency is framed by inherited circumstances.[4]

[2] Peter Sahlins, *Boundaries: The Making of France and Spain in the Pyrenees* (Berkeley, 1989), p. 271.
[3] Marshall Sahlins, *Culture and Practical Reason* (Chicago, 1976), p. x.
[4] Rosser, 3.

Rather than assuming that an artisan found his or her social being defined by his or her labor, then, we might profit from thinking of an artisan's life (and his or her work) as being in important ways a product of what we might call symbolic exchanges, where labor was a sign of social place as well as a means to survival or material accumulation. Such exchanges were brief encounters in continually shifting situations, and so were simultaneously dynamic and structured by a shared system of communication in which meaning inhered. Because incessant change rendered friendships fleeting and social groups fragile, networks and alliances were continually recreated and reconstituted. It was through these infinite encounters and exchanges of "symbolic capital" that artisans continually fashioned and refashioned their sense of a coherent identity, remembering from the immediate past the attributes that defined them while plunging ineluctably into the future, a context forever in flux. Simultaneously and inextricably they established and reestablished their place within the taxonomic structure of society through an apprehension of difference, distinction, and status.

Late medieval and early modern society was increasingly organized across the intersecting axes of hierarchy and subordination, and so it was taken as natural that some people commanded more power, more resources, and more respect than others. Everywhere Europeans divided themselves more and more into a series of graduated ranks. Sometimes this was done formally by institutions authorized by political authorities (for example, through sumptuary laws which dictated what one could wear), sometimes informally. Nor was occupation the only or even the chief determinant of social place or social status, which was mostly determined by a mixture of criteria based on family, office, wealth, or membership in particular institutions (like guilds, or confraternities, which served as devices for social distinction, differentiation, and rank as well as placement in the social and political firmament). Old regime taxonomy was a structured system of hierarchical differences which reached its highwater mark in the seventeenth century, a structure which was nonetheless dynamic, fragile, and unstable. It was within this structure, a product of an incessant interrelationship of prescription and practice, that individuals and groups of individuals made their lives meaningful. Social and self-definition were rooted in cultural experiences which included, but also transcended, production; these definitions were profoundly influenced by shifts in political, legal, intellectual, as well as economic, developments across these centuries. Artisans did not make themselves in isolation, nor were they hapless victims simply molded by forces beyond their control. They were products of their own ceaseless struggle, not just to earn a living, but to maintain rank and a sense of social place in the face of powerful, often inimical forces in their world, turning these forces to their advantage when they could, suffering fragmentation or transformation when they could not.

As society's elites increasingly distanced themselves from the craftsmen, artisans in turn became increasingly keen on defining the distance between themselves and their inferiors. At all social levels, this process of dissociation was visualized by cultural markers, and the key badge of artisanal status could be summed up in the word "honor." This swung on the hinge of respectability, and was the stuff of the dreams of all artisans, be they master, journeyman, or nonguild worker, as they were of the inimitable eighteenth-century French glazier and author of *A Journal of My Life*, Jacques-Louis Ménétra. Honorable, however, could mean a variety of things. For the master craftsman it could mean economic solvency and heading one's own reputable business and respectable household, while for a journeyman it surely meant being subject to no one's discipline, with no restrictions on one's freedom of movement.

Honor carried multiple meanings, but everywhere it cemented cultural ties. It would be difficult to overemphasize the importance of honor in the daily life of medieval and early modern artisans. Honor was society's measure of social standing in the hierarchy as it was a marker of personal self-esteem. At both levels, honor was a paramount social value that enforced standards of accepted conduct and measured an individual's actions and worth against a norm recognized by peers, superiors, and inferiors. Duty and obligation, revenge and redress against insult and humiliation, even vindication by violence, were all subsumed in a code of honor which relied on the notion that the social hierarchy was established by God and was mediated through signs and symbols by which the hierarchy could be "read."

The obverse of the coin of status and honor was discipline and subordination. Indeed, in many ways, as we will see, they were interdependent. These interlocked themes – status, honor, discipline, subordination – are woven like so many colored threads through most of this book.

One thread that can only intermittently be included in this tapestry is the history of female artisans. This book will largely be about men and about their activities and their identities. We now know that huge amounts of artisanal work was done by women, and we know that the household economy, largely the preserve of the woman, was inextricably linked to the craft and market economy beyond the home. All of these activities will receive attention in the pages that follow, but the fact remains that artisanal organization, political expression, public life, and identity in early modern Europe were overwhelmingly masculine, and it is precisely because of the strongly gendered assumptions of the Old Regime and their ubiquitous inscription in the historical record left to the scrutiny of historians that the primary subject of this book will be men.

Bibliography

In the bibliography of this chapter the reader will find general histories of European artisans as well as titles of a more theoretical nature. Some works contain material covered in subsequent chapters, but for the sake of space, those titles will only be listed here.

Entries marked with a * designate recommended readings for new students of the subject.

Baudrillard, Jean. *The Mirror of Production.* Trans. Mark Poster. St. Louis, 1975.
*Berlanstein, Lenard R., ed. *Rethinking Labor History.* Urbana, 1993.
*Block, Fred, and Margaret Somers. "Beyond the economistic fallacy: the holistic social science of Karl Polanyi." In Theda Skocpol, ed., *Vision and Method in Historical Sociology.* Cambridge, 1986, pp. 47–84.
Canning, K. "Gender and the politics of class formation: rethinking German labor history." *American Historical Review* 97 (1992), 736–68.
*Cerutti, Simona. *La Ville et les métiers. Naissance d'un langage corporatif (Turin, XVIIe–XVIIIe siècles).* Paris, 1990.
Coornaert, Emile. *Les Corporations en France avant 1789.* Paris, 1968.
Corfield, Penelope J. "Defining urban work." In Penelope J. Corfield and Derek Keene, eds., *Work in Towns, 850–1850.* Leicester, 1990, pp. 207–30.
Corfield, Penelope J., and Derek Keene, eds. *Work in Towns, 850–1850.* Leicester, 1990.
Crossick, Geoffrey, ed. *The Artisan and the European Town, 1500–1900.* Aldershot, 1997.
Davis, J. "Rules not laws: outline of an ethnographic approach to economics." In Bryan Roberts, Ruth Fennegan, and Duncan Gallie, eds., *New Approaches to Economic Life.* Manchester, 1985.
*Davis, Robert C. *Shipbuilders of the Venetian Arsenal: Workers and Workplace in the Preindustrial City.* Baltimore, 1991.
Epstein, Steven. *Wage Labor and Guilds in Medieval Europe.* Chapel Hill, 1991.
*Farr, James R. *Hands of Honor: Artisans and Their World in Dijon, 1550–1650.* Ithaca, 1988.
"Cultural analysis and early modern artisans." In Geoffrey Crossick, ed., *The Artisan and the European Town, 1500–1900.* Aldershot, 1997, pp. 56–74.
Friedrichs, Christopher. *Urban Society in an Age of War: Nördlingen, 1580–1720.* Princeton, 1979.
Geremek, Bronislaw. *Le Salariat dans l'artisanat parisien aux XIIIe–XVe siècles.* Paris, 1962.
Godelier, Maurice. "Work and its representations." *History Workshop Journal* 10 (1980), 164–74.

Haskell, Thomas L., and Richard F. Teichgraeber III, eds. *The Culture of the Market: Historical Essays.* Cambridge, 1996.

Hauser, Henri. *Ouvriers du temps passé.* Paris, 1899.

Howell, Martha. *Women, Production and Patriarchy in Late Medieval Cities.* Chicago, 1986.

Joyce, Patrick. "In pursuit of class: recent studies in the history of work and class." *History Workshop Journal* 15 (1988), 171–7.

*Joyce, Patrick, ed. *The Historical Meanings of Work.* Cambridge, 1987.

*Kaplan, Steven L. *The Bakers of Paris and the Bread Question, 1700–1775.* Durham, 1996.

Le Goff, Jacques. *Time, Work and Culture in the Middle Ages.* Chicago, 1980.

Lespinasse, René de. *Les Métiers et corporations de Paris.* 3 vols. Paris, 1886–94.

Levasseur, Emile. *Histoire des classes ouvrières et de l'industrie en France.* 2 vols. Paris, 1901.

Lottin, Alain. *Chavatte, ouvrier Lillois. Un contemporain de Louis XIV.* Paris, 1979.

*Lucie-Smith, Edward. *The Story of Craft: The Craftsman's Role in Society.* Ithaca, 1981.

Martin Saint-Leon, Etienne. *Histoire des corporations de métiers.* Geneva, 1976.

*Mackenney, Richard. *Tradesmen and Traders: The World of the Guilds in Venice and Europe, 1250–1650.* Totowa, 1987.

*Ménétra, Jacques-Louis. *A Journal of My Life.* Trans. Arthur Goldhammer. New York, 1986.

Mokyr, Joel. *The Lever of Riches: Technological Creativity and Economic Progress.* Oxford, 1990.

Montias, John Michael. *Artists and Artisans in Delft: A Socio-Economic Study of the Seventeenth Century.* Princeton, 1982.

Moss, Bernard H. *The Origins of the French Labor Movement, 1830–1914: The Socialism of Skilled Workers.* Berkeley, 1976.

Nicholas, David. *Medieval Flanders.* London, 1992.

Poitrineau, Abel. *Ils travaillaient la France. Métiers et mentalités du XVIe au XIXe siècle.* Paris, 1992.

Rancière, Jacques. "The myth of the artisan: critical reflections on a category of social history." *International Labor and Working Class History* 24 (1983), 1–16.

Reddy, William M. *The Rise of Market Culture: The Textile Trade and French Society, 1750–1900.* Cambridge, 1984.

*Rosser, Gervase. "Crafts, guilds and the negotiation of work in the medieval town." *Past and Present* 154 (1997), 8–9.

*Rule, John. *The Experience of Labour in Eighteenth-Century English Industry.* New York, 1981.

*Safley, Thomas M., and Leonard Rosenband, eds. *The Workplace before the Factory: Artisans and Proletarians, 1500–1800.* Ithaca, 1993.

Sahlins, Marshall. *Culture and Practical Reason.* Chicago, 1976.

*Sewell, William, Jr. *Work and Revolution in France.* Cambridge, 1980.

Sonenscher, Michael. *The Hatters of Eighteenth-Century France.* Berkeley, 1987.

  Work and Wages: Natural Law, Politics and the Eighteenth-Century French Trades. Cambridge, 1989.

*Swanson, Heather. *Medieval Artisans: An Urban Class in Late Medieval England.* Oxford, 1989.

*Walker, Mack. *German Home Towns: Community, State, and General Estate, 1648–1871.* Ithaca, 1971.

*Wiesner, Merry E. *Working Women in Renaissance Germany.* New Brunswick, 1986.

Woodward, Donald. *Men at Work: Labourers and Building Craftsmen in the Towns of Northern England, 1450–1750.* Cambridge, 1995.

Zeitlin, Jonathan. "Social theory and the history of work." *Social History* 8:3 (1983), 365–74.

1 The meaning of work: ideology and organization

Worthy or disgraceful?

From the Middle Ages to the industrial age men (and it was exclusively educated men who wrote about this) have had an ambivalent, even sometimes paradoxical, attitude to work. In the contemporary western world where the work ethic is so firmly embedded in our assumptions about nearly all of our activity, it seems peculiar that work could ever have been anything but positively valued. After all, are not the fruits of labor the goods and services western society so voraciously consumes and ostensibly values? And yet, it has not always been so. Indeed, only in the last 200 years has a positive connotation of work held sway, largely because of the triumph of a particular way of thinking about society and the role of economics within it. We call it modernity. As theorists like Adam Smith or Karl Marx reified and abstracted economics as the essential force shaping particular societies (notably their own), work, at least among the educated, was viewed more positively. How did this dramatic transformation in the thinking about labor come to pass? And how did educated men think about labor before?

The Greek philosophers Plato, and especially Aristotle, had an enormous influence on the way medieval men thought about nearly everything, and these Greek sages had considered manual labor as base activity, marking the laborer as inferior to men (like themselves) who did not work. They placed higher value upon intellectual activity than technical skill, and ranked men hierarchically in proportion to their possession of these qualities. Thus the pensive philosopher was superior to the craftsman who was nonetheless, by virtue of his possession of some creative genius, superior to the manual laborer (quite often a slave) who simply carried out the ideas of someone else.

For no medieval philosopher or theologian was work a central preoccupation, but we can glean from the writings of many of the leading minds of the age what work meant to them, and how they believed that it should be organized in society. Not surprisingly, all were influenced by the Classical legacy, and though it was cast now in the Christian mold, the negative connotation about the value of work remained. In the fifth century CE, Saint Augustine incorporated in *The City of God* the Pauline dictum that man's original sin of disobedience had condemned him to labor "by the sweat of his brow." Augustine also asserted that sin had created servitude "by which man is subjected to man by the bonds of his condition."[1] Bringing these two postulates together – sin and servitude – justified the principles of hierarchy and discipline in society and in the workshop. These principles, although eventually purged of their religious trappings, were to guide the thinking of men about work and its organization for the next 1,500 years.

Augustine certainly contributed to the continuation of a negative valuation of work by associating it with hierarchy and servitude, but he injected ambiguity when he also wrote that man's rational faculties were applied in work (thus setting the species apart from and above the animals), and that the products of labor help man to realize God's designs. Both the positive and negative ideas about work were appropriated by medieval theologians, as were Aristotelian teachings.

In the twelfth and thirteenth centuries Hugh of Saint Victor and Thomas Aquinas believed that manual labor protected against the vice of sloth, while Saint Bonaventure even identified God Himself as the first worker. In the twelfth century John of Salisbury envisioned society as a human organism, and represented workers – peasants and craftsmen – as the feet of the *respublica*, lowly but necessary.

Still, despite the tepidly positive spin these thinkers placed on labor, they remained convinced that work must be organized according to hierarchy and discipline. John of Salisbury placed workers at the feet, not the head, of the social organism. Bonaventure may have exalted God as the first worker, but he also viewed work by humans as servile and therefore base activity. Aristotelians in the new universities taught that the liberal and mechanical arts were utterly distinct, that the former dealt with the mind and the latter the hands, and furthermore that the liberal arts were superior to the mechanical. Aquinas may have noted that society was stitched together in part by mutual exchange of goods and services and that artisans thereby made an essential contribution to the good life, but he also taught that the social system must have a ruling part which decidedly did not include the craftsman, and that the equilibrium of the system depended upon hierarchy and obedience.

Indeed, every theologian believed in the Christian virtue of obedience, and agreed that work inescapably must contribute to it. Work was, in

---

[1] Quoted in Peter Anthony, *The Ideology of Work* (London, 1977), pp. 26–7.

short, a spiritual discipline. Medieval theologians, therefore, did not think about work in terms of economic calculation or the material value of production, that effort would somehow create wealth and better one's position in life. Instead, they conceived of work in moral terms, a distinctly premodern notion.

Inherited from the Middle Ages and stamped on the minds of early modern men was, in Michel Foucault's words, "a certain ethical consciousness of labor" which possessed "a certain force of moral enchantment."[2] The theological component of this mentality, as we have seen, held that labor was a penance imposed on humankind for original sin; redemptive, but also a curse. Man did not labor to nurture the fruits of nature. Indeed, in the sixteenth century the Protestant reformer John Calvin taught that labor had no such power, that the fertility of nature was the special and exclusive preserve of God's will. The French Catholic bishop Jacques-Bénigne Bossuet would effectively concur more than a century later: "At each moment, the hope of the harvest and the unique fruit of all our labors may escape us; we are at the mercy of the inconstant heavens that bring down rain upon the tender ears."[3] No, the value of labor was not its productive capacity, but its moral force. This was a view still current in sermons in the late seventeenth and early eighteenth centuries. As the well-known French Oratorian, professor of theology, and influential preacher Jean-Baptiste Massillon succinctly put it at that time, "to work is to be saved."[4]

As Augustinianism enjoyed increased influence in the early modern age, so too did the theological notion that work is spiritual discipline and, as such, is closely tied to ideas of obedience and servitude. Augustine had taught that the greatest enemy of the soul was idleness, and that work was the soul's greatest defense against it. Because God had ordered man to labor "by the sweat of his brow," idleness was rank rebellion against God and society. Labor, in this way of thinking, was at once the bulwark against the social disorder which inevitably followed idleness, and the assault of evil upon the soul. It thus contributed to security in this world and salvation in the next. Louis Bourdaloue, a tremendously popular French preacher and one favored by Louis XIV in the second half of the seventeenth century, said in a sermon: "What then is the disorder of an idle life? It is . . . in its true meaning a second rebellion of the creature against God."[5] For the priest, the jurist, the

---

[2] Michel Foucault, *Madness and Civilization* (New York, 1968), p. 55.
[3] Quoted in Foucault, p. 56.
[4] Quoted in Abel Poitrineau, *Ils travaillaient la France. Métiers et mentalités du XVIe au XIXe siècle* (Paris, 1992), p. 8.
[5] Quoted in Foucault, p. 57.

government administrator, idleness became "the mother of all vices" and the poor and unemployed the *a priori* culprits of disorder. Everywhere in the seventeenth century sloth, the inverse of labor, replaced avarice as the most "deadly sin" and was considered the absolute form of rebellion.

Of course, the men voicing these views on idleness and work were prescribing a regimen applicable not to themselves, but to those of inferior social rank whose lot it was to labor. Here they betray a deeply held belief in a supposed "naturalness" of rank hierarchy, that certain people are naturally situated in society to perform certain functions. Obedience, servitude, and hierarchy were thus thought to go hand in hand and were all legitimated by nature, and thus by God, and labor as a form of discipline suitable to certain ranks of society was assumed to be entirely natural and good. Early seventeenth-century English poets and playwrights Thomas Deloney, Thomas Heywood, and Thomas Dekker all chose craftsmen as subjects of some of their works, and each assumed that diligent labor was neither a good in itself nor a means to escape a lowly social position. Rather, as service and obedience, it was a fundamental prop to right, that is hierarchical, order.

Later in the century the widely read author of treatises on political economy, Sir William Petty, wrote from the same perspective that the poor must be kept at work, however useless, "to keep their minds to discipline and obedience."[6] His contemporary Thomas Firmin wrote in *Some Proposals for the Imployment of the Poor* in 1681 that it matters not "what you employ these poor children in, as that you do employ them in some thing, to prevent an idle, lazy kind of life, which if once they get the habit of, they will hardly leave."[7]

In the next century Voltaire still conceived of work, in *Candide*, not as a generator of wealth, but rather as an agency of social control, an antidote to vice, and, above all, to idleness. For most commentators (although not for Voltaire), industry was seen as a virtue with a religious quality. Josiah Tucker wrote in 1757 that "the rules of religion and the rules of social industry do perfectly harmonize . . . [and] all things hurtful to the latter are indeed a violation of the former." Jonas Hanway added ten years later that "honest industry is an essential part of religion, and the ways of it are a reward of virtue, and an earnest of happiness after death." Indeed, idle persons were vilified; as the eighteenth-century verse put it, "Satan finds some mischief still/for idle

---

[6] Quoted in Joyce Appleby, *Economic Thought and Ideology in Seventeenth-Century England* (Princeton, 1978), p. 144.

[7] Quoted in ibid., p. 141.

hands to do," and idleness was considered by some, like Edward Barry in 1789, to be "the fruitful root of every vice."[8]

People who worked with their hands, of course, bore the brunt of this moralizing. They were often seen as naturally inclined toward idleness, which in turn revealed them as an insubordinate multitude. In 1770 the author of *An Essay on Trade and Commerce* intoned that "the labouring people should never think themselves independent of their superiors; for if proper subordination is not kept up, riot and confusion will take [the] place of sobriety and order."[9]

Already in 1649 Peter Chamberlen was anticipating what the likes of Firmin, Tucker, or Hanway were writing decades later, associating work with discipline. Chamberlen even added the important concept of civility to the mix. He wrote in *The Poore Man's Advocate* "it is certain that employment and competencies do civilise all men, and makes [*sic*] them tractable and obedient to superiors' command."[10] That labor disciplines and contributes to the "civilizing process," a development Norbert Elias, Robert Muchembled, and Georges Vigarello, among others, have shown was grounded in social distinction and thus had profound hierarchical qualities, was an opinion that had become commonplace across Europe in the 1700s. In 1753, in a treatise *On the Utility of the Sciences and the Arts*, the Abbé Talbert wrote that man is distinguished from animal not by soul or morality, but by, among other qualities, his capacity for work which has, he continued, a civilizing effect. Work teaches self-discipline, a hallmark of the civilized individual: "[Work] is the file that smoothes away our rough edges and polishes away... disorder and vice."[11]

Ideas about obedience, discipline, labor, hierarchy, and civility thus came together in the minds of many men of letters, but they also found a home among government administrators. Indeed, perhaps the clearest application of these ideas in the seventeenth and eighteenth centuries is the workhouse, first an institution of punishment for incarcerated condemned criminals, and later a repository of idle beggars and the unemployed. In France in 1611, 1612, 1617, and 1618 for the first time statutes authorized that incarcerated criminals be forced to work. Similarly, many condemned criminals were sentenced to forced labor, either pulling the oars aboard the king's galleys in the Mediterranean, or building the vessels in the vast shipyard in Toulon, the *bagne*.

---

[8] Quoted in Robert W. Malcolmson, *Popular Recreations in English Society, 1700–1850* (Cambridge, 1973), pp. 91, 92.
[9] Quoted in ibid., p. 96.
[10] Quoted in Appleby, p. 144.
[11] Quoted in Cynthia Koepp, "The order of work: attitudes and representations in eighteenth-century France," Ph.D. dissertation, Cornell University, 1992, pp. 395–6.

As the number of beggars increased across Europe in the seventeenth and eighteenth centuries, especially after 1650, workhouses were enlisted more and more to treat this severe social problem. Workhouses like the Hôpital Général system in France, the Spinhuis and Rasphuis in the Netherlands, the Zuchthaus in Hamburg, or the 126 such establishments established in Britain and Ireland between 1697 and 1800, demanded that labor be performed as an exercise in moral reform and discipline. These "fortresses of moral order," as Foucault calls them, were designed during this "age of confinement" first to discipline the interned beggars, infirm, and unemployed – idle all, and many of them children – for their moral well-being and, by their removal from the streets of Europe's cities, for the social order of the world beyond the walls of the workhouse. In 1684 a royal decree concerning the Hôpital in Paris dictated that work must occupy the greater part of the day of the inmates, but it must also be accompanied by "the reading of pious books." Earlier in the century the directors of the Zuchthaus in Hamburg were similarly morally preoccupied: they were to see that "all in the house are properly instructed as to religious and moral duties . . . [The schoolmaster] must take care that they attend divine service, and are orderly at it."[12]

Morality and productivity

From one perspective, quite clearly, labor performed in workhouses had a primarily moral rather than productive purpose – it instilled discipline – and so was in step with what we might call the premodern or traditional view of labor. During the seventeenth century, however, new, what we might call modern, ideas about the meaning of labor which *did* have productive qualities began to gain currency. In the minds of some men, forced labor was thought of not only as a moral tonic, but also as an economic strategy. Jean-Baptiste Colbert, France's Controller-General and mastermind of his king's economic policies in the second half of the seventeenth century, regarded labor in workhouses, beyond its moral contribution, as a remedy for unemployment as well as a contribution to the development of manufactories. Similarly, when the workhouse in Bristol was established in 1697, its founder John Carey hoped that his interned workers would produce cheaply and thus restrain prices in the local markets where the products of the workhouse would be sold. Early the next century Daniel Defoe observed what was becoming apparent everywhere as workhouses competed in local econo-

---

[12] Quoted in Foucault, pp. 60, 61.

mies, usually producing textiles: that such institutions, by their cheap labor and cheap products, provided such competition for nearby trades that it created more of what it was designed to eliminate – unemployment and poverty.

These views on the productive potential of forced labor are but part of more general ideas about the productivity of labor being heard in the seventeenth century. Mercantilists focused on strengthening the state, and sought to organize and regulate its economic life to accomplish this. Increasing the productivity of a regulated society, therefore, garnered their attention more than did the means of distribution, and mercantilists like Colbert concluded that productivity would be increased by employing as many individuals as possible as much of the time as possible. They framed their regulatory ideas according to an intellectual tradition of long standing, that is, corporatively and thus hierarchically, viewing society as an organism, akin to a living body where the parts obey the head. When Antoine de Montchrestien wrote in his *Traité d'économie politique* in 1615 that the kingdom's idle poor were a vast, untapped reservoir of a workforce, he was a harbinger of later voices, some that were mercantilist, others like Adam Smith's that would hypostasize the idea of productivity inherent in labor. When this latter way of thinking became dominant in the late eighteenth century, a seachange in the meaning of labor and its "proper" organization had occurred. Indeed, this rethinking of the meaning of work took a central place in an even broader reconceiving of the role of economies in human affairs. The traditional was giving way to the modern.

Although in 1600 the idea of an abstract "market" as a "representation of countless exchanges that regularly took place" did not exist in the minds of men, it began to take hold shortly after.[13] Paralleling ideas in the sciences that posited motion rather than rest as the natural state of matter, Englishmen like Thomas Mun and Edward Misselden theorized that economies were no less a part of the natural order and thus were naturally in motion. In the 1620s Mun conceived of an economy as "a flow of goods and money," while Misselden, in *The Circle of Commerce* published in 1623, held that there were natural laws that guided economic activity. In the early seventeenth century ideas like these were deeply subversive, for they challenged the inherited mental construct of order on intellectual, social, and political levels. First, these ideas about motion and natural economic laws undermined the belief that the natural and social order were, by God's design, immutable, that God's creation was structured in fixed statuses. Second, as Misselden explicitly

---

[13] Appleby, p. 21.

pointed out, the operation of these laws was beyond the power of the prince, or the head of the body, to control.

Of course, men expressing these ideas were not anarchists; they, like everyone else in the early modern period, believed in a determinable order. Indeed, their theorizing was an attempt to conceive of a satisfying order. They simply but profoundly disagreed on its properties. Whatever the motivation, by 1700 some economic theorists had extracted and isolated economic reasoning, and endowed it with ordering principles of its own. Now the market mechanism, which was thought to obey inexorable economic laws, was the regulator of human activity. It placed a premium upon utility and efficiency, and brought commodities, land, and people within the logic of the market – calculable, quantifiable, and valuated through prices as products of economic processes rather than of moral precepts of tradition and authority.

Bringing people as objects into the logic of the market, of course, had profound implications for how labor was conceptualized. Indeed, fully trusting the market mechanism to regulate labor and discipline laborers was an expectation few men of the early modern period, despite the theorizing about liberty in general and free markets in particular, were prepared to hold. The prevalence of the discourse on idleness and its assumed remedy, forced labor by incarcerated workers, testify to that. Labor was increasingly reified as production, but simultaneously continued to be immersed, in practice and in theory, in moral systems of authority. The English revolutionary, the Digger Gerard Winstanley, for example, in the mid-seventeenth century conceived of a reconstructed society based fundamentally on a particular organization of work associated with a pronounced disciplinary regimen. His society would embody a patriarchal hierarchy, where the first level of enforcement would be the father and master "who is to command [his inferiors in] their work and see they do it." The second level was to be a council of elected overseers who supervised trades, "to see that young people be put to masters, to be instructed in some labour . . . that none be idly brought up . . . " Finally, this disciplinary system was to be backed up by a criminal code which held the draconian provision that runaways from workshops would "dye by the sentence of the Judge when taken again."[14]

Winstanley was, of course, a utopian, but in his reification of work he was in tune with later, less politically revolutionary thinkers, like Daniel Defoe or Adam Smith. In *The Compleat English Tradesman* which Defoe published in 1723, this celebrated novelist and essayist saw work as the

---

[14] Quoted in Anthony, p. 49.

central preoccupation of a tradesman's life, arguing that even the duties of religion "must be kept in their places." Defoe connects hard work with money-making and social advancement:

Nothing can give a greater prospect of thriving to a young tradesman, than his own diligence . . . without application nothing in this world goes forward as it should do; Let the man have the most perfect knowledge of his trade, and the best situation for his shop, yet without application nothing will go on . . . Trade must . . . be worked at . . .[15]

Half a century later Adam Smith carried to his monumental *Wealth of Nations* these same assumptions about the causal links between diligence and "improving." In keeping with the hypostasizing of nature so common in eighteenth-century thinkers, he added that the connection between work and progress was assumed to be a law of nature rather than socially acquired, and he joined these thoughts with perhaps his most famous economic maxim: that labor is "the real measure of the exchangeable value of all commodities," and that gains in productivity were directly related to the division and specialization of labor.[16]

Competing during the early modern centuries, then, were two world views of work. One, which we have called premodern or traditional, emphasized work as a degrading activity, but one that served primarily moral purposes and was structured upon the principles of hierarchy and discipline. The other view no doubt rings more familiar to modern ears since this newer view of work saw it as productive energy in a market economy.

True, eventually the modern view of work would eclipse the traditional, and tracing the trajectory of modern economic ideas to Adam Smith and beyond well illustrates how the abstraction of the market mechanism and the reification of labor became a hallmark of modern economic thinking, but it oversimplifies. It must be emphasized that these ideas co-existed awkwardly and, at times, even paradoxically in the intellectual, social, and political constellation of the seventeenth and eighteenth centuries. This can be seen quite clearly in the Enlightenment thinkers' attempts to reconcile a certain view of the value of work with their beliefs about how society should be properly organized.

William Sewell writes that work was for Enlightenment thinkers the application of the mechanical arts to nature from which all true knowledge and order in society ultimately derive,[17] but, as he has also pointed out elsewhere, this is only partly true. Enlightenment thinkers were

---

[15] Quoted in Laura Stevenson, *Praise and Paradox: Merchants and Craftsmen in Elizabethan Popular Literature* (New York, 1984), p. 197.
[16] Quoted in Anthony, p. 54.
[17] William Sewell, Jr., *Work and Revolution in France* (Cambridge, 1980), pp. 64–72.

much more ambivalent about the value of work in society than this statement suggests. True, one can find in the *Encyclopédie* the view that the value of work springs from its utility to society, and is the bond that unites humanity by way of commerce. One can even find extolled in these pages the craftsman who brings order and progress to the world: "the lowly artisan to whom all society [is] in debt." Indeed, the leading encyclopedist Denis Diderot wrote that the mechanical arts were equal to the liberal because they were equally complex productions of knowledge and order-giving applications of intelligence, and since all useful knowledge was knowledge of nature, the mechanical arts, with their direct contact with production from the materials of nature, were the greatest reflection of this useful knowledge.

Interspersed with these words of praise for artisan production, however, are engravings that visually portray the artisan himself as "alienated, abstract labor power," as a mechanical automaton only ancillary to technology.[18] Indeed, often the text praises the machines as much as the men who operated them. Juxtaposed to praise of the mechanical arts, in fact, one can find Diderot distrusting artisans as obscurantist, secretive, and ignorant guildsmen who jealously clung to obsolete modes of production and who described their work processes in maddeningly inexact terminology. The overarching design of Diderot and his fellow encyclopedists was to "prise the vocabulary of the manual arts away from the domain of the workers, to change it, to bring it under control, and finally, to create a new language of the mechanical arts available to 'all.'"[19]

In this design of separating technical aptitude from knowledge in the production process, the encyclopedists were anticipated by the German alchemist and natural philosopher Johann Joachim Becher. In 1672 he published *Chymisches Laboratorium* in which he described the ideal workshop. Judging the typical organization of artisanal guild workshops chaotic and inscrutable, he elaborated a system that would order the world of work philosophically. He focused on production, and structured his workshop hierarchically. At the top would be the "counselor," a natural philosopher who possessed the necessary knowledge of production and who controlled the men beneath him in ironclad and unquestioning discipline. On the next rung down stood the "dispensator," a man who simply took instructions from the counselor and assigned tasks and materials to the appropriate laborers. He was not to

---

[18] William Sewell, Jr., "Visions of labor: illustration of the mechanical arts before, in and after Diderot's *Encyclopédie*," in Steven L. Kaplan and Cynthia Koepp, eds., *Work in France* (Ithaca, 1986), pp. 258–96.

[19] Koepp, p. 100.

"tinker with [the instructions] or add anything to [them], but should perform [them] as [they] are written . . ."[20] At the bottom of this workshop hierarchy stood the laborer, whose sole responsibility was mindless toil at assigned tasks. Becher's detailed plan, in short, wrested knowledge from the craftsman and lodged it with the counselor in service, in good mercantilist fashion, to his prince.

Becher's workshop organization never became commonplace, but, like the subsequent encyclopedists, for all their praise of the creativity of the mechanical arts and the knowledge of nature that craftsmen possessed, he was in step with many economic theorists, *philosophes*, and government administrators of the eighteenth century. They all sought, in the name of the rationalization of the work process, to replace the inefficient, inarticulate, mysterious, and indisciplined art of the craftsman with a public, open, and widely available mechanical practice that was built upon a strict, mindless, and hierarchically ordered division of labor. These men wanted to encourage productivity while retaining an essentially unchanged social order. But how could the former be unleashed without destroying the latter?

Guilds and the organization of work

When readers first encounter the topic of guilds, most likely an image of a workshop with a master craftsman toiling alongside a couple of journeymen and apprentices comes to mind. Furthermore, the quaint picture is often filled out by an assumption that the workers in the shop turn out items specific to their trade – thus shoemakers shoes and boots, tailors clothing, weavers bolts of cloth, locksmiths locks, and so on. Some readers may even know that specific trades were associated in organizations we call guilds, and that these institutions had regulatory powers governing economic activities. This is an accurate picture – as far as it goes – but the guild was more than an economic institution. More broadly and more fundamentally, in fact, it was a device designed to organize and order society.

Indeed, the guild was a central cog in a theoretical system of order that emerged in the late Middle Ages which historians have come to call corporatism. It may be useful to think of corporatism as a cosmology, or as a rhetorical system for ordering the world and making sense of it. It laid out organizing principles which shaped social, political, as well as economic, organization, embracing the principles of paternalism, hierarchy, and discipline in the social and political realm, and the economic

[20] Quoted in Pamela H. Smith, *The Business of Alchemy: Science and Culture in the Holy Roman Empire* (Princeton, 1994), p. 236.

principle of containing competition to preserve the livelihood of artisans and channel quality goods to the consuming public at a fair price. It may have had only partial and often ineffective hold on economic practice, but as an *idea* corporatism was fundamentally important. As William Sewell has noted, the idea of order is imbedded in the very word *corps*. Like the physical, organic *corps*, or "body," the corporation was a single entity, its members subsumed in a common substance and presumed to possess a united interest. As the human body had a rational and order-giving soul, so the social "body" had its esprit de corps expressed in confraternal solidarity.[21]

Corporatism entailed a view of work, therefore, as a collective social responsibility and one that was public in character. Political authorities everywhere, unlike Marx, did not consider work the "natural and free exercise of the activity of man," but rather deemed its practice a concession of the public authority. That is, they believed it their duty to regulate the world of work for the public welfare, or *la chose publique*, as it was called in France. By law and custom, artisans were to be faithful producers of items for public consumption, and for this reason craftsmen were required to work with their shop windows and doors open, visible to public scrutiny. The corporate guilds to which masters belonged were public bodies whose purpose was to provide the essential needs of society. In return for this service they were granted corporate privileges, among them the power to police their own members in accord with their own statutes and regulations. They were thus tightly linked to the public authority, beginning with the municipality and sometimes ending there, as in Baroque Rome and the cities of the United Provinces like seventeenth-century Amsterdam. More often, the hierarchy of public authority extended beyond the town council, ultimately reaching, as in Germany, England, France, Spain, Sweden, and the duchies of northern Italy, the monarch, since it was theoretically the king's, prince's, or duke's duty to ensure the public good of the entire realm.

Probably the best-known privilege that guilds possessed was the monopoly over the manufacture and sale of particular items. To be sure, guild statutes or by-laws everywhere did specify such a privilege, and specific provisions were made for preventing one guild's craftsmen from encroaching upon another's, a most pressing concern among tradesmen working with the same materials like leather (tanners, curriers, shoe-makers, cobblers), wood (joiners, cabinet-makers, carpenters), or metal

---

21 William Sewell, Jr., "*Etats, corps,* and *ordre*: some notes on the social vocabulary of the French old regime," in Hans-Ulrich Wehler, ed., *Sozialgeschichte heute: Festschrift für Hans Rosenberg* (Göttingen, 1974), p. 55.

(smiths of all kinds). Guild by-laws also regulated economic relations within the guild. No master, for instance, was permitted to monopolize the purchase of raw materials or the hiring of workers. These provisions were to protect the public against abuses by certain masters, but also to shield all masters of a trade from unfair competition, from both within the guild and outside of it. The governing idea of monopoly was therefore moral as much as it was economic, for this privilege was intended to secure public order and harmony by precluding excessive price fluctuation and inordinate enrichment or impoverishment within the guild community. Such harmony was the measure of civic peace, a distinctly Christian value at this time. A guild, as Ellis Knox has observed for Augsburg, was expected to "ensure an income appropriate to one's rank."[22]

Old regime society everywhere in Europe was, as Harold Perkin has said of England, "a finely graded hierarchy of great subtlety and discrimination, in which men [and women] were acutely aware of their exact relation to those immediately above and below them."[23] At one level, without question, life was a struggle for access to material resources, but at another level, and one which had much to do with identity, life was, as Steven Kaplan has noted, a struggle over classification, over accession to or preservation of status. For an artisan of the early modern period, this hierarchical quality was represented by his or her position vis-à-vis a guild – as master, journeyman, apprentice, widow, or wage-worker, each a distinction which related to the securing of a living, but also which conferred a social identity in relation to one's place in the social order.

Whenever men theorize about the meaning of work, its "proper" social classification, like its value, is never far from mind. This was certainly the case in the Middle Ages. In the twelfth century theologians and philosophers increasingly theorized that particular classes of Christians were particularly suited to particular kinds of activity. Moreover, they placed manual labor at the bottom of a valuated hierarchy, to be held in place by discipline. That this kind of thinking clearly emerged in the twelfth century no doubt has much to do with the economic expansion and urbanization that marked that dynamic century. More and more craftsmen flocked to existing trades or created entirely new ones as the population continued to grow. How to order society, and the world of work within it, became an increasingly pressing concern.

[22] Ellis Knox, "The guilds of early modern Augsburg," Ph.D. dissertation, University of Massachusetts, 1984, p. 8.
[23] Harold Perkin, *The Origins of Modern English Society, 1780–1880* (London, 1969), p. 24.

Theologians made their contribution to the resultant social theory, but regarding the theoretical organization of work, the writings of Roman law jurists are more significant, for it is here that we find a discussion of guilds. A century or more before jurists incorporated guilds in their theoretical structure, however, the new communes, or self-governing towns, were assimilating them in their new political firmament. As early as the eleventh century we find in the communes of the Rhineland, the Low Countries, and northern Italy evidence of groups of craftsmen and merchants (significantly not necessarily of the same occupations) in sworn associations which were devotional groups and mutual aid societies. We will return to this in a later chapter, but it should be pointed out that whatever the origin of craft guilds, we would be mistaken in assuming that they emerged uniquely because of economic pressures; rather, they emerged from confraternal associations that organized a way of life, and that gradually incorporated work activity as economic conditions changed. More than anything, they provided their members with a modicum of social security, a moral and, by the thirteenth century, a political identity, and a sense of place in a rapidly changing world.

In the twelfth and thirteenth centuries, jurists, appropriating Roman law for reasons of political theory and governance, associated the guild with the *collegium* of late Roman law and granted to constituted authority (notably the monarchs for whom most of these jurists were writing and who claimed to be descendants of the Roman emperor) the power to create and regulate it. The jurists thereby grafted a Roman legacy of hierarchical political authority on to guild organization. Guildsmen, for their part, clung to a theoretical legacy of autonomy, citing the Germanic custom of sworn, voluntary association and self-governance. Were these bodies of oath-swearing craftsmen and merchants to be self-governing, or political creatures of other authorities?

The answer for the next 600 years was to be both. Medieval and early modern guilds continued to function as devotional and mutual aid societies, but they increasingly became identified with governance as well as the regulation of economic activities. Population growth and commercial expansion accelerated from the eleventh to the early fourteenth centuries, creating ever larger pools of increasingly mobile laborers to be absorbed into the productive and social system. In some places in the twelfth century, and everywhere in the thirteenth, municipal authorities sensed a threat to order from these developments, and responded with regulatory decrees to attempt to secure it. Like municipalities, guild masters also were troubled by indiscipline in the workplace and the home (since most workers, probably until the eighteenth century, lived with their employer, the master) and drafted statutes, or guild by-laws, to deal with it. Municipalities sanctioned these statutes for a fee, oversaw their enforcement by imposing fines for transgressions (in part payable to the municipal treasury), and, in the fourteenth century, increasingly conferred legal status upon the guilds.

This politicizing of the trades for regulatory and fiscal purposes embodies that new theoretical system of order called corporatism. Corporation theory played a vital role in medieval legal and political thought, and although few jurists specifically theorized about guilds as corporations, increasingly in the fourteenth century guilds were referred to, as in French, as *corps de métiers*. For jurists, "corporations" (or *universitas*, which was the generic term these intellectuals invoked to refer to organized groups claiming the privileges of corporations as specified in Roman law in the *Digest*) were quasi-public associations, which were empowered to make their own rules governing their internal affairs and submitting their members to a collective discipline, but which simultaneously gained this privilege from a public authority. A *de facto* situation of confraternal association was thereby appropriated and systematized in a sweeping theory organizing socio-political and, increasingly, economic life. Confraternities and guilds of merchants and craftsmen predated the corporate regime, but corporate theory of the fourteenth century joined hands with demographic and economic forces to formalize a political and juridical system that would last into the nineteenth century.

The idea of confraternal community was a powerful one in the early modern period. Indeed, as spiritual *Gemeinde*, it is expressed time and again in Protestant tracts during the Reformation in the sixteenth century. Moreover, it informs the most substantial exposition of guild ideas of the era, the *Systematic Analysis of Politics* first published in 1603 by Johannes Althusius of Emden. This German Calvinist rooted economic exchange in the moral soil of guild values. He asserted that exchange originates in mutual needs, and that reciprocity is thus inherent in all exchange. When transacted within a political system based upon contract – and thus, he explained, upon the guild values of trust, friendship, and mutual aid – then social solidarity and harmony will result.

No less a champion of the moral values of corporatism, of guilds, but also of hierarchy and status, was the eighteenth-century German Justus Möser. He believed that what naturally governed men's affairs were the values so evident in the guild communities: not unrestrained competition or unchained economic growth, but rather honor, mutual respect, and propriety – *Ehre, Erfahrung, Eigentum*. The respect of the respected was, for Möser, the great mainspring of human affairs.

According to the historian of medieval corporatism Bernard Chevalier, corporatism was a "new system" whose rules expressed by intellectuals at once were inspired by and inspired the "real behavior" of people.[24] The best evidence supporting Chevalier's point is the guild statutes that multiplied everywhere in Europe from the mid-thirteenth century to 1600. These statutes, which originated with guildsmen but were brought to political authorities for sanction, were fundamentally about discipline. They articulated in minute detail how guilds were to be regulated; but the logic of this regulation is social and moral. Dictates on religious practice and mutual aid among "brothers" are central to these by-laws. Even ostensibly purely economic matters, like regulations restricting masters to the operation of only one shop, were informed by social concerns. For example, in eighteenth-century Paris it was argued by officers of the furrier guild that the "common law of the realm" prohibited subjects from holding two social ranks at once and so it followed that any master operating two enterprises simultaneously was seeking unfairly to enrich himself at the expense of his confrères and so to vault himself out of his assigned rank in the hierarchy. This is tortured logic from the perspective of liberal economics, but eminently rational to men who believed that status was the soul of identity and the sign of hierarchical position in the social order.

As we will see, these theoretical prescriptions of guild values had an incomplete hold on economic practice; but we must never discount the moral, juridical, social, and political significance of the corporate idiom during the early modern period. If it never subsumed all work activity in its fold and had only a partial impact on the actual practice of production, distribution, and consumption, it was nonetheless of inestimable moral importance in articulating rank in an increasingly hierarchical society. And, as Steven Kaplan so perceptively observes, the organizing principles of the corporate idiom were imbedded in a social taxonomy, which in turn was closely linked to the exercise of power: "the tools of distinction used to forge the classification system are tools of social and political control . . ."[25] This is why, to take an illuminating example, in eighteenth-century Paris the inspections of goldsmith workshops by the officers of the guild were orchestrated with such pomp. The inspectors

---

[24] Bernard Chevalier, "Corporations, conflits politiques et paix sociale en France aux XIVe et XVe siècles," *Revue historique* 268 (1982), 17–44.

[25] Steven L. Kaplan, "Social classification and representation in the corporate world of eighteenth-century France: Turgot's carnival," in Steven L. Kaplan and Cynthia Koepp, eds., *Work in France* (Ithaca, 1986), p. 177.

wore ceremonial robes and scrupulously kept "in marching line according to rank."[26]

Such a hierarchical system was, then, equally a power structure, and distinction and difference were animated by a concern for subordination and discipline of inferiors, be they journeymen, apprentices, wageworkers, or women. Breach of discipline by journeymen or wageworkers reflected more than instability in the labor market, but also and more dramatically, a perceived threat to hierarchy and the principle of distinction itself. Masters were deeply sensitive to insubordination by journeymen and nonguild wage-workers, and journeymen were keen, in turn, on maintaining the inferiority of noncorporate wage-workers beneath them. As we will see, guild statutes had a great deal to say about this as well.

If regulations over the production and distribution of goods, or even wages, gain minor if any attention in guild statutes, matters relating to labor discipline attract much more. Labor relations come more and more to be submitted to legal formulations, especially, for reasons we will explore in later chapters, in matters concerning disciplining the labor force. Numerous provisions in statutes in guild after guild and town after town throughout Europe strictly regulated the access of workers to the corporation, and to mastership within it. Entry examinations, rising fees, extended periods of apprenticeship, the making of a masterpiece (widespread by the fifteenth century) all pointed to a mounting preoccupation with discipline and an increasing hierarchization in the world of work where the barriers between master and journeyman (that is, a worker with some institutional claim to guild membership) and between journeyman and nonguild worker (those with no guild membership whatsoever) were raised higher than ever before. Master guildsmen and the political authorities (and the theorists that gave them voice) shared these values of hierarchy, status, and discipline, and their common interests came together in the formulation of the corporate regime, enshrined in part in guild statutes.

Already in the twelfth and thirteenth centuries political authorities in France and Germany were increasingly grouping guilds within an administrative structure called a *ministerium* which included guild offices sanctioned by public authority and charged with regulating the world of work. The famous *Livre des métiers* demonstrates this well. Compiled by the *prévôt*, or mayor of Paris, Etienne Boileau in 1268, the *Livre* not only lists the various trades of Paris at the time, but also records the statutes or by-laws governing the various crafts. Its purpose, above all, was to

---

[26] Quoted in Steven L. Kaplan, "The luxury guilds in Paris in the eighteenth century," *Francia* 9 (1981), 262.

enumerate administrative units (the trades or *métiers*) and then authorize their officers to "fulfill their public charge" under the aegis, in this case, of the crown of France.

The history of the corporate regime has been most studied in France, but it was clearly a European phenomenon. In the towns of the various kingdoms in Spain evidence for economic organization along craft lines emerges in the thirteenth century within the institution of the religious confraternity. In the following century, the corporate guild emerged, an administrative unit with the principle of classification of members according to rank finding a constitutional place both within the guild and in the town ordinances and charters drafted by the municipal authorities. Membership in such guilds (often still called *cofradia* and not clearly distinguishable from the spiritual brotherhoods which antedated them) was voluntary until the early fourteenth century, but thereafter obligatory membership and ever sharper hierarchical classifications took hold on the Iberian peninsula. Paralleling the development of corporatism in France, the number of incorporated guilds, increasingly called *gremios*, expanded sharply in the fourteenth and fifteenth centuries, and they became creatures of the king. Monarchs like Peter of Aragon may have granted royal "protection" to "all the artisans of Barcelona" in 1218, but it was one of his successors, James I, who actually conferred privileges on the municipality in 1249 which granted guildsmen the right to participate politically. The first corporate statutes extant from Barcelona date from 1308 (that of an amalgamated textile guild of dyers, woolweavers, fullers, and carders), and after that many follow, each with statutes ultimately sanctioned by privileges emanating specifically from the king.

The situation in Castile was similar. King Peter the Cruel might in the mid-fourteenth century delegate to the municipal authorities the right to issue guild ordinances, but the king reserved the right of final approval, and, of course, exacted funds for the privilege. In the fourteenth and fifteenth centuries both Aragon and Castile witnessed compulsory membership, tightening of apprenticeship rules, and increasing attention to discipline within the guild hierarchy (masters controlling journeymen). With the unification of the peninsula under Ferdinand and Isabella in the late fifteenth century, the corporate regime was systematically expanded, incorporating formerly nonguild trades. As in France, craft corporations served multiple purposes for the authorities: they organized the economy, in conformity with the increasing hierarchization of society they were expected to maintain discipline in their ranks, and they were lucrative sources for fiscal expropriation.

A similar story can be told of the guilds of the towns of medieval

Flanders. The critical date is 1302. Following the defeat of the French at the battle of Courtrai, the French-allied patricians of Ghent, Ypres, and Bruges were overthrown and the craftsmen who had supported Count John of Namur against the French were rewarded for their support of the count with corporate privileges, granted, of course, by the count. Flemish incorporated guildsmen may have had greater rights of political participation in their municipal government than some of their counterparts elsewhere (the range of this across Europe was great), but the guilds of Flanders show similar patterns to those elsewhere in Europe in matters pertaining to the organization of work, the discipline of workers, and accelerating hierarchization. With incorporation came statutes which specified privileges of mastership. Among these were sole rights to own shops, to employ journeymen, and to train apprentices. With an eye toward disciplining the worker, masters were also empowered, subject to the count's approval, to set hours and conditions of work, the length of apprenticeship service, and the number of workers allowed in the employ of a master. Increasingly in the fourteenth and fifteenth centuries masters sought to restrict access to their ranks by workers who were not sons of masters, first by raising entry fees, then by demanding the making of an increasingly expensive "masterpiece" (a requirement waived for masters' sons).

In the city states of Italy guilds had varied constitutional histories. In Venice, already in the 1270s guildsmen swore an oath to abide by guild regulations; but it was an oath that simultaneously declared their allegiance to the republic. Before long, with the Serrata of 1297, they were excluded from exercising any formal political power in the state. Thirteenth- and fourteenth-century Florentine communal politics, in contrast, rested on guilds as autonomous, self-governing corporations composed of equal members. These guilds had extensive powers, ranging from legislative to judicial to regulatory, which were articulated in written statutes and which were in turn delegated to elected officials. The Florentine republic, therefore, according to John Najemy, was effectively "a sovereign federation of equal and autonomous guilds, with each guild free to elect its own representatives to the governmental committees through which the sovereignty of the full community was exercised."[27]

Everywhere in the fourteenth century, even in Florence as guild governance gave way to oligarchy, stratification and differentiation were becoming increasingly articulated, reaching their apogee in the seventeenth century and continuing in many places into the eighteenth and

[27] John Najemy, *Corporatism and Consensus in Florentine Electoral Politics, 1280–1400* (Chapel Hill, 1982), p. 9.

even nineteenth centuries. Chevalier has persuasively contended that in the fourteenth century in the "good towns" of France an internal hierarchy emerged which loosely divided the urban populace into three vertically ranked categories, granting diminishing degrees of "honor" to each rank, from *les bons* (the bourgeois), to *les communs* (including craftsmen of guilds), to *les vulgaires* (including laborers outside the guild).[28] This loose structure heralded the establishment of the corporate regime in which craft guilds became defined constitutionally as the *corps de métiers*. Craft guilds, of course, predated the corporate regime, but only in the fourteenth century do we find them specifically organized as *corps* and correspondingly assuming an *état*, a quality which placed them socially and constitutionally in the city. The *gens de bras*, or workers not organized in *corps*, had no *état*, and thus were *gens sans qualité* (people of no status).

From the outset, then, corporatism as a new system of order was imbedded in the economy, but everywhere it was also inextricably linked to social hierarchy and distinction as well as to politics. It was grounded in a demand for subordination and discipline of inferiors. Indeed, the corporate regime gained definition *by* the principle of exclusion. Workers without *état* were defined outside the system of order, and consigned to the netherworld of disorder. Even journeymen were liminal figures, in some ways part of the guild order, but simultaneously excluded from the respectable ranks of masters. These men and women were imagined to "have in their head only the inversion of all values, the abolition of providential differences."[29] Thus, when workers did challenge their masters over control of the labor market, for example, their actions were interpreted by masters no less than municipal and later royal authorities as violence against order *per se*, and were invested with cosmological and not just narrowly economic importance.

The Middle Ages bequeathed to the early modern era a society politically organized by corporation, in which a host of collective bodies, including guilds, were considered legal persons. Empowering corporations to own property, plead in public courts, and in some locales to participate in governance, corporatism dominated the thinking about and, in some ways, as we will see in subsequent chapters, the practice of economic, social, and juridical life. By the fifteenth century, corporatism was established as the legal armature of nearly every polity of Europe.

Even in the kingdom most commonly associated with weak guilds, England, the corporate regime took hold in the fourteenth century and expanded in the fifteenth and sixteenth. Incorporated by the crown as

---

[28] Bernard Chevalier, *Les Bonnes Villes de France du XIVe au XVIe siècle* (Paris, 1982).
[29] Chevalier, "Corporations, conflits politiques et paix sociale," 36.

"mysteries" or, as they were called in London, livery companies, membership in these bodies entailed a purchase of the "freedom" payable to the municipal authority of the town in which the artisan lived, a payment which in turn granted the right of citizenship (this entailed a range of political rights, depending on the city). Citizenship in turn permitted the practice of a trade within the city. In the fourteenth and fifteenth centuries the freedom was continually extended by municipalities (for fiscal reasons), so that its purchase became essentially obligatory for any craftsman wishing to open a shop. In exchange for purchasing the freedom (and channeling funds to the increasingly financially strapped municipalities), mysteries or companies were granted the right to manage their internal affairs, specifically including the disciplining of subordinates. Within each London company hierarchical status was defined precisely, descending from liverymen, to yeomen (subdivided into "householders" or masters, and journeymen), to apprentices, and authority over others within the structure was clearly stated. Masters, for example, by the sixteenth century were demanding the compulsory employment registration of journeymen, which required the journeyman to remain with the master as long as the master provided work. Indeed, the brewers of London stipulated that no journeyman could be hired without a "passport" from his former master certifying his "lawful departure."[30]

In parts of fifteenth-century France guilds had come to be referred to as *choses du roi*, literally belonging to the king. In 1467, for instance, Louis XI demanded that all new masters take an oath of fidelity directly to him. Still, however important the royal sanction for legitimacy was and would increasingly become, nearly everywhere the first line of authority the guilds encountered was the municipality. The corporate guild system in France, which lasted until 1791, was organized in *métiers statués* (either *jurés* or *réglés*, but in either case regulated by the municipality), that is, guilds with statutes sanctioned by the government. These by-laws, as elsewhere in Europe, stipulated an internal hierarchical structure descending from master to apprentice. The municipal authorities appointed guild officers (or, in some cases like the goldsmiths and pastrycooks of Dijon, approved the officers elected by the guild), called variously *jurés*, *prud'hommes*, *gardes*, or *syndics*, and granted them the authority to "police" their own guild and to assure that their monopoly would not be encroached upon by other trades. These men (usually two per guild, but upwards of six in some guilds in some places, like the bakers' guild in Paris in 1719) were thus empowered to enforce the

---

[30] Steve L. Rappaport, *Worlds within Worlds: Structures of Life in Sixteenth-Century London* (Cambridge, 1989), p. 239.

provisions of the statutes, and their powers could be far reaching. They ranged from inspection of guild shops to guarantee quality of manufacture (with the authority to seize and destroy poorly made objects and to fine the craftsman for shoddy workmanship), to inquiry into the morals of candidates for mastership, to presiding over guild assemblies, to representing the guild's interests before the town council.

Guilds proliferated everywhere from the fifteenth to the seventeenth centuries, while in some places like Sweden or Austria the high point was reached in the eighteenth. The fifteenth century was a time of corporate expansion in most French towns, like Dijon, and the sixteenth century witnessed a similar development in the towns of the southern Netherlands and England. Expansion surged into the seventeenth century, too. In London alone between 1600 and 1640 twenty-seven new livery companies were formed (the crown encouraging their establishment because of the revenues that could be extracted from them). The towns of the new United Provinces in the northern Netherlands had few guilds before the seventeenth century, but by 1700 could count about 2,000 of them. The same growth marked contemporary Catalonia.

Though corporate organization of work in France never included all trades, it was not for want of trying. The Colbertian edict of 1673, "Pour l'établissement des Arts et Métiers en Communauté," attempted to universalize the corporative regime among the trades, a stated goal of the royal edict of 1581 as well as that of 1767. Frederick William I of Prussia endeavored to do the same in his state. From 1736 to 1738 he issued a series of edicts making corporate statutes uniform, each guild being theoretically subjected to the surveillance of the state. Regardless of the incomplete reach of such legislation, or even its paradoxical nature (one can find royal edicts that exempted trades from incorporation), the importance of corporatism *per se* in terms of status and politics should not be underestimated.

Outside of France and Prussia, perhaps no other regions of Europe have been associated so closely with corporatism as the German "home towns," that analytical category created by Mack Walker to encompass a type of town which was relatively small (fewer than 10,000 inhabitants) and marked by relative isolation, both political and economic. The constitutional characteristics of the guilds of these towns and their hinterlands show some divergences from those of most other European towns, notably in their degree of independence from outside political influence (here they are sharply different from their Prussian counterparts); but in important ways they represent the highwater mark of corporatism which crested in much of Europe in the late seventeenth and early eighteenth centuries. Guilds in these polities possessed statutes which stipulated, as elsewhere, the nature of apprentice training, regulations for recruitment of workers and their distribution among the shops of the town, and monopolies. Guild masters were the watchdogs of these rules, and they were empowered by the municipality to prosecute *Böhnhasen* or "groundrabbits," those nonmasters who encroached on a guild's monopoly. Regulating economic competition may have partly inspired this legislation, but it was but a piece of a larger constitution which safeguarded the community by laying out its imagined boundaries. The goal of the guilds of the "home towns" was to secure community peace, to maintain a certain order. They imagined, in its most extreme manifestation, what corporate regimes throughout Europe imagined: an order rooted in definition of social exclusivity and hierarchy. *Ehrbarkeit*, or "honorable status," was the quality that announced this in the "home town," and to possess it, as guild masters did, included one in the orderly community; not to possess it, as the nonguild outsiders did not, allocated the individual to the dishonorable lower elements of society and, generally, to the realm of disorder.

Nuremberg offers an instructive point of comparison, illustrating the similarities as well as the varieties of artisanal regulation in Germany and Europe. A free imperial city, Nuremberg's governing elite never permitted artisans to form independent corporations (having crushed an artisan rebellion in 1349), and the town council directly regulated the work activity deemed essential to the welfare of the community. The so-called free crafts, or *Freie Künste*, had no rules governing apprentices, quality of products, price, and so on, but patrician dominance spelled strict statutes and regulations for the masters, journeymen, and apprentices of the "essential" trades. Admission to mastership, wage levels, and marketing were all overseen by municipal officers. If technically there were no guilds in Nuremberg, there were nonetheless organizations called "sworn crafts," each with a "sworn master" elected by its members and invested by the town council to be its agent in the enforcement of the provisions comprehensively articulated in the *Book of Handicrafts*. In a sense, Nuremberg as a whole functioned like a corporation, as patrician Nurembergers embraced the idea that, as Gerald Strauss put it,

to be in society meant to be in possession of a body of rules and statutes defining one's life and actions. Society . . . was thought to consist of groups and classes, each a legally provisioned component with shared rights and enumerated responsibilities toward itself, toward other groups, and toward society at large. Each constituent group had its distinguishing peculiarities of dress, habit, manner, style.[31]

31 Gerald Strauss, *Nuremburg in the Sixteenth Century* (New York, 1966), pp. 116–17.

Apprentices, journeymen, and women

The rhetoric prescribing the corporate regime was embodied in most polities of medieval and early modern Europe. As creations and creatures of political authority, incorporated guilds were simultaneously empowered and rendered vulnerable to political authority. Throughout the old regime, hierarchy and discipline were joined by paternalism in defining corporatism. Society was theoretically structured on the microcosm of the family, the prescriptive model of which was the *paterfamilias*. A well-ordered society, as theorists never tired of proclaiming, was based upon the well-ordered family, which was supposedly regulated and disciplined by the father, the male head of household. Of course, women were construed to be, in the nature of things, inferior to men, and journeymen and apprentices were treated as children and thus owing filial obedience to their master. Patriarchy as a specific legal construct may have been directly challenged in the late seventeenth and eighteenth centuries, notably by Locke and his followers, but paternalism did not die a sudden death. Indeed, legislation prohibiting worker insubordination continued to be cast in a paternalistic idiom, even in England, from the fourteenth to the early nineteenth centuries.

Insubordination, then, challenged paternalism and undermined hierarchy. Hierarchy rests on vertical distinction, and distinction rests on the definition of otherness. Masterless men (and women) behaving as masters (working in their own "shops," taking on customers) blurred these distinctions which were given meaning by the corporate ethos. To obscure the distinction between a master artisan, an apprentice, and a wage-worker, not to mention a woman, was a threat to the constituted order and the master's place within it. The boundary separating the guild master from the *gens de bras* was societally fundamental because it marked the boundary between order and disorder. This was the meaning and value of corporatism: it was a constitutional system that did not simply organize work, but that translated the various activities of work into a moral representation of status and rank.

Consequently, corporate statutes purported to discipline labor and to erect clear boundaries between masters and nonmasters. The master guildsmen who drafted these by-laws hoped to accomplish such distinction and discipline by regulation of entry to the guild, apprenticeship within it, restrictions on admission to mastership, and control of the labor market.

Admission to the guild and eventual mastership was closely regulated nearly everywhere from the fourteenth to the nineteenth centuries. As Kaplan neatly and correctly observes: "apprenticeship was at the heart of the corporatist conception of work and of hierarchy."[32] It was a moral and political socialization as much as it was an initiation to the trade. Apprenticeship could be a promising avenue to mastership, and masters often made sure that this track was open only to boys who met with their approval (this is why statutes invariably state that only masters may train apprentices). Apprenticeship regulations were enshrined in most guild statutes (of the 101 statutes collected by Boileau in Paris in the *Livre des métiers* in 1268, for example, 82 specifically address apprenticeship), but by no means did every worker within the guild serve one. That was because apprenticeship was to be a means to institutionalize distinctions and hierarchy within the guild. Upon payment of a placement fee (which also varied widely from guild to guild, and in time and place – in Lyons in 1786 such fees ranged from 24 *livres* for a shoemaker to 1,332 *livres* for a hatter), apprentices took their place in their master's household, agreeing to obey and respect him as a father. These hand-picked and potential future masters received food, clothing, lodging, and training in return. Their training, it should be noted, was more than technical aptitude – nonapprenticed "skilled" workers received that, too – but a special education through which these hopeful future masters were introduced to the "mysteries" of the trade. Thus, only rarely do guild statutes or apprenticeship contracts inform us of the skills acquired, referring instead to the "customs" or "secrets" of the trade. This knowledge was not to be shared with everyone (although in practice it was well-nigh impossible to keep other workers toiling shoulder to shoulder with the apprentices from learning these secrets as well), and its possession theoretically set one apart and defined one's sense of belonging, not just to the guild, but more generally to an *état*. This sense of inclusion and exclusion spanned the guilds – indeed, as we will see in chapter 6, master artisans appear to have self-consciously reached across guild lines to secure social bonds by marriage, godparenthood, or the placement of their sons as apprentices with other masters not of their guild.

Not all apprentices reached mastership (many died, ran away, or simply failed to learn adequately the mysteries of the trade), but this does not gainsay the fact that the purpose of apprenticeship was selection and the goal a direct route to mastership. This is why apprentices were often sons of other masters (and usually not of the same guild), boys who learned from an early age that they were distinguished from workers outside the guild – the "unqualified," the "unskilled" – as

---

[32] Steven L. Kaplan, *Le Meilleur Pain du monde. Les Boulangers de Paris au XVIIIe siècle* (Paris, 1996), p. 213. For the recent English translation, see *The Bakers of Paris and the Bread Question, 1700–1775* (Durham, 1997).

well as from nonapprenticed workers within. Upon completion of one's term (which varied widely from guild to guild and place to place, ranging from two years to twelve years, and which began at ages ranging from ten to twenty), the apprentice would be hopeful of acceding directly to mastership. In most places this required the approval of the existing masters as well as sufficient capital to open a shop. It also required the approval of the political authorities – the city magistrates and, in some places, the king. Family connections were all important for gaining guild approval nearly everywhere. In late fifteenth-century Barcelona, for instance, prospective masters had to present their baptismal certificates and full proof of *limpieza de sangre*, or purity of blood, while would-be masters in seventeenth- to nineteenth-century German "home towns" as well as large cities like Augsburg likewise had to demonstrate in writing the legitimacy of their birth.

Would-be masters with insufficient quantities of either capital or goodwill from existing masters found themselves confronting exclusionary-minded masters who were interested in bringing only enough young men into the charmed circle of mastership as were minimally necessary to continue the community. Municipalities or crowns, on the other hand, had good reasons (ranging from fiscal to economic) to be less exclusionary. Masters usually paid an entry fee to the authorities, and on occasion magistrates came to believe that local economies were harmed by too few masters in town. Masters keen on restricting access to mastership and governments (sometimes municipal, as in Dijon, sometimes royal, as in the Holy Roman empire) desiring to open it up is a story that can be told about towns of every country of Europe except England in every century from the fourteenth to the eighteenth – Spain, Flanders, France, Germany, all saw master guildsmen in different times and places raise entry fees, demand exorbitantly expensive banquets hosted by the prospective entrant, or require increasingly difficult and expensive masterpieces of the candidate for mastership. These criteria, as we will see in chapter 6, were all reduced or ignored for sons and sons-in-law of masters.

England was an exception in some respects, for there admission to mastership seems to have been relatively open. In the fourteenth and fifteenth centuries, though apprenticeship was established, many masters bypassed it by purchasing the freedom (and thus the legal right to open a shop and practice a craft) directly from the municipality. In 1563 the Statute of Artificers stated explicitly that an apprenticeship of at least seven years had to be served before anyone could be admitted to citizenship, but the law implicitly allowed that one could legally practice a craft different from the one in which apprenticeship had been served.

From the 1570s this became commonplace among craftsmen, turning apprenticeship more and more into a political institution. But if admission to "householder" or master status was relatively easy to attain, advantageous apprenticeship placement still carried a premium (and required family connections to obtain) because political advancement within the guilds (which were sharply pyramidal in their internal hierarchy), and thus within the city, was eased for those who were placed with masters already well established in politics.

Apprenticeship was clearly an important institution in the world of guilds from the Middle Ages to the nineteenth century. Many future masters passed through it, but demographics, economics, politics, and social ambitions, as we will see in subsequent chapters, created conditions in which, in some circumstances, there were too many candidates for mastership and in others too few. Some local boys and even girls (and certainly many immigrants), then, found themselves with apprenticeship certificates but denied access to mastership. For many, journeymanship (or domestic service for the girls) would be a lifelong state. At other times in other places and in different circumstances, some outsiders might find the gates to mastership wide open. This was the situation in Vienna during the Thirty Years' War among the joiners and corsetmakers, where 70 percent of the men admitted to mastership were immigrants. The admission of outsiders, or "foreigners" as they were called, might follow formal apprenticing. Or it might result from outright purchase. Or it might entail admitting to mastership a man who had simply paid some dues for use of the guild's chapel in the local parish church and had worked faithfully in his master's employ or even in his house for many years, earning the master's trust and favor, maybe even marrying his daughter or widow. Such journeymen who had not completed apprenticeship but who learned the trade through experience, be they local boys or immigrants, occupied an important if legally imprecise status within the guild. They might aspire to mastership when and if the conditions permitted it, and with their sense of community grounded in an identity that was every bit as exclusionary as their masters', they sharply distinguished themselves from the "unqualified" or "unskilled" wage-workers that masters hired on a short-term basis to do prescribed tasks and who clearly were not affiliated with the guilds at all. But, like those "unskilled" workers next to whom these journeymen sweated at the workbench or on the construction site but from whom they were so keen on distinguishing themselves, they, too, were usually paid a wage. Thus, within the ranks of nonmasters, there were many layers. There were apprentices destined to slide smoothly into mastership and apprentices who, for whatever reason, and some despite receiving their certificate, were not so fortunate. There were journeymen who became masters without serving an apprenticeship, and there were journeymen like them who remained journeymen their entire lives. Then there were noncorporate wage-workers, possessing some of the skills of apprentices and journeymen, but jealously excluded from their ranks.

Guild statutes and regulations say very little about journeymen, and when they do both the terminology by which these workers are referred to and the powers within the guild that they possess are imprecise. In the thirteenth-century *Livre des métiers* the men who had completed their apprenticeship but who had not, for whatever reason, become masters, were called *valets* (a term in use in France into the fifteenth century). Such terminology blurred any distinction between a journeyman and a domestic servant and thus carried clear expectations of servile obedience. In most places and in most guilds, journeymen participated not at all. There are, however, some exceptions to this generalization, at least during the Middle Ages. In the textile guilds in fourteenth-century Flanders, for example, journeymen had the right to vote in guild affairs, even if in most other trades there they did not. In a handful of guilds in some towns in late medieval France – Paris, Toulouse, Rheims, Rouen – in exchange for an oath of fidelity and regular payment of dues to the guild, journeymen were granted the privilege of attending guild assemblies, though it is unclear and unlikely that they had any formal power. More rarely, as in Arras, Montpellier, and among the fullers of Paris, journeymen participated in the election of *jurés*. Nowhere, however, did journeymen even approach the masters in terms of institutional or juridical power or privilege, and whatever participation in the guild they were allowed in the Middle Ages disappeared in the early modern epoch. This does not mean that journeymen had no organizational life, for they certainly did, but it does mean that it was primarily outside the guild and sometimes illegal. If journeymen are seldom mentioned in guild statutes, as we will see in chapters 5 and 6, they certainly garner their share of attention from governmental authorities bent on disciplining the workforce.

The institutional world of work was overwhelmingly male, and so women hold a very small place in our discussion of guilds, if not in the world of economic practice, as we will see. In general, all across Europe women saw their formal, independent participation in guilds narrow from the Middle Ages to the eighteenth century. Although their presence was not entirely eroded, guildsmen and magistrates joined to increasingly exclude them from a range of guilds, leaving them in guilds upon which society placed little social value and deemed "unskilled."

This gender division of labor was firmly supported by patriarchal theory and takes its place in the accelerating hierarchical disciplining of society – in this case, women – and increasingly relegated independent women to poorly paid, insecure, and politically powerless, in a word, inferior occupations.

The situation had not always been so gloomy for women. In late medieval Leiden women were well represented institutionally in the cloth industry, sometimes actively organizing production (called "draping") in their own shops with their own apprentices and wage-workers, sometimes involved in large-scale distribution of the finished cloth, sometimes involved in finishing and dyeing. In fourteenth-century Frankfurt am Main ordinances permitted women the right to practice many trades – of twenty, nine had women in their ranks. The formal situation in Cologne was even brighter for some women. In the fourteenth and fifteenth centuries they were constitutionally restricted to certain guilds by the guild regime that took power in 1396, but they dominated four important ones: yarntwisting, goldspinning, silk-weaving, and silkthrowing. Each of these guilds had their own statutes sanctioned between 1397 and 1456 and stipulating what all guild by-laws did – length and terms of apprenticeship, admission to the "mysteries" of the craft, workshop visitation and quality control, regulation of monopoly. The women of these guilds ran their own shops, took on their own apprentices, purchased their own materials, and marketed their finished products, often in wide-ranging import/export businesses. To be sure, Cologne was the only medieval German city to grant women such independence, but even here the male, patriarchal hand rested heavily, for none of the women from these all-female guilds, in contrast to their male counterparts, was permitted a political voice in the municipal governance of this "guild regime." Indeed, the statutes of the silkweavers stipulated that the two female guild officers elected by the guild be joined by two males, although these males had to be husbands of silkweavers.

It would be unwise, therefore, to look upon the Middle Ages as some golden age of female artisans, for not even then were women on a level with men. Indeed, even in Cologne in the fifteenth century women were only represented in six of the forty-two official guilds. In medieval Flemish and provincial English cities the situation was no better. Women were never permitted to hold civic or guild office there, seldom were placed in apprenticeship, and rarely became masters in guilds. In Ghent, Ypres, and Bruges until the fourteenth century a woman was permitted legally to form a business partnership with her husband, and as a widow she could expect her son to accede to mastership. Following the guild revolution of 1302, however, the guilds actively purged women from their ranks, and even denied widows of masters any control over the heritability of the mastership, now relegating it exclusively to the male line.

It would be a mistake, then, to assume that women had easy or widespread access to guilds in medieval cities. As restricted as female autonomy was, however, from the fifteenth to eighteenth century it was to become even more circumscribed. For example, in Frankfurt the number of guilds with women in them dropped from nine in the fourteenth century to three by 1500, to two by 1550. In Leiden, when the linenweavers ascended to *ambacht* status (that is, as an official guild with a charter) in 1563 there were five "mistresses" in their ranks. Five years later there were none.

This trend to exclude categorically women from official guilds occurred in towns all across the Holy Roman empire – Frankfurt, Memmingen, Strasbourg, Stuttgart, Munich. In the thirteenth and fourteenth centuries, many guilds in these towns admitted girls to apprenticeship, but in the late fifteenth and sixteenth centuries some guild ordinances and statutes specifically prohibited the practice, while others simply masculinized the language. Similarly, craft ordinances from the late fourteenth and early fifteenth centuries often mention female masters, and none specifically prohibits women from their ranks. Indeed, women represented 10–15 percent of the membership of some guilds. But in the revised and expanded statutes of guilds in these same cities which appear increasingly after the mid-fifteenth century, reference to female masters has gone the way of female apprentices – they are no longer mentioned.

These same revised and expanded statutes tightened restrictions on widows of masters, too. Whereas the earlier ordinances do not mention widows, these later ones restrict how long they can continue to operate the shop (ranging from two months to two years, depending on the town and guild). By 1550 we often find regulations prohibiting widows from taking on apprentices, and a century later forbidding them to use journeymen at all. Widows in many towns in France seem somewhat better off, in that statutes usually permitted them to keep their deceased husband's shop open and staffed with journeymen (although they were always forbidden to take on apprentices) until remarriage or until a son came of age. Remarriage had strings attached, however, for if a widow married outside of the guild, she had to close her shop, and if she married another master within the guild, the couple could merge their resources but could only retain one of the shops. If a widow married a journeyman, however, she could keep her shop if her new husband became a master.

In England customary law did not officially deny married women or widows the right to carry on a trade, nor were there laws impeding such women from gaining the "freedom." A woman designated legally as a "feme sole" could trade, enter binding contracts, and sue in court just as any man. Even "femes coverts," or women with no legal personality independent from their husband, could exploit a legal technicality that emerged in the sixteenth century called the doctrine of "separate estate," by which women could enter marriage retaining certain property in a separate estate and thus employable in a business independent from that of her spouse. Similar legal latitude was granted to women by the weavers of Copenhagen in 1550. This new guild originally permitted even single women as masters who could hire workers and train apprentices, just like the male masters of the guild. Shortly thereafter, however, mirroring a trend nearly everywhere, female independence was restricted, in this case as the status of mastership was confined to wives and daughters of male guild members.

All across Europe female artisans found their autonomy – never very liberally granted, in any case – increasingly eroded. In 1550 the livery company of London weavers officially excluded women from their ranks, adding to their ordinances the following prescription: "[no weaver] shall keep, teach, instruct, or bring up in the use, exercising, or knowledge of the same art or mystery of weaving any maiden, damsel, or other woman."[33] By the eighteenth century, although women were widely apprenticed in the towns of the southern and eastern counties (Keith Snell finds women in one-third of the apprenticeship contracts in fifty-one trades there)[34] if not in London (very few female apprentices are on the books of the livery companies there), their roles were circumscribed and confined to menial aspects of the trade, and they were seldom taught its "mysteries" or promoted to mastership. Meanwhile, guilds were becoming increasingly masculinized. In Linz, Austria in 1750 an ordinance for the saddlers' guild insisted that "all . . . masters shall take great pains to maintain proper male decorum among themselves, and to instruct their apprentices and journeymen in such male decorum . . ."[35]

Even in places where corporate status was granted women in some trades, as in eighteenth-century Nantes, the picture is still one of inferiority and subordination. As everywhere, women in Nantes worked mostly in textile, food, and female-clothing crafts, but within mixed-

---

[33] Quoted in Rappaport, p. 37.
[34] Keith Snell, *Annals of the Labouring Poor* (Cambridge, 1985), p. 331.
[35] Quoted in Merry Wiesner, "Guilds, male bonding, and women's work in early modern Germany," *Gender and History* 1 (1989), 128.

gender guilds female mistresses were not granted the same privileges as their male counterparts. For instance, the tailors in 1728 amended their statutes to allow female mistresses, but these women could not open a shop and were restricted to only "bespoke" or commissioned work. They could not employ journeymen. It seems that the tailors opened their guild to women because the demand for female clothing (both domestic and colonial, Nantes being a major export center) was outstripping the male tailors' ability to meet it. Clandestine production, much of it by women, was happening anyway, and by bringing the women into the guild (but granting them little power there) the men hoped to better regulate them. The female labor force in the garment trades everywhere was large and growing in the eighteenth century, and masters hoped to control this army of formerly illicit laborers through guild ordinance and police. Admitting women to the guild held an additional benefit, one especially important to a guild that apparently was increasingly in debt: the payment of a mastership fee into the strapped guild treasury.

In the face of the erosion of status, some women struggled to arrest the degradation, and they did so by forming guilds. Here and there in early modern European cities we find female guilds, but almost invariably in textile-related trades, and of low status and relatively poor. In Paris, the seamstresses fit this profile. The seamstresses (*couturières*) established a guild in 1675 with statutes that entitled them to sew and sell clothing for women and small children. Women serving a three-year apprenticeship and a two-year subsequent probationary period as workers could accede to mastership, provided they were at least twenty-two years old. By 1745 there were 1,500–1,700 "mistress" seamstresses in the capital, a number that swelled to 3,000 by 1789. Their poverty should not blind us, however, to the benefits women believed that incorporation provided. In response to the French Controller-General Turgot's abolition of the guilds in 1776, the women of the all-female linendraper guild of Paris protested the policy in terms of status as much as economics. In *Réflexions des marchandes et maîtresses lingères de Paris sur le projet de détruire les jurandes* the linendrapers described their guild as an institution that not only protected the quality of their work, but assured "the decency and propriety [*honnêteté*] of their estate" or rank.[36] They saw their guild as a bastion against subordination and dependence, an inevitable fate, they feared, if their guild were abolished.

---

[36] Quoted in Cynthia Maria Truant, "Parisian guildswomen and the (sexual) politics of privilege: defending their patrimonies in print," in Dena Goodman and Elizabeth Goldsmith, eds., *Going Public: Women and Publishing in Early Modern France* (Ithaca, 1995), p. 56.

The meaning of skill

Until recently, histories of artisans described craftsmen as preindustrial skilled workers destined to be crushed by the juggernaut of mechanized, factory production. In the process they found their skills eroded. But should skills be so objectively defined as a function of production? Clearly female "skills" had been undergoing a process of devaluation for centuries before industrialization, a process which had nothing to do with technology, factories, or fixed capital. Instead, such "deskilling" was a product of particular social and gender relations. It is not enough to define skill as manual facility, as the co-ordination of perceptual and motor activity, although this certainly is an important part of it. The definition of skill also must include knowledge of the properties of materials and how to assemble them into products. Such a definition, as useful as it is, however, is overly production centered and, moreover, ahistorical. Seamstresses, after all, fit this definition but were construed by the men of their world to be "unskilled." This definition tells us nothing, in fact, of the *meaning* of skill, to those who claimed to have it, and to those who wrote about it. To understand the meaning of skill, we must situate it contextually, for it is a relational quality, measured against those who supposedly possessed less of it, or none at all – the semi-skilled and the unskilled.

Two historians – Stephen Marglin and Harry Braverman – have suggested that what the industrial revolution was really about was not the economic efficiency that came from the factory system, the morcelization of the division of labor, or even scientific management, but rather the social power that capitalists achieved from greater control of the workforce and the workplace, effected through hierarchy and the discipline of labor.[37] This may have been true for the industrial revolution when such control derived rather nakedly from extensive and integrated market relations and capital formation, but it was a story with a long history. Perhaps not mediated so thoroughly by the market but also by the framing political and social structures of the guilds, control of the workforce and the workplace had been a fundamental concern of guildsmen since the fourteenth century. Hierarchy and the discipline of labor were principles enshrined in guild ordinances, and these were to be effected through control over skill – both its meaning and its possession. Skill became increasingly masculinized and associated with male independence and female subordination. Apprenticeship as an institu-

---

[37] See Stephen Marglin, "What do bosses do? The origins and functions of hierarchy in capitalist production," *Review of Radical Political Economy* 6 (1974), and Harry Braverman, *Labor and Monopoly Capital* (New York, 1974).

tion, as we have seen, clearly was designed to serve these ends as well, as was legislation demanded by guildsmen against "illicit" clandestine workers. These *faux ouvriers*, *chambrellans*, "chamberers," *Böhnhasen*, or *Störer* as they were variously called in France, England, and Germany, were workers behaving as masters without guild sanction – taking orders from customers, hiring workers, and so forth. Judging from the avalanche of evidence of their widespread existence, these workers were the bane of masters. The master goldsmiths of eighteenth-century Paris complained to the authorities that "an infinity of false workers [diminished] . . . the amount of available work . . . [and took] their clients away with lower prices."[38] Significantly, these unqualified workers were disparaged as "unskilled" and, as the French language of the time tellingly put it, *sans état*, or literally "without rank."

These matters are clearly about skill and division of labor, and they do connect with the world of production, but their significance is about much more than economics. Skill was also a symbol of status, the division of labor placed one socially, and the guild (and corporatism generally) theoretically secured these. These qualities helped define a system that created a hierarchical slot for women, for apprentices, for journeymen, and, of course, for masters. Hegel perceptively pointed out that the evidence of a craftsman's "skill" was not his technical wizardry, but rather his membership in a guild. Such membership conferred a collective status upon the guildsman via his apprenticeship, journeyman status, or mastership, and granted the craftsman a sense of possessing a "property in skill" which marked him off from others without it. Through mastership, it was, in theory, legally secured. Until the late eighteenth century this sense was more assumed and implicit than stated, and during the early modern period it became imbedded in an artisan's identity which was rooted deep in the soil of rank and hierarchy. How this formal, theoretical model of society squared with the messy world of practice is the subject to which we now turn.

Bibliography

Entries marked with a * designate recommended readings for new students of the subject.

*Anthony, Peter. *The Ideology of Work*. London, 1977.
*Appleby, Joyce. *Economic Thought and Ideology in Seventeenth-Century England*. Princeton, 1978.
Biernacki, Richard. *The Fabrication of Labor: Germany and Britain, 1640–1914*. Berkeley, 1995.

---

[38] Quoted in Kaplan, "The luxury guilds," 261.

*Black, Antony. *Guilds and Civil Society in European Political Thought from the Twelfth Century to the Present*. London, 1984.

Braverman, Harry. *Labor and Monopoly Capital*. New York, 1974.

Chevalier, Bernard. "Corporations, conflits politiques et paix sociale en France aux XIVe et XVe siècles." *Revue historique* 268 (1982), 17–44.

Coats, A. W. "Changing attitudes to labour in the mid-eighteenth century." In Michael Flinn and T. C. Smout, eds., *Essays in Social History*. Oxford, 1974, pp. 78–99.

Hunt, Lynn, and George Sheridan. "Corporatism, association, and the language of labor in France, 1750–1850." *Journal of Modern History* 58 (1986), 813–44.

*Kaplan, Steven L. "Social classification and representation in the corporate world of eighteenth-century France: Turgot's carnival." In Steven L. Kaplan and Cynthia Koepp, eds., *Work in France*. Ithaca, 1986.

Klein, Julius. "Medieval Spanish gilds." In *Facts and Factors in Economic History*. New York, 1932, 1967, pp. 164–88.

Koepp, Cynthia. "The order of work: attitudes and representations in Eighteenth-Century France." Ph.D. dissertation, Cornell University, 1992.

Marglin, Stephen. "What do bosses do? The origins and functions of hierarchy in capitalist production." *Review of Radical Political Economy* 6 (1974).

Najemy, John. *Corporatism and Consensus in Florentine Electoral Politics, 1280–1400*. Chapel Hill, 1982.

Ovitt, George, Jr. *The Restoration of Perfection: Labor and Technology in Medieval Culture*. New Brunswick, 1987.

Rule, John. "The property of skill in the period of manufacture." In Patrick Joyce, ed., *The Historical Meanings of Work*. Cambridge, 1987, pp. 99–118.

Seaver, Paul. "The Puritan work ethic revisited." *Journal of British Studies* 19 (1980), 35–53.

Sewell, William, Jr. "*Etats*, *corps*, and *ordre*: some notes on the social vocabulary of the French old regime." In Hans-Ulrich Wehler, ed., *Sozialgeschichte heute. Festschrift für Hans Rosenberg*. Göttingen, 1974.

"Visions of labor: illustration of the mechanical arts before, in and after Diderot's *Encyclopédie*." In Steven L. Kaplan and Cynthia Koepp, eds., *Work in France*. Ithaca, 1986, pp. 258–96.

Stevenson, Laura. *Praise and Paradox: Merchants and Craftsmen in Elizabethan Popular Literature*. New York, 1984.

Thrupp, Sylvia. "The gilds." *The Cambridge Economic History*, vol. III. Cambridge, 1963, pp. 230–80.

2   The craft economy

An overview of the early modern European economy

The map of the late medieval and early modern European economy, as the economic historian Jan De Vries observes, can best be thought of as a collection of regions with cities and towns as their focal points. From the high Middle Ages onwards a process of increasing economic integration occurred first within and later between these regions. The process was uneven, but Europe's cities gradually were stitched together in an increasingly tight commercial system that more and more brought the countryside into its orbit. Within their increasingly obsolete walls, cities constituted the infrastructure of the economy, the site where a great deal of craft production was organized, goods distributed, and capital attracted and invested. Of course, such a process of network creation and integration was far from linear, happening more rapidly in some areas than in others.

The demographic collapse after the catastrophic visitation of the Black Death after 1347 sent shock waves through the economy, but ecological disaster also added to the devastation of wars that had beset Europeans even before 1347. Royal armies, like those of England and France beginning in 1337, counted many mercenaries in their ranks (paid by escalating tax revenues), and during times of peace these "free companies" ravaged the countryside. But it was ecological disaster that most severely transformed the economy. The plummeting of the European population (estimated to have been by at least 25 percent) in the immediate wake of the Black Death was followed by a spike in wages after each epidemic (plague visited in 1360 and again in 1371), and with labor short, prices rose steadily across the board until the 1370s in northern Europe and the 1390s in Italy. Then a relative glut of grain hit the markets, primarily due to the importing of grain into Europe's larger cities from across the Mediterranean by Italian merchants and from the Baltic regions by the Hanse, that league of merchants established in many northern

German cities. Prices then moved in different directions. Those for manufactured goods continued to go up, while those for grain dropped.

The European population stabilized during the first half of the fifteenth century, and then began to grow again after about 1460. It continued to expand into the first half of the seventeenth century. Although reliable figures are hard to come by, it is safe to say that the European population increased by about 20 percent between 1460 and 1650, from an estimated 82 million to about 100 million. More people meant greater demand for goods, especially foodstuffs but also artisanal manufactures. Demand from population growth, coupled with the infusion into the money supply of silver from the mines of eastern Europe and the recently colonized New World, sent prices spiraling upward. The inflation lasted as long as population continued to grow and silver to flow, and one important result was increased polarization of wealth. On the one hand, immiseration and even pauperization tragically captured ever more people (from 1530 perhaps one-third of the population was poised on the brink of destitution, or lived and died within its iron grasp). Yet on the other hand, the growth of the economy during these years tended to concentrate capital increasingly in the hands of a wealthy elite of merchants, lawyers, government officials, as well as some artisans.

In the seventeenth century the flood of gold and especially silver that had flowed into the economy slowed to a trickle, and the population of Europe began to level off. Aggregate demand slackened, especially in the agricultural sector. Indeed, De Vries observes that for a century after 1650 Europe sank into an agricultural depression, with far-reaching ramifications. As food prices dropped and rents declined but real wages went up, more of the household income was disposable for the purchase of manufactured items. Even though the economy as a whole grew little before the eighteenth century and a large sector of the population continued to flounder in the despair of poverty, demand for manufactured goods nonetheless increased.

This consumer demand was stimulated by several changes. As cottage industry spread in the countryside, more and more rural but landless wage-earning households were thrown upon the market for their goods. Equally market dependent were urban dwellers, the number of whom continued to expand, especially in cities of over 10,000 inhabitants. But perhaps the greatest stimulus to consumer demand was the transfer of wealth to the government via ever-increasing taxation, capital which was then immediately redistributed to the state's increasingly wealthy dependents (aristocratic courtiers, officials, bond-holding creditors). Clearly, by the seventeenth century capital was increasingly important, as were those who controlled it.

Many historians have pointed out that market integration proceeded at different paces in different parts of Europe, with the earliest strides taken in northern Italy, southern Germany, and the Low Countries. It is no accident that these regions were also precociously urban, with populations increasingly dependent upon the market for their goods. In the late medieval Low Countries, for example, a growing population and a shift from arable to dairy farming came together to commercialize agriculture as dairy products were marketed in northern Europe's larger cities, and grain was imported from northern Germany and lands at the eastern end of the Baltic Sea. A surplus population (cattle raising was not as labor intensive as arable farming) swelled the cities and stimulated expansion in manufacturing, its products likewise directed through the channels that markets were opening up. Such integration was not seen everywhere, especially in manufactures; indeed, in England in 1500 most manufactured products never reached market at all, the bulk of them being made and consumed in the household. This would change, however, so that by 1600 the European economy was integrated to a degree "unimaginable" in 1400.[1] Of course, population growth, especially in cities, and the development of rural industry and a growing class of landless laborers contributed mightily to this integration during what Fernand Braudel called "the long sixteenth century." Even when the population curve began to level off between 1600 and 1750, however, the proportion of the population dependent on the market continued to grow. During this period the trend was toward concentration of demand in Europe's larger cities.

De Vries has recently called for renewed attention to the economic history of the household unit, and contends that the "consumer revolution" that marked the second half of the seventeenth and the entire eighteenth centuries was in fact driven by what he calls an "industrious revolution," whereby the productive resources of households expanded by more intensive labor and were reallocated. He suggests that households made decisions that "increased both the supply of market commodities and labor and the demand for goods offered in the marketplace."[2] Economic historians like De Vries or Maxine Berg

---

[1] Jordan Goodman and Katrina Honeyman, *Gainful Pursuits: The Making of Industrial Europe, 1600–1914* (London, 1988), p. 64.
[2] Jan DeVries, "The Industrial Revolution and the industrious revolution," *Journal of Economic History* 54:2 (1994), 255. See also Jan De Vries "Between purchasing power and the world of goods: understanding the household economy of early modern Europe," in John Brewer and Roy Porter, eds., *Consumption and the World of Goods* (London, 1993), pp. 85–132.

caution us, then, from thinking about the household economy as being somehow divorced from markets, as historians used to assume, instead suggesting that households were hooked up with other households in a network of complex and reciprocal alliances, and that during the seventeenth and eighteenth centuries households became increasingly market oriented.

Thanks to the vast historiography on proto-industrialization of the past twenty-five years, we know a great deal about households and markets in the context of textile production, but these are primarily rural. How do urban artisans fit into this picture? Clearly by the late seventeenth century, various sectors of the urban artisanal economy had become deeply immersed in expanding domestic and international markets, and some of these sectors took on some of the characteristics of what later came to be called "economies of scale." As we will see, however, some of the characteristics of scale were already emerging in some artisanal sectors in the Middle Ages. Indeed, within small commodity production we can find a wide range of units of production existing side by side and sometimes in interdependent combination, from small-scale, relatively lowly capitalized but highly specialized household-based workshops to complex, highly capitalized entrepreneurial networks involving partnerships and subcontracting.

Certainly the most prevalent unit of production was the workshop where family members and a handful of employees toiled. This is the traditional image of the preindustrial manufacturing economy, and every city in Europe from the high Middle Ages to the twentieth century had multitudes of such units. The German term *Handwerken* describes them well. In contrast to *Manufacturen*, which were enterprises with many workers concentrated in one place and a market with customers that the producer never saw, *Handwerken* suggested small shops which met the needs of local customers and which obeyed a set of norms governing exchange between buyers and sellers who knew each other. Scores of trades in medieval London were little different in their regard for the rules of a community-based economy from their sixteenth-century descendants, or, for that matter, from those in Reformation Augsburg, seventeenth-century Dijon, or eighteenth-century Lleida, Spain. These enterprises were shaped by the local market, supplying the needs of the town and hinterland, catering to a local clientele either by marketing "bespoke" goods (that is, those commissioned by the customer), or products sold directly to the public from the shop window or from a stall in the marketplace near the church or in the central square. Inventories were usually, though not always, small. Guild artisans like bakers, butchers, tailors, blacksmiths, locksmiths, saddlemakers, engravers, cabinet-makers and many others, usually fit this profile, as do, in some respects, nonguild artisans – many of them women – producing and selling inexpensive consumer goods like combs, wooden mugs, thimbles, needles, and so on.

This familiar picture is an accurate rendering of much of the small commodity production in preindustrial Europe, but recent research has probed behind the uncomplicated image of the artisan in his shop to discover that the craft economy could be quite complex, with many sectors of it enmeshed in a diversified and far-flung market economy long before historians have customarily assumed. By the sixteenth century an urban network connected many European cities in systems of commercial transaction which became frameworks for regional development in manufacturing.

As markets expanded and consumer demand increased, the array of manufactured products available diversified, as did the activities of the artisans who made them, ranging from luxury products adorning the bodies and decorating the homes and modes of transport of the increasingly wealthy elite, to the cheaper imitations of them, the so-called "populuxe" goods – silk hosiery, umbrellas, snuff boxes, pipes, ceramic tableware – that also found an expanding market. The eighteenth-century Englishman Tobias Smollett snobbishly moaned that "the general tide of luxury . . . hath overspread the nation and swept [up] . . . even the very dregs of the people. Every upstart of fortune [is] harnessed in the trappings of the mode . . . "[3] Whether all of this constituted a consumer "revolution" we can leave to the economic historians to debate, but there can be no question that the number of Europeans dependent on the market increased, in some places dramatically, across the early modern centuries. Nor is it in doubt that the variety of goods available and the kinds of artisans who made them increased apace. Galloping diversity and specialization would be characteristics that would mark the urban artisanry at least to the end of the nineteenth century.

Demand and supply

The economic categories of supply and demand are, of course, reciprocally intertwined, and must be analyzed, if separately, nonetheless in relation to one another. Economic historians have often privileged one or the other in their quest for explanations of economic trends. For example, until recently most approaches to industrialization have been

[3] Quoted in R. A. Leeson, *Travelling Brothers: The Six Centuries Road from Craft Fellowship to Trade Unionism* (London, 1979), p. 80.

dominated by supply-side considerations (production, technology, and so on). Increasingly of late, however, demand factors have garnered attention, especially those of a cultural cast. Not only are markets – their structures as well as access to them – being explored as formative in the creation of "manufacturing communities," as Maxine Berg puts it, but expenditure patterns dictated by taste and fashion are being granted primary consideration as well.[4] This exploring of the varieties of demand factors informs much of the recent historiography on the "consumer revolution" of the late seventeenth and eighteenth centuries.

The most noteworthy feature of production in early modern manufacturing is its decentralization. Artisans produced according to the logic of "constant returns to scale," an economic rationality whereby "growth of output required proportional growth of the inputs of labor and raw materials."[5] In a system guided by such logic expansion was accomplished by increasing the quantities of labor and materials rather than by expanding the physical plant because concentrated production was cumbersome, increasingly expensive, and fraught with the problem of labor indiscipline. As long as manufacturing operated according to the logic of constant returns to scale, pressures to expand production exerted by increased demand, then, would be accommodated by decentralization, not concentration. Only gradually did manufacturers abandon the logic of constant returns to scale and decentralized production. They did so, as we will see, by experimenting with economies of scale in some product lines where high-volume, standardized, and concentrated production became the rule.

Still, the vast majority of artisanal businesses in the early modern period worked within the framework of constant returns to scale, which meant that expansion of production stimulated by increased demand would take the shape of decentralized enterprises which could be highly varied. Historians generally have categorically separated the "putting-out system" from "small commodity production," and though this may be useful for analytical purposes, we must recognize that in the actual functioning of the craft economy, these modes were often interconnected by elaborate and complex networks of subcontracting. In the putting-out system, production was flexible because labor, in an age (at least since the mid-fifteenth century) of chronic underemployment, was readily available. Labor could be added to or reduced by the employer

---

[4] See Maxine Berg, "Markets, trade and European manufacture," in Maxine Berg, ed., *Markets and Manufacture in Early Industrial Europe* (London, 1991), pp. 3–28; and De Vries, "The Industrial Revolution," passim.
[5] Jan De Vries, *The Economy of Europe in an Age of Crisis, 1600–1750* (Cambridge, 1976), p. 91.

without difficulty to expand or contract the volume of output in response to demand. The putting-out system is usually associated with rural, especially textile, production whereby a merchant orchestrates and controls production by "putting out" raw materials to workers (raw wool to spinners, spun thread to weavers, bolts of woven fabric to fullers and dyers, and so on) who then fashion only parts of a finished product (but it should be noted that this way of organizing production took hold in other trades such as nailmaking and in cities as well). The well-documented transformation of the textile industry into a *Verlagssystem* or putting-out system in Nördlingen between the late sixteenth and early eighteenth centuries illustrates this well. Variations on the putting-out system were also employed by mercers everywhere. These entrepreneurs usually were not artisans, but they would often transform goods before selling them in their "general stores" by farming out the modification work to craftsmen.

In the pure form of this mode of production, artisans had little if any control over the movement of the product to market (that function being performed by the merchant). However, quite often we find variations of the putting-out system where artisans employed subcontracting arrangements, and thereby more greatly preserved their independence by hammering out and closing business deals face to face, without the mediation of merchants. In this mode, products were fashioned in a similar way to putting out (component-part production), but artisans were not as dependent upon merchants. Among most urban craftsmen in most cities, the tradition of independence had deep roots, and so small commodity workshops knitted together through subcontracting arrangements were more common than the putting-out system, which was found mostly in trades – above all, textiles – with export markets about which merchants would be better informed than local artisans. However, in both instances – putting out and subcontracted small commodity – there was relatively modest capital investment in physical plant, and production was expanded by a proliferation of very small and increasingly specialized trades.

As demand increased trades proliferated, specialized, and diversified. For five centuries after the Black Death Europeans witnessed the introduction of a vast array of urban-made consumer products in leatherware, metalware, woodworking, luxuries, textiles, and the like. There is no clear timetable for this transformation, nor was it even over time and smooth from place to place; but cities that experienced it first and with the greatest intensity, establishing new trades and turning out novel goods, were those that felt a quickening of commercial demand for their products. Precocious in this regard were cities that, largely because of their advantageous geographic location, engaged in international trade as early as the high Middle Ages. In thirteenth-century Nuremberg, for instance, we can find within its walls goldsmiths, cutlers, furriers, beltmakers, armorers, swordsmiths, scythesmiths, pewterers, and mirrormakers plying their trades and selling their products to middlemen who carried them well beyond the city's walls. The fourteenth century saw the appearance of, among others, wiresmiths, bottlemakers, brass smiths, and dicemakers. By 1400 the registers of the *Rugsamt*, a municipal tribunal specializing in commercial and industrial affairs, listed 141 separate trades, among them such highly specialized ones as playing-card illuminators, brass-bowl makers, honeycake makers, and scalemakers. The trend continued in the sixteenth century, especially in precision metalware (for which this city became renowned), from bells to candlesticks, hinges, doorknobs, and musical instruments; from curtain rods, scissors, and precision scientific instruments, to pistols and cannon.

With shifting consumer demand, trades came and went. Dijon is a well-documented example of the dramatic reconfiguration the artisanry might undergo. In 1464 the tax rolls list 81 different trade descriptions, 14 of which had disappeared from the rolls of 1556. The other 67 trades from 1464, however, were joined by 20 entirely new crafts. By 1643 21 more trades had disappeared, while 11 new ones were listed, and then by 1750 10 had been lost but 36 new ones had appeared. Thus from 1464 to 1750, as the total number of craft descriptions on the tax rolls increased from 81 to 102, fully 67 new descriptions had appeared and 45 had vanished.

Consumer demand and market expansion went hand in glove with artisanal specialization and, despite the mythical status that the autonomous artisan toiling in his workshop with a handful of workers commands in traditional accounts, no craftsman stood alone. Indeed, the more we learn about their business practices, the more we realize how deeply enmeshed artisans were in interdependent networks. Michael Sonenscher and Steven L. Kaplan have recently demonstrated the complexity of these networks in eighteenth-century France. Consider subcontracting. Sonenscher has convincingly shown that during the eighteenth century an expanding and diversifying market was stocked with products from increasingly specialized artisanal enterprises engaged in widespread and intricate subcontracting networks. Most master artisans still made limited runs of articles sold within a range of variable prices, and depended upon perhaps scores of constantly changing and dispersed market outlets, relying upon personal relationships for information about those markets as well as for all-important credit,

possible subcontracted work, and labor availability. The eighteenth-
century economy was certainly more diverse, extensive, and segmented
than ever before, but the outlines of, and the trajectory toward, such an
economy are clearly discernible in preceding centuries.

Craftsmen in the construction trades, for example, had established
subcontracting arrangements almost as far back as we have records of
their activities. Already around 1300 in the Artois we know that master
masons and carpenters who had engaged in large projects would
simultaneously take on smaller jobs and then subcontract the work to
others, sometimes masters in their own guild, sometimes not, and sometimes to craftsmen of nonmaster status. Certain masons in medieval
Bruges became site managers and as such co-ordinated equally elaborate systems of subcontracting with other masons, stonecutters, hodcar-
riers, carpenters, and all the other workers that thronged construction
sites. Little had changed by the fifteenth century, or even the eighteenth,
as construction in Florence or Lyons illustrates. In each instance, and
no doubt in many other early modern cities, projects were bid for and
then jobbed out by masters with more access to capital and credit than
their fellows, and so in effect the lesser masters who lacked the financial
means to take on large projects were hiring out their labor and expertise,
sometimes as foremen of work crews comprised of journeymen masons
and carpenters.

Everywhere we look at late medieval and early modern artisanal
business practices we see subcontracting. Mercers, as we have seen, are
one example, while luxury craftsmen present another. Master craftsmen
in some luxury trades in sixteenth- and seventeenth-century Delft, for
instance, employed such techniques. Montias's study of the craftsmen
producing luxury goods there crisply illustrates the kinds of business
practices we see elsewhere. Adjusting to a contraction of ecclesiastical
patronage in the wake of the triumph of Protestantism in the Dutch
Republic and a simultaneous rise of a domestic mentality among its
people, many Dutch master painters began to market "ready-made"
paintings destined for home decoration (by 1660 45,000 paintings hung
on the walls of Delft homes). To meet the demand of this market, they
subcontracted with other, specialized master or journeyman painters
(some to do expensive, high-quality work, others to turn out cheap
dozjin werck – the same painting rendered, literally, by the dozen). These
entrepreneurs then sold their standardized and "mass-produced" wares
from increasingly large inventories either directly to the public, or to art
dealers.

Subcontracting, evidently, was widely practiced. We know that sixteenth-century butchers rented the stalls in the Paris *boucheries* from the

municipality, then sublet them to so-called *étaliers*, who also did the actual butchering. The "butchers" provided the animals, paid the *étaliers* for slaughtering them and marketing the meat, and cleared a profit in the bargain. In sixteenth-century Augsburg some master furniture-makers of means, rather than expanding their plant, inventory, and labor costs, subcontracted with smaller masters of the same guild to produce component parts of furniture which would then be assembled in the workshop of the contracting master. Similarly, in many crafts in the same city several shops often collaborated on single orders (especially large ones).

In such systems of subcontracting, finished products thus involved several processes. Consider the complex collaboration between craftsmen in production of a horse's saddle in London around 1300. A joiner made the saddle tree, a lorimer the harness, while painters added decoration. The saddler oversaw and co-ordinated the process providing the investment capital and then retailing the finished product. Similar co-ordination and subcontracting took place in the production of works of art. In late medieval Tournai painters were deeply interdependent in networks of subcontracting, as were their Florentine counterparts. Take, for example, the production of the major altarpiece commissioned for the church of San Pier Maggiore in Florence in 1370. Art history books attribute the piece to Jacopo di Cione, but its production actually involved a host of designers, painters, carpenters, and gilders. The manufacture of the gun further demonstrates interconnected systems of production. Ostensibly made by the gunmaker, by the eighteenth century it in fact involved nine different craft processes as the lock, stock, and barrel passed through different, "independent" shops on their way to final assembly in the gunmaker's shop.

Textiles also witnessed innovation in product and diversity in the trades turning it out, as well as systems of subcontracting. Wool, cotton, flax, and silk fabrics were woven in countless varieties of weaves (often of mixed fabric), designs, shapes, and colors, many of these co-ordinated processes occurring in different urban artisan shops. The *sayetteurs* of Lille worked on commission with merchants, sometimes with groups of other masters who would collectively buy raw materials from wholesalers and then commission work and distribute the materials to other master *sayetteurs*.

The situation in the hardware trades of eighteenth-century Birmingham or the edged-steel tools of contemporary Sheffield is no less a part of a visible trajectory of diversification and specialization traceable to the high Middle Ages, the difference being one of degree rather than kind. The streets of Birmingham buzzed with the activity of metal-working craftsmen turning out of their shops a dizzying variety of buckles, lamps, spurs, candlesticks, metal fittings, or kitchen items. The city was a matrix of small, interconnected, and interdependent workshops. The edged-steel tool industry of Sheffield, likewise, was astonishingly specialized: in 1797 fully 134 artisan enterprises made pocket knives, while 81 others made table knives, 33 more made razors, and yet 34 others made surgical instruments. As with many of their craft ancestors, these eighteenth-century artisans were simultaneously independent (they worked on their own account in their own shops, hiring wage-workers as needed) and dependent (credit was usually necessary to purchase raw materials and to pay wages, while the product from their shops was often a component part of another product).

If decentralized small commodity production was the norm from the Black Death to industrialization, we nonetheless can observe "hotspots" scattered around Europe where enterprises were partially organized according to the modern principles we have come to identify with economies of scale. With an eye toward reducing what modern economists have come to call transaction costs, or consolidating access to a market, some enterprises concentrated production in protofactories like the glass works, dyeworks, and brickmaking operations in East London during the seventeenth century, which were concentrated in plants or yards, and artisans traveled from their homes to these protofactories daily for work. Even some small commodity enterprises, however, can be found that reflect a drift to scale. Some of these small enterprises integrated vertically, while others combined horizontally. The modern economic characteristics of volume manufacture of standardized products and uniform pricing can also be seen.

One path to economy of scale has been vertical integration, a way of organizing production and distribution not unknown in the preindustrial economy. Take the butchers of Bologna as an example. In the late sixteenth century the butchers were accused by the tanners of encroaching on the monopoly the tanners supposedly held in tanning hides. The butchers, as events of the seventeenth century clearly prove, were individuals working in individual shops, but who nonetheless collectively attempted to, and for a time succeeded in, vertically integrating the raw leather trade by bringing together the purchase and butchering of cattle and the tanning and marketing of the hides. Other guildsmen elsewhere tried different tactics, but aiming toward vertical integration nonetheless. In the eighteenth century, in order to free themselves from dependence upon the founders, the painter-sculptors of Paris conferred a mastership upon a journeyman without any training in their trade and then arranged with him to do all of their founding and smelting work in return.

In some product lines increasing volume and standardization of product and pricing are evident. We have already seen the example of "mass-produced" paintings being turned out of painters' shops in seventeenth-century Delft, and we find such production processes in other trades as well. Driven by widening demand in the seventeenth and especially the eighteenth century, consumer goods like hats or pottery were increasingly made in volume and in a standard range of styles. Indeed, from 1500 to 1700 we can observe a drift away from bespoke manufacture (that is, the making of customized items ordered by specific clients) to "ready made." This trend is especially visible in the making of clothing and shoes. By the mid-seventeenth century, a ready-made shoe industry had emerged in Northampton, England, as shoe-makers toiling in their own shops made a standard range of footwear primarily for the burgeoning London market. Merchants placing the orders with the craftsmen, of course, reaped the greatest benefit from savings on transaction costs, but the artisans nonetheless received a steady flow of orders. A similar effect was exerted by demand from the militaries of early modern states as the new and expanding standing armies of the seventeenth century were armed, clothed, and shod. Vast quantities of standardized muskets, uniforms, and boots were turned out of countless artisan shops across Europe.

Capital, investment, and credit

Capital from commerce was the fuel that made the manufacturing economy run. Investment patterns in many product lines across Europe show merchants investing in manufacturing. Merchants could move capital in and out of industrial investments without much difficulty since the fixed investment was low; but this does not mean that capital was exceedingly fluid because a great deal of capital was tied up in credit. Credit could take a multitude of forms, from purchase of government bonds to short-term bills of exchange to advances on orders placed. It was not unusual to find merchants or even master artisans providing short-term credit to masters, or becoming silent partners by investing capital in a master's enterprise, either for start-up costs or for continuing manufacture. We find master artisans everywhere loaning and borrow-ing, like everyone else, through personal *rentes* (as they were called in France), or annuities. Kaplan has found that about one-third of the bakers of Paris invested in such annuities, ranging from such modest investments as 162 *livres* to a sizable 47,390 *livres*.

Elsewhere, as in sixteenth-century Seville and seventeenth-century Dijon, artisans took advantage of a building boom by buying houses, sometimes fixing them up, and then renting them. Luis de Ribera, a silversmith in the Spanish city, even owned all of the houses on one block of the Calle de Vigenes in 1600. Whether the capital returned from such investments was channeled back into manufacturing we have no way of knowing, nor can we say beyond speculation that capital from profits from trade or from dowries did so. Wherever the capital went, however, we know that many an artisan's income derived from more than craft production. Sevillian craftsmen, for instance, joined merchants in investing in overseas trading ventures in the booming sixteenth century. Rich artisans like silversmiths could be substantial investors, even trafficking in the slave trade, while more ordinary craftsmen like shoemakers, clothiers, or leather workers not uncommonly pooled their resources and were involved in the occasional shipping of small quantities of merchandise like hides, soap, wax, or honey to the colonies of New Spain.

Dowries were another infusion of capital into a craftsman's purse. The Sevillian sculptor Pedro Millan bought two houses and a workshop with his wife's dowry. Indeed, marriage contracts frequently stated that the dowry was to be used for starting a business, and as such are very good sources of information about start-up costs. In the current state of research we do not know much about this, but what we do know tells us that such costs could substantially tax the means of an ordinary artisan. In Dijon from the mid-fifteenth century through at least the mid-seventeenth, for instance, costs for entering a guild and setting up shop continually escalated. All of the following required expenses went up: fees to the craft confraternity, capital outlay for the materials necessary for the nonmaster to make the masterpiece, providing the food and drink for the celebratory banquet after admission to the guild, and of course, the costs of outfitting a shop.

Indeed, it cost shoemaker Bénigne Rebourg 300 *livres* – no mean sum to a seventeenth-century craftsman – to buy raw materials and tools to start his business in 1632. Tools, especially in precision trades like coppersmithery, could cost a great deal, even 100 *livres*, as they did in Dijon in 1627. In late seventeenth-century London it would cost a dyer, a mason, or a tailor anywhere from 100 to 600 pounds to set up shop, while the sum would run up to 1,000 pounds for a tanner or pewterer, and perhaps 3,000 pounds for a goldsmith. Jacques-Louis Ménétra, the eighteenth-century Parisian glazier, tells us in his inimitable memoirs that it cost him 300 *francs* (equivalent to *livres*) to buy a presumably equipped shop from a fellow master glazier around 1770, a cost perhaps below market since, as Ménétra informs us, "the deal was closed" because "we had been friends."[6] Such amounts required advantageous marriages (Ménétra's future wife advanced him the money to buy the shop), or access to credit. An inexpensive, marginally equipped, and out of the way bakery in Ménétra's city in the 1760s and 1770s would run to at least 300 *livres*, and a prosperous enterprise could sell on the market for 6,000 *livres*, this in addition to fees to join the guild that could reach nearly 1,000 *livres*. For those artisans who could not afford to buy, renting was an option, but again among the bakers of Paris, the range could be vast, from 140 *livres* annually for a bakery in the faubourg Saint-Lazare to 3,200 *livres* for a prime location in town on the rue Aumaire.

Often overlooked in discussions of small commodity enterprises is the ubiquity of credit relations. These are nonetheless fundamental to our understanding of this economy. Many workshops may have been small, but whatever the size, all were immersed in surprisingly elaborate credit and debit networks of mutual dependence that provided the means of doing business. The Florentine Catasto of 1427, for instance, shows long lists of artisans' debtors and creditors, suggesting an extensive web of credit relations. What Peter Earle has said about the late seventeenth-century English economy can be said about the early modern economy as a whole: there was a cash basis to the economy, but credit permeated every aspect of economic life. No shop stood alone, and ironically, this was the source of both the artisan's precarious dependency and his much-valued independence.

Everything hinged on respectability. As Gervase Rosser has noted,

the single most pressing earthly concern of every medieval artisan was the establishment of a good personal reputation. This imperative was accentuated by a relatively high degree of mobility among the working population . . . Until good repute could be vindicated, it would be impossible to obtain credit – that personal credit without which survival in the urban economy was not to be expected.[7]

Receiving credit secured the independence of the master craftsmen and provided a bulwark against sinking into the ranks of wage labor; but indebtedness had to be managed effectively. The artisan who allowed small debts to become large ones faced the threat of plunging to penury and status ignominy. To avoid such shame, artisans had to pay attention to cash flow. Inventories were relatively small because income, and thus the ability to repay debt, was proportional to the velocity of the circula-

---

[6] Jacques-Louis Ménétra, *A Journal of My Life*, trans. Anton Goldhammer (New York, 1986), p. 169.
[7] Gervase Rosser, "Crafts, guilds and the negotiation of work in the medieval town," *Past and Present* 154 (1997), 9.

tion of capital; it may have been unavoidable for artisans to tie up capital in debt and wages, so turnover in inventory was the critical variable in the enterprise's viability. The key to preindustrial profit for merchant and artisan was increasing the speed of circulating capital.

In short, the cash flow problem was one that every artisanal enterprise had to solve to remain viable, and effective management of credit was the way to do it. In fourteenth-century Bruges bankers provided credit overdrafts to producers of cloth, necessary for the drapers because theirs was a business of frequent purchases of materials for small sums and sporadic sales of cloth for larger sums. Similarly, cash flow was eased through credit in fifteenth-century Florence, a place where the general confidence in the recording system of debit and credit was extraordinarily high. Here artisans often were paid in drafts drawn on their current employer's banker. Alternatively, these same artisans might allow credits with their employer to build up, and then pay off their own debts by channeling them through their employer's banker.

Debt management was no simple task, especially if one's customers were aristocrats. The eighteenth-century luxury economy was what Daniel Roche has called a "deferred economy," where the bills that aristocrats owed artisans could go years in arrears. Craftsmen usually got paid, but often after considerable cajoling, eventual threatening, and even litigating. An artisan would start with a friendly, deferential reminder to settle promptly, or to negotiate some sort of mutual satisfaction. If the aristocrat balked, a threat of legal action was next, and records show that artisans in the 1780s increasingly resorted to this, and almost always found the courts sympathetic to their case. Payment, often with interest, was usually forthcoming.

Every artisan encountered the problem of keeping his debts below his credits, but even though we are sure that the web of credit relations was extensive, indeed ubiquitous even in the late Middle Ages, we know surprisingly little about how artisans managed cash flow. Few artisan account books survive, but those that do point to rudimentary single-entry book-keeping techniques. Household and business expenses and income were thrown together and, even among artisans and tradesmen in late seventeenth-century England, or even eighteenth-century Paris, the periodic "taking stock" was simply meant to measure accumulation, not compute annual profits, much less return on capital.

One bright light has been shone on this dark corner of daily, small-scale credit practices by Steven Kaplan in his extraordinary study of eighteenth-century Parisian bakers.[8] The abbé Galiani observed that

[8] Steven L. Kaplan, *Le Meilleur Pain du monde: Les Boulangers de Paris au XVIIIe siècle* (Paris, 1996), esp. chapter 5, "Le pain à crédit."

"everyone buys bread on credit," not just because of scarcity of liquid capital but also because of the intense competition among bakers which encouraged them to offer credit to customers to win their business. To keep track of how much customers owed the baker, rather than keeping elaborate account books of debits and credits (this was still an age of widespread illiteracy, especially among the poorer of the bakers' customers), bakers employed something called a *taille*. This was a long piece of wood split lengthwise into two strips, one for the customer and one for the baker. As the customer made a purchase on credit, the baker notched both strips in the presence of the buyer. When the *taille* was "declared full" by the baker, no more credit would be extended and it was time to pay up.

To remain viable or to prosper, an artisan had to oversee debt management with a keen eye, keeping his ear to the ground for information that a debtor had come into some money, and to be promptly at his door to collect. Obviously, not every artisan could be first in line. For those who could not manage cash flow, and thus not keep credits beyond debts, two options offered, both of them bleak. First, retrenchment, whereby the strapped craftsman reduced his borrowing. This, however, ran against the need for status spending necessary for the maintenance of the all-important social rank. As Daniel Defoe so succinctly put it in the early eighteenth century: "he must live as others do, or lose the credit of living and be run down as if he was broke. In a word, he must spend more than he can afford to spend, and so be undone, or not spend it, and so be undone."[9] If Defoe is correct, retrenchment was the slippery slope to loss of status and even bankruptcy.

The rise of retail shops

Within Europe's cities we can observe some transformations in the artisanry. Certainly there was specialization in product and producer, and also specialization in market. Fashionable aristocratic consumption drove a greater proportion of artisans toward luxury production, as we will see. The thirst for imitation by the lower orders, in turn, triggered "populuxe" consumption and production which reached a vast scale in the eighteenth century. Moreover, the increasingly standardized products of this expansion and transformation were marketed in new ways, notably from "bespoke" to retail. It is between 1500 and 1700 that we find the emergence, and, if not the generalization then at least the

---

[9] Quoted in Peter Earle, *The Making of the English Working Class* (Berkeley, 1989), p. 132.

spread of the retail shop, described by the Bristol merchant John Carey in 1695 as "the wheel whereon the inland trade turns."[10]

Artisans had for centuries marketed their goods through a combination of individual, open shop windows and market stalls erected on market days in the central square, or at periodic fairs. In most cases (food purveyors being the notable exception), they displayed a few samples of their products and took orders. Such business practices required little in the way of inventory. During the early modern period, however, we find more shopkeeping artisans offering a greater variety of increasingly standardized products, sometimes made elsewhere, as regional specialization and market integration proceeded. By 1550 this transformation was already well under way in London, as it was in most urban centers during the second half of the sixteenth century.

The growth of retail shopkeeping meant that artisan shopkeepers needed a deeper inventory, which in turn required an increase in the scale of operation. Most shops of this nature still could be classified as small commodity, but the demand for capital nonetheless incrementally increased (start-up costs continually rose, for instance, especially during the eighteenth century). One result was further specialization in manufacturing and marketing. For example, among the seventeenth-century London pewterers, we find those with most capital and the largest inventory supplying wholesale customers. Few of these men actually produced what they sold, instead buying the product from small masters who also turned out specialized items (and sold some from their own shops) dictated by the wholesaler and, indirectly, by the consumer market. There were also retailing pewterers with sizable stock who did manufacture the product (or, more accurately, oversaw and organized the production in their workshops) and who sold to both retail and wholesale customers. We can find similar subcontracting and marketing arrangements in many commodity trades, in some instances leading to a complete separation of manufacturing from retailing. The day when the manufacturing artisan no longer retails his product is still long in the future – even in London only about 14 percent of the employed population were shopkeepers in 1700 and even in 1850 – but the trend to purveying increasingly standardized commodities from fixed premises rather than selling bespoke goods in the open, central market was clearly underway in the sixteenth century and was accelerating thereafter.

[10] Quoted in H. Mui and L. H. Mui, *Shops and Shopkeeping in Eighteenth-Century England* (London, 1989), p. 6.

The luxury trades

A closer look at the specific experience of three important and dynamic sectors of the early modern craft economy – the luxury, building, and textile trades – will demonstrate some of the historical characteristics we have been discussing: diversity, extension, and segmentation of market, specialization of producer, and standardization of product. Recent literature on the consumer revolution of the late seventeenth and eighteenth centuries has pointed toward changes in taste and fashion which, on the one hand, intensified consumption of expensive luxury products by an elite that found capital increasingly concentrated in its hands, and on the other, broadened consumption of "populuxe" goods by a growing "middling sort" of well-off tradesmen, artisans, merchants, and legal and medical professionals.

The sixteenth and seventeenth centuries saw a growing aristocratic presence in towns, as a self-conscious refinement, dissociation, distinction, and sense of cultural difference between social strata increasingly marked urban society. Distinction was made visible by consumption, and such consumption, coupled with growth in private building, is considered to be a significant catalyst to economic expansion. Indeed, historians now agree that in the late seventeenth and eighteenth centuries the luxury trades, especially in France but also nearly everywhere else, comprised one of the most substantial sectors of the urban economy. Louis-Sébastien Mercier wrote that in the 1770s and 1780s an "explosion of luxury, taste, and fashion" had rocked Paris, adding that "600 mansions were built, that on the inside looked like a fairyland," as furniture became an important object of luxury and expense.[11] Mid-eighteenth-century Madrid was gripped by similar consuming habits, and over half of its artisans produced items – quality textiles and leather goods, jewelry, objects of precious metal – to meet the demand.

If we know a good deal about such spending during the "consumer revolution" of the 1700s, we are considerably less informed about earlier centuries. Surprisingly, however, scattered evidence suggests that similar cultural forces had been exerted for centuries, if not on the same scale, and in the process had transformed luxury trades and building industries into the complex enterprises we tend to associate only with a later period.

For example, in the low countries of Flanders and Brabant in the fifteenth century, as the textile industry contracted, industrial renewal and the emergence of new guilds centered on luxury goods – painting,

---

[11] Quoted in Michael Stürmer, "An economy of delight: court artisans of the eighteenth century," *Business History Review* 53 (1979), 497.

embroidery, carpets, fashionable clothing – largely because of the domestic demand stimulated by fashionable consumption at the court of the dukes of Burgundy and by members of the urban elite bent on emulation. This economy was, of course, organized corporatively, and the cell of production and distribution was the artisanal workshop. To domestic demand, however, was added an export market, as demand for Flemish and Brabantine luxuries escalated to the point where, according to Van der Wee, they began to flood Europe in the late fifteenth and sixteenth centuries.

Whether or not this constituted a "commercial revolution," as Van der Wee suggests, with the expansion of the market came a transformation of business organization, especially in the direction of specialization and segmentation which carried into the seventeenth century. Surviving contracts commissioning tapestries and paintings, for instance, show that some specialists would weave, embroider, or paint only faces, others only hands, dresses, or landscapes, passing the tapestry or painting from shop to shop as the process was completed. As labor became increasingly specialized, so too did particular towns in the production of particular luxury products. Malines, Brussels, Ghent, and Bruges were renown as centers of the production and export of lace and fine linen. Leiden was famous for cut diamonds, while Delft emerged as the center for majolica.

In their response to demand for luxury items and their cheaper imitations, the artisans of Delft illustrate many of the trends in the artisanal economy we have discussed thus far. We have already encountered the "mass" production of paintings called, appropriately, *dozjin werck*, which found their way onto the walls of tens of thousands of Dutch homes. Earthenware production follows a similar pattern, becoming increasingly specialized as master faience-makers discontinued making the clay tiles in house, opting instead to purchase them in bulk from subcontracted artisans specializing in the task. Once under the master faience-maker's roof, the raw tiles were decorated, baked, and sold in bulk (priced uniformly in 1,000-unit lots). To reduce costs, the painted designs became less elaborate, more standardized, and increasingly in the subsequently famous blue and white, which sold for at most a quarter of the cost of the formerly popular polychrome tiles.

A similar development can be traced in Tuscany, over much the same period. Although Florence had long been known for luxury goods by the sixteenth century, the demand for luxury products grew in the fifteenth, sixteenth, and seventeenth centuries precisely as the woolen industry leveled off then shriveled, bringing a whole new set of luxury crafts into existence. It was during this time, as Brown and Goodman note, that "large numbers of people concerned themselves with the pursuit of fashion and of refined material culture."[12] These fashion-conscious, status-proclaiming consumers (who included many artisan families) exerted a noticeable demand for decorated furniture, glassware, glazed ceramics, musical instruments, silks, and the like, and craftsmen were drawn into these sectors of the economy to satisfy the demand.

Shops of all kinds proliferated. In Benedetto Dei's description of Florence in 1470, he counted eighty-four shops for woodcarving and inlay, fifty-four for decorative marble and stone, and forty-four for gold- and silversmithing. Between 1561 and 1642 the number of shops dedicated to making and selling glassware exploded from ten to thirty-two, ceramic shops from eight to thirteen, lute and harpsichord makers from two to eleven, far outpacing the general population growth of Florence which inched up by about 15 percent over roughly the same period. Sixteenth-century Seville likewise became oriented toward quality production, the result of the demand of an elite which was thriving from the transatlantic trade. The city's most numerous craftsmen, not accidentally, were the embroiderers, painters, silversmiths, engravers, and sculptors.

The growth of a European conspicuously consuming aristocracy during the early modern centuries has been amply documented. Best known are the excesses of the courtly aristocrats. The wealthy inhabitants of large, aristocratic houses were prodigious consumers of luxury goods and services. In Paris in 1760s and 1770s, for instance, five aristocratic houses employed in one way or another 1,800 artisans from 200 different trades. The hotel Kinsky, to take but one of these, underwent constant alterations from the end of the 1770s to the early 1790s, the Princess Kinsky employing in the process over a hundred craftsmen whose ranks included seventeen painters, fourteen sculptors, seven upholsterers, six carpenters, and three cabinet-makers. The Duchess Fitz-James of Paris was a big spender, too. Between 1786 and 1788 she spent 400,000 *livres* in debt settlements to over 200 artisans and merchants, with 20,000 *livres* alone going to one joiner, 17,000 *livres* to a jeweller, 10,000 *livres* to an ironsmith, 9,000 *livres* to a carpenter, 7,000 *livres* to a wheelwright, and 6,000 *livres* to an upholsterer.

Stupendous as this kind of aristocratic consumption was, we should not ignore the importance of the burgeoning numbers of the elite in general in this robust luxury economy – office-holders, financiers, merchants, lawyers, and *rentiers*. These men (and their spouses) were no

---

[12] Judith C. Brown and Jordan Goodman, "Women and industry in Florence," *Journal of Economic History* 40:1 (1980), 75; Richard Goldthwaite, *The Building of Renaissance Florence: An Economic and Social History* (Baltimore, 1980), p. 350.

less intent on proclaiming status by display, and as a great deal of the capital flowing into royal coffers was so often redirected towards these men's pockets, they had ample and growing resources to finance luxury consumption. The artisanal sector of local economies was often transformed in the process. We shall return to this topic when we analyze the workforce in the following chapter, but so dramatic was the impact of this kind of consumption on the organization of work, that it is worth commenting on it here.

In Dijon, which seems a typical example of its kind, from 1464 to 1750 the office-holding class grew from about 3 percent of the total population of heads of households to over 12 percent (the total number of laymen and women in town with tax exemption by reason of office and/or nobility expanded from 57 to 567). Over the same period, the percentage of artisans working in the luxury trades increased from 3.8 percent to 9 percent. Some trades closely tied to fashion witnessed meteoric growth. Whereas goldsmiths, pewterers, and painters comprised 26 of the 31 artisans engaged in luxury production in the fifteenth century, by the mid-eighteenth century these three trades counted for only 29 of 133 artisans in this sector. By 1750 14 sculptors were working in Dijon, as were 32 wigmakers, 15 faience-makers, 14 glassmakers, and 14 carriage-makers. In 1464 there were only two glassmakers in town and only one sculptor, while there were no wigmakers (no one wore wigs then), faience-makers, or carriage-makers at all. Indeed, the one-in-eleven proportion in 1750 probably underrepresents the number of artisans catering to the luxurious demands of members of the elite. Certainly many locksmiths (whose numbers nearly doubled from 13 to 24 between 1643 and 1750) fashioned wrought iron products for elite dwellings, while many tailors (whose numbers swelled from 80 to 144 over the century before 1750) were called upon to make the sumptuous clothes so desired by these members of the elite. During the great period of grandiose townhouse construction commissioned by these magistrates – the seventeenth and eighteenth centuries – the percentage of all artisans laboring in the construction trades increased from just over 10 percent in 1464 to nearly 16 percent in 1643 and 1750. The number of stonecutters – those essential craftsmen in townhouse construction and decoration – mushroomed from zero in 1556 to forty-six in 1750.

Members of the elite with a taste for luxury transformed the artisanry in other towns as well, and well before the eighteenth century. Rome in the early sixteenth century housed a relatively large elite population – the aristocracy and the clergy and courtiers attached to the papal court. Of course, members of the Roman elite spent on luxury items of all sorts; already in 1526 more than one in nine artisan household heads (of

1,760) was producing luxury items, a proportion that no doubt under-represents the actual number catering to the elite since certainly many tailors and leatherworkers (classified in different categories) made luxurious items for these conspicuous-spending men and women (see illustrations 1 and 2). Rome also experienced a construction boom that spanned the sixteenth century and was capped by the Catholic Reformation-inspired building program of Sixtus V after 1585. This free-spending pontiff (and some of his successors) were bent on glorifying the Church of Rome, thus providing work for many carpenters, masons, and tilers (16.4 percent of the 1,760 artisan household heads already in 1526–7), not to mention the thousands of unskilled day laborers thronging the construction sites.

Saint Charles Borromeo had said that in Rome in his day, the late sixteenth century, two things were needed to succeed: to love God and to have a carriage. Many of the elite agreed. By 1594 883 carriages owned by 675 people could be counted on the streets of Rome. In Paris in 1720 there were 15,000 carriages. To meet the demand for this novel and increasingly popular form of luxury, artisans began making them, or rather, making their component parts. In Florence in 1561 there were no coachmakers at all, yet by 1642 there were thirteen. The occupational description "coachmaker," however, obscures the number of artisans who were in fact involved in the manufacture of carriages. Coachmaking ushered in a riot of specialization, and although the final product was assembled in a "coachmaker's" shop, in fact the carriage's constituent parts were produced in a wide array of individual shops. The following eighteenth-century example shows how far specialization had gone, for the London parish of St. Martin's in the Fields was a veritable coach factory without walls. Here fully seventeen trades were found to participate in "coachmaking," with "coachbuilders" assembling the carriage whose parts were made by, among others, coach-frame makers, coach-harness platers, coach-harness makers, coach joiners, coach painters, coach-spring makers, coach trimmers, and coach wheelwrights. In contemporary Paris we find the same, with blacksmiths and ironsmiths forging the axles, springs, and hinges, harnessmakers dressing the leather, and joiners building the body, with saddlers decorating the inside and painters, gilders, and mirrorcutters the outside.

Rapid growth, specialization, and component-part production and assembly mark clock- and watchmaking no less than coachmaking. Weight-driven clocks were developed around 1300, and for 200 years these large timekeeping devices were made by teams of ambulant clockmakers, many who also were locksmiths and blacksmiths (illustration 3). Late medieval clockmakers belonged to no particular professional

Illustration 1 Seventeenth-century tailor. Photo Bibliothèque nationale de France, Paris

Illustration 2   Seventeenth-century shoemaker. Photo Bibliothèque nationale de France, Paris

Illustration 3 Fifteenth-century clockmaker's shop. Biblioteca Estense, Modena (Ms. lat. 209=alfa.X.2.14: *De Sphaera*). Reproduced by kind permission of the Ministero per i Beni e le Attività Culturali

category, and the technical competence for building clocks existed in various crafts (weaponsmiths, goldsmiths, and above all locksmiths). Clockmakers were a mobile lot, often working regions of a diameter of two to four days' journey. Heinrich Halder, for instance, worked in Lucerne, Basle, and Strasbourg between 1373 and 1419.

With the invention of the much smaller spring-powered clocks around 1500 a new market was opened up and increasingly professionalized, corporatively organized, and sedentary clockmakers came into being. Though most towns of any size likely had a few of these resident craftsmen, an export market emerged in the sixteenth century with artisans in a handful of towns in central Europe – which had had a tradition of accomplished metalworking – making and selling timepieces across Europe. Strasbourg, Ulm, Nuremberg, and above all Augsburg emerged quickly as the clock- and watchmaking capitals of Europe. Indeed, between 1550 and 1650 Augsburg licensed 182 master clock-makers, and in any given year this town could count fifty to seventy shops, each shop turning out fifteen to twenty-five timepieces annually. Like coachmakers, clock- and watchmakers everywhere actually as-sembled component parts which had been manufactured in other shops, often through a subcontracted arrangement (thus the importance of skilled metalworkers, especially those accomplished in making gears and transmission devices). These German cities retained pride of place in the timepiece market until the invention and manufacture by the English and the Dutch of the pendulum clock in 1657 and the spring balance pocket watch around 1700. The latter especially had the potential to become a mass-produced consumer durable, as indeed it did by the late eighteenth century. Between 1775 and 1800 300,000 to 400,000 such timepieces entered the market from watchmaker shops in Europe each year.

Building trades

The building industry illustrates the characteristics of diversity, exten-sion, and segmentation that marked preindustrial craft production more than has commonly been realized. The construction market tended in the late medieval and early modern period to be local in nature, in respect both to demand and to supply, where employers tended to hire local craftsmen who in turn relied upon, given the difficulty of transport, a local or regional supply of building materials. Still, the industry saw much specialization and expansion over these centuries.

In late fourteenth- and fifteenth-century Florence, specialization was already the rule (although there was, as elsewhere since the Middle Ages, a remarkably free mobility of individual craftsmen between trades, no doubt following market opportunities). Master wallers headed small crews which specialized in masonry, or tiling, or laying foundations. Like these independent workmen, stonecutters likewise often specialized in specific tasks (illusration 4). Some quarried stone and chiseled it into rough blocks ordered by a builder, while others worked in shops and carved the blocks into decorative pieces to order. Some entrepreneurial wallers and stonecutters had an eye toward expansion. Some wallers performed a range of tasks, while some stonecutters integrated the provisioning of decorated stone vertically by organizing the entire production of quarrying, cutting, and carving. All of this was contracted with a builder, likely the "purveyor" (*provveditore*) hired by the employer to arrange for supplies, check on deliveries, pay for wages and materials,

Der Steynmetz.

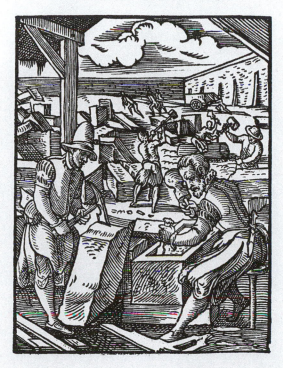

Ich bin ein Steinmetz lange zeit/
Mit stangn/Winckelmäß vñ Richtscheit/
Ich auffricht Steinheuser wolbsinn/
Mit Keller/gewelb/Bad vnd Brünn/
Mit Gibelmauwrn von Quaderstein/
Auch Schlösser vnd Thürnen ich meyn/
Setz ich auff festen starcken grundt/
Cadmus erstlich die Kunst erfund.

Illustration 4   Sixteenth-century stonemason. Reproduced with permission from Jost Amman and Hans Sachs, *The Book of Trades*, New York: Dover Publications, 1973

Illustration 5   Early fifteenth-century builders at work. From *Livre des profits champêtres* by Pierre de Crescent. Bibliothéque de l'Arsenal, Paris. Photo Bibliothèque nationale de France, Paris

and to oversee the foreman who was entrusted with handling the technical aspects of the construction project.

Such an organization of production was probably typical of most construction sites throughout early modern Europe (illustration 5). Often this segmentation was driven, as was the case in eighteenth-century Lyons, by impoverishment of some masters within the trade.

These unfortunates lacked the financial means to purchase materials for large projects, and so hired themselves out to the large builders, sometimes as foremen of work crews of journeymen masons or carpenters.

Most construction in most cities probably dealt with repairs to roofs, doors, and windows, and so most businesses were small and shop-based (illustration 6). Still, like all aspects of the craft economy, the building industry was heterogeneous, with some builder artisans expanding their operations into contracting when possible. With the housing boom for middling and upper-class families, especially in Europe's capitals and port cities that commenced in some places like Seville in the late sixteenth century and continued in other places through the eighteenth, the opportunities to expand for artisans with access to credit were close to hand. In some places there emerged contractors who organized, often speculatively, vast home-building projects. Antwerp, Paris, and London all had such businessmen, many of whom had begun their careers as artisan builders. Large-scale, multicraft building projects linked in a web of subcontracting were not, however, confined to the capitals – witness Dijon – nor, as Elizabeth Musgrave has shown for eighteenth-century Brittany, were all of the contractors men.

A close cousin to construction of buildings was the making of boats and ships. Both trades had a highly fluid workforce that moved from site to site or yard to yard, and in and out of trades. Both were concentrated outside the workshop, though some shipwrights and caulkers, like carpenters, masons, or glaziers, did maintain shops (often run by wives and daughters, as the glazier Ménétra explicitly points out) to house their supplies and tools, and from which to organize business operations (taking orders, keeping the books). Similarly, like building construction, shipbuilding was heterogeneous in organization and scale. In the Low Countries, for example, independent craftsmen with small crews and with access to sheltered waters and a stretch of flat shoreline built small vessels of under 50 tons. Before the mid-sixteenth century this was the overwhelming norm throughout Europe, as ships were relatively small. After that, however, dramatic changes occurred in shipping and shipbuilding, and although small workcrews continued to produce boats and small ships, larger ships were increasingly turned out of yards whose scale dwarfed the traditional operations. Like the large contractors in the general building industry, the scale of operations could be vast.

It is well known that the Dutch were the preeminent shipbuilders of seventeenth-century Europe. During a typical year of that booming century fully 250 shipyards churned out between 300 and 400 ships of 200 tons or more. The seventeenth century had seen a dramatic expansion in this industry, in terms of total tonnage, even as the number

Illustration 6   Carpenter's workshop. From *Les Quatre Etats de la vie de l'homme* by Jean Bourdichon. Photo Bibliothèque nationale de France, Paris

of construction wharves contracted. For hundreds of years before that shipbuilding had been much like other crafts. It required little capital investment, it was urban, and the builder was an independent producer who lived and worked on the property and was assisted by a small workcrew consisting of an apprentice, a handful of hired wage-workers, and a subcontracted master craftsman or two with specialties in making specific objects for fitting out the vessel. Throughout the early modern period, some artisans engaged in shipbuilding were masters of guilds, a status which permitted them to bid for and get a contract for constructing parts of a ship, fitting it out, or undertaking repairs to it.

Before 1600 many small, independent producers could do this, but so dramatic were the changes in the Dutch industry in the seventeenth century that guild masters came to be only those few who owned wharves, rich men with access to capital. There are several reasons for this contraction in the ranks of masters and small-scale independent shipbuilders. First, costs of raw materials, especially wood, rose steadily from the sixteenth to the eighteenth century. Second, Dutch innovation in ship design (notably the flyboat which reduced cargo transport and crew costs) made Dutch ships the prized vessels of not just the expansive Dutch ocean-going fleets, but of many other European states as well. The combination of cost-efficiency and the expansion of overseas commerce spelled demand for Dutch ships. Whereas in 1532 about 400 Dutch ships sailed the seas, by 1636 there were at least 2,500 and perhaps as many as 4,300 of them, and these latter ships were also at least twice the size of the former, topping out at 300 to 500 tons, against the typical 70- to 100-ton vessel of the sixteenth century. Obviously, construction of these vessels consumed more material, more labor, and more capital.

To meet the demand and to keep production costs low and competitive, the industry was reorganized. Orders for larger ships mounted while those for smaller vessels, the construction of which smaller shipbuilders might have afforded, diminished. The industry was increasingly centralized in the hands of a relatively small number of wharf-owners who had the capital and access to credit that would make production of many large ships possible. Capital costs continued to spiral upward into the eighteenth century, driving out of business the smaller, independent producers without adequate capital to own or lease slipways, purchase materials and equipment, or hire a large workforce.

English shipbuilding shared many of the characteristics of its Dutch counterpart, but departed from the Dutch experience in significant ways as well. Unlike Dutch shipbuilding, small-scale English production (vessels of under 50 tons) was not destroyed by firms building larger ships, and few shipbuilders saw the consolidation of manufacture and the concentration of capital that Dutch shipbuilding did. Even ship-builders constructing the larger vessels in the seventeenth century did not have operations on the Dutch scale. Few builders turned out even a ship a year; even the largest, like the Graves brothers of Limehouse or the Foord brothers of Ipswich, only turned out about fifteen 200–300-ton ships each between 1626 and 1637. Like all English-built ships, these were built to order (in contrast to the Dutch where speculative as well as commissioned shipbuilding increased after 1600) and payments were made to the shipbuilder in installments, thus reducing the shipbuil-der's need for large reserves of capital. The shipbuilder (often the master shipwright) subcontracted with various master craftsmen from carpen-ters to caulkers, and hired wage-workers as needed. Only the largest operations would employ as many as 100 men. Unlike the Dutch master wharf-owners, few English shipbuilders made a fortune in the business.

Certainly, since the 1570s and up to the 1640s, the English yards turned out larger ships. Many of these were substantial, heavily masted and well-armed warships built for the navy, while others were the great "East Indiamen," enormous vessels of 600 to 700 tons trading in the Levant and the East Indies. These craft, most of which were built along the Thames in London, were well suited to their purpose, but with the expansion and diversification of English shipping in the second half of the seventeenth century, a merchant fleet consisting of Dutch-style vessels came to be increasingly desired. Flyboats seized by the English from the Dutch in the three Dutch wars between 1652 and 1674 satisfied the demand for a time (and also depressed the home industry, irreparably destroying the Ipswich yards). As these ships began to wear out in the final decades of the century, however, the English ship-building industry, notably on the northeast coast, responded by produ-cing ships modeled on Dutch design and suited to competing effectively with them.

Daniel Defoe observed in the early eighteenth century that "The whole [Thames] river . . . from London Bridge to Black Wall is one great arsenal," estimating that no fewer than thirty-three shipyards operated there.[13] Clearly, London was still a shipbuilding center of importance, primarily continuing to build ships for the navy and the East and West India Companies; but during the eighteenth century the center of gravity of the English shipbuilding industry decisively shifted to the northeast coast from Newcastle to Scarborough. Whereas in 1790

---

[13] Quoted in Earle, p. 24.

and 1791 the yards of this region produced 249 ships (88 over 200 tons) of nearly 41,000 total tons, London was a distant second with 119 ships (25 over 200 tons) of just over 16,000 tons.

Another great seafaring state of the early modern period, the Venetian republic, also was home to a major shipbuilding industry. Its private sector was organized much like the English, and its public sector, the Arsenal, had similarities with the Dutch. Like the English, most master Venetian shipwrights, called squerarioli, were independent owners of shipyards, usually quite modest in size, at which mostly small craft of well under 100 tons were constructed. The smallest of these enterprises and by far the most numerous shipbuilding operations in Venice were simple boatshops, where the squerarioli and a few helpers made small barges, canal boats, and gondolas. Larger operations, building ships of 100 to 250 tons, would find squerarioli directing construction, co-ordinating acquisition of materials, subcontracting sawyers, caulkers, and carpenters, and hiring of wage-workers. There had always been these small operators in Venice, and boatmakers and shipbuilders of modest size continued to exist throughout the history of the Venetian republic.

Larger ships, those of from 250 to 600 tons – first the merchant galleys of the Middle Ages and then the great galleys and roundships of the late fourteenth and fifteenth centuries – were constructed under different conditions. Larger shipyards, more and more expensive materials (larger timbers were needed, often having to be shipped to the lagoons from a distance at great expense), and access to more and more specialized craftsmen (with innovations in rigging, for example, came specialized pulleymakers and mastmakers) meant that few if any master shipwrights could finance the operation. Thus, with these vessels merchant customers commissioned shipwrights to direct and co-ordinate the project, and financed the construction.

Private shipbuilding of great galleys and roundships fared well enough until the second half of the sixteenth century when competition from the Dutch was felt. It was easy enough for a Venetian merchant to transfer funds to the Netherlands and then finance the construction of a Dutch flyboat. To preserve the private Venetian shipbuilding industry, and their own livelihood, entrepreneurial shipwrights like Bernardin Sebastiano Rosso proposed to the republic that credit be extended, not to shipwrights, but to merchant customers who might commission projects. It was hoped that such an inducement would encourage these merchants to keep their capital in Venice, and it would save the shipwright from shouldering a heavy debt. Such creative financing did induce some merchants to build in Venice, but in the long run it did little to arrest the slide in the construction in Venice of private ships of more than 100 tons.

Public shipbuilding in the Arsenal, in contrast to the Venetian private sector and to the English example, became in the sixteenth century increasingly centralized as production grew in scale and the product – the light galley for the war fleet – became increasingly standardized. The Arsenal had begun as a state-owned storehouse for naval supplies which were consigned to private shipbuilders making vessels for the Venetian fleet. In the 1320s the Arsenal expanded operations to include ship-building, but only a dozen master craftsmen were continually employed there. This changed in the 1450s, which saw a new wave of expansion of the war fleet, and then another in the middle third of the sixteenth century (with the Turkish threat), and then again in the seventeenth century. With each wave of expansion shipbuilding was in some way reorganized, but most notable was the shift to an economy of scale, in some ways mirroring the Dutch development. Production of ships, as Frederick Lane and Robert Davis have described so well, followed a line system based on standardization of design and serial assembly of inter-changeable parts crafted by specialists and assembled by work gangs. In the sixteenth and seventeenth centuries the Arsenal turned out an average of seven to ten galleys a year (the sixteenth-century private sector, in contrast, might produce in a good year four or five round-ships), with some notable years far in excess of that average – in 1651 the number was thirty. Of course, in the Arsenal it was the state that owned the operation rather than a wealthy cadre of wharf-owners, but in both the Venetian and Dutch cases capital was concentrated, production was expanded and increasingly standardized (with shipwrights, foremen, and gang bosses delegating the increasingly standardized and specified tasks to legions of artisans), and the range of products was increasingly narrowed (the Arsenal produced only a few types of galleys, galleasses, and cutters, while the Dutch focused on the flyboat).

Royal manufactures and the textile trades

Clearly, then, as luxury trades and especially shipbuilding so starkly illustrate, the heterogeneity of artisanal production in general ranged from small workshops to emergent economies of scale. Indeed, it was often the case with the latter that the state was involved, either as outright owner (as with the Arsenal, the Gobelins in France, the Lagerhaus in Prussia which manufactured uniforms for the military, or the Royal Porcelain Works in Vienna and Berlin), or, as was more common, as financiers or investors providing subsidies, loans, and privileges. Everywhere in Europe, especially in the seventeenth and eighteenth centuries, central governments, in the face of accelerating economic growth and foreign competition, intervened to create and protect useful industries whose viability it deemed important to the interest of the state or the public welfare. Generally, this meant protection from competition for a new industry, and so state intervention usually took the form of granting of privileges, the most important being a monopoly on the production and sale of a particular product. The best-known illustration of this development occurred in seventeenth- and eighteenth-century France, when kings from Henri IV to Louis XVI granted hundreds of privileges establishing protected industries called "royal manufactures." Most of these were privately owned, often by individual entrepreneur artisans (sometimes called "court artisans"), but those that survived were almost always relatively large concerns with a high degree of integration, a network of affiliated workshops and warehouses run by managers and technical directors and co-ordinated by an entrepreneur artisan. These firms reveal labor and product specialization, making long runs of standardized, often luxury goods like porcelain or clothing, sold at relatively uniform prices and marketed through established, durable, and relatively secure channels to a concentrated body of consumers. Often the market was the court and the aristocracy surrounding it, or the state itself.

The sector that benefited most from royal privilege was unquestionably textiles. In France between 1661 and 1683 of the 113 titles of royal manufacturer Colbert granted, 55 went to companies making textiles, several of which specialized in the manufacture of uniforms for the expanding ranks of the French army. Such concentration in textiles continued into the eighteenth century. Between 1683 and 1753 of the 243 royal manufacturers created, 149 were in textiles, and again the state was an important customer as the demand for uniforms continued to grow with the size of armies. Clearly, a viable textile sector was deemed essential to a state's economic health, and small wonder, since this sector was the largest of the early modern, and before that, of the medieval economy.

The well-known history of textiles in Europe from the Middle Ages to industrialization has emphasized the shift of an urban-based industry to the countryside, and a transformation of industrial organization from independent artisanal workshops to a putting-out cottage industry to mechanized factories. There is, of course, a great deal of truth in this general picture (which has received considerable attention in the proto-industrialization literature), and ostensibly, then, because of the rural nature of the textile industry, it lay outside the scope of this study of urban artisans. It is true that in some areas in the sixteenth and seventeenth centuries, like some towns in the Low Countries (Ghent, Bruges, and Ypres, for example), competition from villages like Hondschoote and from countries like England destroyed the textile sector of the economies of the towns that had geared their productive capacities to heavy woolen broadcloth. The competition was destructive because not only was cloth being manufactured more cheaply (rural industry everywhere was organized on a putting-out, piecework basis under which rural workers labored more cheaply than their urban counterparts), but a different kind of cloth was being made.

The "new draperies," as they were called, were not as durable as the traditional broadcloth, but they were lighter and cheaper to make and to sell. The wool comprising the new cloth, which was called worsted, was combed before spinning, but unlike the heavy woolens which were shrunken, beaten, and pressed after weaving, worsted cloth underwent no further postweaving treatment. The production of the new draperies were therefore less labor and capital intensive. They came to dominate the textile sectors of the economies of the Low Countries and England, as they destroyed those of places like Venice and Barcelona. These latter cities had specialized in high-quality woolen manufacture, and saw their prosperity in this sector peak in the sixteenth century. In Venice between 1500 and 1565 wool production increased tenfold, while silk output tripled. In 1570 at least 7,000 people were employed in Venetian textile manufactories, working as many as twenty-five looms in a single shop. Glassworks at Murano and the building industry boomed as well. By 1600, however, the textile markets, notably in the Mediterranean, had been invaded by northern Europeans selling the lighter and cheaper cloths, and as demand for the traditional cloths slackened, the looms of Venice and Barcelona fell increasingly silent.

If the story of the urban textile industry in early modern Europe was simply one of dismal decline and eclipse, then a book like this on urban artisans would have nothing more to say about it. However, once again industrial organization was more heterogeneous than we once thought. Recent research has shown that in many towns and cities the textile industry did not wither and die; in some places, it hardly changed at all, while in others it was dramatically transformed, both in manufacturing processes and in product. We find in many German cities, for example, cloth production continued to be controlled by small-scale master craftsmen with most tasks carried out in small workshops, while in others, like Nördlingen or Lille, we find the putting-out system increasingly entrenched – with all of the economic polarization, dependency, and even proletarianization that this entailed. Indeed, urban putting-out systems in textiles can be found even in metropolises like London, and as late as 1759. In that year weavers, working under piecework conditions, represented the most numerous craft practiced in the capital, and fully 14,000 families depended in one way or another on textile manufacture.

Some cities were not ignorant of the advantages of making the "new draperies." Leiden, for instance, became one of the largest industrial cities in Europe in the seventeenth century, and its dominant economic sector was textiles. Flemish artisans skilled at making the new cloth fled Hondschoote for Holland during the Dutch War of Independence (1568–1648) from Spain, which created religious, political, and above all economic turmoil in Flanders. Many of these migrants settled in Leiden. Here they turned out all types of cloth, but especially inexpensive worsteds and fustians (a combination of linen and wool). The abundant labor supply provided by massive immigration (see the following chapter) and escalating product specialization (in the 1660s over 125 separate textile trades existed there) kept production costs low enough to keep international and domestic markets stocked.

Florence also responded to changing market conditions, and also thereby avoided the collapse of its textile sector. The urban woolen cloth industry, the industrial backbone of the late medieval Florentine economy, suffered in the sixteenth century, like everywhere else, from the dual forces of northern European competition and the relocation of industry to the Tuscan countryside. However, as the urban wool industry contracted, urban silk production expanded. Whereas the ratio of wool to silk output in Florence between 1430 and 1439 was 11:1, by 1600–9 it was roughly 13:10. It reached parity during 1620–9, and for the next century silk output exceeded that of wool, between 1660 and 1669 reaching a 10:3 ratio. Indeed, as woolen manufacture contracted or relocated to the countryside, in many cities in Europe – Venice, Lyons, Tours, Geneva, Zurich, Granada, Valencia, London, Amsterdam, Antwerp – silk production expanded, as did the variety of silk cloth – damask, taffeta, satin, velvet.

Regulation and economic activity

Much of the historical writing on guilds in the early modern era has been bedeviled by a lack of distinction between the theoretical nature of the guild system and actual economic practice. Until recently many historians had assumed that the tight regulatory regime that the guild system pronounced in its statutes and that municipal or royal governments endorsed in law restricted economic growth, and thus straitjacketed the development of free market capitalism in places where the guild system was most firmly entrenched. This proposition has now been challenged, with some historians deeply familiar with archival sources about economic activity asserting that the regulatory reach of the guild system was short and incomplete, and that much, in some places most, economic activity hummed along without being influenced significantly by the guilds and governments one way or another.

Until very recently, most historical studies on work from the Middle Ages to the eighteenth century have viewed it through the optic of the official guild organizations of master craftsmen – the mysteries, the *Zünfte*, the *métiers*, the *arti*, the *gremios*. This in turn has focused attention on the records left by these organizations. However, as some historians now recognize, the statutes promulgated by formally constituted crafts were normative or idealistic, and much historical research now focuses increasingly on the gap between such norms and actual practice, and the relationship between the two. This research agenda has also challenged, by extension, the traditional assumption that the guild system was an impediment to the emergence of capitalism.

What role did regulation play in economic practice? How much did it impinge upon work? There is no question that guilds were empowered and indeed enjoined, by municipal, ducal, ecclesiastical, or royal governments to regulate the economy, and were provided with a sanctioned apparatus of enforcement – workshop inspections and access to courts being the most apparent. Indeed, it is hardly unusual to find instances in the archives of the workshops of artisans being searched for illegal materials and contraband or shoddy products, nor is it rare to encounter litigation between guilds over violation of monopoly privileges, or even journeymen suing masters over what would come to be called "unfair labor practices." Guilds were granted monopolies over the production and sale of given products, and artisans from other guilds and outsiders to the guild system altogether (nonmasters, foreigners) were liable to search, seizure, and prosecution if they encroached upon this privilege. Such a visitation could result in the destruction or confiscation of the offending material or product, "false and deceitful wares," as the London authorities put it in the seventeenth century. A fine upon the offending artisan usually followed, and the result of such regulatory actions could be ruinous to the individual. Indeed, searches were in force everywhere we find guilds, and even in London's livery companies searchers were raiding shops into the eighteenth century. Weavers, for instance, held yearly searches into the 1720s, finally abandoning them altogether only in 1736. The clockmakers had done the same only a year before, and the clothworkers were to follow suit only in the mid-1750s.

Searching generally came to a halt after a committee of the House of Commons ruled in 1753 that searches were "injurious and vexatious to manufactures, discouraging to industry and trade, and contrary to the liberty of the subject."[14]

There is no question that a regulatory apparatus was firmly in place wherever guilds were established, and governments were empowered to intervene directly in the economy by means of their own agencies and officials. Take sixteenth-century Nuremberg as an example. Here a five-man municipal tribunal called the *Rugsamt* specialized in industrial and commercial affairs and had jurisdiction over everything pertaining to the making and distributing of products. One of its members, the *Pfänder*, oversaw all market activity, and administered an army of inspectors and market supervisors. There were twenty wood inspectors, and thirty-six officials assigned to the wine trade alone! Properly weighed and measured goods meeting standards of quality were all inspected and tagged if approved.

The Statute of Artificers promulgated in England in 1563 aimed to regulate the economic life of an entire sector of society, the artisanry, but it clearly had supra-economic intentions as well. Artisans were deemed especially turbulent because of their mobility, and so Queen Betty's Law, as the statute was called, struck a blow for social order by attempting to control entry into most trades by the following regulations. Apprenticeship terms were set at seven years regardless of the trade and skill differential; journeymen had to be twenty-four years of age before becoming masters; justices of the peace were empowered to control wages; and any journeyman who changed jobs was required to have a certificate from his previous master releasing the worker from his employ and attesting to his character. The statute also had an anti-combination clause, outlawing "confederacies and conspiracies" among artisans organized to pressure employers on wages or piecerates.

These regulatory regimes foreshadowed the supposed *dirigisme* of mercantilism, best expressed by Colbertism in late seventeenth- and eighteenth-century France and imitated by nearly every state in eighteenth-century Europe. Between 1673 and 1714 in France, a flood of royal regulation washed across the guilds. There were no fewer than 450 *réglements* on manufacture, and another 500 on the policing of the trades and on jurisdictions between them. Of course, officials had to be created to administer all of this, so legions of offices like inspector of manufactures, clerk of apprenticeships, and controller of weights and measures

---

[14] Michael Berlin, " 'Broken all in pieces': artisans and the regulation of workmanship in early modern London," in Geoffrey Crossick, ed., *The Artisan and the European Town, 1500–1900* (Aldershot, 1997), p. 87.

were created and sold. Ideally, all of this would be part of a structured society, as the eighteenth-century Lieutenant-General of Police in Paris Lenoir put it in his *Mémoires*. Lenoir imagined that society would be held together by a domestic chain whereby *jurés* would be subject to these officials, masters would be subordinate to *jurés*, journeymen to masters, and apprentices to journeymen. "The influence of the police," Lenoir optimistically dreamed, "can act upon a mass of 200,000 men, among whom each must be guided by another, and everyone, from the first to the last individual, will be well classified, well registered, and held in check by the regulations and demands of discipline and subordination."[15]

Of course, long before Colbert or Lenoir, governments had been attempting to regulate certain aspects of the economy. The most extensive and probably most effective government regulation concerned the food trades, especially baking and butchering. Government regulation of production and sale of food items can be traced back to Carolingian times, notably in the assize of bread. For a thousand years hence governments tied the price of bread to grain in an inverse relationship, factoring in production and labor costs and allowing the baker a "reasonable" profit. Early modern Dijon, in France is typical in how the assize worked. Magistrates periodically purchased several measures of variable quality wheat and then oversaw bakers turning it into bread. A fixed margin between the cost of wheat and the allowable price of bread was allotted, and from this margin the baker had to meet expenses for wood, wages, and rent. Whatever was left was the baker's profit. Clearly, this system could squeeze the baker in times of general inflation unless assizes were frequent and the fixed margin adjusted. Judging from the litany of bakers' complaints, such assizes and adjustments were not frequent enough.

As with bakers, so butchers in Dijon and elsewhere were regulated in a similar fashion: the magistrates bought several animals on the hoof, appointed a butcher to slaughter them, and determined from the yield what price per pound was requisite to cover the costs of wholesale production and still allow a "fair" margin of profit to the butcher (from which overhead had to be paid). And like the bakers, the butchers complained about the inflexible relationship between floating wholesale and fixed retail prices, clamoring for adjustable margins and more frequent assizes.

The regulatory regime could be quite elaborate. The eighteenth-century Parisian police had spies and informants to help the *Inspecteurs*

---

[15] Quoted in Arlette Farge, *La Vie fragile. Violence, pouvoirs et solidarités à Paris au XVIIIe siècle* (Paris, 1986), p. 154 (my translation).

des manufactures nab culprits. For sixteen years a police inspector, Poussot, kept a register of those arrested in his jurisdiction, the quartier of the Halles. Of the 2,692 persons arrested by this inspector between 1738 and 1754, about half were picked up based on information reported by his *mouches*, or spies. Most of the miscreants were young immigrants, mostly journeymen and apprentices from every trade.

There is no question, then, that an elaborate regulatory system emerged in the late medieval and early modern period, and that the regulatory arm reached artisans. But does this mean that such governmental action was often enough or punitive enough to impede economic activity and stifle economic growth in general? Indeed, should the logic of regulation just be measured against the standard of economic efficiency? Granted, guilds and municipalities had an institutional apparatus to enforce regulatory statutes; everywhere the archives are full of instances of violation of these regulations, often rampantly so, even in such ostensibly tightly regulated locales like sixteenth-century Nuremberg. However, the very magnitude of violation has prompted some historians to consider the possibility, even the likelihood, that normal economic practice was a freewheeling affair where licit and illicit activity constantly revealed how inadequate the regulatory apparatus was to actual production, distribution, and consumption. What we see in the archives, so this argument goes, is in fact a juridical and administrative distortion, a misleading reflection of economic activity that cannot measure how effective such regulation was, at least in terms of what impact it may have had upon the economy at large.

Indeed, government regulatory action often reflected, paradoxically, an economy that it could not control. For instance, in 1581 King Henri III of France issued an edict which sought to incorporate all economic activity in the kingdom. An inclusive guild system, however, was immediately recognized to be inadequate to actual production and distribution, and so some subsequent royal legislation is a story about legitimating what appears to be a *de facto* unregulated market. Thus, guild production throughout the seventeenth century and beyond was legally supplemented by ad hoc royal patents and privileges exempting some artisans from guild regulation and surveillance. Patents were granted to particular entrepreneurs or manufacturers, concessions were awarded to foreign merchants to market their goods at fairs, mercers were permitted to sell everything from fine art to clothing to pins (there were several thousand mercers in Paris alone in 1789), and privileged areas like the suburbs (called *sauvetats*) St. Seurin and St. André in Bordeaux or the *faubourg* St. Antoine outside Paris were recognized as effectively "free enterprise zones." Even these concessions could not encompass the dynamic economy, as illegal activities like operating multiple shops, smuggling, unlicensed peddling, and clandestine workers working on their own account outside of guilds proliferated everywhere. In 1748 the tailors of Amsterdam, for instance, were troubled by clandestine, nonguild workers – both male and female – who, it seemed to the masters, were making more clothes than the masters themselves.

Part of the trouble for the regulatory minded was the proliferation of mastership letters sold, in fact, by the crown (fiscal demands, as so often happened, contributed to a subversion of the crown's own regulatory intentions). This had been going on for centuries, but by the eighteenth century it had become a speculative market, as individuals bought the letters and then leased them to other craftsmen, usually nonmasters. This was expressly forbidden by guild statutes everywhere, of course, but nonetheless widely practiced. Take the "wigmaker" M. Lacouture from Bordeaux. He bought seven mastership licenses for wigmaking, keeping one (and presumably practicing the craft) and letting out the other six. This practice was encouraged by the fact that increasingly trades abandoned the making of a "masterpiece" as part of the requirements for admission to the guild. With no demonstrated mastery of the craft's skill required, only the money to buy the license was needed.

It was commonplace among tailors of eighteenth-century Bordeaux to run several shops, despite the illegality of this practice. Others formed equally illegal mergers. Likewise the Parisian goldsmiths. They were constrained by their statutes to allow but 300 shops in the city, but in fact there were 800 of them, many of these being enterprises run by "false workers" who, moreover, received subcontracted work from masters within the guild. The bakers were no different, either in Paris or in Amsterdam. The Dutch guild ordered that members could only operate one shop "in one's own name and on one's own account," but in practice many bakers ignored the law. In Paris the bakers' by-laws specifically prohibited masters from "lending their names" or "renting their masterships directly or indirectly" to nonmasters. Master bakers nonetheless did just that, often by notarized lease contracts. To take but two examples of many, the master bakers Guillaume Grand and Jean Theveneau rented their bakeries to, in the one case, a couple not of the guild, and in the other, several journeymen bakers, even giving the master's protection and *couverture* – or cover – allowing these non-masters to operate their enterprises under the name of the master.[16]

Nor was this just an eighteenth-century development, although owing to the expansion of the consumer-based economy it was probably more

16 Kaplan, pp. 317, 131.

commonplace then. In late medieval London an apprentice tailor might run a shop in his master's name or, a couple of journeymen might pool their capital to open a shop, allowing one of them to buy admission to mastership while the other shared in the venture as a silent partner. And this did not occurr just among tailors, for apprentices and journeymen cutlers in late fifteenth-century London were also accused of opening up shops illicitly.

By the eighteenth century, with the "consumer revolution" at full throttle, whole sectors of the European urban economies operated on a day-to-day basis according to rules more akin to the spot market than the tightly regulated guild world prescribed in statute and legislation. The business practices recounted by the Parisian glazier Jacques-Louis Ménétra in his journal amply demonstrate this.[17] Masters employing masters, journeymen working on their own account for private individuals, masters forming partnerships with other masters and even merchants, journeymen employing apprentices; all of these business practices may have been carried out in autonomous shops rather than factories, but they came together nonetheless in a complex network of subcontracting which, in some product lines as we have seen, rendered the street an early version of the assembly line.

Given the incomplete reach of regulation into economic practice in the early modern era, perhaps we should think of the regulatory regime in political and moral terms as well as economic. Robert Du Plessis and Martha Howell are surely right to suggest that the backbone of the economic system of urban early modern Europe was the independent master artisan working in the small shop assisted by family members and a handful of workers.[18] They are also correct to point out that the chief characteristics of this system were an openness to the expansion of commodity markets and product innovation as well as accelerating specialization and division of labor. However, the goals of this economic system of "small commodity production," as they call it, were not unbridled growth or maximization of profit, but rather full employment, producer autonomy (symbolized hierarchically by the independent master distinct from and superior to the piece- or wage-worker), and a reasonable standard of living. Authorities, moreover, attempted to regulate the system to achieve these goals, which thus were moral and political as much as nakedly economic. They were moral, because harmonious human relations, the highly valued Christian peace, were secured by stability – social, political, economic; they were political

[17] Ménétra, *A Journal of My Life.*
[18] Robert Du Plessis and Martha Howell, "Reconsidering the early modern urban economy: the cases of Leiden and Lille," *Past and Present* 94 (1982), 49–84.

because stability was the surest way to perpetuate existing power relations which positioned magistrates in dominance. To be sure, this ideology had an economic face; in 1575 the ruling oligarchy of Lille asserted that small shops were "best attuned to market conditions, for not only was work closely supervised, thus maintaining the desired level of quality, but a close balance was promoted between output and demand, thus avoiding harmful gluts."[19] Still, regulatory intervention was more about fine-tuning, seeking a balance between, than imposing some economic logic on, recalcitrant or obtuse craftsmen.

What was happening in Lille and Leiden was certainly not unique. In sixteenth-century Augsburg we find magistrates interested in shoring up the deteriorating condition of the town's weavers, and they saw the putting-out system, which seemed to lead to concentration and dependency, as the root of the problem. They responded with strict regulation of the number of looms permitted per workshop. Moreover, sometimes the municipality itself purchased cloth from workshops, sold it, and then used the profits to advance loans to artisans in need of operating capital. Clearly seeking to secure the independence of the individual artisan, their objectives were guided by the ideal of the patriarchal household, a unit of production and reproduction that was assumed to be the microcosm of the well-ordered polity. The master artisan, according to this economic, political, and moral vision, had a self-contained business, financial independence, public honor, a spouse, and political adulthood.

Such a vision did not consider the success of a business as unimportant. In fact, all artisans considered business success vitally important, and the guild was far from considered an impediment to a successful business. In fact, it was seen as the appropriate framework for such business success. In the late medieval Low Countries no less than in eighteenth-century Austria, Italy, or even France, in fact, recent research has demonstrated that one of the key variables in the development of new industries was the creation of new guilds or the novel uses of existing ones. Historians like Jean-Pierre Sosson, Marc Boone, Gail Bossenga, Jean-Pierre Hirsch, and Simona Cerutti have shown how guilds responded flexibly to new market conditions and surging demand, and a clear correlation can be seen between the emergence of new guilds and the emergence and acceleration of the demand for their particular products.[20]

[19] Ibid., 72.
[20] See Jean-Pierre Sosson, "Les Métiers. Norme et réalité – l'exemple des anciens Pays-Bas merdionaux aux XIVe et XVe siècles," in Le Travail au Moyen Age (Louvain-la-Neuve, 1990), pp. 339–48; Marc Boone, "Les Métiers dans les villes flamandes au bas Moyen Age (XIVe–XVIe siècles): Images normatives, réalité socio-politiques et économiques," in Pascale Lambrechts and Jean-Pierre Sosson, eds., Les Métiers au

Philippe Minard has recently cautioned us that efficiency is not the best measure of the role of the guild or the state in the economy. Regulation there certainly was, but if we remove the reductive blinders of economism, we can see other uses to which the system of regulation was put. One very fruitful avenue of recent research has explored the relation between the regulatory regime and social status. Minard himself has found that many successful artisans in fact welcomed the regulatory regime because it served as an external verification that their product was free of defect, and that the artisan who made it was of good credit and sound reputation – a man of honor. Such qualities were hardly simply economic, and demonstrate once again how multifaceted the meaning of status was in the world of the artisan.[21]

It seems that guildsmen in seventeenth-century Spanish towns found the regulatory system of quality control useful for announcing and preserving their good name and social status as well. Here master craftsmen believed that fraudulent production by one guildsman sullied the reputation of them all, and explicitly described the logic of inspection in terms of collective prestige. Even a regulatory practice as seemingly explicitly about economic matters – the search – could have been about status and reputation no less. One might imagine that if the logic were solely economic, then the purpose would be to catch malefactors, and this would be done most efficiently by surprise. And yet London livery company ordinances, for example, stipulated when searches were to take place, and though the intervals varied from guild to guild from quarterly to monthly, they were nonetheless known in advance to all. Importantly, these searches were ceremonial, indeed, public occasions, where guild officials were accompanied by legal representatives of the municipality. The inspecting craftsmen, clad in costumes and proudly carrying the guild's insignia on its banner, marched in a procession from the guild hall through the city, stopping at and inspecting shops along the way, finally ending the demonstration of guild integrity at the fairground at Smithfield. Perhaps to ensure the largest audience, often the procession/inspection was held on market days or coincided with the opening of fairs. Willful malefactors might take the risk of escaping detection, but they could hardly have been surprised by an inspection if it occurred. Guilds like that of the coopers

Moyen Age (Louvain-La-Neuve, 1994), pp. 1–21; Gail Bossenga, *The Politics of Privilege: Old Regime and Revolution in Lille* (Cambridge, 1991); Jean-Pierre Hirsch, *Les Deux Rêves du commerce. Enterprise et institution dans la région Ulloise, 1780–1860* (Paris, 1991); and Simona Cerutti, *La Ville et les métiers* (Paris, 1990).

[21] Philippe Minard, "Normes et certification des qualités. Les Règles du jeu manufacturier au XVIIIe siècle," in *Bretagnes. Art, négoce et société de l'Antiquité à nos jours* (Brittany 1996).

did vary their routes on each occasion, and they searched shops where they had heard abuses might be discovered, but on each occasion they still only searched about thirty shops, and even then the inspection could hardly have been thorough. In all trades, if faulty products were found, they were publicly and ritually destroyed, "burned and consumed," as the basket-makers put it when they found faulty products. These inspections, of course, had an economic side, but they were just as much, perhaps more, about the honor and status of the guild and its members. The inspections were a form of public tribunal, and, as the spectacle-makers and basket-makers put it, were even referred to as "trials" with a "jury" and "witnesses." The turners specifically invoked the language of honor in their ordinances when they announced that the production of "faulty commodities sold [to the public were a] great *slander* of the Misterie [the guild]" (my emphasis).[22]

So what can we conclude about regulation and the economy? Certainly it is time to abandon the assumption that guilds suffocated the economy where they were most deeply entrenched. But we should be equally cautious from running to the opposite extreme by assuming that the regulatory regime was ineffective or irrelevant. Perhaps we must recognize that the regime was extremely flexible, responding to the varieties of needs of artisans and governments. We must appreciate that there were different kinds of markets, and regulation fit differently in them. There was the sprawling, freewheeling, and effectively unregulated clandestine and illegal craft economy. Alongside this economy there was the licensed one, but even here within the official organization of the guild we find ample room for flexibility and economic growth. Indeed, within this official structure we find masters of the same guild competing with one another, availing themselves when possible of the regulatory apparatus to compete more effectively. And finally, there is the prestige economy, where regulation was immersed in the world of status, and was strategically appropriated by artisans for purposes that were much more than simply economic.

Historians of artisans have long assumed that guild regulations so clearly articulated in corporate statutes were an accurate reflection of economic activity. A corollary to this assumption is the assertion that such regulations stunted the early modern economy. Recent research has prompted us to question these positions. No doubt guild or governmental regulation affected many artisans in their worklife, but the evidence for artisanal economic vitality is too overwhelming to draw the conclusion

[22] Berlin, p. 81.

that regulation smothered the economy. The traditional picture of the craftsman toiling alongside a couple of workers in a shop turning out finished products that conformed to guild regulations, therefore, is not so much inaccurate as it is incomplete. The craft economy, we now realize, was surprisingly heterogeneous and dynamic. Artisan enterprises from the Middle Ages to the eighteenth century (and beyond) ranged from lowly capitalized but highly specialized household-based workshops deeply enmeshed in elaborate webs of credit relations to complex, highly capitalized enterprises involving sophisticated combinations of partnerships, private and state-financing, and extensive subcontracting arrangements. As consumer markets grew and became increasingly integrated from the Middle Ages to the eighteenth century, the variety and number of artisanal enterprises increased. Already, however, in some cities in the Middle Ages and in many more in the sixteenth and seventeenth centuries the drift toward specialization and diversity of producer and, in some artisanal sectors, standardization of product is evident. Equally apparent are changes in the organization of production. Artisans were guided by a traditional, premodern rationale of constant returns to scale, but their experiments with vertical integration, horizontal combination, and above all economies of scale in some sectors reveal that many craftsmen were surprisingly modern, and more flexible in their approach to business that was once thought.

Bibliography

Entries marked with a * designate recommended readings for new students of the subject.

*Berg, Maxine, *The Age of Manufactures, 1700–1820*. New York, 1986.
    "Commerce and creativity in 18th-Century Birmingham." In Maxine Berg, ed., *Markets and Manufacture in Early Industrial Europe*. London, 1991, pp. 173–201.
    "Markets, trade and European manufacture." In Maxine Berg, ed., *Markets and Manufacture in Early Industrial Europe*, London, 1991, pp. 3–28.
*Berg, Maxine, ed. *Markets and Manufacture in Early Industrial Europe*. London, 1991.
Berg, Maxine, Pat Hudson, and Michael Sonenscher. "Manufacture in town and country before the factory." In Maxine Berg, Pat Hudson, and Michael Somenscher, eds., *Manufacture in Town and Country Before the Factory*. Cambridge, 1983, pp. 1–32.
Bossenga, Gail. "Protecting merchants: guilds and commercial capitalism in eighteenth-century France." *French Historical Studies* 15 (1988), 693–703.
    "Capitalism and corporations in eighteenth-century France." In *Naissance de la liberté économique*. Paris, 1993, pp. 13–31.

Cerutti, Simona. "Group strategies and trade strategies: the Turin tailors' guild in the late 17th and early 18th centuries." In Stuart Woolf, ed., *Domestic Strategies: Work and Family in France and Italy, 1600–1800.* Cambridge, 1991, pp. 102–47.

Cipolla, Carlo. "The economic policies of governments: the Italian and Iberian peninsulas." *The Cambridge Economic History of Europe,* vol. III. Cambridge, 1963, pp. 397–429.

*Clarkson, Leslie A. *Proto-industrialization: The First Phase of Industrialization?* London, 1985.

Clay, C. G. A. *Economic Expansion and Social Change: England, 1500–1700.* 2 vols. Cambridge, 1984.

*De Vries, Jan. *The Economy of Europe in an Age of Crisis, 1600–1750.* Cambridge, 1976.

European Urbanization, 1500–1800. Cambridge, Mass., 1984.

*"Between purchasing power and the world of goods: understanding the household economy of early modern Europe." In John Brewer and Roy Porter, eds., *Consumption and the World of Goods.* London, 1993, pp. 85–132.

*"The Industrial Revolution and the industrious revolution." *Journal of Economic History* 54:2 (1994), 249–70.

Deyon, Pierre, and Philippe Guignet. "The royal manufactures and economic and technological progress in France before the Industrial Revolution." *Journal of European Economic History* 9 (1980), 611–32.

Du Plessis, Robert, and Martha Howell. "Reconsidering the early modern urban economy: the cases of Leiden and Lille." *Past and Present* 94 (1982), 49–84.

Earle, Peter. *The Making of the English Working Class.* Berkeley, 1989.

Fairchilds, Cissie. "The production and marketing of populuxe goods in 18th-century Paris." In John Brewer and Roy Porter, eds., *Consumption and the World of Goods.* London, 1993, pp. 228–48.

*Farr, James R. "On the shop floor: guilds, artisans, and the European market economy, 1350–1750." *Journal of Early Modern History* 1:1 (1997), 24–54.

Friedrichs, Christopher R. "Capitalism, mobility, and class formation in the early modern German city." In P. Abrams and E. L. Wrigley, eds., *Towns and Societies: Essays in Economic History and Historical Sociology.* Cambridge, 1978, pp. 187–213.

Goldthwaite, Richard. *The Building of Renaissance Florence: An Economic and Social History.* Baltimore, 1980.

*Goodman, Jordan, and Katrina Honeyman. *Gainful Pursuits: The Making of Industrial Europe, 1600–1914.* London, 1988.

Hohenberg, Paul M. "Urban manufactures in the proto-industrial economy: culture vs. commerce." In Maxine Berg, ed., *Markets and Manufacture in Early Industrial Europe.* London, 1991, pp. 159–72.

*Kaplan, Steven L. "Reflexions sur la police du monde du travail, 1700–1815." *Revue historique* 261 (1979), 17–77.

"The luxury guilds in Paris in the eighteenth century." *Francia* 9 (1981), pp. 257–98.

*Kriedte, Peter, Hans Medick, and Jurgen Schlumbohm. *Industrialization Before Industrialization.* Cambridge, 1981.

Lane, Frederic C. *Venetian Ships and Shipbuilders of the Renaissance.* Baltimore, 1934.

Mayr, Otto. *Authority, Liberty and Automatic Machinery in Early Modern Europe.* Baltimore, 1986.

Mazzaoui, M. F. *The Italian Cotton Industry in the Late Middle Ages, 1100–1600.* Cambridge, 1981.

Medick, Hans. "The protoindustrial family economy: the structural function of household and family during the transition from peasant society to industrial capitalism." *Social History* 1 (1976), 291–315.

Mui, H. and L. H. Mui. *Shops and Shopkeeping in Eighteenth-century England.* London, 1989.

Murray, James M. "Cloth, banking, and finance in medieval Bruges." In Erik Aerts and John H. Munro, eds., *Textiles of the Low Countries in European Economic History.* Louvain, 1990, pp. 24–31.

Nightingale, Pamela. "Capitalists, crafts, and constitutional change in late 14th-century London." *Past and Present* 124 (1989), 3–35.

Parker, Harold. *The Bureau of Commerce in 1781 and its Policies with Respect to French Industry.* Durham, NC, 1979.

*Poni, Carlo. "Norms and disputes: the shoemakers' guild in eighteenth-century Bologna." *Past and Present* 123 (1989), 80–108.

*"Local market rules and practices: three guilds in the same line of production in early modern Bologna." In Stuart Woolf, ed., *Domestic Strategies: Work and Family in Italy and France, 1600–1800.* Cambridge, 1991, pp. 69–101.

Pullan, Brian, ed. *Crisis and Change in the Venetian Economy.* London, 1968.

Quataert, Jean. "A new view of industrialization: protoindustry or the role of small-scale, labor-intensive manufacture in the capitalist environment." *International Labor and Working-Class History* 33 (1988), 3–22.

Rapp, Richard Tilden. *Industry and Economic Decline in Seventeenth-Century Venice.* Cambridge, Mass., 1976.

Ringrose, David. *Madrid and the Spanish Economy.* Berkeley, 1983.

*Schwarz, L. D. *London in the Age of Industrialization: Entrepreneurs, Labour Force and Living Conditions, 1700–1850.* Cambridge, 1992.

Sella, Domenico. *Crisis and Continuity: The Economy of Spanish Lombardy in the Seventeenth Century.* Cambridge, Mass., 1979.

*Strauss, Gerald. *Nuremberg in the Sixteenth Century.* New York, 1966.

Stürmer, Michael. "An economy of delight: court artisans of the eighteenth century." *Business History Review* 53 (1979), 496–528.

Thomson, J. "Variations in industrial structure in preindustrial Languedoc." In Maxine Berg, ed., *Manufacture in Town and Country Before the Factory.* Cambridge, 1983, pp. 61–91.

Unger, Richard W. "Technology and industrial organization: Dutch shipbuilding to 1800." *Business History* 17 (1975), 56–72.

Dutch Shipbuilding before 1800: Ships and Guilds. Assen, 1978.

*Van der Wee, Herman. "Industrial dynamics and the process of urbanization and de-urbanization in the Low Countries from the late middle ages to the 18th century: a synthesis." In Herman van der Wee (ed.), *The Rise and*

Decline of Urban Industries in Italy and in the Low Countries. Louvain-la-Neuve, 1988, pp. 307–81.

Van Houtte, J. A. *An Economic History of the Low Countries, 800–1800.* London, 1977.

Van Zanden, J. L. *The Rise and Decline of Holland's Economy: Merchant Capitalism and the Labour Market.* Manchester, 1993.

3   The workplace

Cityfolk

The artisans who are the focus of this book lived in Europe's cities and towns. Their way of life was fundamentally affected by the nature, process, and results of urbanization. Just how many people comprised a "town" or a "city" is open to debate, but most historians accept that settlements with fewer than 1,000 inhabitants do not qualify, and some would suggest that the description "urban" requires at least 2,000 or even 5,000 souls. We need not settle that issue here, but we should bear in mind that in 1350, just after the Black Death had catastrophically carried away between a quarter and a third of the European population, no more than 10 million (and perhaps as few as 7 million, depending on which estimate of total European population one accepts) men, women, and children lived in settlements of at least 1,000, a figure that reached between 8 and 12 million by 1500. In that year only four cities – Milan, Venice, Naples, and Paris – held over 100,000 souls each, while eighteen cities counted at least 40,000 (ten of which were in Italy). Perhaps seventy held at least 20,000. France had over thirty cities of at least 10,000 inhabitants.

The sixteenth century would witness growth among cities of all types, sizes, and locations, so that by 1600 there were upwards of 600 European cities with more than 5,000 inhabitants, comprising about 12 percent of Europe's total population. The seventeenth century would see a net deurbanization of cities under 40,000, a contraction partially offset by substantial growth in port cities and capitals. In some of these cases, the growth was enormous, as Madrid, Berlin, Vienna, Amsterdam, and especially London, illustrate. The urban population of England grew from 12 percent of the total population in 1500 to 23 percent by 1700, some of the growth the result of the extraordinary surge of London which ballooned from about 60,000 in 1520 to 200,000 in 1600 to 575,000 in 1700. Amsterdam swelled from 30,000 in 1550 to 175,000 a century later, engulfing a vast acreage in the process (the area of the city expanded from 450 to 1,800 acres). Amsterdam was a great metropolis, to be sure, but the United Provinces as a whole were highly urbanized, as their cities and towns held 464,000 inhabitants in the mid-seventeenth century, and 58 percent of their total population lived in towns of 10,000 or more.

The growth rate of the total population of Europe was relatively flat between 1620 and 1750, after which it rose vertiginously, an increase that was accompanied by widespread urban growth, which now included smaller cities and new cities, in addition to the megalopolises like London (which continued to burgeon, reaching 900,000 by 1801).

Obviously, many of the inhabitants of these cities and towns throughout the period were artisans, men and women whose way of life, moreover, was fundamentally related to the nature, process, and results of urbanization. But just how many of the denizens of these towns and cities were artisans? How many were masters, and how many were journeymen, apprentices, and women? How wealthy were they? What were the conditions of their work life? How and how much were they paid? These are some of the questions we will address in this chapter.

The division of labor

Surprisingly, forty years after the advent of social history and historical demography, it is still beyond our grasp to determine with precision what percentage of the European urban population were artisans. Few sources exist which permit accurate counting (virtually none before 1500), and what records do exist (such as tax rolls, hearth counts, guild memberships, excise papers, mortality bills, and so forth) disproportionately represent the sedentary and proprietary population. Moreover, what modern studies we do have tend not to be directly comparable, because of the different records used as well as the variety of the historians' own assumptions and methods of determining what an "artisan" was. These variables of evidence and method determine which "artisans" have been counted. The imprecision can be seen immediately in the difficulty in distinguishing between "artisans" and "shopkeepers," a difficulty compounded by the expansion of pure retailing in the early modern period. Moreover, any attempt to determine what percentage of an urban population were artisans requires laborious social histories of cities where historians have counted and classified all the inhabitants.

This kind of history has been associated with *annaliste*-inspired methodology, and to date has generated some impressive (if often francocentric) studies for the early modern period. Unfortunately such an approach is inappropriate for the large cities of Europe because of

Table 3.1. *Artisans as percentage of population, selected cities*

City	Date	%	(N=)	(Method)
Rome	1526–7	55.4	(1,760)	(male household heads)
Montpelier	1549	21.3	(350)	(taxed male household heads)
	1640	25.1	(588)	
Dijon	1464	39.7	(851)	(taxed male household heads)
	1750	25.5	(1,183)	
Cuenca	1561	58.0	(2,007)	(all household heads)
	1771	35.1	(598)	
Frankfurt	1587	56.1	(1,247)	(taxed male household heads)
Nördlingen	1579	83.3	(1,054)	(taxed male citizens)
	1724	78.9	(878)	
Madrid	1757	39.4	(16,731)	(property-tax payers)
Mainz	1785	30.5	(582)	(master home owners)

their unmanageable size, and so we have little demographic knowledge of many cities that were undergoing dramatic change.

Still, if we cannot precisely compare the demographic make-up of Europe's cities, what studies we do have do illustrate, *grosso modo*, the range of urban artisanal activity. What emerges is a picture of diversity, variety, and, in some places, sweeping change! Late medieval London, for instance, had an estimated 180 different trades and crafts, and by the early seventeenth century St. Botolph Aldgate, an extramural parish, had 130 of its own. Between 1654 and 1693 St. Giles Cripplegate, London, could count 215 different manufacturing occupations, led by weavers (864), shoemakers (567), tailors (547), and glovers (333). Examples like these could be multiplied.

The percentage of artisanal representation within European cities is a portrait in diversity. In some places artisans represented just 20 percent of the total recorded population, while in others they were upwards of 80 percent. Table 3.1 isolates some examples which illustrate this extraordinary diversity (and the variety of ways historians have counted) in the early modern period.

It seems that diversity is the only generalization that can be concluded from this table. The range of artisanal representation (usually male household heads) in the population at large is wide: one of four or five in Dijon and Montpellier, one of three in Mainz, two of five in Madrid, one of two in Rome, Frankfurt, and, for a time, Cuenca, four of five in Nördlingen. If such differences between cities are surprising, more predictable, given the remarkable specialization that characterized the craft economy that we saw in the previous chapter, is the variety of artisanal activities within the towns themselves.

Generalization about artisanal division of labor is made difficult by the fact that, depending on the city or town, the size of some craft sectors grew while others contracted, and many wholly new trades appeared while others vanished. We have already seen this in the previous chapter in the case of Dijon. Moreover, any attempt to represent numerically the division of labor by craft suffers from the same difficulties as representing the percentage of artisans in towns or cities as a whole. We must also bear in mind the caveat that occupational nomenclature or guild membership does not necessarily describe manufacturing or commercial activity, nor does it completely convey the extent of the division of labor in a town or city. In sixteenth-century Dijon, for instance, we find a man like Hugues Sambin listed on the tax rolls as a cabinet-maker, but we know from other records that he was a distinguished architect, military engineer, and wood sculptor; he was listed as a cabinet-maker in official records because that was the guild to which he belonged, not because he made furniture. Similarly, Adriaen Willeborts van Weena was Delft's principal builder and architect but was listed on the tax rolls of the 1620s as a stonemason. In eighteenth-century Paris, even though the statutes of the bakers' guild formally prohibited its members from practicing more than one profession, we find master baker Pierre Félix trafficking openly in grain, as did master baker Louis Chevalier, the latter in cereals that were rarely used in breadmaking. Many other bakers doubled as *voituriers*, or wagoneers, while "baker" André Le Roux made his living trading in stone for building construction. In some places, like Nördlingen, artisans could be listed in official records with two occupations, which reflected guild membership in one but practice of the other. Moreover, in many cities multitudes of artisans belonged to no guild at all. Wage-earning artisans in the fifteenth century, especially the marginals whom we encounter in criminal records, frequently practiced two or more trades. A man picked up for petty crime, for instance, called himself a tanner, but he also worked as a shoemaker and as a mason. A "tailor" had also worked emptying cesspits, a "baker" had hired himself out as a porter, a "shoemaker" had been employed as a pastrycook at times and as a porter at others. And how are we to classify the builders of Renaissance Florence or those of several towns in early modern northern England who practiced several crafts – masonry, carpentry, stonecutting – depending upon demand, and becoming "jacks of all trades," as they were called in England, in the process?

To make matters worse for the historian bent on counting and classifying, many guilds in many towns and cities were amalgamations of crafts and trades. The cabinet-makers' guild in Rome in 1624, for

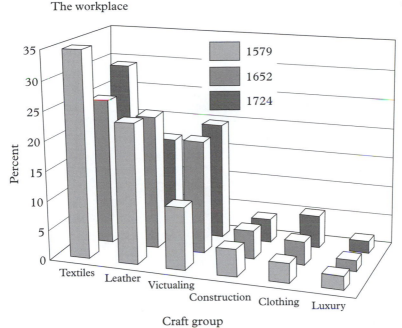

Figure 1   Nördlingen, 1579–1724: percent of all taxed, male artisans, selected craft groups

instance, encompassed twenty-two different trades. And finally, generic labels in the records left to us often veil an extensive subdivision of labor. The label "painter" on craftsmen's bills submitted to aristocratic customers in eighteenth-century Paris, for example, could have referred to one of the following craftsmen: decor-painter, architect, painter carver, gilder, pattern-painter, varnisher, and even stucco-worker.

With such imprecision, need we bother trying to classify and count artisans according to a division of labor at all? Some might suggest that any picture is bound to be excessively nominalistic and ultimately inaccurate, but, since these records are all we have, unless we completely discount any possibility that they might reflect, however murkily, artisanal activity, then perhaps it is worth presenting some examples of the division of labor in some European towns that in recent years have been the subject of scholarly scrutiny.

Nördlingen, as we have seen, held a citizen population that was classified as 80 percent artisan. Moreover, as figure 1 shows, the plurality of artisans was engaged in textiles (most of them woolweavers), and when added to the leather (mostly tanners and shoemakers) and food trades (mostly butchers and bakers), we find that from 1579 to

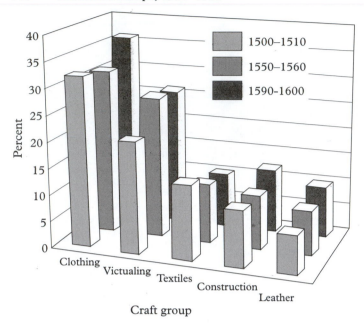

Figure 2   York, 1500–1600: artisans in percent of all admissions to freedom, selected craft groups

1724 the artisans of these three sectors made up no fewer than two-thirds of all taxpaying craftsmen in the town.

The other sectors shown here – clothing, construction, and luxury – also contrast sharply with the division of labor in other European towns, as we will see. For example, the number of tailors plying their trade in Nördlingen (only twenty-four, eighteen, and thirty-six in the respective years) was disproportionately low compared to most other towns, as were the numbers of building craftsmen (only twenty-two, six, and eight masons paid taxes in Nördlingen, and only eight, nine, and thirteen carpenters did) and luxury craftsmen (only ten, four, and eight gold-smiths and gilders were listed as taxpayers, and only five, one, and one painters were, although by 1724 the town could boast two clockmakers and two organbuilders).

Tudor York (figure 2) provides us with a very different picture. True, as in Nördlingen the dominant class in this city was the "freeman," or citizen, a group that was comprised mostly of master craftsmen, traders, and shopkeepers. In the 1530s and 1540s, however, they numbered about half of the adult males in this city with a total population in 1525 of close to 6,000 souls. Throughout the late medieval and early modern period York was among the five largest and wealthiest cities in the kingdom, despite its dramatic contraction between 1377 and 1525. Still, in 1579 this classic regional production center and market town had sixty-four craft guilds within it, and, in partial contrast to Nördlingen, the largest craft sectors were the clothing, food, and by 1600, the building trades that served the city and its hinterland.

Within these groups, the largest craft guilds were tailors and shoemakers in the clothing trades, butchers and bakers in the food trades, carpenters and tilers in the building trades, weavers in textiles, and tanners in the leather trades. York's craft profile conforms to the traditional picture that historians at one time thought was general to the urban artisan population of Europe. To be sure, the division of labor in this example was not unique, for many other towns exhibited very similar patterns; but, on the basis of the mounting evidence in recent studies, we must be wary of assuming that this was the norm, or that there even was a norm.

Looking at Frankfurt am Main in the late sixteenth century (figure 3) we see a city that thrived from transit commercial traffic on the Main river as well as from the fairs held there twice a year. But an examination of the craft sector comprised of 1,247 male, artisan householders finds production geared toward the local market, not for export. Ostensibly, we might expect, then, a profile similar to York's, if not Nördlingen's.

Direct comparison between York, Frankfurt, and Nördlingen is impossible, given the variations in the way the respective historians have chosen to form their craft groups, but certain resemblances are apparent nonetheless. Victualing trades are well represented in each city, and not surprisingly butchers and bakers dominated this sector in all three cities, as they must have in every early modern city. In 1616 in Frankfurt approximately sixty butchers belonged to their guild; unless there was extraordinary growth in their ranks between 1587 and 1616, butchers must have comprised nearly one-half of the food and drink sector there. Similarly, tailors were numerous nearly everywhere. In 1587 there were ninety-four men in Frankfurt's tailors' guild, so tailors undoubtedly comprised nearly the entire "clothing" craft sector there. But note that this craft sector only represents 8 percent of male artisan householders, still twice the representation of this sector in Nördlingen but contrasted sharply with York's 25 percent at roughly the same time. D. M. Palliser counted shoemakers within the clothing sector in York, and Christopher Friedrichs clearly did not for either Nördlingen or Frankfurt; but even if we add the entire leather sector in Frankfurt to the clothing sector there, the percentage still remains well below the combined clothing and

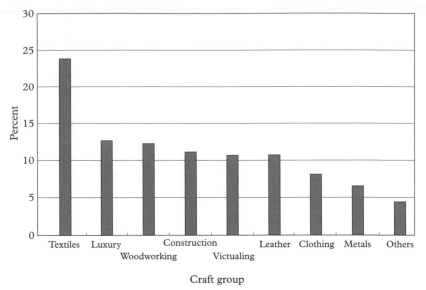

Figure 3   Frankfurt am Main, 1587: percent of artisan householders by craft group

leather trades of York. Ostensibly similar towns, York and Frankfurt turn out to be quite different in the division of artisanal labor.

Like York and Frankfurt, Dijon also was a city that produced for the surrounding hinterland and served as a regional market center (increasingly for wine); but it was also a growing administrative center and a provincial capital during the late medieval and early modern centuries. How different was its artisanal sector from our previous examples?

Certain similarities with York, Frankfurt, and even Nördlingen are evident where we would expect them, but more instructive are the differences. In Dijon, with the population of office-holders, merchants, lawyers, and *rentiers* exploding between the mid-fifteenth and the mid-eighteenth century, crafts that catered to their consumption needs grew. Recall that this elite comprised only 5 percent of the heads of households in 1464 (artisans comprised about one-third), but by 1750 these same elite groups equaled about a quarter of the population, as did the artisans. Given that this elite was also increasingly wealthy and fully immersed in a culture of conspicuous luxury consumption from at least the mid-seventeenth century, we should not be surprised to find that the division of artisanal labor would shift to sectors satisfying these demands.

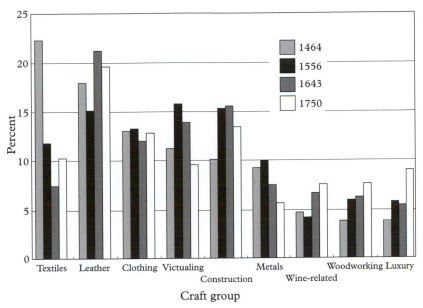

Figure 4   Dijon, 1464–1750: percent of artisan heads of households (male and female)

Clearly, as figure 4 shows, the textile industry in Dijon collapsed in the sixteenth century (victim to rural industry and competition from other textile towns), but other sectors grew. This was notable in the building trades. Dijon's streets in the seventeenth century rang with the clang of masons' chisels and pounded to the thud of carpenters' hammers and adzes as sumptuous townhouses sprang up all over town. The woodworking sector grew, too, as many joiners and furniture-makers fitted out the interiors of these townhouses. Above all, however, the growth is clearest in the luxury sector.

Rome in the early sixteenth century had some similarities to the Dijon of later centuries, but departs from the profiles of some of the other examples described thus far (figure 5). Both Rome and Dijon housed relatively large elite populations (unlike Nördlingen) – in Rome's case, the Roman aristocracy and the clergy and courtiers attached to the papal court – both experienced construction booms, and both supported a relatively large sector of artisans producing luxury goods.

As nearly everywhere, there were more tailors than any other craftsmen in Rome, but the building boom that Rome experienced throughout the sixteenth century provided work for many carpenters,

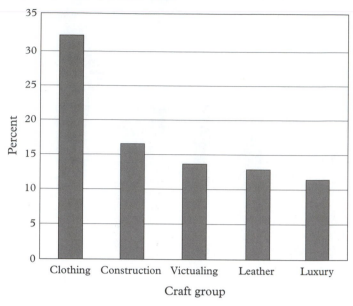

Figure 5   Rome, 1526–7: percent of artisan household heads

masons, and tilers, not to mention the thousands of unskilled day laborers thronging the construction sites. Many of these craftsmen found work as a result of the Catholic Reformation-inspired building program by Sixtus V and his successors who, after 1585, were bent on glorifying the Church of Rome. No doubt as in Dijon, many Roman tailors made clothes for the Roman elite and so the percentage recorded on the chart on Rome (and Dijon) probably underrepresents the proportion of artisans producing luxury goods. Even underrepresented, however, these ranks were large relative to what we know of other towns of sixteenth-century Europe, no doubt a testimony to the precocious luxury consumption of the denizens of the aristocratic and papal courts.

Like in Dijon and Rome, luxury consumption in Madrid restructured the artisanry as well (table 3.2). In the eighteenth century it was so pronounced in Spain's capital that well over half the artisans there were engaged in making products for this market. In contrast to Madrid but typical of most Castillian cities, Cuenca witnessed a radical contraction of its total population from the sixteenth to the eighteenth century (from nearly 15,000 in 1561 to barely 6,000 in 1707, then creeping slightly upward to just over 7,500 by 1771) and with it the collapse of the export-oriented textile and metallurgical industries (figure 6). Local service industries (leather, clothing, and construction) remained fairly

Table 3.2. *Madrid, 1757: distribution of occupations by product, in percent*

	%
Quality textiles, leather, and final products	44.7
Precious metals, jewelry	10.7
Mechanical and metallurgical	19.8
Rough textiles, leather, semi-finished goods	17.7
Other crafts	6.6

Source: David Ringrose, *Madrid and the Spanish Economy* (Berkeley, University of California Press, 1983), p. 69.

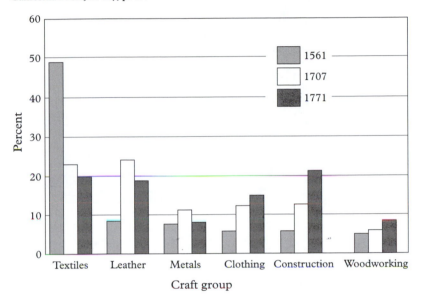

Figure 6   Cuenca, 1561–1771: percent of artisans by craft group

constant in absolute numbers, suggesting that by the eighteenth century Cuenca's artisans were providing for the town and its immediate hinterland only.

A final example, sixteenth- and seventeenth-century London, again challenges our desire to generalize, and the historian who arrived at the following numbers used yet another kind of source to do so: mortality bills (figure 7).

Masters, journeymen, apprentices

The sources social historians have at their disposal for numerical representation are usually biased toward the sedentary and proprietary

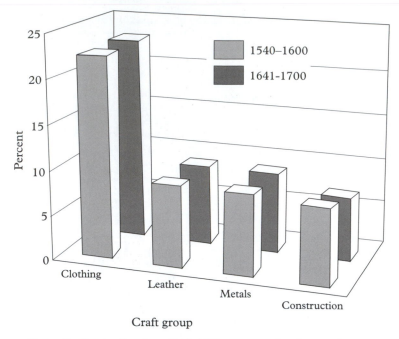

Figure 7   Greater London, 1540–1700: percent of artisans, selected craft groups

artisan, that is, the male master. From these, we can gain some knowledge of the numbers and proportions of masters in Europe's urban populations. In contrast, seldom do we capture journeymen, apprentices, or women methodically enough in our records to count them and to determine their representation in the population. The example of the apprentices of seventeenth-century London is interesting, but unfortunately nearly singular. London in 1600 had about 15,000 apprentices and 12,000 journeymen in its artisan shops, the apprentices swelling to 20,000 by 1650. Untold thousands more, however, fled beyond the northern, eastern, and southern edges of the city (areas which grew dramatically in population) to evade guild regulation. It has been estimated that in 1600 apprentices comprised about 15 percent of the population of London, but by 1700 they were only 4 or 5 percent.

If we cannot offer much more than this in the way of apprentice and journeyman representation in the towns and cities of Europe, we can present ratios of master to apprentice and master to journeyman. Here again, however, diversity is the rule. In some places, like early modern Dijon or eighteenth-century Bordeaux, apprentices were very few, while in Rome in 1622 they outnumbered the masters 17,584 to 6,609. At the Venetian Arsenal in 1630 within the three major guilds of shipwrights, caulkers, and oarmakers the proportions of masters to apprentices were, respectively, 217:165, 277:121, and 56:20.

Heterogeneity describes master to journeyman ratios, too, since in some places the masters outnumbered the journeymen, while elsewhere it was the inverse. In Coventry in the 1520s there were 63 master capmakers and 47 journeymen, but 37 master weavers and 45 journeymen. In Augsburg in 1615 the master shoemakers outnumbered the journeymen 111 to 62, while in the same year in the same town the master joiners outnumbered their journeymen 119 to 80, a proportion that shifted four years later to 104 to 85. In the towns of Bavaria in 1792 there were three to four master artisans for every journeyman.

Elsewhere, journeymen outnumbered the masters. In the faience workshops in Delft in 1640 there were about 15 *knechts* (apprentices and journeymen) in each of the ten registered potteries. In Bologna in 1697 236 journeymen were spread (unevenly) among the 49 master shoemakers' shops. In Rouen in 1752 journeymen hatters outnumbered the masters 100 to 18, while in Paris in 1739 the proportion was 546 to 63, an imbalance that was even more exaggerated in 1790–1 when there were 1,602 journeymen hatters and only 67 masters.

Women

If we know little about the numbers of journeymen and apprentices, we know even less about female artisans. Two central problems in the history of women's work have been, first, to explain the changes in the gender division of labor in the European workforce from the late Middle Ages to the era of industrialization, and second, to determine whether these changes entailed a devaluation of women's work and a marginalization of their activities from the market economy. Although, given the nature of the sources, we can never know the full extent of female involvement in the early modern economy, recent local studies are confirming the impression that we should not think of the family economy and the market economy as somehow separate, nor should we think of women as confined to the former and cut off from the latter. Indeed, a consensus is emerging among historians that women's economic activity changed in the early modern centuries and a gendered division of labor appears to have rigidified. Female participation in the economy, however, was certainly not confined to the household. Or rather, we should say that the household economy was closely and dynamically connected to the market economy and so that a female role in the "family economy" often meant a pronounced contribution to the market economy itself.

A recent study of women in the construction trades in eighteenth-century Brittany by Elizabeth Musgrave neatly illustrates the ambiguity of the female role in the artisanal economy and the blurred distinction between the household and market economy. She points out that on-site construction was performed by mobile and transient artisans who formed craft associations that were "free" and thus not officially guilds. She contrasts this organization of work with the sedentary off-site construction trades which were workshop based and formally incorporated. The nonguild, on-site work was monopolized by men, while, surprisingly, female builders were fairly common in the off-site sector. These female builders were not members of guilds, but as wives of master guildsmen they could act legally in the marketplace if they did so with the permission of their husbands. Widows had even more freedom. In any case, Musgrave finds women working independently, supplying on-site enterprises with raw materials, sometimes even engaging in general contracting, bidding for and undertaking large-scale, multicraft building projects. The only evident participation of the husband in these enterprises is his requisite signature.

One can see in the example of the construction trades of Brittany the outlines of the traditional picture of the wife of the master craftsman as his helpmate in the family workshop, but closer scrutiny reveals a more complex picture where women were more independent than previously thought. Of course, not all wives became independent contractors or wholesalers of supplies. Indeed, in the countless small household workshops that dotted most medieval and early modern streets husbands and wives were partners, the women often having an adjunctive role in production. Bakers' wives would set out loaves baked by their husbands, while butchers' wives would boil the tripe and bones of the beasts slaughtered by their spouses. Similarly, weavers' wives were often spinners, providing the thread needed by their husbands in the making of cloth (illustration 7). Wives of artisans everywhere can be found as the keepers of the accounts of the family enterprise, often making purchases of raw materials and paying workers.

As we saw in chapter 1, guild history shows a trend toward exclusion of women from guilds from the late Middle Ages, but many early modern cities still had mixed membership guilds. The weavers of Augsburg in 1600 are one example, where 15 percent of the masters were women (although they employed only 5 percent of the journeymen and apprentices). The guilds of spinners, ribbon-makers, and lace-makers in eighteenth-century Rouen counted many women in the ranks

Der Weber.

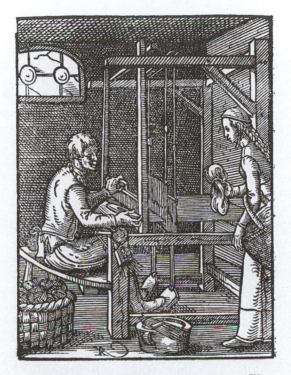

Ich bin ein Weber zu leinen Wat/
Kan wircken Barchent vnd Sponat/
Tischthůcher/Handzwehl/Facilet/
Vnd wer luſt zu Bettziechen hett/
Gewůrffelt oder Kamaca/
Allerley gmodelt Thůcher da/
Auch Flechſen vnd wircken Haußthuch/
Die Kunſt ich bey Aragnes ſuch.

Der

Illustration 7 Sixteenth-century weaver. Reproduced with permission from Jost Amman and Hans Sachs, *The Book of Trades*, New York: Dover Publications, 1973

of masters, too. Indeed, in this city of 85,000 inhabitants there were 600 female masters in various trades, or about 7 percent of all of the city's guild masters.

The evidence of women artisans in mixed guilds is just the tip of the iceberg of their actual artisanal activities, however, for recent studies have shown that, despite legal exclusion from most guilds, many women practiced artisanal trades nearly everywhere. In fourteenth-century Flanders, for instance, women may have been increasingly excluded from guilds, but precept was not always practice. The dyer guilds there specifically excluded women, but we know nonetheless that many women worked as dyers in Flemish cities, some even owning dyeing enterprises. Similarly the famous London silkwomen, though they had no guild status, dominated silk manufacture and trade in the late medieval and early modern period. In Oxford between 1500 and 1650 no women were admitted to the freedom and thus none could legally practice a trade independently, but there is evidence for widespread female involvement (even their taking of apprentices) in glovemaking, shoemaking, and tailoring. In York between 1560 and 1700 we find women silkweavers, pinmakers, joiners, curriers, pewterers, and tailors. In Lyons in 1781 many women practiced aspects of the hatting trade, as *eplucheuses*, *cardeuses*, and *coupeuses*, and even had formed "combinations," perhaps with the intention of one day receiving guild status.

Clearly, women practiced a wide range of artisanal crafts, but alongside this diversity is a trend toward an increasingly gendered division of labor as women were concentrated more and more in particular artisanal sectors. Peter Earle presents us with a cross-section of female artisanal activity in London between 1695 and 1725, and it neatly sums up a picture that should be noted for the diversity of female artisanal activities as well as the concentration of women in cloth and clothing production and sale. He bases his profile on 613 depositions of female witnesses (unmarried women, wives, and widows) before the London church courts.[1] Not all of these women claimed to practice artisanal activities (many of which were casual, intermittent, or seasonal, and none of which was organized in livery companies or guilds), but 12 of the women were involved in some form of manufacture other than textiles, while 28 were involved in textile manufacture (mostly as silkwinders) and another 124 made or mended clothes. A further 47 were retail shopkeepers (many of them were milliners, who employed apprentices and journeywomen to do needlework to stock their shops).

---

[1] Peter Earle, "The female labour market in London in the late 17th and early 18th centuries," *Economic History Review* 2nd ser., 42 (1989), 328–53.

In sum, about one-third of Earle's sample was involved in artisanal and shopkeeping activities, most in cloth and clothing production and sale.

This female concentration in textiles can be traced to the late Middle Ages, but so can diverse female participation in other artisanal activities. In late medieval England, for instance, there is scattered evidence of women working as smiths, and female bakers (probably as managers) are not unusual in late medieval London. Sixteenth-century German cities had many independent women working in the "free arts," or crafts not organized into guilds, doing, for example, light metalwork (making needles, thimbles, or rings).

In mid-fourteenth-century Florence, women could be found in a wide variety of artisanal occupations, too, but by the early fifteenth century a significant change had set in, a change that was not unique to Florence. Women became increasingly concentrated in particular artisanal sectors and excluded from others. From the early fifteenth century until the late sixteenth there is scant mention of working women in the Florentine records, but just before 1600 rather suddenly account books of woolen manufacturers show a rising percentage of female workers. By 1604 62 percent of weavers and 40 percent of woolworkers were women, the majority of whom were married. This surge of women back into the workforce resulted from the "bidding away" of men from the textile trades into the booming luxury trades. By 1663 women were confined to woolweaving and warping; of 550 woolweavers, 447 were women, as were 26 of the 27 warpers. Conversely, all beaters, cleansers, scourers, tenterers, dyers, shearers, and menders were men.

The Florentine silk industry shows a similar gendered division of labor. All master dyers were men, as were their apprentices, but 65 percent of the 100 master throwsters were women (as were 78 percent of the 480 apprentices), 78 percent of the nearly 2,000 master silkweavers were women and 59 percent of the 775 apprentices were, and every one of the nearly 5,000 master silkwinders was a woman, and nearly all the 3,300 children who worked in the trade were female. The vacuum drew women in, and in the process constructed a gendered division of labor, not between the household and the market economy, but within the market economy itself.

A similar trend toward concentration of women in certain textile trades occurred in German cities. In fourteenth-century Frankfurt twenty-four different "free arts" were the preserve of women, mostly in cloth and clothing production. The fifteenth and sixteenth centuries witnessed a gradual crowding of women into fewer and fewer free arts as incorporation took over formerly free crafts and masculinized them. Even in the sixteenth century there were still women tailors in at least thirty German cities, but by the end of the century everywhere they had been reduced to seamstresses working for male tailors. The same trend of exclusion, concentration, and increasing gendered division of labor can be seen in stocking-knitting as men took over the trade and excluded women from it. Ultimately, quite often women artisans were left only with spinning. Indeed, in the sixteenth and seventeenth centuries, the most common female artisanal occupation in German towns, and probably nearly everywhere else, was spinning.

Clearly the early modern trend was toward concentration of female artisanal tasks in certain sectors, but within these sectors women did, in some cities, expand their activities. Maxine Berg asserts that in eighteenth-century England women dominated all aspects of textile manufacture. Across the channel in France women were independently participating in the expanding clothing trades. Certainly this is the case with seamstresses and linendrapers (*lingères*). The seamstresses of Paris established an all-female guild in 1675, carving out of the male tailoring world the privilege to sew and sell clothing for women, and for children under the age of eight. As we have seen, their numbers expanded throughout the eighteenth century reaching 3,000 by 1789. The linendrapers, the oldest women's guild in Paris (they traced their statutes to the fifteenth century), rode the increasing demand for underclothing in the seventeenth and eighteenth centuries to expansion and, in some cases, prosperity, for some women organized themselves into a well-heeled group with large networks of suppliers and workers. By the 1780s there were 800 mistress linendrapers in Paris employing another 1,200 *lingères*.

As the cases of the seamstresses and linendrapers of Paris illustrate, all-female guilds existed in the early modern period. However, the history of guilds reveals the trend across these same centuries toward a gendered division of labor and the concentration of women artisans in fewer craft sectors. Already in the fourteenth century we can see a trend toward excluding women from guilds in which hitherto they had been members. In the towns of fourteenth century Flanders guilds were steadily excluding women from their ranks, while in late medieval Cologne guilds likewise imposed restrictions on female membership. Cologne also reveals the trend toward a more rigid gendered division of labor, for in Cologne several all-female guilds were in fact created. The yarntwisters were organized as a guild between 1370 and 1397, receiving statutes in 1397, while spinners of gold thread were chartered also in 1397 and silkmakers in 1437. From the time of incorporation until 1504, 116 mistress silkmakers with independent shops employing 765 apprentices made and marketed silk, and joined a thriving export industry. This was not just a medieval or German phenomenon, since in eighteenth-century Rouen several of the seventy guilds were exclusively female as well: the hand-knitters, the fashionable plume-makers, the embroiderers of religious vestments, and the linendrapers.

Nearly everywhere widows of masters of guilds were permitted to continue their husbands' businesses, although usually, as we have seen, there were statutory restrictions on their activities. It is probable that in most places most of the women in the mixed guilds that had master status gained it through widowhood. In Nantes between 1620 and 1650 at least 10 percent of the bakeries and butchers' shops were run by mistress widows, while in York between 1581 and 1660, according to guild account books, 49 of the 257 bakers were widows. Similarly, in Frankfurt am Main in 1696 30 of 180 master tailors were widows.

Despite the evidence of widows running independent artisanal businesses, we should not draw the conclusion that most widows of master artisans did so. The evidence from London between 1695 and 1725 suggests that few did there, a situation that held for sixteenth-century Augsburg as well. No doubt some widows ran businesses in areas related to their husband's occupation, as was the case in early modern construction in northern England where it was not unusual for widows to run building supply businesses. Still, a life of penury confronted many a widow.

Wealth and poverty

In 1741 Pierre Anquetin, one of the poorest of Paris's master bakers, died. The modest dowry of 1,500 *livres* that his wife had brought to the marriage in 1719 and an equal sum he had contributed had long since been depleted, so that he left his six children and his widow with no assets and saddled with a debt of over 4,200 *livres*. In the same trade at about the same time we find Pierre Lepage, one of the richest bakers in all of Paris but who was not even a master but a *faubourien*, a denizen of one of Paris's guild-free suburbs. He boasted a net worth of 82,818 *livres*, which included uncollected debts of customers of more than 25,000 *livres*, *rentes* worth over 24,000 *livres*, and a house, complete with a library of 200 books, worth 13,000 *livres*. Such a range of wealth and poverty within the same trade was, in fact, typical of most trades in most cities, and once again impresses upon us the rule of diversity and heterogeneity in the early modern European artisanry.

Because of the scarcity of the kinds of sources needed to ascertain wealth (above all tax rolls and notarial records) and the painstaking and time-consuming research needed to compile and interpret them, we can

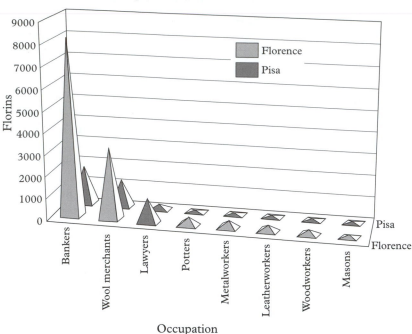

Figure 8   Florence and Pisa, 1427: average per capita wealth in florins, selected occupations

say little about artisanal wealth during the Middle Ages. Of course, we can surmise that opening and stocking a shop and staffing it with workers required a level of wealth that was significantly greater than that commanded by the propertyless migrant laborer or vagrant, but we have no way to compare quantitatively the relative wealth of various artisanal occupations, or artisans with other occupations in medieval cities before the fifteenth century. With the early modern centuries, however, this changes.

When we examine quantitatively the distribution of wealth in various early modern European cities, we find, as we might expect, that artisans nearly everywhere rank well below the elite of their city (patricians, royal officials, merchants, lawyers), but also appear as owners of enough property to place them clearly above the propertyless underclass of society. In this "average" sense they were a "middling sort," but closer examination shows a wide disparity in the wealth of different artisans in given towns, even within the same occupation.

Fifteenth-century Florence and Pisa conform to these generalizations (figure 8). There was an enormous chasm in terms of wealth between

Illustration 8 Nailmaker, 1529. Reproduced with permission from Jost Amman and Hans Sachs, *The Book of Trades*, New York: Dover Publications, 1973

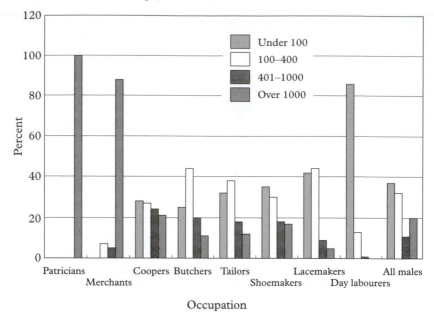

Figure 9   Frankfurt am Main, 1587: distribution of wealth by assessed worth in *gulden*, selected occupations

the Florentine and Pisan elite (bankers, merchants, and lawyers) and the artisans, and when we note that the *sottoposti* (or unincorporated and essentially propertyless occupations) of Florence in 1427 overwhelmingly clustered at the bottom of the wealth scale where fully 65 percent of them had an assessed individual net worth of one florin or less, we get a picture of a vertical distribution of wealth, with an artisanry clustering in a lower middle rank. Many of these artisans, however, were closer to the *sottoposti* than at first appears because of indebtedness. If we deducted their debts from their net worth we would find over 40 percent of them in the "1 florin or less" category. In other words, these artisans owned property, but for many it was entirely mortgaged. The difference between a tailor with an assessed worth of, say, 100 florins, and a propertyless *sottoposto* was narrower than one might initially assume. No wonder artisans were so keen on proclaiming the status differences between themselves and their "inferiors." They were closer to them economically than they wished to admit.

In its heterogeneity, Frankfurt in 1587 is similar to Pisa and Florence of 150 years earlier (figure 9). Once again, the artisans are distinctly placed between the patricians and the day laborers, but the Frankfurt

Illustration 9 Shoemaker, 1520. Reproduced with permission from Jost Amman and Hans Sachs, *The Book of Trades*, New York: Dover Publications, 1973

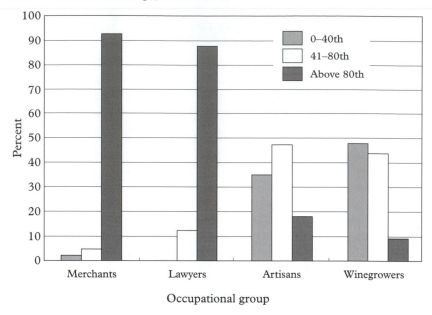

Figure 10   Dijon, 1556: distribution of wealth, by percentile, in percent of selected taxable occupational groups

records show that distribution of wealth among and within trades was wide. Here the coopers, butchers, tailors, shoemakers, and lacemakers, to name some prominent trades, cluster together relative to the rest of society, but, as we will discuss below, also saw their wealth spread widely across the guild.

Much the same can be said about Dijon in the sixteenth and seventeenth centuries (figures 10 and 11). The artisans are placed between the winegrowers below them and the mercantile and legal elite above. As a group relative to the rest of society, artisans appear a middling sort, but within the artisanry the range of wealth is once again wide, with one of every five artisans in the top 20 percent, and about one of three in the bottom third. Between 1556 and 1643 there is little change in the artisans' relative position, but by the mid-seventeenth century more merchants and lawyers have clustered in the top end of the wealth scale.

A final example, Madrid in the mid-eighteenth century, at first glance seems to suggest that artisans were the poorest occupation in town, oddly, having a greater proportion in the lowest annual income category of 0-1,000 *reales* (according to the *Catastro* of 1757) than even unskilled

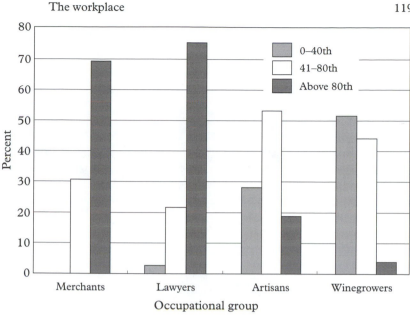

Figure 11   Dijon, 1643: distribution of wealth, by percentile, in percent of taxable selected occupational groups

laborers (figure 12). However, artisan wealth in this table is skewed by the disproportionate representation of poor construction workers who were especially numerous in Madrid (and 80 percent of whom were not masters). These artisans account for fully two-thirds of the 0–1,000 *reales* category, and when they are subtracted from the remaining artisans in the overall sample, a profile similar to that found in most other early modern cities emerges, with a clumping of artisans on average toward the lower third of the scale but with representation across the wealth spectrum.

Within the European artisanry we also find a range of wealth *between* trades. The butchers of Dijon, for instance, from 1464 to 1750 were consistently more wealthy as a group than the tailors, shoemakers, or furniture-makers, although the bakers had surpassed all artisans by 1750 (table 3.3).

Many towns are like Dijon in the wide range of wealth possessed by different master artisans. Nördlingen in 1579 (table 3.4), Delft in the 1620s (table 3.5), Reutlingen in 1745 (table 3.6), Madrid in 1757 (table 3.7), or Lyons from 1728 to 1789 (table 3.8) are characteristic. The difference between tanners or butchers and woolweavers in Nördlingen,

Illustration 10   Reliquary maker, 1458. Reproduced with permission from Jost Amman and Hans Sachs, *The Book of Trades*, New York: Dover Publications, 1973

Illustration 11 Turner, 1485. Reproduced with permission from Jost Amman and Hans Sachs, *The Book of Trades*, New York: Dover Publications, 1973

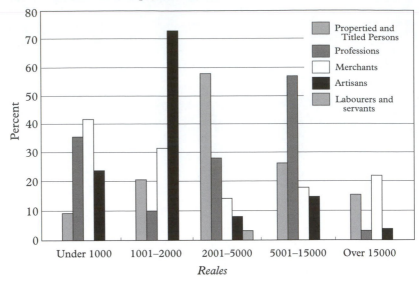

Figure 12   Madrid, 1757: distribution of wealth (assessed worth) by percent of occupational category

Table 3.3. *Dijon, 1464–1750: median tax assessment (the* taille, *a tax on personal wealth), selected trades (minimum ten instances)*

	1464 (in *gros*)	1556 (in *sous*)	1643 (in *sous*)	1750 (in *livres*)
Butchers	22	17	110	12
Goldsmiths	12	10	55	–
Bakers	6	9	60	20
Tailors	6	4	30	7
Shoemakers	5	4	50	7
Furniture-makers	4	4	30	7

Source: James R. Farr, "Consumers, commerce and the craftsmen of Dijon," in Philip Benedict, ed., *Cities and Social Change in Early Modern France* (London, 1989), pp. 134–73.

or between silversmiths or painters and carpenters or pinmakers in Delft, or between coopers or bakers and carpenters or masons in Reutlingen, or luxury craftsmen and construction tradesmen in Madrid, or shoemakers and bakers in Lyons, for example, is visibly dramatic.

If wealth was widely distributed among the trades, so too can that be said *within individual* trades. The shoemakers, butchers, bakers, and woolweavers of Nördlingen in 1579 show this clearly (figure 13). Even the relatively wealthy butchers had one in four of their brethren assessed

Table 3.4. *Nördlingen, 1579: average wealth of male citizens, selected occupations, in florins*

Tanners	652
Butchers	622
Bakers	512
Finecloth weavers	398
Shoemakers	310
Woolweavers	184
All males	438

Source: Christopher Friedrichs, *Urban Society in an Age of War: Nördlingen, 1580–1720* (Princeton, 1979).

Table 3.5. *Delft, 1620–31: average real estate taxes paid, selected occupations (number of taxpayers in parentheses)*

Occupation (N)	Average taxes paid (in *stuivers*)
Silversmiths (10)	179.6
Painters (39)	177.8
Faienciers (14)	142.8
Carpenters (39)	103.2
Pinmakers (5)	44.0

Source: John Michael Montias, *Artists and Artisans in Delft* (Princeton, 1982).

Table 3.6. *Reutlingen, 1745: average value of homes owned, selected occupations, in florins (number of home-owners in parentheses)*

Bakers	963 (60)
Coopers	669 (17)
Shoemakers	440 (41)
Furnituremakers	390 (4)
Tailors	343 (16)
Carpenters	313 (8)
Masons	275 (5)

Source: Douglas Dekker Hall, "Craftsmen in Reutlingen, 1740 to 1840," Ph.D. thesis, University of California at Berkeley, 1977.

Table 3.7. *Madrid, 1757: percent of occupational group with income above (in reales)*

	1,000	5,000
Luxury crafts	84.7	24.7
Construction	31.1	6.6

Source: David Ringrose, *Madrid and the Spanish Economy, 1560–1850* (Berkeley, 1983).

Table 3.8. *Lyons 1728–89: average* apports (livres) *brought by males to marriage, bakers and shoemakers (number of marriages in parentheses)*

Bakers	1,923.5	(183)
Shoemakers	514.5	(552)

Source: Maurice Garden, *Lyons et les lyonnais au XVIIIe siècle* (Paris, 1975).

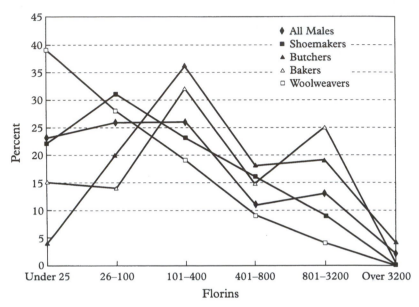

Figure 13   Nördlingen, 1579: distribution of wealth, in florins, in percent of taxpayers in selected crafts

in the lowly 0–25 florin category, while nearly an equal number were assessed on a worth of over 800 florins, and 1 in 25 of over 3,200 florins. At the other end of the artisanal wealth scale we find the woolweavers where predictably nearly two of five were assessed on 25 florins or less; but even in this poor trade more than one in eight were assessed on over 400 florins.

The same disparities of wealth can be seen within the crafts of Frankfurt in 1587 (figure 9). As we have seen, there was a considerable gap between the coopers in general and the lacemakers, but even among the relatively wealthy coopers and the relatively poor lacemakers, note that wealth within the guild was scattered from the top to the bottom of the scale. The same could be said about most trades in most European towns from the fifteenth to the eighteenth centuries. Entirely typical in this regard are the shoemakers and tailors of Dijon in 1556 and 1643

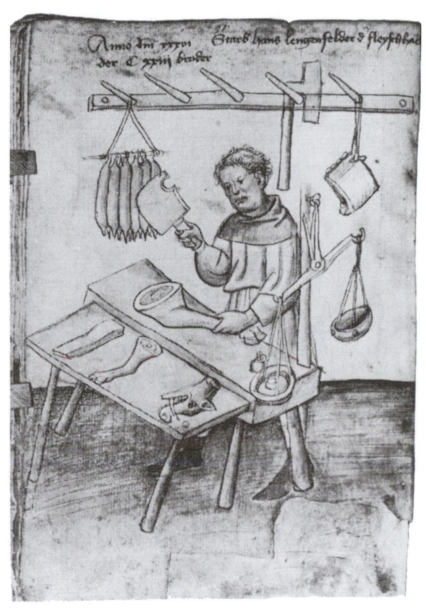

Illustration 12   Butcher, 1436. Reproduced with permission from Jost Amman and Hans Sachs, *The Book of Trades*, New York: Dover Publications, 1973

Table 3.9. *Dijon, 1556, 1643: distribution of wealth by percentile, in percentage of taxpaying shoemakers and tailors (number of taxpayers in parentheses)*

| | Percentile | | |
	0–40th	41–80th	over 80th
Shoemakers			
1556 (34)	35.5	44.1	20.6
1643 (45)	24.4	64.4	15.6
Tailors			
1556 (70)	31.4	54.3	14.3
1643 (71)	38.6	49.3	12.1

Source: James R. Farr, *Hands of Honor: Artisans and Their World in Dijon, 1550–1650* (Ithaca, 1988).

Table 3.10. *Frankfurt, 1701: wealth assessment of master tailors, in florins*

Assessment	Number of masters	Percent of all masters
Under 300	2	2
300	60	44
301–2,000	59	44
Over 2,000	14	10

Source: Gerald Soliday, *A Community in Conflict: Frankfurt Society in the Seventeenth and Early Eighteenth Centuries* (Hanover, NH, 1974).

Table 3.11. *Paris, 1773: distribution of wealth, goldsmiths, in percent of goldsmiths paying capitation asssessment*

| | | Assessment in *livres* | | |
1–5	6–25	26–50	51–100	Over 100
21%	49.8%	16.9%	7%	2.8%

Source: Steven L. Kaplan, "The luxury guilds in Paris in the eighteenth century," *Francia* (1981).

(table 3.9), the tailors of Frankfurt in 1701 (table 3.10), or even the goldsmiths of Paris in 1773 (table 3.11). If one of the functions of guilds in preindustrial Europe was to ensure an equitable distribution of wealth among its members as guild statutes suggest and historians have asserted, they were doing a demonstrably poor job of it.

The sources that historians have used to describe the distribution of wealth – usually tax rolls, notarial contracts, or property registers – inevitably privilege the sedentary resident and head of household. In

Table 3.12. *Dijon 1464–1750: distribution of wealth among female artisans, by percentile of total taxpaying population*

| | Widowed | | Single | |
	N=	Percentile	N=	Percentile
1464	18	36th	0	–
1556	36	50th	4	26th
1643	25	43rd	8	15th
1750	174	42nd	105	36th

Source: Farr, "Consumers, commerce and the craftsmen of Dijon," in Philip Benedict, ed., *Cities and Social Change in Early Modern France* (London, 1989), pp. 134–73.

most cases when the resident is an artisan, this means that males and masters are disproportionately represented. How can we determine the wealth of journeymen, many of whom were migratory and did not establish households of their own? And what about women? Theoretically, the wealth of independent women should be easier to ascertain than that of journeymen since they were heads of households, but the male preponderance as household heads in the extant records has guided historians in search of norms away from quantitative analysis of female artisanal wealth. True, the number of female household heads before the seventeenth century who were not widows was rather small, but no studies that I am aware of besides my own on Dijon have even correlated widows with occupation and taxable wealth. Most studies generally refer to artisan widows as invariably poor, and no doubt many were, but the evidence from Dijon cautions us from making sweeping generalizations. It shows that widows tended to be better off on average than single female artisans, and though generally below their male counterparts, many of these women were definitely above the threshold of poverty.

If we can say little about the wealth of artisan women, we can say more about that of journeymen. Tax rolls are not much help here because rarely do these sources indicate whether the taxpaying artisan was a journeyman. Other sources, like marriage contracts or property registers, are more helpful, however, and though the evidence is sparse, in each of the following cases, predictably, we see a picture of significant differences between the wealth of masters and that of journeymen. For instance, in Dijon from 1550 to 1650, the average *apports* that daughters of master artisans brought to their marriage was 278.6 *livres* while that of daughters of journeymen was 95.5 *livres*. A ratio of about 6:1 is evident in the values of dwellings owned by masters and journeymen in Delft between 1620 and 1644. Here master painters' homes averaged

1,800 *gulden* in value, while the homes of journeymen painters averaged
275 *gulden*. The gap between master faience-makers and their journeymen in this European capital of majolica production was not as wide,
but it was substantial nonetheless, for the average master's home was
worth 1,650 *gulden* while that of a journeyman was 672 *gulden*. Looking
at Lyons over a century later a similar relative disparity is evident. From
1749 to 1751 the daughters of master artisans in general brought *apports*
of 1,870 *livres* to marriage, while those of journeymen averaged 600
livres. In each of these cases – Dijon, Delft, Lyons – the ratio of master
to journeyman wealth was usually about 3:1. Of course, this evidence
disproportionately reflects the sedentary artisan of whatever status (one
would have to assume that the gap between the sedentary master and
the migratory journeyman must have been greater still), but as with tax
rolls, these averages also obscure the fact that there were many masters
who could scrape up no more assets for their daughters than journeymen could, and must have crowded into dwellings little different
from those inhabited by their "inferiors."

At this end of the spectrum of wealth we come up against artisans
perilously close to sliding out of the world of the artisanry altogether (as
we have come to understand it) and into the world of proletarianized
waged labor. These workers are not the subject of this book, of course,
but their existence (which has been amply documented by many
historians, particularly in the textile industry) calls our attention to the
volatility and precariousness of the world of the artisan, for penury and
economic dependency were never far away from many a craftsman.

Working conditions

Our best evidence telling us what the workplace was like is visual. Rich
as images can be (illustrations 13–17), unfortunately they still leave to
our imagination the sounds and even the smells that round out what life
in the artisanal shop was like. Or perhaps we should say shops, for the
working conditions varied widely from trade to trade. The construction
industry was noisy with the sawing, stonecutting, chiseling, and hammering that took place at crowded sites full of bustle, while tanneries
were renowned for noxious odors, shoemakers' shops for being cramped
and ill lighted, butchers' shops, obviously, not only for the raw meat
carved off the carcass of an animal dispatched with little concern for the
suffering the beast might feel, but also for the rivers of blood and globs
of fat that accompanied the process. Indeed, although butchers were
everywhere enjoined to do their work only in slaughterhouses, they often
out of convenience simply slaughtered the brutes in the alleys behind

Illustration 13   Cabinet-maker, 1484. Reproduced with permission from Jost Amman and Hans Sachs, *The Book of Trades*, New York: Dover Publications, 1973

Illustration 14   Sixteenth-century wood turner by Jan Joris van der Vliet. ©
Kupferstichkabinett. Staatliche Museen zu Berlin – Preussischer Kulturbesitz.
Photo Jörg P. Anders

Der Läderer.

Die Heuwt die henck ich in den Bach/
Werff sie in den Escher darnach /
Dergleich die Kalbfel auch also/
Darnach wirff ich sie in das Loh/
Da sie jr ruhe ein zeit erlangn/
Darnach henck ichs auff an die Stangn/
Wüsch darnach ab mit ein Harwüsch/
Vnd habs feyl auff dem Leder Tisch.

Der

Illustration 15   Sixteenth-century tanner. Reproduced with permission from
Jost Amman and Hans Sachs, *The Book of Trades*, New York: Dover
Publications, 1973

Illustration 16 Seventeenth-century edge-tool maker. Photo Bibliothèque nationale de France, Paris

Illustration 17 Seventeenth-century carpenter. Photo Bibliothèque nationale
de France, Paris

their shops, turning these byways into impassable morasses of fly-infested, coagulated blood.

The working conditions in artisanal workshops, large or small, were, in Arlette Farge's words, "violent and deadly."[2] Overcrowding, poor or

---

[2] Arlette Farge, "Les Artisans malades de leur travail," *Annales. Economies, sociétés, civilisations* 32:5 (1997), 994.

non-existent ventilation, the use of chemicals emitting noxious, even incapacitating, and sometimes deadly fumes, all afflicted the early modern workplace. Risks on the job were high, prompting historian John Rule to observe "The labouring poor you always had with you, but not, in many occupations, for very long."[3] Building trades had the ever-present risk of a fall, as Gaspare Nadi well attested. This fifteenth-century waller from Bologna records in his diary several falls he suffered, the most serious being a plunge down a chimney.

An English pamphleteer lamented in 1782 that manufacturing produced a "mournful scene of the blind and lame and of enfeebled, decrepit, asthmatic, consumptive wretches crawling half alive upon the surface of the earth."[4] Allowing for hyperbole, there is, nonetheless, little doubt that working for piecerates, as many craftsmen did, encouraged long hours at work and resulted in fatigue, and thus accidents on the job. Negligent or tired printing shop workers passing too close to a press in operation could find their ribs, arms, or legs broken or their skulls fractured by whirling levers. Clothcutters lost fingers while woolcombers often punctured theirs.

Different occupations had specific risks, depending upon the nature of their work, but all work took its toll upon the artisan. Hernial ruptures plagued craftsmen doing heavy lifting, while prolonged and repeated muscular action or working in the same posture for hours at a time, day in and day out in trades like shoemaking, saddlemaking, or tailoring contributed to cramps sometimes known as "craft palsies." Cruelly, to modern sensibilities, a part of the Black Country in England was known colloquially as "humpshire" because of the deformed posture of the locksmiths that concentrated there. Equally insensitive by modern measures, in 1700 the Italian physician Ramazzini wrote a treatise of occupational medicine in which he observed that

It is a laughable sight to see those guilds of cobblers and tailors in their own special feast days when they march in procession two by two . . . Yes, it makes one laugh to see that troop of stooping, round-shouldered, limping men swaying from side to side; they look as though they had all been carefully selected for an exhibition of these infirmities.[5]

Disabling chemicals – especially lead and mercury – also afflicted artisans who came into contact with them. Ramazzini described the effects of lead poisoning contracted by pottery workers who used lead in their glazes: "First their hands become palsied, then they become

[3] John Rule, *The Experience of Labour in Eighteenth-Century English Industry* (New York, 1981), p. 76.
[4] Ibid., p. 74.
[5] Quoted in ibid., pp. 82–3.

paralytic, splenetic, lethargic, cachetic and toothless, so that one rarely sees a potter whose face is not cadaverous and the colour of lead."[6] Ramazzini surmised that gilders, who also used lead in their work, would pray for death if they did not die young, for an uncontrollable trembling of fingers, hands, legs, and head would begin to afflict craftsmen after just months on the job. Mercury brought on nervous and mental disorder, too. Used in the making of felt hats, "hatters' shakes" and the mental symptoms of depression, loss of memory, and paranoia resulted from mercury poisoning, and contributed to the proverbial image of the "mad hatter."

Amid such perils, nonetheless, work did get done. Artisanal techniques everywhere were protected by craftsmen themselves as the "mysteries" of the trade, so we know surprisingly little about the actual work done by artisans. They operated by "rules of thumb," learned by apprentices through experience from a master or a journeyman, and by a journeyman from his fellows or from a master. Techniques were therefore highly varied, secretive, and far removed from the systematic, scientific basis that mechanical production would gradually acquire during the era of industrialization. Perhaps the best way to describe artisanal technique would be in a manner familiar to the craftsmen of the age themselves, by example, by exploring the techniques, sights, sounds, smells, and conditions of a few, specific trades.

Let us begin with ubiquitous baking, its eighteenth-century Parisian ambience recently so magisterially examined by Steven Kaplan.[7] Most of the production of loaves of bread took place in the bakehouse (fournil), a dark and ill-ventilated place behind the boutique or sometimes underground. Usually the baker's brick or refined-clay oven was in the bakehouse, and so bakers and their workers toiled in exceedingly hot and often cramped conditions (sometimes so hot that the dough did not rise properly, having partially cooked from the heat, and sometimes so cramped that bakers could wield the long-handled baker's shovel only with difficulty). Bakers, stripped to their waists (see illustrations 18 and 19), grunted, groaned, and sweated over hardwood, non-porous kneading troughs (usually one or two per establishment) which were, after the oven, the most important piece of equipment in the bakery. Here the dough was confected. Flanking the trough were cauldrons of water, along with salt, yeast, and flour, these being the four formal ingredients (although by the eighteenth century some doctors were complaining about the unhygenic additive of sweat that liberally dripped

---

6 Quoted in ibid., p. 79.
7 Kaplan, *Le Meilleur pain du monde, Les Boulangers de Paris au XVIIIe siècle* (Paris, 1996), esp. ch. 2, "Panification."

Illustration 18   An eighteenth-century bakery: kneading bread. Division of
Rare and Manuscript Collections, Carl A. Kroch Library, Cornell University,
Ithaca, NY

Illustration 19   An eighteenth-century bakery: weighing, shaping, baking
bread. Division of Rare and Manuscript Collections, Carl A. Kroch Library,
Cornell University, Ithaca, NY

off the bodies of the four or five workers). Mixing of these ingredients required an enormous intensity of physical effort. Time was of the essence, for taking too long to mix the dough could upset the fermentation process and the dough would then not rise properly. The rule of thumb of one Parisian bakery was forty-five minutes for a doughball suitable for 200 loaves. During the last half of the eighteenth century kneading machines made their appearance, but only gradually came to dominate the trade in the following centuries.

Experience in the trade, not scientific manuals or mechanical clocks, tutored noses, and eyes informed bakers when the dough had risen properly and was ready for weighing and cutting, and later when it was well baked. A certain odor to the dough signaled the first stage, just as a certain golden appearance signaled the latter. No mistakes could be tolerated, for bread that had not risen properly baked densely, and loaves removed from the oven prematurely could not be reinserted without damaging the product. Then as now, a baker's livelihood rested squarely on the quality of his product.

Baking was laborious and physically taxing – something we can say about nearly every trade during the old regime. Hatmaking certainly was, to cite another populous trade, the processes of production of which we are well informed about thanks to the work of Michael Sonenscher.[8] Making a hat in eighteenth-century France involved three dozen processes, all performed by workers in the same place (see illustrations 20–24). The stripping of fur from the beaver or rabbit pelt (the most common raw materials for hats in that age) was done mostly by women, despite the labor-intensive nature of this task. The fur was then sorted and sent along to felters who "bowed" it, stirring it with a bow-shaped implement. These men had to work in closed, airless rooms to prevent the fur from blowing away. Fullers washed the felt, which was then placed on a mold the shape of which shifted according to fashion, and left to dry. Once dry, hats were singed by fire, rubbed to raise the nap, trimmed, and then sent to be dyed and further stiffened. The process concluded with another group of female artisans trimming and tidying up the hat before it was sent for final decoration, with ribbons, feathers, or gilt.

Close scrutiny of many artisanal workshops and of the production processes within them reveals a picture of an extensive division of labor and a high degree of integration. Moreover, production was often spatially quite concentrated, the literature on proto-industrialization which has emphasized dispersion not withstanding. Baking and

[8] Michael Sonenscher, *The Hatters of Eighteenth-Century France* (Berkeley, 1987), pp. 20–5.

Illustration 20   Hatmaking: tearing and shaving fur from pelts. Reproduced with permission from Michael Sonenscher, *The Hatters of Eighteenth-Century France*, Berkeley: University of California Press, 1987

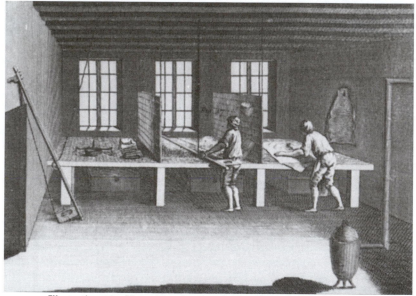

Illustration 21   Hatmaking: bowing the fur. Reproduced with permission from Michael Sonenscher, *The Hatters of Eighteenth-Century France*, Berkeley: University of California Press, 1987

Illustration 22   Hatmaking: building a hat. Reproduced with permission from Michael Sonenscher, *The Hatters of Eighteenth-Century France*, Berkeley: University of California Press, 1987

Illustration 23   Hatmaking: felting a hat. Reproduced with permission from Michael Sonenscher, *The Hatters of Eighteenth-Century France*, Berkeley: University of California Press, 1987

Illustration 24 Hatmaking: dyeing and finishing hats. Reproduced with permission from Michael Sonenscher, *The Hatters of Eighteenth-Century France*, Berkeley: University of California Press, 1987

hatmaking make this point, and so does papermaking. As Leonard Rosenband observes, "during the eighteenth century [papermaking] still consisted of centuries-old artisanal procedures performed in a mill."[9] Here we find, amid dangerous and unhealthy conditions, artisans hard at work in tasks that had changed little for centuries. Craftsmen and women toiled at various tasks, from converting old linen into pulp, to creating sheets, to preparing the paper for ink and for shipment. As with the women who stripped the fur from pelts in hat manufacture, so others were put to relatively "unskilled" tasks in papermaking, first called upon to pull the knots out of old linen after they had removed the caked dirt and other foreign matter from the raw material. The linen was then rotted in a fermentation process, and beatermen then monitored the rythmic stamping mallets as they hammered the rotted linen into filaments and pulp. Vatmen then took over as the pulp was transformed into paper. Dipping a rectangular, wire-mesh mold into a

[9] Leonard Rosenband, "Hiring and firing at the Montgolfier paper mill," in Thomas M. Safley and Leonard N. Rosenband, eds., *The Workplace Before the Factory* (Ithaca, 1993), p. 226.

vat of watery pulp, the vatman then "lifted the mold and shook it according to custom so that the fibers of the infant sheet 'shut.' "[10] From the vatman to the coucher went the nascent sheets of paper where they were "flipped" six or seven times a minute, each onto a "hairy felt." Together the felt and the paper were then pressed. The layman then took over, separating the sheet from the felt. This was a delicate operation, according to a contemporary authority who wrote a book on the art of papermaking, "suitable only for people who have practiced it from an early age and not for . . . inexperienced country-folk."[11] Women then resumed a role, hanging the paper on cords of horsehair for drying. Later, the sizerman collected them and plunged them into an emulsion which filled the pores of the paper and thereby prevented inkblots. Women then sorted the sheets by size, weight, and quality and helped the loftsman wrap them up in reams for shipping.

In each of these examples – baking, hatmaking, and papermaking – we catch a glimpse of the workshop that, perhaps surprisingly, is more readily seen in illustrations than read about in written sources. Of course, each trade has its unique characteristics, but these three well depict qualities of old regime artisanal production which have been underemphasized in the traditional literature – its extensive division of labor and its high degree of integration. These trades were far from unusual in this regard.

Cores and peripheries in the workforce

For all but the wealthiest master craftsmen, economic insecurity was a constant fact of life for artisans from the late Middle Ages into the age of industrialization. For most masters and journeymen of most trades, employment was uncertain and irregular. Weather and seasonal cycles of demand affected a variety of trades, and chronic warfare added a further disruption. In the preindustrial economy demand for manufactures was inconstant, compounded by the technological and distribution bottlenecks that beset the putting-out system (variants of which, as we have seen, were employed in more trades than simply textiles). Of course, the conjuncture of historical conditions determined the level of employment, underemployment, or unemployment. The immediate aftermath of the Black Death, for example, found labor in demand beyond available supply, and so employment was high. A contrasting example would be London in the 1570s as a wave of unemployment swept most trades as the international demand for English products –

---

[10] Ibid., p. 227.   [11] Quoted in ibid., p. 227.

especially cloth – slackened. There are countless examples of these cycles.

In general, however, an analysis of early modern employment reveals a picture of precarious insecurity. This was especially the case for the artisans we have called "peripheral." Proportions and ratios between masters and journeymen are informative about the division of labor, but it is also helpful to see the early modern workforce in terms of cores and peripheries. It appears that from the Middle Ages right into the eighteenth century master artisans in many towns, fully in keeping with the economic logic of "constant returns to scale," had kept a core of well-trained workers (sometimes fellow masters jobbing themselves out) in permanent employment, and added only modestly or incompletely trained workers from the mass of migrants when business was good, and laid them off when business slowed. As Michael Sonenscher has shown, Parisian masters taught only a select few workers the "knowledge" of the trade, and in so doing maintained discipline in the workforce by keeping it "dis-integrated."

In many towns master artisans retained in their employ a central core of highly trained workers, some who were small masters in the guild, others who often had been picked as apprentices (and frequently were sons of other master artisans) and were destined for eventual mastership. Surrounding these workers who knew or were taught the "mysteries" of the trade were "peripheral" workers, men who were briefly trained in only certain tasks and were summarily hired and fired as employers, operating according the logic of "constant returns to scale," sought to keep production in balance with demand. When faced with increased demand, preindustrial employers did not expand the physical plant; they simply hired more workers. Conversely, when demand slackened, they laid them off. Given the fits and starts of short-term supply and demand cycles and the scarcity of investment capital available to most master craftsmen, this was a business practice that was entirely rational, if harsh for the laid-off worker.

Of course, what this strategy created were islands of skilled and relatively continuously employed small masters and journeymen surrounded by a vast sea of semi-skilled craftsmen, many with no distinct occupation, who were underemployed and could and did switch jobs and trades readily. Censuses and tax rolls, useful as they are, are just a snapshot of a shifting, dynamic, and unstable world of employment. Such a core and periphery situation is already evident in sixteenth- and seventeenth-century Dijon, and no doubt existed elsewhere. Here we find a clearly segmented labor force of journeymen, a core destined for mastership who remained in the employ of their master for several years.

This privileged sector of the workforce was surrounded by a much more transient body of workers with little hope of entry into the masters' ranks.

A dynamic correlation existed between available investment capital, demand, and workforce concentration. The tapestry works in Audenarde in 1541 (a town with a population of about 8,000) were run by 41 masters who employed 29 apprentices, 209 journeymen, and 905 unskilled workers, an average of 29 workers per enterprise. This average hides a polarized situation, however, for, as the chronicler Joos Vandenbroucke observed, some masters with available capital employed more than 300 men in one enterprise, while others less economically advantaged ran small shops with only a handful of journeymen or workers.

In 1630 in the textile industries in Holland we find similar structures of workforce segmentation and concentration, where a master/entrepreneur called a *reder* owned relatively large workshops employing as many as forty workers under one roof. The Venetian glassmaking and fur and wool industries likewise had seen labor segmentation and concentration, in their case since the late Middle Ages.

Of course, the traditional picture of the artisan's workshop – a master toiling alongside a journeyman or two and an apprentice – is not an entirely inaccurate one, but it must be complemented by one of shops that, depending upon the vagaries of demand, could reach considerable size. Even a bakery, like one in seventeenth-century London, might bustle with thirteen people at work, including maidservants, a wife, and children, in addition to five or six apprentices and journeymen. Contemporary guild statutes from German cities occasionally specified how many workbenches a shop might contain (typically three) and everywhere statutes restricted the number of journeymen a master may employ in his shop (often only two, sometimes a few more); but we know from other sources that these restrictions were often ignored, no doubt by the more successful enterprises. By the eighteenth century it was not at all uncommon to find workshops with twenty workers within. This was certainly true in the emerging "ready-made" clothing and shoemaking industries, but it was also the case in both English and French hatmaking. In Paris in 1739 ten of the sixty-three master hatter shops employed one-half of the journeymen, an average of between twenty-five and thirty journeymen per shop. By 1791 the fifteen largest hatmaking shops were huge by preindustrial standards, employing an average of over sixty journeymen each. Such a scale calls the terminology of "workshop" into question, suggesting protofactories instead, more akin to the textile enterprises which in some places housed under one roof several artisanal operations. The Linz woolen manufactory in

Austria in 1786 illustrates this well, for 102 dyers and cloth finishers toiled inside its walls.

Thus, when we speak of cores and peripheries, we should bear in mind their double meaning. On the one hand the terms reflect a segmented labor force of select journeymen with relatively permanent employment surrounded by a sea of transient, short-term, unskilled workers. They also describe a concentration of workers unevenly distributed across the enterprises of particular trades in a particular town. In Nantes in 1738, for instance, 2.6 percent of the master locksmiths employed more than four journeymen in their shops, while 81.5 percent employed one or none at all. The locksmiths of Marseilles in 1782 show a similar profile: 80 percent of the masters there employed one-half of the journeymen in shops with three or fewer journeymen, while about 4 percent of the masters employed almost 20 percent of the journeymen in shops with nine or more. Or take the joiners of Amiens in 1765–6, where the pattern of concentration and peripheralization is even more pronounced. There 90 percent of the masters employed half of the available journeymen and put them to work in shops where they worked alongside 3 or fewer of their fellows, while three percent of the masters hired nearly a quarter of the available journeymen, putting them to work in shops where they were joined by more than ten of their fellows.

Peripheralization and incompletely trained workers were the products of, but also contributed to, segmentation of labor. In some sectors of manufacture, like textiles, shipbuilding, or ceramics, we find the division of labor deeply segmented, resulting in a loss of independence for many craftsmen. A great deal has been written about this development in the eighteenth century, the best-known example being the Wedgwood potteries. Extensive specialization where workers were trained to a particular task contributed to standardization of production, but it also fragmented the artisanal work process and eliminated any claim to independence an artisan may have had. Josiah Wedgwood, the man behind the system, sought "to make machines of the men as cannot err" and referred to his workers, tellingly, as "sett[s] [sic] of hands."[12] His system rested upon ironclad discipline. In exchange for job security (a powerful incentive, given the chronic insecurity of employment most artisans faced), master potters lost all authority, conforming to a discipline secured by written rules and regulations that demanded punctuality, cleanliness, sobriety, and fixed hours of work.

No doubt the eighteenth century witnessed an expansion of disci-

---

[12] Quoted in Neil McKendrick, "Josiah Wedgwood and Factory Discipline," *Historical Journal* 4:1 (1961), 34, 46.

plined systems of production and advancing specialization and fragmentation of the labor force – but these trends did not originate then.
Already in early Renaissance Florence we find a convergence of political,
economic, and technological changes that altered production and the
division of labor in the textile industry fundamentally. The diffusion of
the loom and the spinning wheel in the late thirteenth century and the
expansion of the wool industry created more steps of production, and
labor was increasingly fragmented into menial tasks. Many formerly
skilled and independent artisans were subsequently pressed into a mass
of wage-earners.

Some historians have called this process "proletarianization," but
whatever its label, we can find this development in several sectors of the
early modern economy. The Venetian Arsenal provides a vivid example,
mirrored in some respects in seventeenth- and eighteenth-century
Dutch shipbuilding. From the mid-fifteenth century and culminating in
the seventeenth the Arsenal workforce was increasingly disciplined to
the demands of an integrated production schedule. An elaborate state-
administered bureaucracy regulated production at the expense of guild
self-government. Standardization of design and production of inter-
changeable parts crafted by specialists and put together in "assembly-
line" fashion by workgangs converted the task of the artisan into a one-
dimensional and repetitive one (this was true in Holland's shipyards,
too, where workers did not have to be versatile or knowledgeable).
Anticipating Wedgwood's system in many ways by more than a century,
in exchange for job security (the Venetian state guaranteed life-long
employment), craftsmen lost to the Venetian government any claim to
control over apprenticeship, working conditions, wages, or quality
standards. Indeed, by 1650 the *arsenalotti* were no longer even called
"masters" (*maestri*) any more, just "workers" (*operai*).

Specialization of task, labor segmentation or fragmentation of skill,
and employers' disciplinary production systems are but one side of the
coin of employment practices, for on the other we find a countervailing
but related trend toward a growth in the peripheral labor force, an
increase in the scale of artisanal mobility and, as we will see in the next
chapter, mounting "insubordination" among journeymen.

Mobility and migration

As far back as records take us, we can see that many artisans in Europe
were highly mobile. Indeed, it was not just artisans that thronged the
roads of late medieval and early modern Europe, prompting one
historian to refer to a "culture of mobility." As David Reher notes,

people's propensity to move about has emerged as perhaps the single most noteworthy trait of urban populations. Migration levels were extremely intense for people of all ages, sexes, and social categories . . . [a] pattern [that] . . . quite possibly [was] typical of most pre-industrial urban areas in Europe, regardless of their size.[13]

No doubt immigration into cities was needed to fill the ranks of populations that, owing to the high mortality rates there, could not reproduce themselves.

Migration of laborers was a significant part of this ambulant population, and be it skilled, semi-skilled, or unskilled, it was a constant feature of the manufacturing economy of Europe's cities. Migratory patterns were sometimes seasonal, but throughout the year one could find multitudes of workers tramping from town to town seeking work, with a chosen few gaining access to mastership or citizenship, and thus permanent residence. In the two years of 1779 and 1780, 2,836 journeymen tailors registered in Rouen, while the registrations of journeymen wigmakers in Nantes between 1783 and 1785, for example, show peaks of over a hundred in the months of May, September, and January, and troughs of under twenty in June and December. Some of these artisans, like their brothers everywhere had done for centuries, settled in to semi-permanent employ with one master (thus forming a relatively stable "core" of trained journeymen), but by far the most found only short-term jobs and drifted into town and out again after a brief stay. Whatever the city in Europe – large megalopolises like London or Paris, or smaller towns like Nördlingen or Dijon – the demographic situation regarding migration was always the same: vast waves of migrants in search of work flowed into town; some stayed, but most, like an ebbing tide, floated out of the town gates and drifted along the road toward the next nearest town.

The construction industry was notoriously mobile. The stonemasons of central France trekked annually to Paris during the construction season (by 1694 6,000 made the trip from the Haute-Marche), and returned home at the end of it. Mobility may have been marked in construction, but it pervaded all the trades. The workforce of the printing craftsmen at the Société Typographique in Neuchâtel, Switzerland, turned over every six months in the eighteenth century. Similarly, 80 percent of the journeymen hatters working in Marseilles in 1782 were not born there, while 85 percent of all journeymen in Frankfurt am Main in 1785 were outsiders, many from France, Hungary, Denmark, and even England.

[13] David S. Reher, *Town and Country in Pre-Industrial Spain, Cuenca, 1550–1870* (Cambridge, 1990), p. 302.

Since the late Middle Ages, and probably before, London had been a
city of immigrants, but when the city government opened up the
freedom in 1531 (responding to a demand for labor), the magnitude of
immigration increased dramatically, fueling a massive population
growth that would continue for centuries. It has been estimated that by
the seventeenth century 70 percent of Londoners had been born elsewhere. So powerful was London's magnet for people that by 1700
immigration to metropolitan London absorbed 50 percent of the natural
increase of the entire population of England. Countless numbers of
these immigrants were artisans. Indeed, in London in 1650 fully 85
percent of the 20,000 apprentices there were immigrants.

As sixteenth-century Venetian industries boomed (glassmaking,
building, shipbuilding, and above all textiles), the queen of the Adriatic
became a magnet for itinerant and immigrant labor; but it was not the
only destination. The silkweaver Francesco Cazuolo in the 1550s and
1560s wandered from Milan to Mantua, Bologna, Florence, Naples,
and Messina on the island of Sicily, before finally reaching Venice.
Fellow silkworker Francesco Fontana likewise made a stop in Milan, but
his itinerary included Turin, Lyons in France, Geneva in Switzerland,
Brescia, and then Venice. Venice also became home to foreigners in
other trades. Most of the bakers and many of the cobblers and tailors
came from Germany, many butchers from the Grisons in Switzerland,
and many journeymen printers from France.

The common aspiration of most skilled workers was to become a
master and establish residence, but, even though emigration is nearly
impossible to document quantitatively, we can be sure that only a
minority of artisans formed a sedentary core of workers, and that many
migratory workers must have remained so throughout their lives. Europe's workshops were largely peopled by a floating population of casual
labor. Wherever records of turnover in the workplace exist, we see short-
term employment as the norm, with longer stays reserved for far fewer.
Construction workers in the towns of northern England, for instance,
were commonly hired by the week or the month, and many remained on
the job for less than a year. One-half of the journeymen joiners in
Chester between 1600 and 1640 stayed for less than a year, and another
30 percent for less than three. But one in five remained for longer than
three years. Renaissance Florence was little different. For example, of
the eighty-nine stonecutters employed in the first 600 days of the
construction of the Strozzi palace, one-fourth worked fewer than 50
days, one-half fewer than 100, but two were still on the job after 450
days. A clear example of a resident core of workers trained for eventual
mastership comes from Dijon. There is no question that workshops, like

their counterparts in Paris and no doubt everywhere else, were sites of constant coming and going of workers, but the sixty-nine journeymen who acceded to mastership amid all this flux in Dijon between 1590 and 1642 had spent an average of three years in the service of their last employer. The eighteenth century shows the same profile. Almost one-third of the tailors hired in Rouen between 1778 and 1781 stayed on the job for a week or less, while another 40 percent were gone before month's end. Of the 500 to 750 journeyman wigmakers who annually registered in Rouen between 1783 and 1790, almost three in ten stayed on the job for less than a month, almost 60 percent for three months or less. Fully 90 percent were gone within the year.

Marriage contracts also point toward a minority core of immigrant craftsmen entering the charmed circle of residency and mastership, surrounded by a majority of peripheral transients. Between 1551 and 1650, of the 168 immigrant journeymen who married in Dijon, 51 or about 30 percent found brides who were daughters of masters resident in Dijon, a clear inside track to mastership for the groom, while 58 married immigrant women. Of those who married masters' daughters, the price was mounting; indeed, the average amount of *apports* these men brought to the marriage between 1601 and 1650 was 363.3 *livres*, a far greater sum than the 68.3 *livres* that their counterparts of the second half of the sixteenth century had to muster.

Nördlingen provides further evidence of this core/periphery phenomenon in the working community, and once again wealth mattered. Between 1580 and 1700 one in six of the 4,700 men admitted to citizenship were immigrants; but we know that the city's standards of admission were high and getting higher. Before 1585 the city council had required prospective citizens to have a minimum of 50 florins in cash, but this figure was doubled in that year, and then in 1607 doubled again. This meant that many craftsmen remained itinerant, with mobility accelerated by the upheavals of the Thirty Years' War. Records show that few migrant journeymen gained mastership and citizenship in Nördlingen, the overwhelming majority staying in town no more than a year, and often for far briefer stays.

The towns of Holland provide another illustration of mobility, cores, and peripheries. Massive immigration fueled dramatic population growth in these cities (from 247,000 in 1600 to 464,000 in 1650 to 489,000 in 1700, despite a negative intramuros natural rate of increase), the first wave in the late sixteenth century triggered by the war with Spain and a huge exodus from the southern provinces of Flanders and Brabant. Many of these migrants were skilled craftsmen with capital, and the towns of Zeeland and Holland swelled with artisanal enterprises which in turn created a demand for labor. The towns of Holland and Zeeland became vast labor markets, by the seventeenth century expanding so that workers were pulled from a wide geographic area. On average from the late sixteenth to the early eighteenth century one in four men living in the Dutch republic had not been born there.

Amsterdam, the fastest growing city of the republic, illustrates this well. Many hatters and silkworkers destined for "the warehouse of the world" came from France, while many construction tradesmen migrated from the coastal provinces of Germany as well as those of the Netherlands itself. Inland Germany sent many bakers, smiths, tailors, and shoemakers to Amsterdam. Of course, once again, some of these immigrants became burgher masters, but many more were, and remained, journeymen. For example, of the 4,139 craftsmen married in Amsterdam between 1641 and 1650, five out of eight were immigrant journeymen (one in eight of the masters marrying in this decade were born elsewhere as well), whereas only one in twenty-five was a master Amsterdammer.

Eighteenth-century Vienna presents a similar picture. In 1742 only 13 percent of the guild masters had been born in that town of well over 160,000 souls. Indeed, in most central European cities of that century we find that three-quarters of the journeymen were immigrants. Vienna was a magnet that pulled many sons of rural artisans to it for at least temporary stays, most of the newcomers hailing from the German lands to the west in the upper Rhine region, followed closely by lower and alpine Austria. Few, however, came from nearby Hungary, but wherever their point of origin, most would tramp from city to city and eventually either join ranks of lifetime wage-workers or return to their roots in the countryside and become village craftsmen.

The urban labor market was flexible and open, and everywhere gave rise to a core and periphery phenomenon, with permanent privileged jobs of high wages for relatively extensively trained workers surrounded by relatively unskilled workers in short-term employment. As specialization increased, the labor market everywhere became more segmented, and as the market grew (urban manufacturing was attracting labor away from agriculture for centuries before the industrial age), it became increasingly anonymous. This spelled difficulty for authorities and employers alike, who were keen on maintaining discipline in the ranks of hired artisans. Of course, employers had long been concerned about this; the seventeenth- and eighteenth-century labor market was different in degree more than in kind. As early as 1354 in Paris master artisans and royal authorities had tried to regulate the labor market spatially by demanding that all wage-workers in clothmaking, tanning, carpentry, masonry and "generally all manner of work" present themselves "at the hiring square" (*sur la place d'embauche*) that was customary in their trade. In Milan and Antwerp workers were required to report to special hiring locales, and by the sixteenth century the Dutch shipbuilders were demanding that all unemployed journeymen report to a specified place daily for a "shake-up," as the hiring practice was called. Throughout the early modern period construction workers in Chartres were expected to gather by the porch of the town's magnificent cathedral, while their counterparts in Dijon were required by municipal statute to report to St. Michel Square at daybreak. Laggards or workers trying to arrange employment elsewhere were to be expelled from the city if apprehended. This was still the practice in the eighteenth century, for the place de Grève was the traditional gathering place for construction workers seeking employment (ironically, the expression *faire la grève* meant looking for work, not going on strike), while the rue de la Poterie was the place for pastrycooks, and the rue des Ecouffes for joiners. Other trades required that their workers seeking employment gather in front of the guild hall (if one existed), or in front of the home of one of the officials of the particular guild. Verbal contracts were then often concluded between master and worker on the spot.

Not all trades had a geographic "hiring place," but, with an eye toward worker discipline, by the seventeenth century many had guild officers whose job it was to place workers in shops in need, and many guild statutes were amended to require journeymen to report immediately to the placement officer upon their arrival in town. Several Parisian guilds already had employment clerks in the sixteenth century, and in the seventeenth we find them in Dijon (the master cabinet-makers created the office in 1624, the shoemakers in 1633), Toulouse, Montpellier, and Nevers (in the latter two towns the clerk was appointed by the municipality and the crown respectively). A police ordinance in Paris in 1639 ordered all journeymen of whatever craft to present themselves upon arrival to the employment office of their trade. This was not just a French phenomenon, for the shoemakers of seventeenth-century Augsburg, to take but one example among many, had a *Zuschickmeister*, a master whose job it was to register incoming journeymen and to place them in the employ of masters needing labor.

Masters and journeymen lived in perpetual tension between need and (in)discipline. By the eighteenth century, masters had come to believe that insubordination had reached crisis proportions. Placement clerks and mandatory reporting to hiring places were now deemed inadequate to stem the rising tide of worker sedition. To keep track of the churning, shifting world of work and workers, authorities and masters generalized and expanded upon a system of obligatory worker registration. Vestiges of this system can be traced back to the fourteenth century. The Statute of Labourers in England in 1349 and 1351 laid down that artificers who changed employer must have a certificate from their previous master. In the sixteenth century the brewers of London required workers to carry a "passport" signed by masters verifying that the worker had left his employ in good standing, while the goldsmiths required workers to produce letters from their former employers attesting not to their training or skills, but rather certifying their good conduct and behavior. There is evidence in France of the use of such documents, called *billets de congé*, in the late sixteenth century as well, but it was during the eighteenth century that the system was increasingly standardized and generalized across the guilds. These *billets* were records of previous employment, and no journeyman was permitted to seek work unless the previous master had signed the certificate releasing him from his employ. To force mobile journeymen to seek work promptly and there-fore come quickly within the disciplinary arms of the masters, these certificates expired after fifteen days, whereupon a journeyman who had not found work was plunged into the dreaded, floating population of *gens sans aveu*. Journeymen were later told to keep the certificates together in a small booklet, called a *livret* which, as in the case of the bakers of Paris, could only be acquired from the placement office of the guild. When signed, these *billets* verified that the journeyman had completed his work and legitimately departed his previous employment. Journeymen were required to carry these documents with them, and present them to guild employment officers upon arrival.

In 1739 the French crown prohibited master papermakers from hiring any worker without a *billet de congé*, and then royal patent letters extended this requirement to all guilds in 1749. The preamble to this regulation explains its fundamental purpose, which was to combat worker insubordination:

We are informed that a number of workers in the trades and in manufacturing are leaving the manufacturers . . . employing them without first having obtained in writing notice to quit, or without completing the work in hand and, in many cases, without reimbursing advances [on wages] made to them on the basis of earnings from their output. We are also informed that some of these people having formed a kind of body are holding meetings and laying down the law to their masters, doing as they choose, depriving them of workers and preventing them from [hiring] . . . whom they want.[14]

---

[14] Arlette Farge, *La Vie fragile. Violence, pouvoirs et solidarités à Paris au XVIIIe siècle* (Paris, 1986), p. 126 (my translation).

It should need no emphasizing that this system was designed to oversee and, as the French legislation of 1781 requiring *livrets* put it, "to contain" the working population by identifying, classifying, and, it was hoped, immobilizing it. The *livret* signified a bureaucratic surveillance system that intended to "classify all the workers," to render them all visible to the disciplinary eye of the authorities. Given the swirling, dynamic complexity of the world of work and workers of eighteenth-century Paris, such a system could only be a dream, if perhaps a reassuring one, in the minds of the authorities.

A similar situation was developing in Germany. To control the migrations of journeymen and so limit their independence and indiscipline, in 1724 the Saxon ducal government required journeymen to keep a *Wanderbuch* (identical to the *livret*), and then in 1731 the emperor issued an edict that created the *Kundschaft*, a document all journeymen were required to carry on which was recorded their name, age, place of birth, a brief description of physical appearance, and the particulars of employment history, complete with signatures of previous masters releasing them from employ. This booklet had to be presented to guild placement officers upon a journeyman's arrival in a new town. The *Kundschaft* was issued by the guilds, and had to be signed by a guild officer when the journeyman wished to depart. Without a signed, and therefore validated *Kundschaft*, a journeyman could not legally work elsewhere in the empire.

Wages

The urge and need that masters felt to discipline workers did not, of course, begin in the eighteenth century. Indeed, already in the fourteenth century we see deep tensions between masters and workers over the duration of the working day. Workers were usually paid a daily wage (usually distributed weekly, on Saturday), or sometimes "by the piece," but in either case the hour was not the unit of measurement for payment. Masters, therefore, were keen on controlling how much and when their workers worked, and workers' resistance movements in the late fourteenth and early fifteenth centuries, as we will see in chapter 5, focused on the duration of the working day as often as the wage itself.

This is not to say that wage levels were unimportant, but several factors affecting an analysis of wages in the preindustrial European economy must always be borne in mind. First, we should not equate wages as the monetary equivalent of the necessities and conveniences of life, for wages were often only a fraction of a worker's income (and an unknowable one at that), since nonmonetized payment for work (the provision of lodging and/or food and drink) was far from unusual. Obviously, then, we must avoid applying liberal Ricardian "iron law" assumptions about wages to the preindustrial economy.

Second, the increasing economic specialization and the segmentation of the labor market coupled with an economy that was only sporadically becoming integrated meant that wage differentials from place to place, season to season, craft to craft, and even within the same craft in the same place, could be significant. Most masters did not even work for wages, but those who did were generally paid higher wages than journeymen in their trade. We know that during the eighteenth century rates varied among journeymen, not just in the same trade, but even in the same shop, with higher wages going to the semi-permanent core of workers. But even the transient journeyman earned more than the "semi-skilled" or unskilled migrant wage-worker. Such differentials had been around for nearly as long as we have records of wages. At a construction site at Caernarvon in Wales in 1304, for example, fifty-three masons received seventeen different rates of pay. Nowhere, in fact, do we find standardized systems of wage payments, not even in the eighteenth century, nor can we trace a linear trend from payment in kind or by piecerate to payment in cash, since this fluctuated as the schedules of production were affected by shifting demand and the conditions in the labor market itself. All of these variables make comparisons between wage levels highly speculative and only informative in very general ways.

Third, real wages are not an accurate measurement of standard of living because, not knowing the nature of workdays (specifically how many there were in a year), we cannot extend with any confidence daily wages to annual income, nor do we know what percentage wages may have been of household earnings (we know that women contributed to household budgets, and that often the men had by-employments, even agricultural ones, that brought added income to the family).

So of what use to us are wage indicators? Certainly data exist, especially in the building trades, to show that from the fourteenth to the nineteenth centuries generally across Europe nominal wages were extraordinarily "sticky," sometimes remaining stagnant for a century, and that though they lagged behind food price increases, they almost never fell. We can also demonstrate that real wages moved in accord with population movements. Thus from the Black Death to the late fifteenth century real wages were relatively high everywhere, but this "golden age" was followed by a disastrous "long sixteenth century" where, by the early 1600s, price inflation had cut real wages to half what they had been in the late 1400s. Gradually falling prices to 1750 and periodic wage increases boosted real wages, but then inflation resumed and only in the early nineteenth century did real wages begin rising again.

These trends more or less accurately describe the movement of wages during the early modern centuries (with the exception of the Netherlands where the demand for labor, especially in the early seventeenth century, drove real wages up faster than elsewhere, giving the Dutch wage-earner, in Jan De Vries's vivid words, "a privileged position" trapped in "an iron cage").[15] The data tell us two things of great importance. First, whether a wage paid was above or below subsistence. Knowing this tells us whether the artisan in question needed nonmonetized payment, a working wife, or by-employment to make ends meet. Second, we know that the ratio of a craftsman's wages to those of "unskilled" laborers remained fixed for centuries at roughly 3:2. Within the ranks of the craftsmen, moreover, we find, predictably, that the wages paid to masters were and remained superior to those paid to journeymen. This tells us that "skill premia" reflect not simply the monetary worth of dexterity and training or even the relative supply or demand in the labor force, but reveal just as much a powerful concern for status and relative position. Given what we know about nonmonetized payments in the workplace, we can conclude that wages paid were as much symbolic cultural indicators of appropriate place in a hierarchy as they were economic indicators of subsistence and convenience needs.

Historians have traditionally assumed that artisans were a "middling sort," numbering about a third of a town's inhabitants and occupying a position in society that was determined by the wealth they possessed – considerably less than the elite above them, not greatly more than the propertyless underclass beneath them. There is some truth in this profile, and one can safely say that, given the incertitude of employment and bottlenecks in production and distribution, economic security was precarious for most artisans. Research over the last thirty years, however, forces us to recognize nonetheless that the artisan community was extremely heterogeneous. Artisans did comprise about one-third of the population of some towns, but their numbers ranged from 20 percent in some places to 80 percent in others. Likewise, it may be true that many artisans in many towns occupied the lower middle rank in the wealth hierarchy, but we also know that many of their brethren spread across the wealth scale, from the very wealthy to the very poor, so that

---

[15] De Vries, "Between purchasing power and the world of goods: understanding the household economy of early modern Europe." In John Brewer and Roy Porter (eds.), *Consumption and the World of Goods* (London, 1993), pp. 85–132.

we must jettison any preconception that guilds effectively distributed wealth among their members.

Diversity describes the history of apprentices, journeymen, and women artisans, too, for the number of apprentices and journeymen (and their ratio to masters) varied widely from town to town and from trade to trade. Until recently we knew almost nothing about female artisans, but research in that area has revealed that women practiced more trades than was once supposed, and we now realize that dichotomizing the household economy (the supposed female sphere) and the market economy (the purported male sphere) is misleading, for women participated in both and their economic activities blurred distinctions between the two.

Amid all of this variety, are there any general trends that can be identified and supported by a body of research? One identifiable trend across the early modern centuries concerns the experience of women. Although we can find as late as the eighteenth century women working in a wide variety of trades, we can also perceive in many cities a concentration of women in a narrower sector of craftwork, that of textiles and clothing manufacture.

Second, even though mobility marked the lives of most artisans at least since the Middle Ages, it does appear that the numbers of artisans on the move steadily increased at least from the sixteenth century, so that by the early eighteenth century masters and political authorities became especially concerned about the disorder and indiscipline that, from their perspective, accompanied such mobility. Of course, complaints about insubordination among workers can be found throughout our period, but the masters' voices became more shrill and the legislation of central authorities more coercive as the numbers of migrant workers apparently increased, and institutional changes (placement bureaus, *livrets*, and *Wanderbuchen*) were created to attempt to bring order and stability to this world of flux and turmoil.

A third, related, trend that emerges from all of this diversity is an increasing segmentation in the labor force, with a core of trained workers remaining in the employ of masters for relatively lengthy periods (and perhaps even gaining mastership eventually) surrounded by a swelling population of incompletely trained and transient workers who stayed on the job for a considerably shorter time. Of course, the logic of 'constant returns to scale' contributed to this core–periphery situation in the workforce as masters laid off and hired workers in response to demand (the first to go were the incompletely trained transients); but the result of such marginalization was expansion in the ranks of mobile and "indisciplined" workers. The problem of discipline, as we will see in chapter 5, informed the construction of institutions of authority from the Black Death to the era of industrialization.

Bibliography

Entries marked with a * designate recommended readings for new students of the subject.

Archer, Ian W. *The Pursuit of Stability: Social Relations in Elizabethan London.* Cambridge, 1991.

Bennett, Judith M., Elizabeth A. Clark, Jean F. O'Barr, B. Anne Vilen, and Sarah Westphal-Wihl, eds., *Sisters and Workers in the Middle Ages.* Chicago, 1989.

Brown, Judith C. "A woman's place was in the home: women's work in Renaissance Tuscany." In Margaret Ferguson, Maureen Quilligan, and Nancy J. Vickers, eds. *Rewriting the Renaissance.* Chicago, 1986, pp. 206–24.

Brown, Judith C., and Jordan Goodman. "Women and industry in Florence." *Journal of Economic History* 40:1 (1980), 73–80.

*Clark, Alice. *The Working Life of Women in the Seventeenth Century.* New York, 1920.

Clarkson, Leslie A. "Wage labour, 1500–1800." In K. D. Brown, ed., *The English Labor Movement, 1700–1951.* Dublin, 1982, pp. 1–27.

Coffin, Judy. "Gender and the guild order: the garment trades in 18th-century Paris." *Journal of Economic History* 54:4 (1994), 768–93.

Cohn, Samuel K. *The Laboring Classes in Renaissance Florence.* New York, 1980.

Coleman, D. C. "Labour in the English economy of the seventeenth century." *Economic History Review* 2nd ser., 8 (1956), 280–95.

Collins, James B. "The economic role of women in 17th-century France." *French Historical Studies* 16:2 (1989), 436–70.

*Davis, Natalie Z. "Women in the arts mécaniques in sixteenth-century Lyons." In Barbara Hanawalt, ed., *Women and Work in Preindustrial Europe.* Bloomington, 1986.

Delumeau, Jean. *Vie économique et sociale de Rome dans la seconde moitié du 16e siècle.* 2 vols. Paris, 1957–9.

De Roover, Raymond. "Labour conditions in Florence around 1400: theory, policy, and reality." In Nicolai Rubenstein, ed., *Florentine Studies.* London, 1968.

Dolan, Claire. "The artisans of Aix-en-Provence in the sixteenth century: a micro-analysis of social relationships." In Philip Benedict, ed., *Cities and Social Change in Early Modern France.* London, 1989.

Earle, Peter. "The female labour market in London in the late 17th and early 18th centuries." *Economic History Review* 2nd ser., 42 (1989), 328–53.

Hafter, Daryl. "Gender formation from a working-class viewpoint: guildswomen in 18th-century Rouen." *Proceedings of the Western Society for French History* 16 (1989), 415–22.

Hanawalt, Barbara A., ed. *Women and Work in Preindustrial Europe.* Bloomington, 1986.

Hill, Christopher. "Pottage for freeborn Englishmen: attitudes to wage labour in the sixteenth and seventeenth centuries." In C. H. Feinstein, ed., *Socialism, Capitalism, and Economic Growth*. Cambridge, 1967, pp. 338–50.

Honeyman, Katrina, and Jordan Goodman. "Women's work, gender conflict, and labour markets in Europe, 1500–1900." *Economic History Review* 44:4 (1991), 608–28.

*Hudson, Pat, and W. R. Lee. *Women's Work and the Family Economy in Historical Perspective*. Manchester, 1990.

Hufton, Olwen. "Women and the family economy in eighteenth-century France." *French Historical Studies* 9:1 (1975), 1–23.

"Women, work and marriage in 18th-Century France." In R. B. Outhwaite, ed., *Studies in the Social History of Marriage*. New York, 1981, pp. 186–203.

"Women without men: widows and spinsters in Britain and France in the 18th century." *Journal of Family History* (Winter 1984).

Jacobsen, Grethe. "Women's work and women's role: ideology and reality in Danish urban society, 1300–1550." *Scandanavian Economic History Review* 31:1 (1983), 1–20.

Kaplan, Steven L. "Les Corporations, les 'faux-ouvriers,' et le faubourg Saint-Antoine au XVIIIe siècle." *Annales: ESC* 43 (1988), 453–78.

Kaplow, Jeffrey. *The Names of Kings: The Parisian Laboring Poor in the Eighteenth Century*. New York, 1972.

Lacey, Kay E. "Women and work in fourteenth and fifteenth century London." In Lindsey Charles and Lorna Duffin, eds., *Women and Work in Preindustrial England*. London, 1985, pp. 24–82.

Levine, David, ed. *Proletarianization and Family History*. Cambridge, 1984.

Lis, Catharina. *Poverty and Capitalism in Preindustrial Europe*. Atlantic Highlands, NJ, 1979.

Social Change and the Laboring Poor: Antwerp, 1770–1860. New Haven, 1986.

Lucassen, Jan. "The Netherlands, the Dutch, and long-distance migration in the late sixteenth to early nineteenth centuries." In N. Canny, ed., *Europeans on the Move: Studies on European Migration, 1500–1800*. Oxford, 1994, pp. 153–91.

McKendrick, Neil. "Josiah Wedgwood and factory discipline," *Historical Journal* 4:1 (1961), 30–55.

Milward, R. "The emergence of wage labour in early modern England." *Explorations in Economic History* 18 (1981).

Moch, Leslie Page. *Moving Europeans: Migration in Western Europe since 1650*. Bloomington, 1992.

Musgrave, Elizabeth C. "Women in the male world of work: the building industries of eighteenth-century Brittany." *French History* 7:1 (1993), 30–52.

Pallach, Ulrich-Christian. "Fonctions de la mobilité artisanale et ouvrière. Compagnons, ouvriers, et manufacturiers en France et aux Allemands (17e–19e siècles)." *Francia* 11 (1983), 365–406.

Palliser, D. M. *Tudor York*. Oxford, 1979.

*Phythian-Adams, Charles. *Desolation of a City: Coventry and the Urban Crisis of the Late Middle Ages*. Cambridge, 1979.

Pike, Ruth. *Aristocrats and Traders: Sevillian Society in the Sixteenth Century*. Ithaca, 1972.

Prior, Mary. "Women and the urban economy: Oxford, 1500–1650." In Mary Prior, ed., *Women in English Society, 1500–1800*. London, 1985,

Quataert, Jean H. "The shaping of women's work in manufacturing: guilds, households, and the state in Central Europe, 1648–1870." *American Historical Review* 90 (1985), 1122–48.

Rappaport, Steve L. *Worlds Within Worlds: Structures of Life in Sixteenth-Century London*. Cambridge, 1989.

Reher, David S. *Town and Country in Pre-Industrial Spain, Cuenca, 1550–1870*. Cambridge, 1990.

Roper, Lyndal. *The Holy Household: Women and Morals in Reformation Augsburg*. Oxford, 1991.

Rosenband, Leonard. "Hiring and firing at the Montgolfier paper mill." In Thomas M. Safley and Leonard N. Rosenband, eds., *The Workplace Before the Factory*. Ithaca, 1993, pp. 225–40.

Sharpe, P. "Deindustrialization and reindustrialization: women's employment and the changing character of Colchester, 1700–1850." *Urban History* 21:1 (1994), 77–95.

Snell, Keith. *Annals of the Labouring Poor*. Cambridge, 1985.

Soliday, Gerald. *A Community in Conflict: Frankfurt Society in the Seventeenth and Early Eighteenth Centuries*. Hanover, 1974.

Sonenscher, Michael. "Work and wages in eighteenth-century Paris." In Maxine Berg, Pat Hudson, and Michael Sonenscher, eds., *Manufacture in Town and Country Before the Factory*. Cambridge, 1983, pp. 147–72.

"Weavers, wage-rates, and the measurement of work in eighteenth-century Rouen." *Textile History* 17 (1986), 7–17.

Torras, Jaume. "From craft to class: the changing organization of cloth manufacturing in a Catalan town." In Thomas M. Safley and Leonard Rosenband, eds., *The Workplace Before the Factory*. Ithaca, 1993.

Truant, Cynthia. "Parisian guildswomen and the (sexual) politics of privilege: defending their patrimonies in print." In Dena Goodman and Elizabeth C. Goldsmith, eds., *Going Public: Women and Publishing in Early Modern France*. Ithaca, 1995.

Vigo, Giovanni. "Real wages of the working classes in Italy: building working wages (14th to 18th century)." *Journal of European Economic History* 3 (1974), 378–99.

Wensky, Margaret. "Women's guilds in Cologne in the later Middle Ages." *The Journal of European Economic History* 11:3 (1982), 631–50.

Wiesner, Merry. "Spinsters and seamstresses: women in cloth and clothing production." In Margaret Ferguson et al., eds., *Rewriting the Renaissance*. Chicago, 1986, pp. 191–205.

"Women's work in the changing city economy, 1500–1650." In M. J. Boxer and J. Quataert, eds., *Connecting Spheres*. New York, 1987, pp. 64–74.

"Guilds, male bonding, and women's work in early modern Germany," *Gender and History*, 1:2 (1989), 125–37.

Willen, Diana. "Guildswomen in the city of York, 1560–1700." *Historian* 46:2 (1984), 204–18.

Woodward, Donald. "Wage rates and living standards in pre-industrial England." *Past and Present*, 91 (1981), 28–46.

4 Authority and resistance (I): artisans in the polity

The internal governance of guilds

From as far back as we have records of internal guild governance, we find evidence for guild officials, called variously *jurés*, *gardes*, *syndics*, or *prudhommes* in France, *consuls* or *gastaldi* in Italy, *promens* in Spain, wardens in England, *Vorgehern* in Germany, and *juiz de povo* in Portugal. Whatever their title, these men were empowered to inspect the workshop of fellow guildsmen (and sometimes those of a closely competitive guild – the shoemakers of Dijon, for instance, had the right of inspection of cobblers' shops). During such inspections the officials, the numbers of whom ranged from two to six or more, depending upon the guild, the time, and the place, in principle sought to uphold the dictates of the guild's statutes. This meant above all scrutiny of products for quality and investigating whether the master in question was abiding by the rules which usually restricted the numbers of apprentices and journeymen to be employed. If violations were detected, these officers were empowered to impose fines, in some places one-half of the fine going to the officials themselves. The typical term of office was one year, sometimes, as in Paris, two, but equally typical was the same man serving in the post year in and year out.

These were powerful men. In many guilds they administered guild property, collected dues, kept the account books, and in some places served as judges in the guild court hearing and decided cases of disputes between guild members. Often they also judged the quality of masterpieces presented by journeymen for admission to mastership, and, thus empowered to approve or turn away candidates, they were gatekeepers to the guild. With such powers, one might reasonably ask how these privileged men attained such an office. Not long ago, historians of guilds generally believed that during the Middle Ages guilds were democratic bodies that elected their officials in annual assemblies, but that in the more "absolutist" early modern period they lost these freedoms. There is some truth to this generalization. We know that in fourteenth-century

Arras and Montpellier, for instance, *jurés* were elected by and from among the masters and even the journeymen. The best example of guild democracy, however, is Florence. In the wake of the communal revolution, thirteenth-century guilds embodied what John Najemy has called "popular republicanism" because the legislative, judicial, and regulatory powers exercised over their members were conceived to be collectively possessed by the guildsmen.[1] Moreover, the guild's officials, called consuls, were elected by the members and were strictly constrained by the statutes of the guilds.

The essential principles of the Florentine guilds – equality among members and collective rule by them – were not, however, embodied everywhere. We know, for example, that in Paris in the thirteenth century *jurés* were not elected by the membership but rather named by the *prévot* with the king's approval, while in the medieval city of London guild wardens were approved by the mayor and his aldermen. Indeed, the trend of the future would be more along the Parisian or English experience than the Florentine (even in Florence). One can safely say that guild officials nearly everywhere after 1350 were vested with their authority, and increasingly appointed outright by the civic or royal authority.

Particularly well-documented examples of internal guild governance in the late medieval period and the emergence of oligarchy, stratification, and hierarchy within it can be found among English cities. Smaller guilds in medieval England were more democratic than the larger ones, with journeymen and masters more or less equal. In 1370, for example, the Chester bowyers stated explicitly in their statutes that in the election of the guild's officials a journeyman had equal voice to a master. Among the larger guilds, however, democratic principles, if they ever existed, were clearly eroding by the late fourteenth century as increasingly sharp distinctions between masters and journeymen emerged. This development was accompanied by the growing involvement of governments in the trades, a situation encouraged by masters who feared the growing "indiscipline" of their employees. In exchange for relinquishing to town councils or even kings any claim to autonomous self-governance, masters gained the use of municipal courts, and above all government sanction in the discipline of labor. Even in guilds where officials continued to be selected by the guildsmen, they had to be approved by the city council. Furthermore, these guild officials were usually drawn from among the more substantial masters, a harbinger of the crystallization of ranks within the guild that would set in during the fourteenth

[1] John Najemy, *Corporatism and Consensus in Florentine Electoral Politics, 1280–1400* (Chapel Hill, 1982), p. 9.

century whereby first the journeymen and later the small masters would be set off from and deemed inferior to the substantial masters.

Already in 1396 journeymen saddlers had been so distinguished, and had formed their own organization. The master saddlers of London complained to the mayor that the guild's "serving men called yomen" were not only holding meetings, but were wearing a common livery and appointing an officer (a "bedel") of their own.[2] By 1415 the "yomen" tailors also had such an organization, and during the rest of the century they were joined by yeomen founders, curriers, bakers, and clothworkers, each of these groups fighting running battles with the masters of their guilds over elections, control of funds for the poor, and the use (or abuse) of workshop inspections. During this century the yeomen and masters worked out a compromise, but one which nonetheless embodied a drift toward oligarchy, hierarchy, and stratification. Yeomen received some guild privileges (access to burial funds and poor relief), but only masters, and only some of them at that, reserved the right to wear the status-laden guild livery. These masters, increasingly called "of the livery," or "liverymen," monopolized the election of guild officials, and so controlled the governing body of the guilds, the Court of Assistants, while the yeomanry comprised of all the journeymen and increasingly the small masters were denied any voice in guild governance. Emblematic of this development, in 1487 the carpenters went from election "by common consent" to "such as the livery think convenient."[3]

By the sixteenth century the yeomanry had become a rank for journeymen of the guild awaiting promotion to mastership, and for small masters to the livery, a wait in vain for many since it required capital and family connections. The livery came to be more and more dominated by merchants. Such control of governance by the livery did not, however, go uncontested. As late as the 1620s the yeomanry of the weavers and the founders, for example, were demanding political participation. Guild statutes, reflecting a more democratic past, often stated that guild officials were to be chosen by the "commonalty," but by the seventeenth century liverymen of these guilds disputed what "commonalty" meant. As opposed to the definition of "freeman" (that is, an individual admitted to the "freedom" of the city) that journeymen and small masters ascribed to it, liverymen of the weavers, clothiers, and founders defined it as only including a "certain select number of rank and degree." For the clothiers, this meant specifically only the "Master

[2] R. A. Leeson, *Travelling Brothers: The Six Centuries Road from Craft Fellowship to Trade Unionism* (London, 1979), p. 43.
[3] Quoted in ibid., p. 47.

and Wardens." The founder yeomanry might counter that their liverymen were "reading the charter at their pleasure."[4] Maybe so, but they were doing it, so the weaver liverymen said, to restrict the electorate and thus the governing stratum of the guild in order to avoid "popular disorder." Indeed, the fear of indiscipline in the lower orders – and not just in England – insistently lurks behind every justification for hierarchy and oligarchy in the guilds.

The drift to an oligarchic ruling elite within guilds is everywhere apparent. In Venice the *gastaldo* was sometimes elected by the masters of the guild, sometimes (as with the bellfounders) appointed by the city magistracy, but never were his assistants of judges, deacons, and stewards elected by the guild membership, being selected instead by the outgoing officials. Selection for office in early modern Rome was even more circumscribed. There, through a process called *imbossolazione* which was generalized among the guilds in the fifteenth and sixteenth centuries and was still in place in the eighteenth, every three years the "notables" of the guild drew up a list of candidates whom they believed were worthy of guild office. The candidates' names were then inscribed on wax tablets and placed in an urn. Each year the current officers drew tablets from the urn, thereby electing the officers of the guild for the year to come.

Hierarchical stratification occurred in the guilds of Bologna, too, at about the same time. Until 1500 most masters were full members of the guilds and participated in guild governance, but over the next two and a half centuries the ranks of full membership contracted sharply, leaving a situation where most craftsmen became *obbedienti*, a status akin to yeomanry in England and with a meaning immediately redolent of hierarchy. These men paid an annual fee (the *obbedienza*) to the guild council which was controlled by an oligarchy that ran guild affairs.

In France there is some evidence that assemblies of guildsmen were active in internal guild politics in the Middle Ages. According to the Parisian *Livre des métiers* of the thirteenth century, the master goldsmiths and pinmakers gathered annually to elect their *gardes et jurés* (although in other trades of the time *jurés* were already named outright by the *prévôt*, or selected by a committee appointed by the *prévôt*), and most trades required their *jurés* to convene a general assembly if a modification of the guild's statutes were to be proposed. Evidence of such democratic procedures, however, disappears in France in the sixteenth century and is replaced by clear evidence of oligarchization. Many *jurés* of Paris were drawn from among the "notables" of their guilds through a

---

[4] Quoted in ibid., p. 70.

process of co-optation whereby previously selected masters and former *jurés* replenished their ranks by "electing" hand-picked newcomers. This restricted electorate then elected the jurés. The democratic past when all guild members participated was supplanted in the sixteenth century by oligarchy. Among the goldsmiths, for instance, the leadership of the guild decided that, as Steven Kaplan notes, "only experienced and respected masters – 'prudhommes' – would have the right [henceforth] to deliberate upon corporate affairs." Such a coup did not go without objection by the rank and file masters, who denounced their exclusion as "arbitrary" and continued to attend assemblies until they were definitively ousted in 1648.[5]

There is only a trace of guild democracy in sixteenth- and seventeenth-century Dijon, too. The extensive records of those appointed as *jurés* by the town council there (only the goldsmiths and pastrycooks were permitted election, and even then it was for only one of the two *jurés*) point toward a domination of guild politics by a handful of individuals and families. Indeed, the town magistrates repeatedly drew their appointments from the same narrow circle of master artisans, a form of political patronage from which both artisan and magistrate benefited, the former through wealth and status, the latter through a hoped for quiescence in the all too turbulent world of work. Indeed, everywhere in early modern cities, guild officials were integrated into political patronage systems, empowered to deliver peace and stability in the ranks in exchange for their privileged perch atop their corporation.

The escalation of the fear of worker insubordination to crisis proportions in the eighteenth century only served to further ensconce a corporate elite. Some guilds brought more masters into the charmed circle than others, but always the decision of whom to include in electoral or business assemblies was made by current and/or ex-officers of the guild. The Parisian painter-sculptor officers no doubt spoke for all the guild elite when they said that the reason the entire guild membership was not convoked in assembly was "in order to prevent plots and cabals that could influence the . . . elections."[6]

Less fortunate masters, as those among the Parisian goldsmiths, denounced the oligarchs for their monopolization of power. In many guilds in eighteenth-century Paris, as Kaplan has discovered, "one can detect a sort of structural political insurgency latent in many guilds," the primary cause of contention being "questions of accountability and participation." Such complaints seem an echo of former, more

---

[5] Steven L. Kaplan, "The luxury guilds in Paris in the 18th century," *Francia* 9 (1981), 270.
[6] Quoted in Kaplan, "Luxury guilds," 258.

democratic practices, and it may be that lesser guildsmen were leading "a democratic movement . . . in response to a sort of aristocratic resurgence . . . within the guilds – echoing broader social and political trends."[7] The self-appointed elite was at times accused of malfeasance of office, at other times rebuked for taking "the posture of Absolute Masters of the community" and for "regard[ing] the other masters as being far beneath them . . . totally dependent on their will, and [for] thus reply[ing to them] with haughtiness and contempt."[8] Often bound by blood or marriage, this corporate elite was refilled by co-optation, with new, younger men named to the ranks of the "council of elders," there to await "election" by former officials to some administrative post.

Artisans in the polity

As oligarchy and hierarchical stratification increasingly took hold within guilds and characterized internal guild governance from the late Middle Ages to the end of the old regime, so, too, was artisanal participation in the larger municipal political arena increasingly circumscribed. Both developments had much to do with a demand for order that increasingly marked the late medieval and early modern era, cresting during the seventeenth century. Cities and their inhabitants more and more came to be viewed by rulers of increasingly integrated states as parts of a coherent social order, and a preoccupation with social discipline informed this vision. The urban elite came to believe that, as Christopher Friedrichs observes, "[its] own interests were better served not by struggling to defend urban liberties but by functioning willingly as agents of the prince's will."[9]

It is true that urban governments were increasingly subordinated to state control, but one would be wise not to exaggerate the extent. We will return to this shortly, but here we should note that the relationship between the urban elite and outside, higher political authorities affected the political role of artisans within the municipality because outside powers became increasingly concerned about social disorder (often associated with the turbulent world of the craftsmen), and believed that oligarchy and bureaucratic municipal governance would facilitate good "police." As power on the urban level was increasingly concentrated in

---

[7] Steven L. Kaplan, "The character and implications of strife among the masters inside the guilds of eighteenth-century Paris," *Journal of Social History* 19 (1986), 635, 642.

[8] Kaplan, "Luxury guilds," 271.

[9] Christopher Friedrichs, *The Early Modern City, 1450–1750* (London, 1995), p. 57.

the hands of the elite, artisans found themselves, in the name of social discipline, progressively excluded from the constitutionally politically active community.

The constitutional structure of European cities, despite countless variations that were products of unique traditions and historical circumstances, were similar in that they were all rooted in a conciliar system. This meant that authority was collective, and though there were mayors, consuls, and burgomasters, these individuals, if not always named to their office by a council, invariably worked in close conjunction with it. Given the collective nature of authority, the pressing constitutional issues were which groups (including guilds) were permitted political participation (to elect or select its leaders), and who was permitted to belong to such groups. The composition of the political community varied from one town to the next, with more guildsmen included in some places than in others, but over time the trend everywhere was toward an oligarchy of an elite and the exclusion of guildsmen. This does not mean that artisans lost all political power, but it does mean that such power had to be exercised for the most part either through petitioning and litigating in courts of law, or outside of constitutional channels altogether through the threat or action of rebellion.

The trend toward excluding artisans from the constitutional political community began early in Italy. However, even in places where, as we will see in the next section of this chapter, a wave of rebellions by craftsmen in the fourteenth century altered the constitutional balance in favor of guildsmen against patricians in some towns in Germany and the Low Countries, the gains in most places were rolled back in the early modern period. Indeed, nearly everywhere during the sixteenth and seventeenth centuries, from Ghent to Vienna, from London to Nördlingen, Frankfurt, or Augsburg, from York to Barcelona, from Strasbourg to Florence or Venice, from Leiden or Lille to La Rochelle, artisans were increasingly excluded from the world of political participation. Only, it seems, in the "home towns" of Germany did guilds continue to play a significant constitutional role in local government. For the rank and file masters, the late medieval and early modern age was a time of denial of political privileges once possessed, within both the guild and the city.

The exclusion of craftsmen from political participation happened first in Italy. Whatever constitutional position guilds had acquired in the aftermath of the "communal revolutions" of the eleventh and twelfth centuries, in most places it was lost by 1400, in other places even earlier. In Venice the Giustizia vecchia was created in 1173 to supervise the guilds, and by the 1270s upon promotion to mastership a craftsman swore an oath of allegiance not to the guild, but to the state, promising not to form any "organization, company, armed band or conspiracy by oath, bond, or any other sworn commitment against the honor of the Doge and his council, the commune of the Venetians, or any other person."[10] With the *Serrata* of 1297 by which a circumscribed patriciate secured control of the governance of the city, guilds were definitively denied constitutional access to political power.

Such exclusion took longer in Florence – the fourteenth century was seared by a bitter struggle over the constitution of the commune between craftsmen and a mercantile elite – but the outcome – oligarchy and the exclusion of craftsmen from political power – was the same. One legacy of the communal revolution in Florence was government of the city by the direct participation of its citizens. The raging point of controversy henceforth became which inhabitants had the right to participate. The focal point, as John Najemy has explained in such lucid detail, was elections. Most craftsmen in the guilds held to a collectivist and egalitarian position and thus advocated a broad electorate and envisioned the "Florentine republic as a federation of equal and autonomous corporations."[11] The great merchants, bankers, and landholders, in contrast, rejected the decentralized popular republicanism of the guilds and advocated instead a communal society and a polity based not upon the corporation but upon the family, an "organism [that] naturally produced a beneficent elite of trained and experienced leaders who were identified with the patricians of the oldest and most prominent families."[12] These spokesmen and leaders of the "civic family" would be obligated to rule in the interest of all. We will return to this conflict later in this chapter when we discuss the revolt of the *ciompi*, but we should note here that the conflict between these two very different constitutional visions raged from 1293, when the guild forces were ascendant after the promulgation of the Ordinances of Justices, to 1382 when, in the aftermath of the failed corporatist *ciompi* revolt, the oligarchic elite won control of the commune. Never again would artisans participate significantly in Florentine politics. In 1434 the Medici gained control of the city, and then in 1532 the Medici grand duke of Tuscany abolished all distinctions between citizens based on guild membership. Two years later he consolidated the guilds further, and used them as bureaucratic agencies of ducal power, a situation that would exist into the late eighteenth century.

The constitutional exclusion of artisans from political power occurred

[10] Quoted in Richard Mackenney, *Tradesmen and Traders: The World of the Guilds in Venice and Europe, 1250–1650* (Totowa, 1987), p. 25.
[11] Najemy, p. 10.   [12] Ibid., p. 13.

later in other cities of Europe, but the outcome was the same. In Nördlingen, for instance, craftsmen found themselves increasingly restricted from the city council – the fifteen-member *Innerer Rat* – between 1580 and 1700. In the former year craftsmen comprised one-third of this powerful council, a representation that lasted until the beginning of the Thirty Years' War. After that a sharp reduction in their numbers set in, so that by 1652 only one artisan was appointed to it (since 1552 appointment had been made by a committee of seven sitting council members). By 1700 not a single artisan, or even the son of one, sat on the council which was now dominated by lawyers and professional bureaucrats.

In Augsburg, too, oligarchy triumphed. A free imperial city since 1276, Augsburg experienced a *Zunftrevolution* in 1368, a bloodless coup against the patricians led by merchants and artisans who then intro-duced a new constitution to the city. The new order granted certain guilds direct representation in municipal government, and alongside merchants, weavers, bakers, and other craftsmen and shopkeepers now held a majority in the Great Council and the Inner Council. This fortunate constitutional situation for artisans lasted until 1549 when, in punishment for resisting the victorious Emperor Charles V in the Schmalkaldic war that the Catholic Charles waged against the Lutherans, guild representation on the councils was ended. A similar fate befell Memmingen in 1551 and, indeed, twenty-five other imperial free cities between 1548 and 1552, leaving municipal government in the hands of an oligarchy of merchants and patricians. This constitutional structure lasted in most of these cities into the nineteenth century.

The formal political power of Viennese artisans was extremely limited as well. A municipal law of 1526 had excluded artisans from the city government, and, indeed, most artisans were not even citizens. In 1736 only a third of the craft masters were burghers and freemen of the city, and almost an equal number were *Störer*, those craftsmen operating on their own account illicitly outside of guilds.

The seventeenth century also saw the eclipse of artisanal political participation in Barcelona. Municipal government there comprised a Council of 100 (actually 144 representatives or *jurats*) and various municipal officers led by a committee of five councilors. One half of the *jurats* were artisans, but the formal political power of craftsmen was less than might appear at first glance. Only one of the five councilors was an artisan, and few craftsmen were permitted to hold important municipal offices (and only these officers could bring proposals for discussion to the Council of 100). Between 1600 and 1630, as Barcelona plunged into a recession which hit the crafts especially hard, the patricians and merchants on the city council came to hold the view "that some artisans were unworthy of holding high city offices by reason of their 'vile' trades."[13] Countering such oligarchic and exclusionist sentiments, the artisans pressed for the creation of a sixth councilor who also would be an artisan. In 1641, as part of the Catalan revolt that Barcelona's craftsmen supported, they won their sixth councilor – from Louis XIII of France, although the new constitutional arrangement was subsequently confirmed by Philip IV of Spain. The presence of this new councilor, however, did nothing to halt the oligarchic control of municipal government, and in 1716, when Catalan privileges were revoked by Philip V and the province – and Barcelona – were henceforth governed by the laws of Castile, artisans were left entirely out of city government whose officers now were royal appointees.

The same story of the triumph of patrician oligarchies dominated by merchants, legal professionals, or in some places royal officials, can be told about the cities of England and France. In England since the Middle Ages, towns had received their privileges by charters granted by the crown. These charters defined the relationships between the rulers and the ruled both within the city and between the city and the crown. The most prized privilege was incorporation, which granted the town's rulers the status of representing the interests of the entire citizenry. Though many charters had been granted before 1500, 160 more cities received theirs between 1500 and 1700.

One historian has called charters of incorporation "tools of an irresistible tendency towards exclusiveness," and indeed they did encourage the growth of oligarchy as power was vested in the hands of a small civic elite that perpetuated its grip on municipal governance by co-optation rather than by general election by the citizenry, often retaining their seats for life. Fear of the disorder that was assumed to ensue should the 'commons' be allowed to participate is voiced clearly enough by the magistrates of Nottingham in 1512: "If you shall suffer the commons to rule and follow their appetite and desire, farewell all good order." This fear was reiterated in Gloucester in 1584: "Experience hath taught us what a difficult thing it hath always been to deal in any matter where the multitude of burgesses have voice." [14]

In the fifteenth century many English towns heard freemen, many of them artisans, clamoring for a greater voice in municipal governance; but the best artisans could hope for from such demands was the creation

[13] Luis R. Corteguera, "Artisans and politics in Barcelona, 1550–1650," Ph.D. thesis, Princeton University, 1992, p. 153.
[14] Peter Clark and Paul Slack, *English Towns in Transition, 1500–1700* (Oxford, 1976).

of a large, supposedly consultative council comprised of a broader group of citizens. In practice, however, this body was usually ignored by the inner council controlled by the oligarchic elite. Councils of the sixteenth and seventeenth centuries met in secret and made decisions without any pretense of consulting the citizenry. More and more they tuned their municipal decisions to the chord being struck at court, as powerful political patrons rewarded municipal elites for their loyalty.

Charters in France, too, were granted by the crown, and brought with them a degree of self-government vested institutionally in councils called variously *échevinages*, *consulats*, *jurades*, or *capitoulats*. As in England, theoretically the charter sanctioned the council as representative of the community or, as it was sometimes called, the *respublica*. Often there were small, inner councils headed by a mayor, and larger councils, those, too, usually socially circumscribed to include only "notables." These small councils were called to meetings to deliberate on pressing issues, but everywhere the trend was the same as in seemingly every other city in Europe: toward oligarchy, which meant that if any artisan participated, he was among the most affluent.

Perhaps half of French towns in the Middle Ages had been established as "communes," but historians have come to recognize that even in these supposed havens of independence from seigneurial lords, autonomy was less complete than once imagined and institutions of self-government were extended to only a part of the town. In any case, by the early modern period, most towns had received whatever independence they had by concession from the king, usually in exchange for money or, in the case of militarily strategically located towns like Angers or Langres near the outer reaches of the kingdom, for loyalty. Nonetheless, municipal self-government was unequivocally a royal concession, and, moreover, whatever autonomy it had was circumscribed by competing royal administrative bodies within the walls – above all *bailliages* or *sénéchausées*, and, in some cities, *parlements*.

Within this constitutional framework, local power was vested in the hands of an elite who were perpetuated in office by various systems of election and co-optation. Sometimes, as in the towns of the southeast, seats were allotted to certain social or occupational groups, even at times including artisans (although always drawn from the wealthiest ranks of them). In Romans, for instance, one seat each in the council went to the *laboureurs*, the artisans, the merchants, and either the nobility, medical or legal professions, or men called *rentiers* who lived off their investments. More common, however, were cities whose councils were controlled by merchants or men of the law, as was the case in Lyons, Poitiers, Dijon, and Paris.

Resistance

Urban elites had always known that their city – wherever in Europe – was part of a larger political system and owed its privileges to some higher authority, be it a king, a duke, a bishop, or a lord, but they also knew that their relationship with that power was one of give and take. This was as true of the Middle Ages as it was of the early modern period.

Artisans, too, were aware that power was negotiated, perhaps between unequals, but negotiated nonetheless. They may have been formally excluded from politics, but this does not mean that they were politically powerless. Municipal authorities had few means of physical coercion (indeed, the backbone of the urban militia were usually the town's artisans), and artisans had a very high level of group cohesiveness and self-consciousness of their traditional rights. When collective demands were voiced they could carry considerable leverage. Artisans usually entered the political process by petitioning authorities for changes in laws or statutes, and if the demands went unheeded, then craftsmen were known to appeal up the political hierarchy, even to the king or prince himself.

One area of disagreement between guilds and municipal governments concerned access to mastership. Indeed, in 1619 in Dijon many guilds joined to file a collective grievance with the king against the town council, protesting the city fathers' attempt to expand the ranks of masters within the guilds by easing the requirements for admission. Fearing disorder among journeymen denied opportunities for mastership, the civil authorities had pressed for openness, while for decades the masters had been moving in the opposite direction, with considerable success. This single issue had been and would continue to be the most contentious one between the city magistrates and the master guildsmen. Guilds and government squared off over the same issue in Reval (present day Tallinn, Estonia) in 1659, the guilds appealing to the king of Sweden to forbid the municipal authorities from trying to force them to lower their requirements and costs for mastership. Only when they received no satisfaction did they turn to violence. In 1662 a group of artisans attacked the twenty-odd soldiers the town council had sent to break up a demonstration by these same artisans.

Artisans in rebellion

From the Middle Ages through the seventeenth century, towns all across Europe from time to time were rocked by rebellion. Some of these disturbances were riots, the result of poverty and the desperation that so often attends that dismal condition. Many other disturbances, however, were uprisings by substantial citizens. Craftsmen played their part in both kinds of disturbances, sometimes leading and usually filling the rank and file of the rebels. What was the nature of these rebellions? And why were artisans so prominently represented in them? Were these expressions of mass discontent in times of crisis, even of economic depression, perhaps as some historians have asserted, challenging an unjust economic system and a repressive social structure? Or were they, as other scholars have contended, the attempts of a lesser bourgeoisie to democratize town government? In fact, both explanations have some elements of truth in them. Some insurrections did clearly have economic and social discontent behind them, but in others we find no propertyless wage-workers in the ranks of the rebels at all. In these latter uprisings, however, even though citizen artisans often were responsible for them and their explicit demands usually focused on opening government more to their participation, we must be cautious about labeling them "democratic." The craftsmen who led or participated in these insurrections were drawn from the more substantial ranks of the artisanry, and the regimes that were installed, even ephemerally, were still oligarchic.

Given the current state of research, then, we can observe, quite generally, that the urban insurrections that were so numerous from 1300 to 1700 and that concern us here because of the prominent role artisans played in them, were of two sorts, not always distinct. First, there were anti-tax revolts which escalated into insurrections, resulting in ephemeral attacks upon the homes, and less often, the persons of the wealthy. The second type of insurrection was the result of a convergence of factors, the most salient being opposition to new taxes, fiscal maladministration by the existing and almost invariably patrician city government, and the demand for wider political participation in the urban polity. In fact, these issues were often related, for rebels demanded constitutional changes as a way to guarantee greater attention by the ruling elite to the interests of the citizenry, and the interests that were most prominent in these demands were fiscal. Revolt after revolt in town after town centered on these explosive issues. Such protests were often a direct result of expensive wars and thus the town's foreign policy, and they ranged from presentation of petitions asking for redress to the burning of palaces and the execution of patrician councilmen.

The fourteenth and early fifteenth centuries have generally been viewed by historians as a period of crisis, one marked in part by many urban uprisings. Around 1400 the Liegeois Jean d'Outre-Meuse observed that "all the common people every where in France as elsewhere have risen up . . ."[15] In France alone during the second half of the fourteenth century urban disturbances rocked Provins, Chalons-sur-Marne, Amiens, Rheims, Orleans, Lyons, Toulouse, and elsewhere, and artisans were the principal actors in them. Many of these uprisings were clearly about taxes, and artisans were clearly responsible for most of the urban uprisings, especially during "the years of revolution" of 1378–83 when a large part of Europe was shaken by conflicts perceived as unprecedented in the seriousness of their threat to the social order.

In 1378 in Le Puy in eastern Languedoc, for instance, the first salvo of the Tuchin revolt, which would rage throughout the province until it was definitively crushed by the duke of Berry in 1384, erupted over taxation matters. Subsidies granted by the Le Puy town council to the king of France for the seemingly interminable war with England were to be collected as indirect taxes on consumption, a flat tax that would hit artisans especially hard. It led to a rising of, as one letter of remission after the revolt was suppressed said, "a great number of workmen . . ." Another letter recorded that after the tax was announced "Many people cried aloud: 'O blessed Virgin Mary help us! How shall we live, how shall we be able to feed our children, since we cannot support the heavy taxes established to our prejudice through the influence of the rich and to reduce their own taxes?'"[16] In September of 1381 the revolt reached Béziers, the rising there triggered by unfair "estimates" used for assessments of direct taxation. A crowd led by artisans stormed the town hall, set fire to the tower so that some councilors were burned alive while others plunged from the heights to their deaths. Suppression came quickly from the duke of Berry who ordered the execution of forty-five rebels (among whom were sixteen weavers and a host of other "workers and artisans"), four by beheading on a winepress in the town square, and the rest hanged.

In the north of France at about the same time artisan-led anti-tax rebellions also erupted. A royal decree for the collection of new *aides* in 1382 in Rouen provoked a riot from 200 *gens méchaniques*, mostly from the textile crafts. These "men of low estate [*homines vilis status*] . . . coppersmiths, cloth-workers . . . hands engaged in work shops," as a local chronicler put it,[17] attacked the king's tax-collecting officers first, but soon the anti-fiscal riot took a social turn as the rebels targeted wealthy bourgeois, former mayors, the cathedral chapter, the monks of St. Ouen monastery, and the Jews. The rising, called the *Harelle*, lasted

---

[15] Quoted in Michel Mollat and Philippe Wolff, *The Popular Revolutions of the Late Middle Ages*, trans. A. L. Lytton-Sells (London, 1973), p. 99.
[16] Quoted in ibid., p. 180.
[17] Quoted in ibid., p. 176.

three days, and though it resulted in only two deaths, chroniclers, moralists, and judges who commented upon the insurrection and its suppression seem to have feared the worst from it – total subversion of the social order.

Perhaps the best known of the medieval rebellions is the English Peasants' Revolt in 1381. As the name suggests, this was largely a rural rebellion, but we should note that it also involved many artisans from towns, and eventually spread to London. In the repression that followed masons, tailors, dyers, and tilers were interrogated for their participation. Just as the One Hundred Years' War had triggered revolts in parts of France, so, too, did it play a part in this one. By the mid-1370s the war had turned defensive for the English as they tried to retain their territories on the continent; consequently the costs fell upon those at home, the fruits of pillage abroad having dried up. In 1377 and again in 1379 Parliament levied a poll tax to finance the war, a flat rate of 3 groats on all but the destitute. This assessment was higher than any previous tax, equal to a laborer's wages for three days, and rumblings of discontent burst in to the open in June of 1381. When it came to light that many taxable people were not on the tax rolls and thus escaped assessment, an insurrection erupted, one soon led by Wat Tyler that then quickly engulfed all of Kent and Essex as rebels sacked and burned manor houses and castles. Within days the rebels marched on London, and there found citizens, many of them artisans, sympathetic to their cause. When pressure from within the walls forced the aldermen to open the gates to the rebels, many of the rebels were given food and drink by the city's craftsmen and shopkeepers. As is well known, Tyler's demands to the young King Richard II were rooted in egalitarianism, but more germane to our concerns was his demand dear to artisans: the revocation of the Statute of Labourers of 1351 which had restricted wages. Once again, an incipient tax revolt had overflowed its banks and taken a turn toward social warfare. The rebellion was eventually suppressed, but in partial response to it and a reflection that artisans were a part of it, in 1388 the crown ordered all guilds to report to their sheriffs the details of their "brotherhoods," including the "origins, governance, oaths, meetings, liberties, ordinances, usages and any charters or letters patent as well as how much money they had."[18] This was a clear attempt to bring the guilds under public authority.

Popular protest, whatever its form, was a central feature of the power relations between superiors and inferiors in medieval and early modern towns. This was of political importance because, first, it gave voice to

[18] Quoted in Leeson, p. 40.

ordinary people who otherwise could not be heard, and second, because it revealed in the reactions of the authorities the deep fears they harbored about the stability or fragility of the political or social order. As with many medieval insurrections, their early modern counterparts often focused on fiscal issues. In many cases they remained anti-tax revolts with no apparent or extensive political program or aims other than redress of immediate fiscal grievances (usually a new, and perceived unjust, tax), although they commonly were laced with social antagonism so that the riots often escalated quickly into a spasm of social conflict between the rich and the less fortunate (though not necessarily the impoverished or propertyless). Between 1616 and 1647 in France alone 203 urban revolts and riots have been counted, many of which conform to this type. The rebellion in Montpellier in 1645 is a classic example of this sort of insurrection.

This important royal and provincial administrative town of 20,000 inhabitants had been suffering from the combined financial burdens caused by France's involvement in the Thirty Years' War and depressed agricultural conditions. Then, in June of 1645, a new tax was announced. Local accounts say that the first to protest were artisans' wives. A crowd of them led by Monteille, the wife of a tilemaker, chased the tax-collector out of town under a shower of rocks. The protesters, whose ranks began to swell now with male artisans (who clearly predominated in the crowd of rebels), descended upon houses of taxfarmers and pillaged them. A locksmith and a miller were arrested by the provincial lieutenant-general, and were sentenced to death the next day by the royal presidial court. Before they could be executed, however, they escaped from jail, freed by a crowd of women and helped by a locksmith. Violence escalated further when a crowd of protesters was fired upon from a window of one of the tax-collector's houses. A plasterer and a master mason fell dead in the street, and the enraged rebels, provided now with martyrs, exploded in violence. They sacked two more houses of tax officials, and this time two people were killed, the widow of a councilor at the royal financial court in Montpellier who reportedly had insulted the rebels, and the son of one of the tax-collectors. A bonfire stoked by the furnishings of these sumptuous houses blazed into the night. This was the end of the insurrection, for the next day the lieutenant-general suspended the new tax, and when the magistrates simply told the people to go home, they apparently did.

Artisans, as we have seen, were prominent in the ranks of rebels with fiscal grievances, and certainly can be found erupting in violence directed against their social superiors. But this is only one type of urban insurrection, and though it is difficult to determine the social or economic status of the artisans involved in these kinds of disorders, it is likely that they were drawn from the lower ranks. These kinds of insurrection were, of course, deeply troubling to the authorities, but even more grave to the wielders of public power were those occasions when *substantial* artisanal householders raised the standard of rebellion, because this kind of insurrection could challenge the very legitimacy of the ruling elite and bring in, if successful, significant changes to the urban polity in terms of the families that governed it. Often, then, revolts involving artisans had a political side, and were usually coupled with fiscal grievances and social antagonism.

Years ago the distinguished Belgian historian Henri Pirenne wrote of the *Révolution des métiers* of the fourteenth century. He observed that in cities in the Low Countries, northern and southern France, the Rhineland of Germany, Italy, and the Mediterranean shores of Spain, insurrections led by guildsmen carved places for craftsmen in municipal governments. Since Pirenne wrote, historians have come to question just how "revolutionary" these rebellions were, and how successful; but there remains little doubt that artisans were especially restive in that tumultuous century and that the insurrectionary aims of guildsmen often had a clear and bold political cast.

The commercial development that the cities of thirteenth-century Europe experienced increasingly concentrated wealth as it generated it, creating powerful dynasties of merchants, bankers (moneychangers), and financiers. At the dawn of the fourteenth century, these men controlled municipal governments nearly everywhere, and retained their grip on local power through co-optation. This self-perpetuating patriciate was in fact comprised of dynastic family groups – tellingly in Germany called simply the *Geschlechter*, or "the families" – interlocked by marriage and clientage. The constitutional arrangements in which patricians dominated town councils was only challenged if the ruling elite was perceived not to be ruling in the collective interests of the citizenry. Dissatisfaction with these regimes invariably focused on fiscal issues, usually triggered by an increase in urban expenditure and taxation, but often quickly broadened into accusations of malfeasance of office or maladministration of civic finances. In these revolts of householders, substantial craftsmen often led the discontented, usually a grab bag of other social groups, including merchants, but rarely including the very poor and the destitute. On the political plane, all of these rebellious factions complained of being excluded from town management, and their demands for reform always redrew the map of political participation by broadening its social base.

Early in the fourteenth century precisely these issues were joined in the rebellion that shook the major towns of Flanders. In 1300 French armies under the banner of King Philip IV invaded Flanders. His quick success was crowned by what the king imagined to be a magnanimous gesture, the abolition of unpopular taxes on foodstuffs in Ghent. He did not reward Bruges in this way, however, and as soon as the French king was out of Flanders, the Brugeois raised the standard of rebellion. Led by the weaver Pieter de Coninck and the butcher Jan Breidel, early in 1302 the rebels gained control of the city and set up a magistracy stocked with supporters of the count of Flanders, who was held captive at the time by his lord, Philip. Meanwhile in Ghent, a pro-French municipal government attempted to reimpose the food taxes in April. In response, artisans declared a work stoppage there, an act of resistance which then escalated into riot, ending in the killing of two aldermen. Then in Bruges on May 18, pro-count forces ambushed and massacred pro-French forces; uprisings exploded everywhere except in Ghent, as men sympathetic to the French were driven from power. That summer the French invaded, but were defeated in the famous battle at Courtrai in July. Pro-French patrician regimes in Ghent and Ypres were deposed within a few days. The new regimes that were installed recognized the important role the craftsmen had played in the rebellion and so had broader social representation, though the councils remained, as before the rebellions, the preserve of families with property. Guilds won the most extensive rights in Bruges, which had led the rebellion, their members gaining the right to serve on the town council. Nine of thirteen new aldermen there were probably guildsmen, and a fuller even became the new burgomaster.

On the surface this looks like a triumph of, if not democracy, at least of the representative principle in governance, but before we hasten to acclaim this rebellion a "revolution of the trades," we should examine more closely just what kind of regimes emerged from this rebellion. The landowning patriciate was hardly banished from the town councils, and the constitutional arrangement was still structured to favor oligarchy. In both Bruges (where magistrates came to be appointed directly by the count's commissioners) and Ghent oligarchies re-emerged, the same men and families remaining in the magistracy for years despite the requirement that the offices rotate. Unlike before the rebellions, constitutionally the magistracy could and did include guildsmen, but we find that guild aristocracies came to dominate. For example, in Ghent the carpenter Arnoud van der Varent occupied a seat on the council for seventeen consecutive years after 1360. The firm hold of the propertied classes (guild or otherwise) on the Flemish oligarchies continued in the

Burundian period of 1384–1477, when ducal appointment and co-optation combined to keep the leading families entrenched in local government.

The German version of the *révolution des métiers* were the so-called *Zunfterevolutionen*, but once again we must ask how revolutionary, and how advantageous to artisans, these insurrections really were. Between 1300 and 1550 historians have counted 210 uprisings in 105 different German towns, and true to classic form, most were triggered by anti-tax sentiments. They also incorporated political frustrations stemming from exclusion from municipal government. The object of these rebellions was fiscal reform and governments made responsible to the citizenry by popular participation, not revolution.

Generally, the results of the wave of rebellions that shook German towns in the fourteenth and fifteenth centuries can be classified as follows. First, in some cities artisans failed to gain a constitutional foothold in government, as town councils remained solidly patrician. This was especially true of the Hanseatic towns in the north. In some towns in the southwest, like Strasbourg and Basel, guildsmen were more successful, winning representation on town councils, while in other places like Ravensburg in 1346 and Speyer in 1349 or Cologne in 1396 no patricians at all remained on the councils after the rebellions as all of the seats were captured by guilds. Indeed, in Cologne guild membership became the sole route to a council seat, and council members were elected by the guilds.

This seeming triumph of the artisans requires closer scrutiny before we can declare a halcyon day of the artisan. Let us look at both ends of the spectrum, first at two Hanseatic cities, Brunswick and Lübeck, and then Cologne. In Brunswick in 1374 craftsmen (led by tanners) rose against the patrician town council, protesting an increase in taxation to finance what the rebels took to be misguided and expensive territorial acquisition and defense policies. The ruling elite of this Hanseatic city was committed to maintaining and supplying a series of castles well beyond the walls, and this imperial posture involved the city in continual feuds with the local nobility and, in 1374, an unsuccessful war against the archbishop of Magdeburg. In the wake of the war the town found itself swamped in a debt of 10,000 marks, thus prompting the new tax, and the charges leveled against the patricians by the artisan-led citizenry of unnecessary imperial commitments and mismanagement of the town finances.

A special meeting of the citizens was called by a group of tanners and cobblers, and heated discussion and recriminations ignited a crowd to action, bursting from the meeting and storming the town hall and the homes of some councilmen. Eight councilmen were executed, while fifty patricians, fearing for their lives, fled town. A new council was named by the rebels. The rebellious town was promptly expelled from the Hansa, and as patrician families that had fled and even many of the former patrician councilors gradually came home, the situation was altered and internal pressures to return to the *status quo ante* were exerted. By 1380 only one rebel from the newly installed council of 1374 still sat in government. In 1386 a new constitution granted fixed guild representation on the council, the composition of which included a wider range of families, albeit from society's upper ranks.

Just as the situation in Brunswick was simmering down, the "butchers' rising" flared in the fellow Hanseatic town of Lübeck. As the name suggests, this insurrection that raged from 1380 to 1384 was instigated by the town's butchers who opposed an annual tax paid on the stalls they rented from the city and from which they were forced to market their meat. In 1380 the butchers presented a petition to rescind the tax, but in the same petition they also requested an alteration of the town's constitution, demanding their representation on the town council. When their demands were not met, a reported sixty to sixty-five men conspired to lead a rebellion to topple the current government and install a new regime with broader social representation. The ranks of the rebels were dominated by artisans. Not surprisingly, many were butchers (at least twenty-seven), two of whom also joined two furriers and two bakers among the leaders of the revolt, although it was Heinrich Paternostermaker, a merchant, who was the chief of the conspirators. The would be rebels planned to storm the town council while it was in session and arrest the councilmen and kill those who resisted, but the plot was uncovered before it was hatched, and of the forty-seven men subsequently arrested, nineteen were executed. Testimony to the butchers' leading role in the abortive coup, their guild was dissolved in its aftermath.

For a time Lübeck returned to the *status quo ante*, but with a new tax levied in 1403 the citizenry grew restive again, and true to form, fired complaints about mismanagement of civic finances at the town council. Like the citizens of Brunswick thirty years before, citizens of Lübeck accused the patrician council of foolishly and expensively maintaining distant possessions, and couched their complaints in political demands. Like the artisans of the "butchers' rising," this group of citizens comprised mostly of lesser merchants and artisans renewed the demand that they be formally represented on the council. Claiming not innovation but tradition, these men asserted that the patrician families that currently dominated the municipal government in fact contravened

Lübeck's charter granted by the Emperor Henry the Lion in 1340, which supposedly granted all citizens the right to stand for and to elect the town council. Regardless of the appeal to tradition, fearing armed rebellion some councilors fled. An entirely new council was set up with merchants and craftsmen in its seats, but enough former councilors remained in town and, by refusing to step down, left a situation where two councils were struggling for power and vying for legitimacy. The other Hansa towns sided predictably with the patrician council, as did the Emperor Sigismund, and when the situation was resolved in 1416 with a new council in which some rebels were accepted, not one of these new elites was an artisan.

If the political fates of artisans in Hanseatic cities like Brunswick and Lübeck force us to reconsider how appropriate the epithet "revolutions of the trades" is when describing the uprisings in those towns, perhaps the situation in Cologne would be more suitable. For here, it seems, guilds fully triumphed in 1396. From the mid-thirteenth century until 1396 Cologne's municipal government was controlled by an entrenched patriciate that monopolized the fifteen seats on the inner council (the *enger Rat*) and perpetuated their grip by co-optation. A larger council (the *weiter Rat*) with eighty-two seats was selected from the town's parishes. In both bodies artisans had little voice. In 1396, however, artisans were joined by a group of new merchants who likewise had been effectively excluded from government. Beginning with complaints voiced by artisans and lesser merchants about taxation and extending to allegations of fiscal mismanagement by the patrician oligarchy, protest escalated. Several guilds, led by those of the weavers and the goldsmiths, toppled the sitting government and installed themselves in power. They drafted a new constitution called the *Verbundbrief* which established guild government and ostensibly announced victory for artisans. A new council was henceforth to be elected by twenty-two *Gaffeln* which were political guilds comprised of craft and merchant guilds. The new weaver *Gaffel* had four seats, the merchants two, with the remaining seats being distributed among other craft guilds.

Such a new political order, which lasted until 1513, appears to confirm the estimation that this was indeed a *Zunfterevolution*. However, despite the constitutional arrangement of guild representation, the families that came to dominate government were drawn from the upper ranks of their guilds. Indeed, recent research demonstrates that the political movements of the fourteenth century capped by the successful coup in 1396 were the work of the entrepreneurial, even capitalist elite within the ranks of the merchant and craft guilds. These guilds were hierarchical organizations, and once legitimated by the new constitution, they became the organs through which the government was run and the crafts themselves were regulated and, thus, through which labor was disciplined.

None of the German revolts was about equality, and everywhere oligarchy endured, even if the personnel changed and in some cases widened. These revolts, like most other uprisings by householders across Europe, were about responsible government and, if the current regime was perceived to be failing in providing that, constitutional remedies to include the formerly excluded from politics were usually advanced. This, in fact, was the norm of all rebellions from 1300 into the early eighteenth century. It certainly describes the central issues of perhaps the best-known insurrection of the fourteenth century, the *ciompi* revolt in Florence. Historians still disagree whether this revolt was essentially economic or political, but there are more than hints that dissatisfaction over taxation and restriction of political participation in government by significant taxpayers were involved in this revolt.

By the mid-1370s a combination of factionalism in the ruling elite, an economic downturn, and a costly war against the papacy had destabilized the patrician regime dominated by the seven major guilds (the leaders of which were not artisans) then in power. In the summer of 1378 the regime collapsed. The *ciompi* revolt of that summer actually consisted of two distinct phases, but both centered on electoral and thus constitutional reforms. In June and early July the fourteen minor guilds demanded greater political representation (the current regime restricted them to only one-fourth of the civic offices), by being given a voice in the selection of candidates standing for election to civic office. These guildsmen, the leaders of whom *were* artisans, were equally keen to keep the unincorporated *sottoposti* from forming guilds and thereby legitimately being able to claim the right to participate in governance as well. However, once the first demand was forced upon the current regime in July, the feared demands of the *sottoposti* quickly followed. Under the threat of violent insurrection, on July 22 the petition submitted by the *sottoposti* was accepted, and three new *popolo minuto* guilds were created. A dramatically expanded political class resulted and a constitutional regime comprised of three groups of guilds – major, minor, and *popolo minuto* – which theoretically were autonomous and equal came temporarily into being. The new regime was immediately undermined by faction within the ranks of the guilds of the *popolo minuto* as one of them, that of the *ciompi*, or woolworkers, felt that they were being unfairly excluded from the electoral process. Violent insurrection again reared its head, but this time it was crushed by a coalition of the other guilds. The *ciompi* guild was dissolved, a fate that also awaited the remaining two *popolo minuto* guilds a month later as the substantial artisanal community represented in the fourteen minor guilds and the seven major guilds rolled back the gains the *sottoposti* had made in July. Though exclusionary in its own right, this guild regime which controlled Florence until 1382 had a broader base which included many artisans than did the preceding regime. This regime, however, in turn met its demise when disgruntled guildsmen of the seven major guilds sided with the ousted patricians and ushered in a new regime. Artisans were convinced henceforth to abandon their corporatist loyalties and to accept the new regime because of its system of open nominations which slated thousands of citizens for election to civic office. The ruling elite was narrow, no less oligarchic, and no less powerful than that of the pre-*ciompi* days, but it was a governing elite that was drawn constitutionally from a group three to four times larger, and so rested upon the legitimizing fiction of a broad-based system of political opportunity. In practice, the days of any significant artisan participation in government were gone forever.

Though the insurrections of the summer of 1378 depart from the norm of most rebellions of the fourteenth century in that they were not clearly triggered by a new tax, like rebellious artisans everywhere these Florentines wanted something from their municipal government that they were not getting. Political participation had its rewards – attention to the interests of those represented – and though these interests and rewards certainly were economic in many instances, in the Florentine experience we can see the rebels trading in another coin as well – honorable status. The victorious minor guildsmen of late June and early July demanded political *inclusion* so they could maintain *exclusion* of the *sottoposti*. They were fearful of the latter's incorporation because it blurred social distinction, and honorable status was rooted in such distinction. They may have been forced to accept the *sottoposti* (after all, the principles undergirding the *sottoposti*'s demand for incorporation were the same that legitimated the demands of these minor guildsmen), but judging from their subsequent actions they immediately began preparing the ground for the eventual exclusion of *sottoposti*, which happened within two months. The threat from below must have been felt more greatly than from above by 1382, and thus the minor guildsmen cast their lot with a statist regime that could guarantee the hierarchical order that the propertied guildsmen so desired.

Artisans expected their municipal governments to safeguard their interests, and protested, sometimes violently, if the ruling elite failed them. Often, as we have seen, these interests were explicitly fiscal, but the fact that anti-tax sentiments leaped to constitutional levels so quickly suggests that artisans were also deeply concerned about issues that went beyond their pocketbooks and reached the level of the structure and maintenance of the community. How well the government secured the kind of order that artisans needed to maintain the security of their place in the community was an issue worth fighting, and even dying, for. Medieval rebellions, then, were very much about maintenance of community of a particular kind (stratified). Early modern artisanal insurrections were little different in this regard.

We search in vain in English cities for artisanal rebellions with anti-tax sentiments or political goals, but nearly everywhere else we find insurrections strikingly similar to those of the fourteenth century. The *communero* revolt of 1520 launched by Castilian cities was the biggest urban rebellion of early modern Europe, and found artisans deeply engaged in it. Spain's recently crowned king, Charles I (who even more recently had become Holy Roman Emperor Charles V), promptly quarreled with the cities represented in the Cortes over a proposed levy of new taxes. The cities rejected his demands, and instead countered with demands of their own, including not only a reduction of taxes but also a reform of the entire taxation system, the latter calling for prior approval by the Cortes of taxes sought by the crown. Many Castilian cities united behind these demands, and formed a junta that co-ordinated their resistance. Of course, as everywhere the cities (and thus the junta) were dominated politically by oligarchs (*regidores*), but the ruling elite was followed into revolt by many artisanal householders. Indeed, the *communero* cities were the artisanal manufacturing centers of the interior of Castile (the commercial cities of the periphery tended to oppose the revolt). But if the oligarchs were intent on redrawing the map of power between crown and Cortes, the artisan rebels rallied to the cry of *communidad*. In other words, they seized the opportunity of this revolt to press for political, even constitutional, changes on the local level which would better secure their interests by better securing their conception of the community. Politically, this meant broadening the base of political participation among the community of citizens, and constitutionally, by instituting changes that would force the ruling elite to govern in the interests of all the citizenry. In typical fashion, this meant approval of all town council policies and decisions by popular municipal assemblies.

In Avila, to take but one *communero* city, initially this coalition of oligarchs and artisans held, but as artisans began expanding their denunciation of fiscal injustice from the royal taxation policies to the fiscal privileges of the local elite, and then demanded expanded political participation to rectify such abuses, cracks in the coalition opened.

Then, when crowds rioted and sacked the homes of some city councilors, the coalition collapsed. Avila then withdrew from the *communero* movement shortly before the rebel forces were destroyed in the battle of Villalar by the armies of Charles in April 1521. The newly discovered loyalty of Avila's oligarchs to their king spared them; Avila's artisans who led the local insurgency were not so fortunate. Eleven of them were executed in the autumn of 1521. Needless to say, none of the cities of Castile found any room for artisanal participation in governance hence.

One hundred and twenty years later elsewhere in the kingdom of Spain, another rebellion erupted similar to the *communero* revolt and those of the fourteenth century in the centrality of taxes and political demands for broadening the base of participation. Everywhere in the sprawling Spanish dominions the 1640s were a time of crushing fiscal burdens brought on by a governmental fiscal policy seeking revenues to reverse the staggering military misfortunes of the Habsburg forces in the waning years of the Thirty Years' War. These burdens were felt everywhere in the Spanish kingdom, including Naples, then a city of 300,000, the largest in Europe.

In 1647 thousands of Neapolitans exploded in rebellion, triggered by a new tax on fruit. A classic anti-fiscal revolt at the outset, it became much more as time wore on. Initially led by a fishmonger named Masaniello, the rebels plundered the palaces of tax officials and then issued demands for the elimination of taxes on consumption items like grain, wine, oil, and cheese. The cry for tax reform, however, quickly gave way to political demands that any new taxes must first be approved by a popular assembly. From there the rebels expanded their demands to a popular election of magistrates, challenging both the local oligarchy and the crown whose viceroy approved the town councilors who had been chosen by co-optation by the existing council. The viceroy also appointed the royal officers called *corregidores* to oversee the municipal government. The local viceroy had no troops to quell the insurrection, and so was forced to accede to the rebels' demands. Not even the assassination of Masaniello could stem the tide of the insurrection. As Spanish troops disembarked in October and laid siege to the city, the mantle as rebel chief was picked up by a blacksmith named Gennaro Annese who then proclaimed the city and kingdom of Naples a republic, but under the protection of the king of France. French protection never materialized, and the republic collapsed from internal dissension as much as from outside pressure. In April 1648, following a promise of amnesty to the rebels, the removal of taxes on food, and the appointment of a new viceroy, the rebels capitulated and the gates were opened to the Spanish troops. What became of Annese we do not know, but, once again, no room was allocated to artisans in the constitutional regime after the revolt.

The seventeenth century has long been identified as a century in crisis, and a salient illustration of that crisis was the rebellions that swept across most of Europe at that time. The most-studied insurrections have been the rural ones, especially in France, but towns of France and especially Germany did not escape upheavals, most of which, once again, found artisans filling the ranks of the rebels. Typical as well were the anti-tax sentiments of the rebels and the quick escalation of the uprisings to constitutional levels. We could illustrate this in any number of towns. Friedrichs estimates that two-thirds of Germany's imperial cities in the seventeenth and early eighteenth centuries experienced these kinds of conflict, but for the sake of clarity and brevity, we shall confine our attention to especially well-studied rebellions in two important cities: La Rochelle from 1612 to 1628, and Frankfurt in 1612–16 and again in 1703–32.

As the seventeenth century dawned on La Rochelle, patricians dominated the town council, called the *corps de ville*. A thriving port city with a growing population of merchants prospering from commerce, the stage was set for a restive group of merchants and many substantial artisans to begin demanding greater influence in town government. As in most patrician-dominated cities, La Rochelle's councilmen were named by co-optation. What these merchants and artisans cared dearly about was fiscal administration that protected their interests; their complaints about city government, then, often focused upon import taxes, duties, and tolls that might restrict the flow of goods into port. The late sixteenth century was punctuated with just these kinds of disputes, and to preclude any insurrection the *corps de ville* attempted to alter the command structure of the militia which heretofore had been controlled by the merchant and artisan opposition. Nothing could be done about the rank and file of the militia (overwhelmingly artisan householders), but in 1598 councilmen were commissioned as the militia's commanders and lieutenants.

In 1608 another episode further embittered the increasingly alienated merchants and craftsmen. In that year the town council spent 20,000 *livres* to purchase from the crown the privilege to collect taxes on goods entering the port. The unenfranchised merchants and artisans saw this as an attempt by the *corps de ville* to arbitrarily manipulate import duties once again to their detriment, and launched allegations of patrician malfeasance. The breaking point came in 1614 when several of the town's wealthiest but disenfranchised merchants, led by Jean Tharay, raised the banner of insurrection. Justifying their resistance in terms that would have sounded familiar to rebels in nearly every city that had witnessed insurrections since 1300, they claimed that the *corps de ville* had ruled the city, not as it should in the interest of the community of citizens, but rather in its own interests. Wishing not "to govern ourselves insolently, but to be governed equitably," they thus demanded a reform of the town council by broadening the social base of political participation.[19]

The rank and file of the militia companies were artisans, and this force became the backbone of the rebellion that erupted on March 22. Militiamen barricaded the town hall with councilors inside, and six days later the council capitulated and accepted twenty-eight articles reforming town government which brought the formerly disenfranchised into the halls of government. In August, the patricians attempted a counter-coup, and fighting in the streets quickly followed. Tharay was seen in battle helmet and "covered in cutlasses" spearheading an assault on the patrician forces who were holed up in the town hall. The patricians were routed, and sixty of them were apprehended and imprisoned.

The new regime was headed by Tharay who rewarded his followers with formal inclusion in the government, which completely excluded the patricians. Tharay commanded a deep and broad network of clients that included many artisan householders (this was how he could secure the loyalty of the militia), and in the new regime about 10 percent of the Council of Forty-Eight (a large council that paralleled a new, smaller inner council and which possessed significant checks upon the smaller council) were craftsmen. This was not a *révolution des métiers*, but certainly a constitutional arrangement more advantageous to artisans than most urban regimes afforded them. The regime lasted until royal victory in the siege of 1628, after which the inner council, the Council of Forty-Eight, and, significantly for the artisans, the militia companies, were all abolished. The new regime that supplanted the old installed, predictably, a new patriciate drawn from a narrow social base.

Bernd Moeller, the distinguished historian of the imperial cities of Germany and the Reformation, contended that the Protestant Reformation in the imperial cities was rooted in a desire of ordinary citizens to preserve a traditional conception of community life. He argued that these citizens still embraced the concept of "commune" so dear to their medieval forebears and, therefore, the Reformation had strong political links to the medieval past.[20] Other historians have added that the Reformation era saw the eclipse of the communal spirit and henceforth

---

[19] Kevin Robbins, *City on the Ocean Sea: La Rochelle, 1530–1650* (Leiden, 1997).
[20] Bernd Moeller, *Imperial Cities and the Reformation* (Philadelphia, 1972).

citizens increasingly became subjects of authoritarian regimes in which power descended from king or duke to city magistrate.

As we have seen, citizens, householding artisans represented among them in great number, fought violently at times to assert or defend the interests of the community, and not just in Germany or in the Middle Ages. Indeed, although it is true that political unrest of this type was especially pronounced in the imperial cities (forces for the *Gemeinde* or community of citizens squaring off against those of the *Obrigkeit*, or rulers). This is the leitmotif that runs through nearly every rebellion in European cities from 1300 into the eighteenth century.

In German cities this defense of the privileges of the *Gemeinde* was given institutional voice in different ways. In many cities there were constitutional arrangements for *Bürgerschaft* to oversee the governance of patricians. In Erfurt, for example, four *Vierherren* were so invested. In Cologne twenty-two guild masters served as *Bannerherren* who were expected to meet periodically to determine if the interests of burgher-citizens were being served, while in Brunswick in 1513 a committee of *Zehnmänner* to be selected by guild masters was instituted to oversee collection and expenditure of civic revenues. Above all, there was the *Ausschuss*, an ad hoc committee that could be convened by citizens when it deemed that the council was not ruling in the interests of the community. Typically an *Ausschuss* would claim the right to review decisions handed down by the council and to participate in council deliberations. These committees were usually convened when financial maladministration was suspected, but they quickly raised fundamental constitutional questions about the council's responsibility to the citizens, and the citizens' right to participate in their own governance. The convening of such a committee could be, and often was, the first step toward challenging the existing regime, and it often launched demands that by now should sound quite familiar: fiscal reform and broadened representation on the council.

Conflicts that pitted citizens against magistrates over these issues did not end with the Reformation. Indeed, citizens excluded from govern-ance and dissatisfied with their magistrates rose between 1550 and 1700 in Aachen, Brunswick, Bremen, Cologne, Frankfurt, Lübeck, Straslund, and a host of other towns. The experience of Frankfurt well illustrates the salient issues.

From the fourteenth century patrician families had dominated the city government of Frankfurt, challenges to their rule from the artisan-led citizenry in the 1350s and 1360s, and again in 1525 having been repelled. Another challenge was mounted in 1612, and this time, at least for a while, it was successful. Disgruntled burghers, many of whom were established artisans, formed an *Ausschuss* to vent grievance and to press for reforms. Typically, the dissatisfaction focused on fiscal mismanagement, and from the outset was laced with anti-Semitism since the rebels assumed that the city's Jews and its patricians worked together against the interests of the lesser burghers. An imperial commission arrived to negotiate a settlement, a compromise between the burghers and the patricians being reached the day before Christmas, 1612. Of the seventy-one articles in the so-called Citizens' Agreement, the most important to the burghers were those that limited the number of patrician seats on the town council and added burgher seats, and that created two burgher committees that were charged with, among other things, overseeing the city's finances. These changes would benefit the well-to-do burghers who then secured their place in the new constitutional arrangement by a system of co-optation.

For lesser artisans who were still excluded from politics, these reforms were unsatisfactory, and so, led by the pastrycook Vincenz Fettmilch, the challenge to authority took a radical turn. Fettmilch, who had sought and been denied a municipal office in the new regime, led a group of men left out of the new constitutional arrangement. In May 1614 Fettmilch and his followers stormed the town hall and, after capturing the councilors, held them captive until they resigned. Fettmilch then declared himself *Gubernator* of Frankfurt. Not surprisingly, neither the title nor the regime was recognized by the emperor. In fact, after a group of artisans and their journeymen plundered the Jewish ghetto and Fettmilch expelled the Jews from Frankfurt (recall that the Jews were suspected of profiting from the fiscal malfeasance of the previous regime and so became the scapegoats of the fiscal troubles experienced by the town), the emperor placed a ban upon the regime and threatened military intervention. Goaded by the specter of imperial troops invading the city, a group of burghers turned on Fettmilch and arrested him.

An imperial commission restored the patrician council, which hastened to abolish the burgher committees which had been established in 1613. The Jews were permitted to return to the ghetto under imperial protection, and the leaders of the uprising were hanged. Then the emperor, seeking to expurgate the trouble at its source, decreed the Transfix of 1616 which abolished the guilds. They were replaced by *Handwerke*, organizations that had to answer to the town council for everything. Creatures of the government, all officers of the trades henceforth were to be appointed by the council. Even business meetings required prior approval.

Between 1705 and 1732 Frankfurt was shaken by yet another

challenge to patrician government. This time, however, the changes were lasting. What did not change, however, was the exclusion of the rank and file artisan from politics. A new constitution established consultative bodies of citizens and requirements that the council consult it on substantive issues, especially tax increases. The key differences between this challenge to patrician power and Fettmilch's uprising were two: first, the eighteenth-century rebels did not seek to displace the patricians from power, but rather to force them to share power with them. Second, the composition of the rebels was different. Technically both were burgher uprisings, but under Fettmilch the "burghers" in question were mostly artisans, while in the eighteenth century they were merchants and entrepreneurial artisans who had become deeply engaged in commercial activities, often practicing more than one "trade." Not surprisingly, the constitutional settlement of 1732 balanced conciliar power between the patricians and the wealthy men of commerce. Artisans, like their colleagues in most other European towns and cities, were effectively excluded from political decision-making.

After 1680, though disputes between citizens and magistrates in fact increased, recourse to violence declined. A different arena for disputes became increasingly dominant, the courts of law, and artisan demands, at least before the French Revolution, ceased to have high constitutional stakes. The basic structure of guild internal governance – oligarchy – remained the same everywhere, but also widespread was another trend, the intrusion of civic, ducal, or royal government in internal guild affairs.

One trend plainly visible in the political history of medieval and early modern artisans is toward oligarchy, both within the guilds themselves and within the urban polity. Increasingly guilds were dominated by the wealthier craftsmen, the same families tending to run a guild's affairs for generations. Within the urban polity, however, we find artisans increasingly excluded from the constitutional political community. Artisans may not have welcomed these developments, but they saved outright political resistance – rebellion – for matters of even deeper importance. As we have seen, the hundreds of artisanal rebellions that dot the calendar throughout Europe from the late Middle Ages to about 1700 centered on two interrelated concerns – a perceived overtaxation of artisans, and fiscal maladministration by the municipal elite. It may seem that the history of artisanal rebellion is one of dreary failure – after all, the so-called "revolution of the trades" turn out not to have been so revolutionary, and early modern rebellions seem to end monotonously in returns to the *status quo ante*, after a perfunctory execution of some of the rebels. Artisan success, however, perhaps should not be measured simply in revolutionary terms. Artisans expected their municipal governments to safeguard their interests, and protested if the ruling elite failed them. Sometimes artisans tried to carve places for themselves in the constitutional arrangement, and sometimes they found short-term success, but usually rebellious artisans were sending a message that violence against the ruling elite was always an option and that too great a disregard for artisanal interests and concerns would ignite it.

Often, as we have seen, the spark that ignited a rebellion by artisans was fiscal, but the fact that anti-tax sentiments or concerns about fiscal maladminitration leaped to constitutional levels so quickly suggests that artisans were also deeply concerned about issues that went beyond their pocketbooks and reached the level of the structure and maintenance of the community. True, they may have wished to insert themselves officially in the constitution of their polity, but failing this (and they almost always failed), they still hoped to protect and preserve something else, their social status. How well the government secured the kind of order that artisans needed to maintain the security of their place in the community – their status, in a word – was an issue worth fighting, and even dying, for. Medieval and early modern rebellions, then, were very much about the maintenance of a stratified community and of the artisan's place within it.

Bibliography

Entries marked with a * designate recommended readings for new students of the subject.

*Beik, William. *Urban Protest in Seventeenth-Century France: The Culture of Retribution*. New York, 1997.

Bercé, Yves-Marie. *Fête et Revolte*. Paris, 1976.

Boone, Marc, and Maarten Prak. "Rulers, patricians, and burghers: the great and little traditions of urban revolt in the Low Countries." In Karel Davids and Jan Lucassen, eds., *A Miracle Mirrored: The Dutch Republic in European Perspective*. Cambridge 1995, pp. 99–134.

Briggs, Robin. "Popular revolt in its social context." In Robin Briggs, *Communities of Belief*. Oxford, 1989, pp. 106–77.

Carlin, N. "Liberty and fraternities in the English Revolution: the politics of London artisans' protests, 1635–1659." *International Review of Social History* 39 (1994), 223–54.

Duke, Alistair. *Reformation and Revolt in the Low Countries*. London, 1990.

DuPlessis, Robert S. *Lille and the Dutch Revolt: Urban Stability in an Era of Revolution, 1500–1582*. Cambridge, 1991.

Friedrichs, Christopher R. "German town revolts and the seventeenth-century crisis." Renaissance and Modern Studies* 26 (1982), 27–51.

"Urban politics and urban social structure in seventeenth-century Germany." *European History Quarterly* 22 (1992), 187–216.

Kaplan, Steven L. "The character and implications of strife among the masters inside the guilds of eighteenth-century Paris." *Journal of Social History*, 19 (1986), 631–47.

Le Roy Ladure, Emmanuel. *Carnival in Romans*. New York, 1980.

Moeller, Bernd. *Imperial Cities and the Reformation*. Philadelphia, 1972.

*Mollat, Michel, and Philippe Wolff. *The Popular Revolutions of the Late Middle Ages*. Trans. A. L. Lytton-Sells. London, 1973.

Robbins, Kevin. *City on the Ocean Sea: La Rochelle, 1530–1650*. Leiden, 1997.

Scott, James. *Domination and the Arts of Resistance: Hidden Transcripts*. New Haven, 1990.

Te Brake, Wayne. *Shaping History: Ordinary People in European Politics, 1500–1700*. Berkeley, 1998.

Tilly, Charles. *The Contentious French*. Cambridge, Mass., 1986.

Trexler, Richard C. *The Workers of Renaissance Florence: Power and Dependence in Renaissance Florence*. Binghamton, 1993.

Underdown, David. *Revel, Riot, and Rebellion: Popular Politics and Culture in England, 1603–1660*. Oxford, 1985.

5 Authority and resistance (II): masters and journeymen

> The idea that work in medieval cities was characterized by a developing polarization between . . . masters and journeymen has for over a century provided the prevalent framework of historical debate . . . However, "masters" and "journeymen" continued throughout the medieval period, up to and beyond the sixteenth century, to be heterogeneous groups with shifting and partially overlapping interests. The widespread received view which identifies the former as entrepreneurial owners of capital and the latter as a nascent working class is undercut by so many local varieties of experience that this bipolar model remains an insufficiently explanatory historical tool.[1]

So contends Gervase Rosser in a recent article, and he has a point. Masters and journeymen were not always at each others' throats, small masters often having as much in common with their two or three journeymen as with the large masters of their guild. As Ménétra's journal testifies for the eighteenth century, some masters stood ready to share a drink with their journeymen, to make loans to them, to protect them, to help them escape after a brawl, even to bring them food in prison. For Ménétra, a good master who earns his men's respect is one who treats them fairly, eats with them, and works alongside them. Certainly, in the competitive labor markets which characterized European cities at least from the late Middle Ages, masters, especially the smaller masters who were at a competitive disadvantage to the larger employers, found it in their interest to cultivate the goodwill of journeymen. We know as early as the fifteenth century in Basel that some small masters and journeymen in the smith trade regularly worked out employment agreements in open breach of the rules of the guild and in defiance of the large masters.

Small masters falling in league with some of their journeymen was encouraged by the drift to oligarchy within the guilds, and by the simultaneous formation of cores of large masters and peripheries of

---

[1] Gervase Rosser, "Crafts, guilds and the negotiation of work in the medieval town," *Past and Present* 154 (1997), 4.

smaller ones. Certainly the story of strife between masters *within* guilds is one that needs to be told (we already know a great deal about conflict between guilds), even if in the present state of research we cannot say much about it. Kaplan has shown that in the eighteenth-century Parisian bakers' guild a tension existed between the *chefs* and the rank and file of masters, the primary point of dispute being governance of the guild. He finds that the rank and file were demanding more "democracy," challenging an aristocratic oligarchy's domination of guild politics. He points out that

in a manner that recalls the revolt of the Parlement against royal absolutism, the reforming masters intended to clean the corporation of its corruption, oblige the directors to render their accounts public, and to force them to conform to the fundamental laws of the corporation and to renew the moral foundations of the community by restoring a climate of collective participation and of responsibility.[2]

To be sure, then, when we discuss "labor relations" in the preindustrial world of the artisan we must consider the varieties of forms of association and solidarity between masters and journeymen as well as conflict between and among masters. To suggest that the only form of conflict worth studying was that between master and journeyman does indeed, as Rosser has warned, blind us to the varieties of labor relations. But, perhaps Rosser's criticism is overdrawn, for what is the historian to make of the countless instances in the historical record of conflict between masters and journeymen and, indeed, evidence that masters and journeymen saw themselves as quite fundamentally distinct status groups, and seem to have constructed identities that were very much rooted in a sense of status that was generally shared by fellow masters and fellow journeymen? Violence and conflict often functioned as a means to make inclusion and exclusion in these groups clear, and even the most cursory glance at the workshop shows it to be a site of frequent conflict, a place, as we will see, where antinomies existed side by side with solidarities. To recount the history of conflict between masters and journeymen is not to fall into the teleological trap of tendentiously isolating the origins of the conflict between capital and labor, but rather to give the weight of historical evidence its full due.

Time and labor

In the mid-eighteenth century Josiah Wedgwood transformed pottery manufacture in England, a change that in two important respects

---

[2] Steven L. Kaplan, *Le Meilleur Pain du monde. Les Boulangers de Paris au XVIIIe siècle* (Paris, 1996), p. 207.

reflects a trend in worker discipline that had been sporadically unfolding for centuries. In his desire to "make machines of the men as cannot err," Wedgwood instituted a clocking-in system to track and regulate his workers' use of time, and he sought to instill a sense of punctuality by enforcing an uninterrupted attendance on the job for a fixed duration of the workday. In the name of discipline and efficiency, he countered the trained worker's (or journeyman's) traditional sense of the relationship between time and labor, and he robbed the journeyman of his most powerful weapon and most cherished "right" against the employer in the workplace and, indeed, the basis of his sense of honor as a counterpoint to discipline and subordination, the freedom of movement. In exchange for the higher wages Wedgwood paid, his workers were trained to a particular task, and had to stick to it for the entire workshift. Such a system, by no means common in the workshops of Europe at this time, or even a hundred years later, was profoundly at odds with traditional work practices. Wedgwood may have been successful in his venture, but for centuries before his experiment masters and journeymen, employers and workers, had been at loggerheads over precisely these two fundamental issues. Who would control movement of labor (and thus the labor market)? And how would the relationship between time and work be defined?

In yet another pathbreaking article that so gracefully flowed from the pen of E. P. Thompson, this unparalleled English historian of work asked how a clock-based "time sense" that so clearly emerged during the early modern age affected work in general and labor discipline in particular. "And how far," he continued, "did it influence the inward apprehension of time of working people? If the transition to mature industrial society entailed a severe restructuring of working habits – new disciplines, new incentives, and a new human nature upon which these incentives could bite effectively – how far is this related to changes in the inward notion of time?"[3] It is true that workers complained about wage rates as far back as we have records of disputes in the workplace, but rates were daily, not hourly, and were paid weekly or even biweekly. This meant that wage disputes were often about the length of the work day, or the density of work within that day. These disputes suggest that employers and workers did not always share the same perceptions about the relationship of time and work activity.

Thompson contended that the transition to industrial society was characterized in part by a shift in the notation of time from "task-orientation" to "timed labor." In task oriented work regimens, laborers

[3] E. P. Thompson, "Time, work discipline, and industrial capitalism," *Past and Present* 38 (1967), 57.

"attend upon what is an observed necessity," and make no clear demarcation between work activity and other social pursuits. The working day "lengthens or contracts according to the task." Thus, typically in such work regimens, we find unstructured movement in and out of the workplace, irregular working weeks, and bursts of activity followed by lulls. In the "timed labor" work regimen, in contrast, such work habits are deemed wasteful and inefficient.[4] A Newtonian conception of time notation as abstract, absolute, and mathematical, "flowing without relation to anything external," was far from this cultural world which embraced a plurality of time-reckoning modes, each rooted in varying routines of experience. Ménétra once again poignantly demonstrates this observation. In his journal he almost never mentions precise clock-time, although he certainly was familiar with watches. For him, it seems, owning a watch was a sign of prestige rather than of timekeeping practicality. Judging from his journal, he cared not at all about measuring time, other than in a rough sense of time on the job and time in recreation. But even here he saw no sharp boundary and no set cycle, time at work expanding and contracting as needed.

Thompson, then, poses the key historical question: how effectively and universally was the sanctioned discourse on time imposed or appropriated? His answer perhaps gives too much weight to the employers' ability to impose the timed-labor regimen, and it inappropriately assumes a too linear progression in the transformation of the workplace from task-based time to clock-time (after all, not all employers were Josiah Wedgwoods, for task-oriented work routines persisted in the widespread handicraft industry of the nineteenth century). Still, despite the overly tidy picture that Thompson presents, one cannot gainsay the accuracy of his observations that such a transformation over the centuries was occurring, that it did have something to do with employers disciplining workers, and that workers resisted such disciplinary measures.

Historians have long been aware that the crisis of the fourteenth century had a profound impact on the world of work, not least in creating conditions which led to confrontations between employers and workers, between masters and journeymen. In the late medieval period we find a rising tide of regulations that deal with time and work, and at the same time we find workers resisting such laws. Jacques Le Goff has pointed out that an important point of contention focused on the measurement and use of the working day.[5] This was especially acute in

---

[4] Ibid., p. 60.
[5] Jacques Le Goff, "Labor time in the 'Crisis' of the 14th century: from medieval time to

the textile trades where employers sought greater discipline over how much and when their workers worked.

That the timed-labor regimen appeared first and most strikingly in the textile sector probably has something to do with the regularization of expanding demand and the pressure that demand exerted upon production schedules. Whatever the reason, in Germany the *Werkglocke* or "workclock" was introduced first in the textile workplace, and at regular intervals it rang bells which demarcated periods of work and rest. Work bells became common at construction sites, too. We hear of such a bell in 1354 sounded at the Tower of London "to ring the hours for the workmen," and for similar purposes in 1365 at the cathedral in Florence, in 1390 at the cathedral of Milan, and in 1396 at the Certosa monastery in Pavia.[6]

This new method that hourly marked the work day suggests a new mentality where the work day was conceived as the sum of equal hours, and as such it represented the imposition of an alien, timed-work regimen that was associated with the discipline of labor. Not surprisingly, the workclocks were often the targets of worker resistance. In the late fourteenth and early fifteenth centuries worker uprisings were characterized by the destruction and silencing of the workclocks, an indication that the struggle between master and journeyman was not so much about wage levels as the control of labor time. Nor was the contest over time and work activity just a German phenomenon. In France masters and journeymen squared off over this matter as well. In Troyes in 1358 masters in the textile trades complained that their workers had decided collectively not to begin the work day until after morning mass, while weavers in Rheims formed an *entente* against their employers over the same thing, as did the fullers of Saint Denis in 1321.

The struggle between masters and workers (increasingly the trained workers who came to be called journeymen) over control of the relationship between time and labor extended beyond the Middle Ages into the early modern centuries, and seems to have been experienced most notably, once again, in the manufacturing sectors where regular, substantial, and increasing demand was exerted upon production practices and schedules. Worker protests in the Low Countries, for instance, erupted in shipbuilding and textiles, and focused on the length of the work day rather than wages *per se*. The journeymen shipwrights of Amsterdam in 1625 called a work stoppage to force a reduction of the

   modern time," in Jacques Le Goff, *Time, Work and Culture in the Middle Ages* (Chicago, 1980).
[6] Gerhard Dohrn-Van Rossum, *History of the Hour: Clocks and Modern Temporal Orders*, trans. Thomas Dunlap (Chicago, 1996), p. 299.

work day from fourteen hours to twelve, and enforced their demand by boycotting any masters' shops that resisted it. Labor unrest was frequent among Dutch journeymen clothshearers, too, as the strikes in Hoorn in 1639 and Leiden in 1643 attest. Though the municipal authorities always supported the masters and saw the protests as "revolts plain and simple," closer scrutiny once again reveals that the disputes were quite often about control of time in the workplace.[7]

Instances of worker resistance to authority, called *cabales* in France, proliferated in the eighteenth century. They may never have led to general uprisings, but their almost daily frequency upset the world of work nonetheless. Their sporadic and ephemeral nature – often spreading no further than to a couple of shops, the street, or the neighborhood – provided no solace to the authorities who feared that a general breakdown of order was imminent. Indeed, words about worker indiscipline run like a red thread through the *Dictionnaires de police*, judicial treatises, chronicles, memoirs, and of course, police ordinances of the eighteenth century.

Whether the workers' "strikes" against their employers were about hiring practices, a daily wage (in French, *le prix de la journée*), piecerates, hours in the working day, or the freedom to come and go as they pleased, workers' resistance was in one way or another about working as they understood it, and this meant working according to the rhythms of life that structured their existence and framed its meaning. This understanding entailed an assumption about freedom of movement in and out of shops, and worker discretion about the pace of work. When employers tried to restrict that movement (for example, by requiring "passports," *certificats de congé*, or *Kundschaften*, or by demanding that their workers stay in the shop and at work continuously during the work day), the most normal form of resistance was simply to ignore the regulations and dare the masters to do anything about it. In the face of widespread behavior of this sort, masters, even with the support of the police, could do little. In the face of such problems, masters might, alternatively, attempt to alter the mode of payment, either by reducing the daily wage, by attempting to pay workers in kind (in "truck"), or by altering the payment of piecework by retaining the rates but enlarging the quantum, thereby leaving in place the "customary" rate.

Directly or indirectly, these work practices were about a certain relationship between labor and time. Workers understood the relationship one way, masters quite often another. An extended working day coupled with workers on the job more continuously than had tradition-

---

[7] A. T. Van Deursen, *Plain Lives in the Golden Age*, trans. Maarten Ultee (Cambridge, 1991), p. 10.

ally been the case, was an imperative more and more masters embraced as demand exerted its pressures on production schedules in more and more trades. For more and more masters, a morality of industriousness began to attend this imperative about time, and the competing imperative embraced by workers was disparaged as laziness and idleness. As some masters in some sectors of manufacturing increasingly demanded a closer correlation between work performed and units of time, workers resisted by stopping work, their demands usually focusing on maintenance of current wage rates or a reduction in the hours of the work day. Examples of such resistance can be found throughout the early modern period, but become almost constant and ubiquitous in the eighteenth century.

In the sixteenth century in the printing industry, to maintain or increase profits in an expanding and increasingly competitive market, master printers tried to reduce wages and increase working hours. A reduction in wages could be accomplished by changing the method of payment to monetary wages entirely, rather than a mix of wage and board at the master's table. In an age of rising prices (especially for foodstuffs) and "sticky" wages, masters obviously benefited from such methods of payment. Compounding the disadvantageous position of the workers, sometimes masters added extra unpaid apprentices, thereby reducing the demand for trained workers. In most cities where printing was an important industry – Lyons, Venice, Geneva, Paris – masters employed these kinds of practices, and everywhere the laborers' response was the same: work stoppage.

An especially well-documented strike in the printing industry occurred in Lyons in 1539 when the work stoppage was orchestrated by a "company" of journeymen pressmen, typesetters, correctors, and proofreaders called the Griffarins. In response to masters' attempts to eliminate the traditional payment arrangement of monetary wage plus meals at the master's table, the Griffarins co-ordinated an industry-wide strike that lasted almost four months, and in the end they forced the masters and publishers to return to the traditional food and wage arrangement for another thirty years. Some work stoppages were shop based, but reveal no less than the industry-wide strikes the collective organization of the Griffarins. If, for example, a master put an apprentice to work pulling a press against express complaints by the journeymen pressmen of the shop, at the signal of "*tric, tric*" all the journeymen of the shop would walk out. Until the master agreed to adhere to the demands of the Griffarins, the shop would be boycotted, and any journeymen or apprentices who tried to work there would be beaten by the Griffarins if apprehended.

The Griffarins of Lyons were not the only journeymen who co-ordinated strikes in the sixteenth century. At the end of the century the journeymen bakers of Colmar struck, and strengthened their hand by forging a prior alliance with their fellows in Strasbourg and Basel who agreed not to come to Colmar seeking work. Journeymen bakers walked off the job in Paris in 1579, while the journeymen tailors did the same ten years later. In the next century we find journeymen blacksmiths and hatters in Paris boycotting the masters who had lowered their wages. Boisguillebert, the Lieutenant of Police in Rouen disapprovingly observed that "One sees in commercial towns 700 to 800 workers of one trade stop work simultaneously because [their employers] wish to lower the daily wage by a sou."[8]

Labor unrest tore at the textile industry as well. For three centuries beginning in the 1300s we find widespread evidence of clashes between workers and employers in this industry, especially in the Low Countries. Fullers were the most active of the protesters, and if their demands were not met, they would call an *uitgang* where all the workers would simply leave town. The twin objectives, of course, were to deprive masters of workers and to escape the jurisdiction of the local government. In 1478, for example, the fullers of Leiden collectively left town and went to the city of Gouda when their thirty-four demands went unsatisfied. This was certainly not the first *uitgang*, for they referred to similar walkouts "staged by our forefathers." Nor was it to be the last, for we know that the weavers of Amsterdam staged one in 1523.

Whatever the strike activity – issuing demands, stopping work, leaving the city – solidarity was required. Sometimes this was forced upon colleagues, and strikebreakers risked their health, reputation, and future prospects of employment, for they were often roughed up, and then blacklisted.

Fullers lost their prominence as strikers in the sixteenth century, but the shearmen picked up where the fullers left off. In Venice in 1556 the shearmen organized a strike, while in 1643 the shearers of Leiden staged an *uitgang*. It seems, however, that mass exoduses of workers from towns were losing their effectiveness in the seventeenth century. When the shearers of Leiden left town, for example, the authorities immediately wrote to other nearby cities notifying them that their shearers might be en route, and asking them to deny them entry. The Leiden magistrates had good reason to expect compliance, for not only did they promise other towns that they would do the same if the situation were reversed, but growing specialization had meant that the cities were not

---

[8] Quoted in Abet Poitrineau, *Ils travaillaient la France, Métiers et mentalités du XVIIe au XIXe siècle* (Paris, 1992), p. 172.

as competitive with one another as they had been before. *Uitgangs* also lost their effectiveness because after 1637 manufacturers of woolens in different cities in Holland began to collaborate on an unprecedented scale. The resulting employers' organizations had a primary goal of enforcing labor discipline and obedience.

Still, worker resistance did not disappear, for *uitgangs* gave way to strikes, and a wave of the latter in the mid-seventeenth century show that the co-ordination of the workers' activities no less than that of the employers spanned cities. From 1636 to 1639, for example, strikes led by shearers were staged in Haarlem, Hoorn, Gouda, and Rotterdam, the strikers holding clandestine meetings to co-ordinate their actions and to determine the means of enforcement. They determined that those who disregarded the decisions of the group were declared "foul" and so were deprived of their honor and expelled from the community of workers. Not only were strikebreakers blacklisted, but no one would even drink with a "foul" shearer. We find the same kind of coercion and, indeed, the same dishonoring language invoked by workers in English, French, and German towns and cities.

Leiden was the scene of frequent strikes during the turbulent seventeenth century. Work stoppages occurred there in 1619, 1637, 1644, 1648, 1700, and 1701. Leiden was Europe's largest clothmaking center, and it was a terrifying prospect indeed if many of its textile workers stopped work, for they numbered 45,000 strong in 1670 when the total population of Leiden was 70,000. Not surprisingly, like municipal authorities everywhere, the regents of Leiden supported the master manufacturers in their conflicts with labor which, again, turned on issues of wages and the length and density of the working day. In 1700, after a half-century of underemployment and real wage decreases, over 1,000 weavers assembled outside the city walls to discuss their wages and then issue demands for higher ones. When their demands were not met, strike funds were collected. The strike was called the next year; it was eventually suppressed, and four strikers were hanged while another six were flogged.

In the eighteenth century worker resistance to the masters' imperatives of time and labor were more frequent yet. Strikes were called for a variety of reasons – wages, length of working day, numbers of apprentices allowed, even technological innovations. The shearers of Leiden protested between 1716 and 1718 against a new method of shearing which was easier than the traditional method. The shearers held that this was a violation of "their ancient freedom," and feared that the new method diminished their skill by lowering the qualifications to do their job, which in turn spelled a loss of status.

Even state-supported enterprises were not immune from work stoppage. The French royal cloth manufactory established in 1665 in Abbeville was a large, capital-intensive enterprise that almost immediately experienced cash-flow problems. Servicing an enormous debt (more than a million *livres*) and paying 120,000 to 200,000 *livres* annually to its diverse workforce (the manufacture of the fine cloth passed through fifty-two different processes) strapped the enterprise. The employer's usual recourse was to lay off workers who, predictably, protested. The first such protest occurred in 1686, followed by a full-scale strike in 1716 which was only suppressed when royal troops were called in. The judicial officer who tried the rebels in court clearly sympathized with the employers, castigating the workers as a "licentious" lot "who do not seem to realize that the manufactory is not there for them, but that they are there for the manufactory." The strike militarily crushed, workers were expected to – and apparently did – fall in line and adhere to the work regimen dictated by the employers, a regimen which was described by a traveler who observed the manufactory in 1728. The witness reported that he had never seen a manufactory "better-ordered or more cleanly kept," and he was especially impressed that the 3,500 men and 400 girls executed their tasks "to the sound of the drum."[9]

If the Abbeville textile workers succumbed to a discipline in the workplace that resembled that of the Wedgwood potteries, elsewhere their colleagues continued to resist. In Sedan in the 1730s and 1740s the shearmen struck repeatedly against their masters over the masters' attempt to intensify their work without additional pay. Specifically, shearmen were ordered to carry pieces of cloth from the workshop to the drying racks in addition to the normal work required of them. The shearmen protested that they had never before had to do this – this had never been part of their customary practices "since time immemorial" – and they drove their point home by walking off the job on more than one occasion. In 1759 in Verviers the shearmen struck, too, and part of the dispute there concerned the calculus of time and labor that had divided masters and workers in so many other places. Statutes had nominally fixed wages for shearmen at 20 *sous* for a 12-hour and 40-minute work day, but masters had undercut the wage by buying inflated German coins at a discount and then forcing the shearmen to accept them at face value.

Most of our examples thus far have been drawn from industries that were more integrated than most, and so were more sensitive to the

9 Quoted in Fernand Braudel, *The Wheels of Commerce*, trans. Siân Reynolds (New York, 1986), p. 338.

pressure of demand schedules. During the eighteenth century and from the stimulus of the "consumer revolution," however, this pressure spread to many more trades than ever before. Not surprisingly, the number of strikes increased proportionally, and can be found in nearly every trade. At times the number of striking workers was enormous, as the 20,000 silk workers who shut down production in Lyons in 1779 attested. In France alone between the 1720s and 1780s we can count work stoppages and boycotts in over sixty towns, and in Paris we know of over fifty different incidents. Citing only a few of the most notable and large Parisian strikes, we find scores, sometimes hundreds of workers throwing down their tools and walking out of their shops, often insulting the master and his wife as they left: stockingcap-makers in 1724, blacksmiths in 1731, locksmiths in 1746, cutlers in 1748, hatters in 1764, bookbinders in 1776, and masons and stonecutters in 1785.

Similar circumstances occurred in England. On the docks of Deptford yard between 1733 and 1737 the most common offense of the workers there was "basseying," that is, "escaping over the wall after first answering the morning call." The second most common offense was "idling at the tap-house."[10] Taking all the trades together, however, the most remarked upon practice of worker resistance to their employers was what subsequent labor historians have called "industrial disputes," conflicts that mostly meant work stoppages. These erupted all over Great Britain in most trades. One historian counts 373 disputes between 1717 and 1800 (120 in London alone), the lead taken by woolen workers (64 instances), followed by ship's carpenters (37) and tailors (22).[11] Weavers were especially well represented in protests against wage reductions. Weaver riots swept Somerset and Wiltshire in 1726 and 1727. Strikers from Wiltshire calling themselves "regulators" descended upon some employers' houses in the woolweaving town of Frome in Somerset, and presented a list of demands about wages. If an employer rejected the demands, "the windows paid for it," as a local commentator put it.[12]

Workers struck over many issues – manipulation of the relationship between the length of the work day and the daily wage, depressed or stagnant wages in the face of rising prices, denser working days, and especially payment in truck whereby masters overvalued the goods and so effectively depressed wages. The tailors of London complained about

---

[10] John Rule, *The Experience of Labour in Eighteenth-Century English Industry* (New York, 1981), p. 135.

[11] Ibid., pp. 148–9.

[12] Robert W. Malcolmson, "Workers' combinations in 18th-century England," in M. Jacob and J. Jacob, eds., *The Origins of Anglo-American Radicalism* (London, 1984) p. 152.

the impact of the statute of 1721 which fixed their hours of work and divided the working day into two, unequal parts. The afternoon session was an hour longer than that of the morning, and since the masters could pay equal wages for each shift, it was obviously in their interest to let their journeymen "play in the morning" and call them to work in the afternoon, thereby picking up a free hour's work and avoiding the required penny and a half breakfast allowance in the bargain.

Complaints about payment in truck had been heard for centuries. In the 1500s journeymen furniture-makers of Strasbourg protested collectively against their masters who tried to convert payment from cash to truck, a complaint indistinguishable from the one lodged in 1726 by the weavers of Somerset who were grieved by "their masters . . . paying their wages in goods, and setting extravagant prices on such goods." The Devonshire weavers in 1743 were "up in arms . . . on account of their masters forcing them to take corn, bread, bacon, cheese, butter and other necessaries of life, in truck, as it is called, for their labour."[13] And cutlers in Sheffield rioted in 1756 against masters trying to force them to take half their wages in truck.

Job placement

Obviously, collective work stoppage, even if unsuccessful, requires organization and co-ordination, and incidents of strike activity that pepper the historical record since the high Middle Ages tell us that workers had been organizing against employers – mostly in industries like textiles where expanding and increasingly integrated demand was affecting production schedules – long before the age of industrialization. Timed-work regimens, wages, piecerates, length or density of the working day, forms of payment (in truck, debased coinage, etc.) – any of these issues could be and were cause for worker grievance against what we today called unfair labor practices, and on countless occasions ended in work stoppage. However ephemeral and unsuccessful most of these "strikes" were, they do tell us that workers were not infrequently at odds with their employers.

Journeymen artisans joined in these collective actions, but journeymen flexed their muscles in the contest with masters in another arena besides work stoppage; they were also interested in controlling job placement. Journeymen and masters realized that control over conditions, hours, or wages derived from access to and control of the labor market, and in northern, western, and central Europe they openly

---

[13] Quoted in Rule, p. 138.

struggled with one another over control of this all-important market. Journeymen recognized that mobility was their greatest weapon in this contest, and consequently everywhere they struggled to defend their freedom of movement. They well knew, as did their masters, that unimpeded mobility between shops and from town to town allowed them to dictate in some measure the conditions of labor demand. Masters, for their part, saw such demands as rank disobedience, typically conflating economic issues with the social and political, and masters invariably responded to journeymen demands with counter-demands for discipline and an unquestioned respect for hierarchy.

Given the importance of mobility to the labor market objectives of journeymen, it is no surprise that journeymen associations cropped up first in cities in the late Middle Ages where urban production required a flexible supply of trained workers. Thus weavers and fullers were among the first trades to organize, but we also find evidence of associations of journeymen coopers, for instance, in 1321 in Rostock, Lübeck, Hamburg, Wismar, and Straslund. As well-trained workers became more mobile after the demographic crisis of the mid-fourteenth century, brotherhoods of journeymen, called *Gesellenvereine*, mushroomed, so that by 1400 shoemakers, tailors, furriers, bakers, and smiths each had their own organizations in the towns along the upper Rhine.

Journeymen brotherhoods seemed to have emerged as religious confraternities that were isolated cells, not connected to confraternities in other cities. With the mobility of journeymen in the late Middle Ages, however, some of these pockets were increasingly being stitched together between towns, the confraternities thus probably serving historically as the core of what came to be called in France *compagnonnages*, or journeymen brotherhoods directly interested in labor market issues. Journeymen confraternities and *compagnonnages* overlap, and are difficult to distinguish historically, for their interests and rituals were almost indistinguishable from the fifteenth century on. Ostensibly, journeymen confraternities were organizations for devotion and charity, and they do seem to have performed these functions; but they also were the institutional cells of what the French authorities called *cabales*, and thus the seat of sedition and the site of a perceived libertinage and insubordination. These organizations, whatever their origins and historical convergences, were forged in the crucible of corporatism, and it is not accidental that the emergence of urban corporatism was accompanied by the rise of journeymen brotherhoods, nor that they almost always emerged in trades with corporate statutes.

Despite their confraternal function which, ostensibly, merely declared these brotherhoods to be pious, mutual aid societies, in the eyes of the

masters and civil (and ecclesiastical) authorities they were deeply troubling for the disobedience they implied, which, in baldly economic
terms, was evidenced in the covert challenge to labor market control
that they portended. Whenever we find evidence of journeymen associations acting to influence job placement, we find masters responding
vociferously. Already in 1352 we find master bakers from eight towns
along the middle of the Rhine trying to join forces to combat the
journeymen over precisely this issue. These masters ultimately could not
agree among themselves (divisive competition among masters being a
problem that would dog them everywhere for centuries), but they clearly
intended to co-ordinate their hiring practices in an effort to deny their
workers the power to dictate to them what these would be. In the 1380s
master tailors from twenty-eight towns along the upper Rhine tried to
do the same thing that the downstream bakers had tried a generation
earlier, and they agreed in principle not to hire any journeyman who had
left his previous employer without permission. These masters even
formed a *Handwerkerbunde*, but it was largely ineffective for the same
reason that it had been for the mid-Rhine bakers – because of discord
among the masters themselves. When trained labor was in demand,
masters competed among themselves for the best workers, and masters
with larger enterprises and more access to capital often were in a
position to bid away journeymen from the smaller masters by offering
higher wages or better or more plentiful board. The masters' collective
front against worker control of the labor market was undermined by the
masters who might accept journeymen controlling placement in exchange for concentrated or expanded production.

Journeymen brotherhoods were not just a German phenomenon in
the late Middle Ages, for we find these organizations popping up in the
fourteenth century and proliferating in the fifteenth in the Low Countries, England, and France. In 1350 we find London shearmen walking
off the job and none agreeing to return until the grievance in question
with a master was settled, clearly evidence of an association among these
workers that was solidary and had some teeth. In 1362 some London
weavers did the same thing. We do not know the specifics of their
grievances, but this is clearly evidence of collective worker action, and
sounds like the tactics of nascent journeymen brotherhoods elsewhere.
In 1396 the master saddlers of London complained to the mayor that
since 1383 their "serving men called yomen" not only had been holding
meetings, but had taken to donning a common livery and had even
named an officer (a "bedel") to call their meetings and to organize their
activities. By 1415 yeomen tailors apparently had such an organization,
too. And at about the same time in York shoemaker "serving men" had

set up, as the municipal authorities said, "a contentious conventicle . . . [which] publically, proudly and boastfully den[ied] the authority of their masters . . . [and were] gretly disposed to riot and idelness."[14]

It is difficult to say given the scarce evidence whether journeymen (or yeomen, "young men" as they were called in England) were squaring off against masters over control of the labor market in the fourteenth century, but the compromise many masters and journeymen worked out in the fifteenth suggests that this was an important issue by then. In many English cities journeymen agreed to affiliate their organizations with the guilds, the yeomanry taking an inferior position to the liverymen in the guild. Acceptance of hierarchy, however, was exchanged for certain privileges, the extent of which depended upon the strength of the yeomen's organization. For instance, in 1434 the blacksmith journeymen of London and in 1458 their colleagues in tailoring were granted control over labor placement, empowered by their guilds to "search for forrens," that is, to determine that no outsider was working in a shop without their approval.[15] The master blacksmiths also allowed a journeyman to meet and then escort new arrivals to masters in need of laborers, a privilege that their colleagues in York, Hull, and Exeter also extracted from their masters.

In France we find parallel developments, with the appearance in the fourteenth-century workplace of concerted worker activity against masters, and a proliferation of journeymen brotherhoods in the fifteenth. Depending on the trade, the degree of connectedness between the organizations (usually called *confrairies*) in different towns varied widely, but as we move through the early modern centuries there is no question that tighter networks of more bureaucratically organized institutions developed. Worker migrations, often seasonal, were common in the fourteenth century in France as elsewhere, and mobile workers increasingly organized to advance their interests in the workplace against those of the employers. Fundamentally, we see control over the labor market as the prime objective for journeymen and master alike. For instance, by the mid-fifteenth century fuller journeymen had organized into a "league" that embraced forty-two towns, including Paris, and the primary objective of the journeymen was to regulate labor supply and control employment placement. The journeymen dyers of Bruges in 1453 similarly had led the creation of an international league that boasted members in forty-two towns. A journeyman traveled from

[14] Quoted in Heather Swanson, *Medieval Artisans: An Urban Class in Late Medieval England* (Oxford, 1989), p. 56.
[15] R. A. Leeson, *Travelling Brothers: The Six Centuries Road from Craft Fellowship to Trade Unionism* (London, 1979), p. 45.

one town to the next supported by these networks and, depending upon the demand for labor in any particular locale, was either placed in a master's shop by the resident journeymen or sent on to another town in the network. In this way demand was manipulated to exceed supply, but such a system was dependent upon the free mobility of the journeymen. This network of fullers resembles what will come to be called the *tour de France*, a route that itinerant journeymen traveled to learn their trades, but also, through mobility, to ensure access to, and control over the labor market by regulating its supply.

These organizations of worker solidarity, in France called *confrairies* and eventually *compagnonnages*, were not, as we will see in the next chapter, exclusively economic institutions, but they did serve throughout the early modern period nearly everywhere in Europe except Spain and Italy to help workers control the labor market and, indirectly, the conditions of work and the wages paid. One possible reason for the absence of journeymen tramping in Spain, and thus of *compagnonnages*, is the severe economic disunity of the peninsula in the late Middle Ages and the early modern period. Iberia consisted of a multitude of small commercial regions with small towns with little contact with each other. Moreover, traveling from town to town, particularly on foot as a journeyman would, was extremely difficult. Distances between towns were great, the terrain was often rugged and dry, and in few places could a journeyman go more than 50 miles without having to climb a mountain.

If we find no *compagnonnages* in Spain or apparently Italy, we do find them in England, Germany, and especially France. Worker solidarity *across* trades would have to wait for the eighteenth century, and we cannot speak yet of a confrontation between "labor" and "capital," nor of conflict between "classes" of master and journeyman. The relations between masters and journeymen, permeated as they were with paternalism, were too ambivalent for that. Antagonism over job placement could be muted and the solidarity in the ranks of the journeymen divided, for example, by traditions of *fidelité personelle*, particularly if a journeyman felt his prospects for admission to mastership were reasonably bright. Similarly, competition between masters for labor often drove a wedge through the ranks of the masters. On the other hand, negligible or declining prospects for admission to mastership (a situation, as we have seen, that attended the demographic changes in Europe after 1450) prompted other journeymen to struggle for control of the labor market, a control that could at least improve their conditions as lifelong workers. Unmistakably, however, amid all of this variety, in an increasing number of trades more and more journeymen were squaring off against their masters.

There is ample evidence in England, Germany, the Low Countries, and France that these independent journeymen associations existed and became more formally organized in the sixteenth and seventeenth centuries, complete with treasuries and officers, and with pretentions to control the labor market. The *Reichspolizeiordnung* of 1530 prohibited journeymen in the Holy Roman empire from administering justice to their fellow workers and from collectively abandoning their masters' workshops, while an English law of 1549 and the French edict of Villers-Cotterets of 1539 sounded the same note. The English law declared illegal all "confederacies and conspiracies of working people to determine wages or amount of work to be done," a law that would stay on the books until its repeal, along with the famous Combination Acts of 1799 and 1800, in 1826.[16] Villers-Cotterets, similarly, specifically prohibited "any alliance or *intélligence* between journeymen, any assembly on their part for whatever cause, in short, any coalition directed against the masters," stipulations that were repeated in subsequent royal legislation in 1560, 1566, and 1579.[17]

The basic characteristics of the brotherhoods (*compagnonnages* in France, *Gesellenverbänden* in Germany) were much the same throughout Europe. Their roots, as we have seen, were in the migrations of artisans that accelerated after the Black Death, and in many cities and towns it was becoming difficult for journeymen to become masters. The important factor of the conditions for journeyman mobility was, of course, demand for trained labor, and by the sixteenth century it had become customary that they would seek favorable situations, moving on if work was unavailable and being drawn to areas where trained workers were in short supply. It was within this force field of supply and demand that journeymen organized to manipulate the conditions.

In the late fifteenth and sixteenth centuries the institutional trappings of brotherhoods became more clearly defined. The Parisian journeymen tailors, for example, elected a "king" of their company in 1505, while in Burgundy at about the same time we find journeymen cutlers, saddlers, and shoemakers organized and levying dues on newcomers (called a *bienvenue*) in exchange for placing them in jobs. The cutlers were doing this in Dijon as early as 1464. In 1540 we find a newcomer arriving in town and being met by a resident fellow journeyman and escorted to the house of the *mère*, an inn or tavern. Here he was temporarily lodged while it was determined whether employment were available for him. This journeyman was placed with a master, but on other occasions

---

16 Quoted in ibid., p. 27.
17 Quoted in James R. Farr, *Hands of Honor: Artisans and Their World in Dijon, 1550–1650* (Ithaca, 1988), p. 68.

where work was not available, journeymen were instructed to *passer outre*, that is, to go on to another town where employment prospects might be brighter. Eventually there emerged a network of these *mère* lodges and labor clearinghouses throughout the realm.

By 1579 such a network was probably established among the cabinet-makers, and among the locksmiths, tailors, and shoemakers before 1600. The evidence comes from Dijon and Troyes, but given the nature and function of the these organizations they must have extended beyond these towns in a network that extended well beyond Burgundy. In 1469 we find reference already to a *tour de France* among some journeymen, and Dijon was an important stop on this journey of no prescribed route. By the early seventeenth century a shoemaker reported that he had journeyed south from Dijon to Chalon, Tournus, Mâcon, Lyons, and Vienne, while a glover said that he had worked in Paris, Lyons, Avignon, Marseilles, and other towns including Dijon. One remarkably itinerant cabinet-maker had stopped in Lyons, Provins, Grenoble, and had even wandered down into Italy before eventually arriving at Dijon.

In 1579 Dijon's *syndic* (the chief police officer) reported to the city's magistrates that the journeymen cabinet-makers had drawn up "laws and statutes" for themselves and had elected a captain, a lieutenant, a receiver, and a sergeant as their officers. The magistrates were so alarmed that they called a special meeting of the town council to proceed against these rebellious workers. They summarily banished the captain, Jean Champignon of Rennes, as well as "Little John," the brother in charge of the treasury, and they confiscated a rollbook as well as the contents of the brotherhood's treasury held in a strongbox (which contained $10\frac{1}{2}$ *sous*). No doubt suspecting journeymen of other trades of similar clandestine organizing, the council then prohibited all journeymen of whatever trade from assembling, electing officers, collecting dues, or making among themselves "any deliberations or resolutions" to establish prices for their products, to set wages, "or to prevent journeymen of their trade from seeking and finding masters [to work for] that seemed good to them."[18]

Prohibitions like these, be they municipal or royal, were futile, for journeymen brotherhoods not only survived, but thrived. In 1585 again in Dijon the authorities arrested ten journeymen cabinet-makers who had gathered to watch a newcomer display his competence in the craft, a ritual typical of *compagnonnage*. In 1605 the town council again prohibited assemblies of more than three journeymen and forbade journeymen to draw up articles of governance of their organizations and *rolles* of their

[18] Quoted in Farr, pp. 68–9.

members. They were not to prevent newcomers from seeking work in whatever shop they wished, nor were they to take newcomers to taverns or inns upon their arrival. In 1619 these prohibitions were repeated in response to continual violations.

Shoemaker journeymen had a *compagnonnage* nearly as early as the cabinet-makers, as did, apparently, the locksmiths. In 1581 Dijon's municipal authorities prohibited all journeymen shoemakers, locksmiths, and cabinet-makers from assembling in groups greater than three, and the following year, in response to a complaint by the master shoemakers and cobblers, they prohibited the journeymen of those trades from naming provosts, captains, or chiefs of their "companies" or collecting dues from their fellows. Sometime in the next forty years the shoemaker and cabinet-maker brotherhoods became worker placement services, for in 1621 the masters of both crafts appended to their guild statutes a clause making it illegal for journeymen to practice *embauchage* (labor placement), to convene assemblies, and to collect dues from newcomers (the locksmith journeymen were prohibited from doing precisely this as well in 1635). According to these masters, the journeymen and their organization were the principal causes of the "disorder" that reigned in their trade.

Among the journeymen tailors there was apparently a national network by 1588. In that year, Jean Philippe, innkeeper of the Fatted Capon in Dijon, was arrested after an alderman had raided the place and discovered eight journeymen tailors in a room upstairs, some playing cards, some making stockings, others just lying about. Interrogation of Philippe and the journeymen revealed that the journeymen tailors throughout the realm knew that the Fatted Capon was their house of call in Dijon, and Philippe their *mère*. They reported that they knew that they could stay there temporarily until they were placed with a master. Failing that, they would move on. Philippe was ordered to provide this service no more, but to no avail, for in 1599 the master tailors complained to the magistrates that Philippe was still at it, and was "accustomed to receive and retain in his house the journeymen [tailors] . . . Indeed, at present he has six there . . . which is the reason that they [the masters] are badly served."[19] The authorities again ordered Philippe to evict his guests and henceforth to lodge journeymen for no more than one night. We hear no more of Philippe, but in 1603 the master tailors amended their statutes to require newly arrived journeymen to present themselves *directly to the masters* for work, and specifically forbade innkeepers from receiving them first. A fruitless law,

---

[19] Quoted in ibid., p. 71.

it seems, for in 1612 these same masters lodged a grievance with the town council that precisely this clause in their statutes was being egregiously violated by their journeymen.

As the *compagnonnages* developed their distinctively institutional trappings, especially concerning control of the labor market for trained workers, masters were slow to react. Eventually, after royal and municipal measures had clearly proved insufficient in crushing the worker organizations or even stemming the tide of their growth, masters began to institute labor placement programs of their own. In 1624 the cabinet-makers of Dijon created the office of hiring clerk (*clerc embaucheur*), and the master shoemakers followed suit in 1633. This guild officer's job was to receive incoming journeymen and to place them in shops in need of trained labor. In 1626 the master cabinet-makers complained to the authorities that the journeymen still controlled the placement of incoming workers, and were united among themselves which allowed them to stage collective walkouts from the shops. Indeed, they alleged that the unity was coerced, that membership in the brotherhood was mandatory, the journeymen in question "constrain[ing] all who were inscribed on their *rooles* [sic] to follow them."[20] These workers, the masters alleged, enforced their control of master and worker alike by forming "troops" of twenty to thirty journeymen who roamed the city and threatened a beating for any master or worker who dared challenge their control. Workers not inscribed on their rolls but trying to work in town anyway risked being "expelled from the town by cudgel blows," as one journeyman rather boldly admitted to the authorities in 1626.

During the seventeenth and eighteenth centuries all across France labor exchanges and placement offices often engendered conflict between guild officials and ordinary masters, and disputes over corruption and favoritism in the placing of journeymen in shops were frequent. But without a doubt, most of the conflict engendered by this struggle for control of the labor market saw journeymen squaring off against masters, and journeymen coming to blows with one another as they tried to maintain "closed shops."

The issue of placement was perhaps the most divisive fact that a guild could face. As Kaplan has shown, among the bakers of eighteenth-century Paris, it "shook the community" more than any other.[21] Journeymen usually despised and resented the masters' placement clerk, sometimes to the point of murderous rage. In 1742, for instance, the master bakers' placement clerk Estienne Berton was spied in a tavern by

---

[20] Quoted in Cynthia Maria Truant, *The Rites of Labor: Brotherhoods of Compagnonnage in Old and New Regime France* (Ithaca, 1994), p. 64.

[21] Kaplan, p. 225.

a group of journeymen who, their propensity to violence perhaps lubricated by drink, set upon him and beat him senseless with their canes. Berton died the next day of a fractured skull.

For journeymen labor placement exchanges to work in the worker's favor, defection from the ranks had to be either prevented or punished. The same went for workers respecting prevailing wage rates. Violence among journeymen over renegades working "under price" can readily be located in the historical record. A local commentator reported in 1733, for example, that the journeymen weavers in Bristol

being irritated against one of their fraternity for working under price . . . rose in a great body, and seiz'd the delinquent, who underwent the marks of their revenge in the usual manner of ducking in the river, and a hearty drubbing, by which usage he had the misfortune to have one of his eyes beat out.[22]

In 1679 in a smithery in Bedfordshire the blacksmith Nicholas Browne testified in court that a certain journeyman named Thomas Crawley was accused by fellow journeyman John Winch thus: "Hee's the rogue that workes for eight pence a day when others have 12d. a day." When Crawley countered that Winch was lying, Winch, who at that moment was "lighting a pipe of tabacco [sic] with an iron rod being red hott, did run the same into the eye of the said Thomas Crawley, and told him that [that] . . . would teach him . . ."[23]

Effective control of the labor market from the perspective of journeymen demanded such "closed shop" techniques and methods of enforcement, supported by institutional trappings like rolls and treasuries, fixed meeting places for assemblies, and strong leadership (reference to *premiers*, chiefs, captains, and the like are common). Equally clearly, the masters' complaints about the indiscipline, rebelliousness, and violence of their journeymen, and the institutional changes the masters made were attempts to counter this function of the journeymen brotherhoods and to wrest control of the labor market from them. Infighting and competition for good workers often divided the ranks of the masters and blunted the effectiveness of this master counter-offensive, and in some trades the two institutions co-existed, if uneasily, whereby a journeyman would arrive in town and proceed to the house of call and then either be sent on his way or sent to the hiring clerk for placement. In any case, the *compagnonnage* was a fixture.

Master reaction to journeymen organization appears to have been more effective in Germany than in France. Despite the similar institutional trappings of journeymen organizations to those of their counterparts in France, they do not seem to have exerted the same degree of

[22] Quoted in Malcolmson, p. 125.
[23] Quoted in ibid., p. 126.

power over the labor market, at least not before the eighteenth century. The tramping system, or *Wanderjahr*, was made obligatory in some trades as early as the sixteenth century, legislated sometimes by guild statute, sometimes by state regulations. Clearinghouses and waystations called *Herbergen* or *Trinkstuben* popped up everywhere in Germany in the sixteenth and seventeenth centuries, but here these inns were sometimes owned by the guild and were operated by one of its masters. This officer was variously called the *Herbergsvater*, revealing the paternalistic assumptions of these institutions, or, as in Augsburg among the joiners and shoemakers around 1600, the *Zuschickmeister*. Whatever the name, when an itinerant journeyman arrived in town he proceeded to the *Herberge* where he was temporarily lodged, sometimes at the expense of the guild. Journeymen *Trinkstuben* that remained independent of masters employed the *Auszug*, the German equivalent of the French *passer outre*, to attempt to regulate the labor supply. In that event the journeyman was sent on his way, perhaps with a bit of money drawn from the journeymen's treasury. Journeymen who remained in town did so when their labor was in demand. Masters who needed trained laborers came to the *Herberge* or *Trinkstube* to interview prospective workers. In places where the masters owned the house of call or the placement officer was a guildsman, both master and journeyman had the right of refusal of the terms of any contract, but if the journeyman refused to accept the conditions of the work offered, he had to wait a week to be reassigned, and in any case he could only refuse three times, then being assigned anyway.

In the eighteenth century in Germany as elsewhere, the pace of change in the conditions of labor accelerated, and the journeymen adjusted their tactics. Tramping and geographic mobility continued to serve as a pressure tactic, as did strikes and boycotts aimed at particular workshops. But the population was growing, and accelerating product demand and increasing capital concentration led to larger workshops. Organized journeymen, sometimes joined by small masters, began to target specific, large employers for work stoppages or labor shortages, figuring that alteration of working conditions here would have a ripple effect through the industry. Linked together in networks of brotherhoods organized along craft lines, now called *Bruderschaften*, journeymen flexed the muscles that came with increased organization and collective action, calling strikes and labor boycotts against masters they deemed to be unfair. In Leipzig in 1763, for example, 200 journeymen tailors packed up and left town, while their colleagues in Danzig boycotted the city from 1751 to 1798. The Danzig interdiction was unusual for its duration – most boycotts were much shorter – but such boycotts were no more unusual than strikes within towns. In Nuremberg alone between 1786 and 1806 ninety-seven different strikes were called by journeymen.

The authorities continued to rail against such "insubordination" as they had done since the sixteenth century. As we have seen, the imperial edict of 1731 prohibited assemblies of journeymen while it also attempted to control their mobility – recognized to be their most potent weapon in the battle over the labor market – by the *Kundschaft*. Employers also were called upon to report whether the journeyman had "conducted himself in a diligent, quiet, peaceful and honest manner as befitting a journeyman in the crafts and trades . . . "[24] Journeymen countered the *Kundschaft* with a document of their own, the *Gesellenschein*, that verified the journeyman's adherence to the solidarity of the brotherhood. This document spread across the Holy Roman empire in the eighteenth century.

In England, journeymen brotherhoods developed many of the same institutions found elsewhere, and these appear in full flower in the eighteenth century. Hatters had a national network of "turn houses," a "turn" being the English equivalent of the French *tour*, while felt-makers, weavers, brushmakers, curriers, millrights, and, for centuries, masons, to mention only a few of many trades, likewise had stitched together similar networks of inns where tramping and "rambling" brothers would stay. An age and nation of a supposed *laissez-faire* economy, the eighteenth century in England was actually a time when many laws were enacted to control labor, especially journeymen, and this legislation sometimes directly attacked these "lawless clubs." The royal proclamation against journeymen's clubs in 1718, the Act of Parliament of 1721 against journeymen tailors, and the Act of 1726 proscribing workingmen's "unlawful clubs and societies" are but three examples of no fewer than forty laws directed specifically at the regulation of workers that were on the books by the end of the century.[25] From the perspective of the masters and the authorities, the most alarming institution was the house of call, a labor exchange controlled by journeymen that can be found in many trades in eighteenth-century England. The Hole in the Wall on Fleet Street in London, the house of call of the printer compositors, is a colorful example of a common and widespread institution.

The Parliamentary Act against the journeymen tailors in 1721 capped

---

[24] Quoted in Josef Ehmer, "Worlds of mobility: migration patterns of Viennese artisans in the eighteenth century," in Geoffrey Crossick, ed., *The Artisan and the European Town, 1500–1900* (Aldershot, 1997), p. 193.

[25] Leeson, p. 86.

a dispute between London's masters and journeymen that had flared since the turn of the century. Journeymen tailors had long had their own houses of call which, as in France and Germany, served as clearing-houses for workers. Masters had accommodated themselves to the institutions, but around 1700 the five houses of call of the journeymen tailors of London confederated themselves and aggressively restricted the labor supply. In 1720 they also demanded a reduction of hours and a pay hike, and when the masters responded by organizing their own houses of call and demanded that the journeymen use them, the journeymen called a general strike. The parliamentary Act sought to quash the journeyman confederation, but it persisted, largely because of a lack of a united front among the employers (several of whom were eager to use the labor unrest as a weapon to destroy their competitors). By 1760 the journeymen tailors had gone from five to forty-two affiliated clubs in London, and during the general strike of 1764 they had the clout to send 6,000 journeymen tailors out of town, thereby choking the labor supply. Sir John Fielding cogently if tendentiously wrote just four years previous that

the master taylors . . . have repeatedly endeavored to break and suppress the combinations of their journeymen to raise their wages and lessen their hours of work, but have ever been defeated . . . and this has been in some measure due to the infidelity of the masters themselves to each other; some of whom, taking advantage of the confusion, have collected together some of the journeymen, whose exorbitant demands they have complied with, while many other masters have had a total stop put to their business.[26]

The truth was that successful masters had to accommodate these "unions," and many did. In 1811 the radical draper Francis Place observed that "in large concerns, it is very common for the master to send to a house [of call] for a 'squad' of 10 men and a captain, and to another for 6 men and a captain, and so on . . ."[27]

Outside of London, though the evidence is more spotty, similar conditions prevailed among the tailors as well as many other trades. In 1777 the master tailors of Birmingham tried to replace day rates by piecework, and were met with a strike by their journeymen, and the house of call was the focus of the conflict. The masters' opening salvo had been a general call to all journeymen that they would only be hired if they came directly to the masters' shops for work, bypassing the house of call: "none will be employed but such as call at the masters' houses,

---

[26] Quoted in Catharina Lis and Hugo Soly, "'An irresistible phalanx': journeymen associations in Western Europe, 1300–1800," in Catharina Lis, Jan Lucassen, and Hugo Soly, eds., *Before the Unions: Wage Earners and Collective Action in Europe, 1300–1850*, *International Review of Social History* 39 (1994, Supplement 2), 45.

[27] Quoted in Lis and Soly, 46.

and are free from all combinations."[28] The journeymen responded that the house of call was an ancient and customary institution that existed in all the major towns of the realm, and they called a general strike to protect it, and its role in job placement. There is evidence that among these tailors, as well as among tinplaters and woolcombers in other labor disputes that, to control the labor supply in their turn, journeymen were sent on their way.

Owing to the work of Cynthia Truant, Steven L. Kaplan, Michael Sonenscher, and of course the inimitable, memoir-keeping journeyman Jacques-Louis Ménétra, we know more about journeymen brotherhoods in late seventeenth- and eighteenth-century France than at any other time and in any other country. Though injunctions against these "fraternities" date back centuries, during the eighteenth century we find more of them than ever before, populating dozens of trades. Not surprisingly, we also find the authorities more explicitly concerned about the behavior of their members, both in their disruption of the economy – specifically the labor market – as well as a more cosmic fear of insubordination and thereby the dissolution of the social order. Their fears, though shrill, were not far fetched nor wildly exaggerated, for not only were *compagnonnages* growing in membership, but they had also split into sects that spanned corporate boundaries, with the *gaveaux* (sometimes spelled *gavots*) and the *devoir* (or *devoirants*) being the largest and best known.

Geographic mobility – tramping – stiffened by the starch of brotherhood organization continued to be the journeymen's most potent weapon, but they were all the more effective with a noticeable increase in the degree of the almost bureaucratic organization that these brotherhoods adopted to control their own ranks and to co-ordinate collective action against the masters. Ménétra writes often about the job-securing function of these brotherhoods, and refers to networks through which correspondence flowed and job offers were transmitted, creating the itineraries of the *tour de France*. Organized and thus prepared to parry the innumerable prohibitions pronounced by masters and secular authorities alike against their brotherhoods, journeymen, as Kaplan points out, "resisted and contested on countless occasions." He adds that Le Cler du Brillet, a theorist who opined about the policing of society, wrote aphoristically that where there were workers, there was an "esprit de cabale."[29] Indeed, the fear of worker conspiracies became an obsession of many masters and of the police, and with good reason, for

[28] Quoted in Rule, p. 156.
[29] Steven L. Kaplan, "The luxury guilds in Paris in the eighteenth century," *Francia* 9 (1981), 293.

the evidence suggests that *cabales* proliferated during the eighteenth century, "seriously upsetting public order and troubling the world of work almost every day."[30] *Cabale* is the general term employed for workers disobeying their masters and resisting discipline, and it took the form of strikes and walkouts, but *cabales* of journeymen took different shapes. There was the *cabale-bravade*, of which the objective was defense of respect and status (we will return to this in the next chapter). Then there was the *cabale pour l'emploi*, whereby journeymen defended their employment by opposing dismissals of their fellows. There was also the *cabale pour les salaires* which was about wages and piecerates. But above all there was the *cabale-placement*, which focused on control of the labor market.

Legislation restricting journeymen mobility – by imposing the *congé* and *livret* system discussed in chapter 3 – theoretically placed control of job placement in the hands of guilds and their officers. Given the number of journeyman strikes or just simple refusal to abide by the restrictions that pepper the eighteenth century, such legislation could only have been partly successful. In 1699 the officers of the hatmaker guild in Paris complained of a plot by their journeymen who had conspired to force the masters to accept certain workers. If any master refused to accept these men, then the rest of the journeymen would "damn," or boycott, the violating master. In the middle of the eighteenth century Ménétra's companions, the journeymen glaziers, boycotted Nantes, a collective action that brought the masters of the town to their knees, and to the negotiating table. In a drawn out conflict over hiring practices in Bordeaux in the late 1750s, journeymen of many trades engaged in collective action, the co-ordination of which Ménétra boastfully claims to have accomplished himself. Other examples of worker resistance abound. In 1739 a journeyman guilder newly arrived in Paris had refused to report for work at the shop to which the masters' placement office had assigned him, his crime compounded by his inciting of several of his fellows to follow his lead. In 1756 the officers of the bakers' guild in Paris complained to the authorities that their journeymen were harassing the *jurés* and some masters over unfair hiring practices, while other journeymen were operating a job exchange "to place their comrades." Attacks on masters and even guild placement officers had been occurring for decades. These acts of disobedience were bad enough, but the job exchange was more than the masters could bear because it revealed collective, planned action on the part of the journeymen. In 1786 500 or so journeymen *épiciers* simply refused to abide by the obligatory registration and labor placement system that the guild officers tried to implement. Clandestine meetings, threatened reprisals against journeymen who refused to honor a boycott, and renegade masters employing unregistered journeymen undercut the effectiveness of the legislation.

Black-market hiring by masters was far from infrequent, and evidence for it can be found in many trades, the bakers being one example among many. Some master bakers hired black-market labor for various reasons – it was quicker and simpler, and it permitted the master to recruit a specific man who may have had skills the master particularly needed, or because he mistrusted the guild officer who might favor his competitors. Ménétra recounts an incident after he had become a master about how a guild officer unjustly fined him for employing an unregistered journeyman (Ménétra alleged that the placement officer had just sent the man to him), but the real reason for the fine, according to Ménétra, was the enmity that the officer held for Ménétra because Jacques-Louis had "done a job that [the officer] could not do." Ménétra alludes to some support he had from some other masters in this affair, suggesting the rifts that could split the ranks of masters. Indeed, the role of renegade masters in these examples of labor disputes should caution us from too quickly assuming that the battle lines were drawn clearly and categorically between journeyman and master. Indeed, the evidence often points toward conflicts that arose from *specific* "unfair" practices of *specific* masters. Guild policy reflects the interests of certain masters who dominated the politics of the guild, and other masters within the guild, the evidence confirms, not infrequently objected to policies that they estimated were detrimental to their business concerns.

Clearly, confrontation between journeymen and masters over the early modern centuries was expressed in actions in the workplace – work stoppages, boycotts, and the like – and such occurrences were far from infrequent. Disputes between journeymen and masters, however, found another venue as well, and could be wrangled about without any evidence of work stoppage or any reference to conspiracies and *cabales*. This venue, as Michael Sonenscher has explored in some detail for France in the late eighteenth century, was courts of law. In the current state of research Sonenscher's contention that the "typical form of protest in the eighteenth century trades was neither the food riot nor the strike, but . . . the lawsuit" is perhaps a bit overdrawn, but certainly it was one important forum of dispute about the workplace.[31]

Scattered evidence from the late Middle Ages and during the early

---

[31] Michael Sonenscher, "Journeymen, the courts, and the French trades, 1781–1791," *Past and Present* 114 (1987), 77–109.

modern period shows in England and on the Continent that some confrontations between masters and journeymen were indeed fought and settled in court. Journeymen sued employers over violations of guild statutes (for example, when masters retained more that the permitted number of apprentices, clearly an unfair labor practice that depreciated the value of trained labor by lowering the demand for journeymen), sometimes showing a canny familiarity with the legal system by pitching rival jurisdictions against one another. Natalie Davis has found that the journeymen printers who formed the company of the Griffarins in sixteenth-century Lyons used the courts against their masters in salary disputes, sometimes appealing to Parlement, sometimes playing rival jurisdictions off against one another, all the while hiring lawyers to present their cases in court. Indeed, the Griffarins were far from singular, since we have found many instances where journeymen re-tained solicitors and displayed a shrewd sense of playing rival jurisdic-tions against one another, efficiently using legal arguments in the process. In the cities of the Austrian Netherlands in the eighteenth century we find journeymen as plaintiffs on the dockets of even the higher courts.

Sonenscher points out that in Paris in the 1780s journeymen were "regularly challeng[ing] corporate decisions and appeal[ing] to one or other of the parlements." We can safely conclude that many labor disputes, which Sonenscher defines from the perspective of the jour-neyman as "a concerted action to affect conditions in a trade as a whole," often took the form of legal proceedings whereby journeymen used the law to affect a variety of working conditions and wages.[32] Such legal actions could be enormously collective, as demonstrated by the case in 1785 where 2,000 journeymen painters, decorators, and sculp-tors appealed to the Parlement of Paris contesting a lower court decision that required these journeymen to pay 8 *sous* for a *livret* (that booklet that recorded a journeyman's employment history and contained written permission from employers to change jobs) and a further 3 *sous* every time they changed jobs. In the same year the journeymen hatters of Paris appealed to the Parlement against a ruling by the *Lieutenant-général de police* that reduced their piecerates. In neither case, nor in any legal disputes, is there evidence of work stoppage, and never is the term *cabale* invoked to describe the journeymen's actions; but the actions are no less a part of the history of confrontation between masters and journeymen than the better known work stoppages, boycotts, and *cabales*.

[32] Ibid., p. 85.

Whatever the venue or the means, masters and journeymen were often at odds. Leaving aside whether this is part of the history of the conflict between labor and capital, or part of the story of the formation of the working class, we can nonetheless see that *collectively* masters and journeymen had squared off against one another. It is the collective nature of this conflict that is significant, and this raises the issue of bonds of solidarity in artisan life. In the varieties of dispute between masters and journeymen, we often find the question of honor bulking large, its importance signifying status. It is no accident that disgruntled journeymen often smeared the reputation of former masters. Insults were usually loaded with status signifiers, like *misérable* (low-life), or *gueux* (beggars). They might spread rumors in the street, as the eighteenth-century Parisian journeyman baker Le Roux did against his former master Augustin Legrand, bruiting it about that Legrand was married to "a slut and a whore." Or they might threaten their former masters with vengeance. After being fired by his master, François Breton, an eighteenth-century French journeyman buttonmaker, went from street to street swearing to any who would listen that to get back at his master he "was going to join the French Guards so that he would have the right to carry a sword and to run it through [his master's] body." His intent was not simply to kill his master, but also to do it with a status symbol, the sword. The murder of a master with the preeminent symbol of independence would annul his servile status.[33]

Animosity toward masters was not confined to journeymen, for apprentices might also feel the degradation of inferior status and appalling working or living conditions. One episode made famous by Robert Darnton demonstrates the complex interrelationships between worker protest, honor, and community.[34] Apprentice and journeymen printers in Paris by the early eighteenth century were working in fewer and larger shops, among larger workforces, and with less opportunity to advance to mastership than ever before. The frustrations of these workers erupted one night in a paroxysm of ritualized violence directed against the cats in the neighborhood, with the primary target being *La Grise*, the pet of the wife of a certain master. Behind this grisly episode, we find journeymen increasingly aware of their particular status in society, and keen on defending it. As their situation was deteriorating, journeymen became

---

[33] Quoted in Farge, *La Vie fragile. Violence, pouvoirs et solidarités à Paris au XVIIIe siècle* (Paris, 1986), p. 144. An English translation exists: *Fragile Lives: Violence, Power, and Solidarity in Eighteenth-Century Paris* (London, 1993).

[34] Robert Darnton, "Workers revolt: the great cat massacre of the rue Saint-Séverin," in Robert Darnton, *The Great Cat Massacre and Other Episodes in French Cultural History* (New York, 1984), pp. 75–106.

more and more set on distinguishing themselves from the *alloués*, or the simple wage-workers who increasingly thronged the printshops. The narrator of the cat massacre, Nicolas Contat, repeatedly contrasts the world of the apprentice and journeyman with that of the *alloué* and, of course, with that of the masters. As we will see in the next two chapters, ritual, ceremony, community, and status were at the heart of artisan experience.

Bibliography

Entries marked with a ⋆ designate recommended readings for new students of the subject.

Coornaert, Emile. *Les Compagnonnages en France du Moyen Age à nos jours.* Paris, 1966.

Darnton, Robert. "Workers revolt: the great cat massacre of the rue Saint-Séverin." In Robert Darnton, *The Great Cat Massacre and Other Episodes in French Cultural History.* New York, 1984, pp. 75–106.

⋆Davis, Natalie Z. "A trade union in 16th-century France." *Economic History Review,* 19 (1966), 48–70.

Dekker, Rudolph. "Labour conflicts and working class culture in early modern Holland." *International Review of Social History* 35 (1990), 377–420.

Garrioch, David, and Michael Sonenscher. "Compagnonnages, confraternities, and associations of journeymen in eighteenth-century Paris." *European History Quarterly* 16 (1986), 25–45.

Hauser, Henri. *Les Compagnonnages d'arts et métiers à Dijon aux XVIIe et XVIIIe siècles.* Paris, 1907.

Kaplan, Steven L. "La Lutte pour le contrôle du marché du travail à Paris au XVIIIe siècle." *Revue d'histoire moderne et contemporaine* 36 (1989), 361–412.

⋆Leeson, R. A. *Travelling Brothers: The Six Centuries Road from Craft Fellowship to Trade Unionism.* London, 1979.

⋆Lis, Catharina, and Hugo Soly. "'An irresistible phalanx': journeymen associations in Western Europe, 1300–1800." In Catharina Lis, Jan Lucassen, and Hugo Soly, eds., *Before the Unions: Wage Earners and Collective Action in Europe, 1300–1850,* International Review of Social History 39 (1994, Supplement 2), 11–52.

⋆McKendrick, Neil. "Josiah Wedgwood and Factory Discipline." *Historical Journal* 4:1 (1961), 30–55.

Malcolmson, Robert W. "Workers' combinations in 18th-century England." In M. Jacob and J. Jacob, eds., *The Origins of Anglo-American Radicalism.* London, 1984.

Neufeld, Michael J. *The Skilled Metalworkers of Nuremberg: Craft and Class in the Industrial Revolution.* New Brunswick, 1989.

Sonenscher, Michael. "Journeymen, the courts, and French trades, 1781–1791." *Past and Present* 114 (1987), 77–109.

⋆"Mythical sork: workshop production and the compagnonnages of eighteenth-century France." In Patrick Joyce, ed., *The Historical Meanings of Work*. Cambridge, 1987, pp. 31–63.

Thamer, Hans-Ulrich. "On the use and abuse of handicraft: journeyman culture and enlightened public opinion in 18th and 19th century Germany." In Steven L. Kaplan, ed., *Understanding Popular Culture*. Berlin, 1984.

*Thompson, E. P. "Time, work discipline, and industrial capitalism," *Past and Present* 38 (1967), 57.

Truant, Cynthia M. "Solidarity and symbolism among journeymen artisans: the case of the compagnonnage." *Comparative Studies in Society and History* 21 (1979), 214–26.

"'Independent and insolent': journeymen and their 'rites' in the old regime workplace." In Steven Kaplan and Cynthia Koepp, eds., *Work in France*. Ithaca, 1986.

The Rites of Labor: Brotherhoods of Compagnonnage in Old and New Regime France. Ithaca, 1994.

Whipp, Richard. "'A time to every purpose': an essay on time and work." In Patrick Joyce, ed., *The Historical Meanings of Work*. Cambridge, 1987, pp. 210–36.

Wiesner, Merry. "Wandervogels and women: journeymen's concepts of masculinity in early modern Germany." *Journal of Social History* 24:4 (1991), 767–82.

6   Communities

Around 1740 Flegel the tinsmith, a citizen of the German "home town" of Hildesheim, wanted to marry.[1] As for any master craftsman, the proper pursuit of his trade required a household supporting and surrounding his workshop. Such a domestic establishment of hearth and shop signaled to a master craftsman's customers, neighbors, and fellow guildsmen that he was industrious, trustworthy, and morally sound. He thereby could expect to be considered a worthy member of the overlapping communities that gave the artisan his status and his life its meaning and security – family, neighborhood, town, and above all, guild. But when Flegel went to his guild officers to register his intention to marry his chosen bride, the daughter of a fellow citizen named Helmsen, he was barred from doing so on the grounds of indecency. Flegel's future father-in-law, the officers discovered, had been born illegitimately, and Flegel's guild demanded that all masters and their wives prove their descent from four sexually irreproachable grandparents. Flegel's bride, despite the fact that her father had been legitimized after his birth by territorial law, could not do this, and so she was too impure to belong, by way of her future husband, to the tinsmith community.

Not to be deterred, Flegel married her anyway, and promptly found himself barred from his guild's meetings and ceremonial functions. Flegel demanded from the local authorities that they force the guild to recognize his marriage and allow him to take his rightful place in the guild as one of its masters. The town council turned a deaf ear to Flegel's entreaties for three years, but when Flegel appealed to the territorial lord of Hildesheim, the bishop, who ruled in his favor, the town council caved in and ordered the guild to convene a meeting of masters to readmit Flegel and recognize his marriage. On the appointed day, however, not one master showed up, and in the teeth of another order from the council to convene and to admit Flegel, all the officers of the guild resigned.

[1] Mack Walker, *German Home Towns: Community, State, and General Estate, 1648–1871* (Ithaca, 1971), pp. 73–6.

Flegel had been cast from his guild community because, as Mack Walker points out, "he had defied the procedures upon which community peace was founded." Nor were the tinsmiths the first of Hildesheim's guildsmen to bar unseemly masters from their communities. The master shoemakers had cast from their ranks a fellow master whose marriage plans concerned a socially inferior piper's daughter. The master tailors did likewise to a fellow craftsman whose mother's reputation was suspect, and the smiths did the same to a master who tried to register a miller's daughter as his wife. Marriage was a matter of honor for these guildsmen, and this community took as one of its sacrosanct rules of membership the possession of *Ehrbarkeit*, or honorable status, which was rooted in a common understanding of, again in Walker's words, "domestic, civic, and economic orderliness." These morally upright master craftsmen also assumed that these irreplaceable qualities were irreparably damaged by "the promiscuity and irresponsibility implied by illegitimate birth." This sense of honorable status, then, was linked to a sense of purity, and marital purity was a "caste mark" that guildsmen embraced to distinguish themselves from their social inferiors. This fervid preoccupation with morality and its link to status and social exclusiveness apparently was accentuated in the "home towns" more than ever in the second half of the seventeenth century and into the eighteenth. In the degree of their moral intensity and overriding preoccupation with the purity of the guild community, German "home townsmen" were probably an extreme example among the master craftsmen of Europe, but the general concern to define communities and to invest a great deal in the need to belong to them was, as we will see, typical of artisans, master and journeyman, all across Europe.

The artisan experience, even among sedentary masters, was a shifting world marked by ephemeral alliances alongside more lasting and permanent bonds, as well as overlap and competition between loyalties and solidarities. As Steven Kaplan has written, guildsmen had a "split personality." On the one hand, all the masters were bound by an oath to the guild which made them brothers of one another and spiritual sons of the guild's patron saint, and as such they were "supposed to feel a sense of unity and solidarity." On the other hand, however, such brotherliness was seriously undermined by strife between masters within the guild, often, as we have seen, flaring up in disputes over guild governance, with the lesser masters bristling "under the yoke of leaders who treated them as inferiors and/or dependents."[2] Paradoxically, then, the dynamism of the social interaction of artisans destabilized communities which were

---

[2] Steven L. Kaplan, "The character and implication of strife among the masters inside the guilds of eighteenth-century Paris," *Journal of Social History* 19 (1986), 641.

nonetheless necessary. This tension between the fissures that continually threatened to rend the bonds of community and the desire of craftsmen to construct, usually with great attention to ritual and ceremony, bonds of loyalty and solidarity underlies the various nodes of community in artisan lives that we will explore in this chapter – guilds, craft fellowships, the organs of spiritual brotherhood, neighborhood, and family.

Lines of solidarities and counter-solidarities crisscrossed through the artisan world of master and journeyman, a craftsman's daily existence being full of moments of alliance and rupture. Sociabilities were dynamic, moving, unstable and often short lived, stitched together in networks that were constantly being constructed, renewed, and dissolved.

Community rests on mutual awareness of its members of belonging or not, of inclusion and exclusion, of insider and outsider, and such membership is secured by a conformity to agreed upon, unwritten, and often tacit rules. Members simply were expected to know the unspoken rules, and to abide by the norms and constraints they imposed. To violate was to exclude, as the unfortunate Flegel discovered. Community, of course, is embodied in institutions and takes shape through often highly ritualized practices that are further structured by being situated in particular places and occurring at specified times.

Guilds and craft fellowships

Given the emphasis on guilds in most scholarship on artisans, it should not be surprising that historians have for years suggested that artisan identity and sense of belonging to a community were defined by guild membership. No doubt this is true, in part, but we must bear in mind two things: first, that the guild was not the only node of community for artisans, as has so often been assumed, and second, that we ought not be overly hasty in assuming that guild identity was another way of saying that artisan identity was work based. In fact, guild membership signaled social, and sometimes political, status and thus a sense of place and belonging in society, and not just a means of earning a living.

Guilds or corporations everywhere were described juridically as a social rank united by oath in order to become, as it was said in France, "a body, a confraternity, and a community." To be a "body" implied a deep, indissoluble bond among members; to be a "confraternity" brought members together in spiritual brotherhood; and to be "a community" conveyed a sense of belonging to a distinct group in society and a loyalty to that group measured against other categories of the population. It was through membership in a corporation that an artisan acquired social rank, or, as the French called it, *état*, which in turn fixed the person's place in the hierarchical social order and defined his privileges, duties, and, above all, his dignity. Charles Loyseau, that great theorist of social order and ordering of the early seventeenth century, spoke for all Europeans when he defined one's *état* as "'the dignity and the quality' that was 'the most stable and the most inseparable from a man.'"[3] This sense of status was enshrined in the corporate idiom which encouraged solidarity *within* a corps, but also created sharp boundaries *between* corps, and between corps and the undifferentiated mass of the noncorporate population. The idiom also arranged all of this hierarchically.

Of course, the corporate idiom expressed an ideal of amicable social interaction and unquestioned loyalty and solidarity within the body. Lived experience did not, could not, measure up to this ideal, and so it is hardly surprising to find guilds and corporations shot through with tensions and riven by fissures that continually threatened to give the lie to the corporate idiom. All of the sites where guildsmen gathered – the workshop, the tavern, guild assemblies, to mention a few – were fields of power relations and thus sites where alliances were constantly being fractured, but also reinforced. The corporate idiom was a static construct and was valued because of its power of hierarchical positioning; but it was continually destabilized by the shifting vagaries of everyday social life. The result was an unsettling, even paradoxical tension at the heart of artisan identity. It is this tension which gave rise, as we will see, to the pronounced, almost exaggerated, rituals and ceremonies which visibly defined the communities which were such important anchors of stability to people immersed in a dynamic world of ephemeral and often contentious interaction.

The seventeenth-century Lillois weaver Pierre-Ignace Chavatte reflects this paradoxical tension. In his remarkable journal he reveals a deep sense of dignity for being a member of his guild and possessed a sense of *esprit de corps* that bound him to his fellows. Clearly the ideal of the corporate idiom beat deeply in this man's breast, and permeated his sense of social rank and sense of honor. Equally clearly, his sense of belonging to the community of *sayetteurs* was defined in large measure by rigorous distinction from others in the social firmament, above all the dependent wage-workers (the *salariés*) and the corps of *bourgeteurs*, those weavers who were perilously similar to the *sayetteurs* in the kind of weaving they did. In Chavatte's mind, wage-workers and *bourgeteurs* were "beneath" him, the inferiority of the former stemming from their

---

[3] Quoted in William Sewell Jr., *Work and Revolution in France: The Language of Labor from the Old Regime to 1848* (Princeton, 1980), p. 35.

dependent, unincorporated status. The inferior status of both groups derived from their inferior *stil*, a word Chavatte uses repeatedly to describe not just his skill as an artisan, but more profoundly and sweepingly, a way of life. Chavatte acted out on the public stage a behavior that said who he was, a public identity which he expressed through the communities to which he belonged.

Chavatte shows us very clearly that the corporate idiom, with its function of social placement and emphasis on dignity, was not just a juridical ideal confined to the world of the jurists and political authorities. But Chavatte also shows us in his journal that such neat distinctions were undermined and confounded by powerful forces at work in artisan lives. Chavatte prided himself on his independent status; juridically, as a master craftsman, he may have been independent, but economically he was not. He had no workshop of his own, employed no workers, and in fact, worked "under," dare we say despondently, other masters of his trade. Indeed, Chavatte's journal reveals the divisiveness among craftsmen even of the same guild that tore at the idealized fabric of solidarity of the community, and shows us how one craftsman, but so typical of countless others all across Europe, struggled to secure moorings of community in a world that constantly threatened to cut them.

The corporate idiom, aside from its importance in defining rank in a hierarchical society, had other practical uses. The emphasis on solidarity and mutuality served to safeguard perceived collective interests, and especially to keep peace between brothers who all too often were necessarily immersed in competitive relationships. Guild ordinances in towns in the north of England, for example, required peaceable relations between members. The bricklayers of Chester were forbidden "to call any of the brothers worse than his proper name in wrath or anger," while their colleagues in Newcastle fined any member 6 shillings 8 pence "who shall at any time scandalise, demean, vilify or otherwise abuse any other of the said company in the meeting house."[4] Similarly, in the 1330s the London carpenters agreed to "work his brother before any other."[5] Such co-operation, however, required discipline and, for those brothers who resisted it, sanction. The ultimate sanction was exclusion from the community – again, Flegel's tale shows this disciplinary tactic employed by masters in full color – but the ways of community discipline had countless variations among masters and journeymen (who, though their collective organizations were often illegal nonetheless

---

[4] Quoted in Donald Woodward, *Men at Work: Labourers and Building Craftsmen in the Towns of Northern England, 1450–1750* (Cambridge, 1995), p. 78.

[5] Quoted in R. A. Leeson, *Travelling Brothers: The Six Centuries Road from Craft Fellowship to Trade Unionism* (London, 1979), p. 25.

appropriated for their own uses and to their own end the form and spirit of corporatism) throughout the early modern period in every city in Europe.

Let us take a few illustrative examples of discipline and sanction among journeymen, a subject we will return to shortly when we explore the ceremonies and rituals of journeymen brotherhoods. Solidarity and tensions in the workshop were reflected in treatment of newcomers. In late medieval London coppersmiths examined and admitted a stranger to the trade only after he had promised to abide by the rules of the trade, to pay a set fee into the common fund for the poor or the unemployed of the trade, and finally, to demonstrate his competence in the craft. If he fulfilled these requirements he and the rest of the members of the craft swore a "covenant" which, among other things, guaranteed the newcomer employment.

Joseph Moxon wrote in 1683 in his *Mechanick Exercizes* that "every printing-house is by the custom of time out of mind, called a chappel . . . all the workmen that belong to it are members of the chappel."[6] Certainly this was true at the Plantin printing-house in Antwerp where, since the sixteenth century the "chapel" functioned to preserve a "closed-door social harmony," and where workshop rules required journeymen seeking work there to join the local chapel which involved, as with the London coppersmiths centuries before, payment of a schedule of fees, demonstration of competence, and the swearing of an oath to the community.

Once installed in the workshop, rules continued to govern the workers with an eye toward solidarity. Seventeenth-century London journeymen printers, for instance, were also required to join the "chapel," and once a member one had to agree to obey the senior compositor, called the "father of the chapel," whose job it was to maintain "good mutual work habits" in the shop. Illustrative of the emphasis on mutuality and communal solidarity, all compositors were organized into a "companionship" of three to six men which was paid collectively. Journeymen resisting these customary rules could be expelled from the chapel, and the workplace. Indeed, most conflict in the Plantin-Moretus printing-house was not between master and journeyman, but among journeymen. Negligent workers found themselves sanctioned by their fellows in a variety of ways, but primarily by fines which were collected

---

6 Quoted in Jan Materné, "Chapel members in the workplace: tension and teamwork in the printing trades in the seventeenth and eighteenth centuries," in Catharina Lis, Jan Lucassen, and Hugo Soly, eds., *Before the Unions: Wage Earners and Collective Action in Europe, 1300–1850*, International Review of Social History 39 (1994, supplement 2), 55.

and spent collectively. The goal of punishment, however, was solidarity, for offenders were often shown mercy, the aim of discipline not being to impoverish a colleague, but to bring him back into the communal fold.

Spiritual brotherhood

Membership in guilds was obligatory in most places to practice a craft legally, and perhaps the lack of choice (as well as the competition for markets and labor that so many masters had to engage in with their fellows) threw men together in a collectivity not ideally suited to the demands of solidarity. And most likely this is why another institution of association and brotherhood emerged and developed almost indistinguishably from the guild, the craft confraternity. Confraternities in general were religious sodalities comprised, as Richard Mackenny writes, of "voluntary groups of laymen who met together at regular intervals to do pious and charitable works in honour of a patron saint."[7] Historically they appeared on the scene before the craft guilds and flowered everywhere thereafter. For example, craft sodality among shoemakers existed in Barcelona already in 1218, while the shoemaker guild only made its appearance late in that century. Even very small towns were honeycombed with confraternities. In the fourteenth century, for instance, the small English town of Bodmin already had forty. In Venice, though virtually all trade guilds (*arti*) had confraternities (*scuole*) officially attached to them by the fourteenth century, there were other sodalities (*scuole piccole*) that were not affiliated with guilds but counted guildsmen from different trades among their members. These *scuole* cut across parish and class lines, although their membership decidedly did not include the disreputable wage-laborers or beggars. The four *scuole piccole* of S. Anna, Celestina, S. Cris. and Apostoli between 1337 and 1520 drew their membership from over seventy parishes, and among the 1,269 brothers of the *scuola piccola* of Celestina over the same period 132 nobles rubbed shoulders with 123 textile craftsmen, 41 merchants, and 81 artisans in assorted luxury crafts.

All across Europe in the fourteenth and fifteenth centuries the number of guilds and confraternities – craft and otherwise – expanded. Likewise everywhere guilds and craft confraternities became officially affiliated. No doubt this flowering had something to do with the expansion and diversification of the artisanry, and the accelerated mobility of many craftsmen. This, in turn, meant that, as Gervase Rosser points out, "the single most pressing earthly concern of every medieval artisan

---

[7] Richard Mackenny, *Tradesmen and Traders: The World of Guilds in Venice and Europe, 1250–1650* (Totewa, 1987) p. 44.

was the establishment of a good personal reputation," an imperative born of the intensified struggle to gain a foothold in the medieval urban environment that mobility brought in its train.[8] Establishing trust, and thereby personal credit, was vital for successful entry into the cherished world of respectability and the social status that went with it, and membership in confraternities was one way to establish the social connections that would provide these.

It is no accident that the vocabulary employed by confraternities (and by guilds) emphasized the qualities of family, brotherhood, friendship, peace, charity, and above all trust, reputation, honor, honesty, and fairness. Indeed, craft confraternities and guilds as early as the thirteenth century in Italy and everywhere thereafter will be described in this vocabulary. Confraternities stood at the intersection of economic and religious life. Moreover, guildsmen assumed that honor had a religious side, and worshipping in the guild's chapel in the church, as Kaplan reminds us about eighteenth-century Parisian artisans, "was no less a guarantee of masterly character than success in business."[9] By serving as an association of individuals through which trust, reputation, and salvation could be simultaneously pursued, the confraternity was the conscience of the guild, shoring up the solidarity that countervailing tensions within the guild continually challenged.

Guilds and craft confraternities effectively merged in the high Middle Ages and would remain joined to the end of the eighteenth century. Everywhere, in the late Middle Ages craft confraternities and guilds increased in number and overlapped, with the statutes of each supporting the other, with the same masters dominating both. Guild statutes everywhere from then on usually make stipulations about affiliated confraternities, including the dues owed by current masters, and fees paid by new ones. Often the officers of the guild administered the confraternity, frequently not even separating the account books. For example, the statutes of the confraternity of the hosiers of Marseilles required that masters could only give work to journeymen who had sworn to obey its rules and embraced the devotional expectations of the brotherhood, while the guild statutes stipulated the payment of dues to the confraternity. The statutes of the cobblers' confraternity of Aix-en-Provence in the fifteenth century required that any master or journeyman who was a thief or a *fraudeur* be "expelled and chased from this craft," recalling the importance of honor and reputation as a part of the

---

[8] Gervase Rosser, "Crafts, guilds and the regulation of work in the medieval town," *Past and Present* 154 (1997), 9.

[9] Steven Kaplan, "The luxury guilds in Paris in the eighteenth century," *Francia* 9 (1981).

ethic of solidarity that these bodies pronounced. Similarly, in Barcelona between 1500 and 1650 about a hundred trades formed confraternities, and, again there was an indistinguishable administrative overlap between guild and confraternity. Four guild officers (called *promens*) presided over both, and confraternal dues were spent not just on devotion and charity, but also on legal expenses incurred by the guild in its litigation over trade privileges. Even during the Enlightenment, the new statutes of the Parisian bakers' guild in 1719 required new masters to pay 12 *livres* to the confraternity during their reception ceremony, as well as provide a 3-pound candle in honor of their patron Saint Lazare. Current members had to pay 45 *sous* in annual dues to the confraternity.

Craft confraternities, like all religious sodalities, were about salvation as well as solidarity, or, rather, melded the two values inextricably into one. Stipulations of mutual aid for living members and their families and prayers and masses for the souls of dead colleagues appear in documents establishing craft confraternities or in contracts with the clergy for performance of such functions. In 1560 the artisans of the confraternity of Saint Honoré in Dijon, for instance, paid the Jacobins for services "for the . . . salvation of the souls of the said master pastrycooks and bakers as well as for all the brothers and sisters of the confraternity of the said Saint Honoré, living and dead." The same sense of devotion and solidarity is evident in a contract drawn up by Dijon's locksmiths in 1651 for masses to be said "in order to pray to God for the whole *corps* of the said trade, and for the salvation of the souls of their deceased predecessors as well as for those and their wives who will die hereafter."[10]

Dispensing charity brought devotion and solidarity together, too, for it fulfilled the supreme theological virtue of the late Middle Ages, charity, as well as providing mutual aid to brethren, and when directed toward needy guildsmen and their families, it also proclaimed solidarity among brothers. By excluding nonguildsmen and above all wage-workers, even those who worked in the craft, mutual aid also defined boundaries of a community and announced a claim to a certain place in the social hierarchy. Many craft confraternities had hospitals and thus institutionally dispensed charity to brothers and their dependents or survivors. Venetian tailors, silk throwsters, painters, and bakers all maintained such establishments in the fifteenth century. In 1500 the tailors' hospital sheltered seventeen members and their families. Similarly, craft confraternities in sixteenth-century Seville had their own hospitals to help their poor and infirm, including widows and orphans. Such institutions,

---

[10] James R. Farr, *Hands of Honor: Artisans and Their World in Dijon, 1550–1650* (Ithaca, 1988), p. 243.

like their counterparts in Strasbourg, Lille, or Augsburg, often explicitly excluded wage laborers. The expenditures of eighteenth-century Parisian craft confraternities show that time had not dulled the charitable fervor, as large sums on subsistence for the poor and needy continued to be doled out. The cabinet-makers, for instance, came up with 7,200 *livres* from its members to be spent toward the construction of four civic hospitals in 1787 – a significant sum, given that in 1778 the guild's total income was 13,253 *livres*.[11]

Many confraternities spent half, perhaps more, of their revenues on charity for fellow members. In 1616 the master masons, carpenters, roofers, and plasterers of Dijon who had established a new confraternity pledged to set aside half their dues "to the profit of the poor of their . . . trades." In 1482 the York carpenters "ordained that if any of the [guild] fraternity fall to poverty, so that they may not work, or happen to be blind, or to lose their goods by unhap of the world, then the foresaid brotherhood [shall] give them 4 pence every week, as long as they live, by way of alms . . ." In 1619 the joiners of Chester voted to give alms to a destitute brother, and in 1637 the smiths of the same town gave 8 shillings "to the widows of our company."[12]

What percentage of the brotherhood's treasury such charitable expenditures represent, unfortunately, we have no way of knowing, but such expenses were not the only drain on fraternity treasuries. Upkeep and decoration of the brotherhood's chapel could draw down guild or confraternal reserves, too. In sixteenth-century Venice part of guild dues were dedicated to devotional expenditures like paying for candles burning before the shrine of the guild's patron saint, or, as the guild of the caulkers did in 1454, payment to the monastery of San Stefano for an altar and a tomb in the church. A year later the same guildsmen were assessed a special fee to pay for the construction of the altar and decorating its chapel. By 1578 this chapel counted among its sacred objects a variety of images fashioned in gilded silver and studded with precious stones. Ceremonial pomp accompanied decorative splendor, all geared toward honoring God, the guild, and its members. After 1461 among the duties of the chief guild official (the *gastaldo*) was to summon all the guildsmen to mass in their resplendent chapel, and to hire (again, paid from guild fees) trumpeters and pipers to glorify in music the celebration of that mass. Clearly a great deal of money collected by the guild from its members was spent on religious services and decorative and devotional objects.

[11] Kaplan, 265, 268.
[12] Donald Woodward, *Men at Work: Labourers and Building Craftsmen in the Towns of Northern England, 1450–1750* (Cambridge, 1995), p. 82.

As in Venice hundreds of years before, confraternities, like that of the Parisian goldsmiths in 1771, continued to spend considerable sums on religious services and sacred objects. These guildsmen spent 1,261 *livres* on salaries for clergy, choirmaster, and choirboys, and kept in the guild office, as Kaplan discovered, "two reliquaries of their patron Saint Eloy, two large silver images of the saint, and chandeliers decorated with his image."[13]

Before the late sixteenth century the church had played almost no official role in confraternities of any kind, but after the Council of Trent this changes in the Catholic parts of Europe. As part of the attempt of the institutional Church to bring behavior into obedience to Rome in Catholic lands, confraternities were to be more closely tied to parishes and thereby brought under episcopal surveillance and control. After 1604, in fact, confraternities had to have episcopal approval for their existence, without which the Church declared they had no salvatory effect and hence no spiritual function.

Venice saw its *scuole piccole* more closely tied to parishes in the post-Trent second half of the sixteenth century, and after 1591 they were subject to episcopal visitation. The Counter-Reformation church also tried to force parochialism on craft guilds, and if guilds resisted, which they did at times, they found themselves investigated by the Inquisition. We find the same offensive in sixteenth-century Florence. Here, too, craft confraternities were increasingly tied to parishes, but, as in Venice and elsewhere, other institutions of collective devotion were encouraged and thereby competed for the spiritual allegiances of artisans. A cult of the Eucharist was encouraged by the Church (emphasizing collective membership in yet another corps, the spiritual body of Christ), the success of this venture evidenced by the growth of eucharistic brotherhoods, above all the confraternities of the Holy Sacrament. In Florence after 1530 twenty-four new sacramental confraternities were quickly founded, counting many artisans in their ranks. In Venice the confraternities of the Holy Sacrament (*scuole del Santissimo Sacramento*), which were comprised almost exclusively of artisans and were parish based, multiplied rapidly as well. By 1581 one-third of Venice's nearly sixty parishes had such an institution. These confraternities were dedicated to intensifying devotion to the sacraments, and woe to the artisan who did not show reverence to a procession of this confraternity which carried the body of Christ through the streets. It was precisely such irreverence that landed a certain Venetian jeweler named Girolamo before the Inquisition in 1548 for heresy, for he and his workers threw their hats on

13 Kaplan, 267–8.

the floor and turned their backs on the procession as Christ's body passed the shop.

In Spain the same trends toward confraternal growth and diversification are visible, as medieval brotherhoods were joined by new ones whose foundations were encouraged by the reforming Catholic Church. Valladolid, for example, a town of 30,000 souls, had about a hundred confraternities, while Toledo had 143 for 60,000. In Barcelona in 1519 we find thirty craft and professional confraternities, a number which grew to fifty-one by 1588 and, when added to the number of new devotional brotherhoods, brought the total to around eighty. In Zamora in 1400 there were about ten confraternities, but vigorous growth in the late fifteenth century and throughout the sixteenth pushed the number to 150 by 1600, when the population of the town still hovered below 10,000. There confraternal membership cut across occupational lines. In 1400 the confraternity of Santa Catalina included among its brothers a blanket-maker, a blacksmith, a sculptor, a tanner, a woolcomber, a carpenter, and a weaver. That of Nuestra Señora de Yermo counted among its seventy-eight members admitted in 1595 three coppersmiths, five weavers, five woolcarders, two fullers, a carpenter, a shoemaker, and a locksmith. All confraternities were occupationally heterogeneous, and even socially, as these brotherhoods also embraced surgeons, servants, silkmercers, teachers, and even a washerwoman.

In France, too, the seventeenth-century Catholic Church encouraged the formation of confraternities and sought to control them through parishes, and as in all other parts of Catholic Europe, their ranks swelled, including many artisans, although increasingly the craftsmen in these sodalities were just masters. In Dijon the Confrérie des Trespasses in the parish church Saint Jean had 49 active members in 1590, but had bulged to 251 by 1629, while the Confrérie des Rois in the parish church of Saint Michel mushroomed from 99 brothers and sisters in 1583 to 492 by 1650. Many of the new members were master artisans.

Despite the competition of alternative religious sodalities, craft confraternities continued to thrive, especially in the seventeenth century when, in fact, some, like that of the locksmiths of Dijon, were reestablished. The corporate nature of craft confraternities had long been apparent, and no doubt shored up guild solidarity, but many craft confraternities, like the new ones sponsored by the Counter-Reformation Church, had long provided spiritual and social bonds that transcended guild boundaries. This was true in large cities as well as small towns. In the fifteenth century 65 percent of the members of the London tailors' fraternity of St. John the Baptist were not tailors, while the weavers of Coventry admitted artisans of other crafts as "love brethren" to their confraternity of Saint Osburga. In 1596 in Piera in Catalonia a confraternity dedicated to Saints Jacinto and Lucia was founded for tailors, clothiers, shoemakers "and many other individuals," while the year before in Sabadell one dedicated to Saints Joseph, Eulàlia, Eloi, and Crespi had been established for shoemakers, carpenters, and smiths. In Dijon, the drapers, fullers, and dyers all belonged to the confraternity of Saint Trinité, the sword-polishers and cutlers shared that of Saint-Jean Baptiste, while, as we have seen, the master masons, carpenters, roofers, and plasterers, contending that their crafts depended upon "une mesme société," sought to establish a confraternity in 1616 to "solemnize the holy days of Saint Joseph and of the Four Crowns," patrons of their crafts "since time immemorial."[14]

Although in late medieval France masters and journeymen both belonged to the same craft confraternities (for example, the tailors, doublet-makers, cobblers, and windowpane-makers of Paris), increasingly from the fourteenth century journeymen began forming their own (as among the Parisian forge-operators, roofers, and shoemakers), complete with ceremonies that betray a sense among them that they belonged to an *état* distinct from the masters above them and the wage-workers below. Journeyman confraternities existed in the netherworld of clandestinity and quasi-legality. As long as their functions were strictly spiritual they were accepted, grudgingly, by the authorities, but gatherings of journeymen for whatever purpose always met with suspicion. As early as the 1320s the Florentine commune banned journeymen from making "constitutions or statutes . . . within the guise of a fraternity or otherwise, and under the pretext or cover of religion, or of providing for funerals or religious offerings . . . except by special license of the consuls of that [officially organized] craft under whose authority they stand."[15] In 1365 in Freiburg the master clothworkers complained to the authorities that journeymen weavers and woolbeaters were gathering in seditious meetings under the cloak of religious confraternity. When Charles V suspected in 1525 that journeymen confraternities were actually cells of sedition, he prohibited them in the Holy Roman empire. In 1539 his royal rival Francis I of France followed suit for his kingdom. Both were ineffective, and journeymen confraternities in Spain, Catholic Germany, France, and probably elsewhere increased in number in the later sixteenth century and throughout the seventeenth.

The associational brotherhood of confraternities, no less than any other institution of solidarity in the craft world, was additionally secured through festive celebration. Most confraternities held an annual festival

---

[14] Farr, p. 244.   [15] Quoted in Rosser, 25.

on their patron saint's day, beginning with a mass that all members were expected to attend, and then continuing with the secular communion of feasting and drinking. Not surprisingly from the late sixteenth century on, increasingly in the eyes of reforming authorities intent on tightening the screws of moral discipline and public order, such celebrations easily and apparently often became bouts of extensive and excessive consumption. Such bacchanalian celebrations were typical of confraternal festivals since the Middle Ages, but what changed in the sixteenth century was the attitude of the authorities toward them. Increasingly the proponents of the new morality, both clerical and lay, saw in these events opportunities to indulge in pleasures of the flesh and violence, offensive behavior in and of itself, but all the more heinous when it occurred on holy days. A proclamation by the town council of Dijon in 1600 is typical in its content and sweep:

The confraternities . . . of the *arts et métiers* . . . [were] introduced to honor God and the patron saints . . . with the intention of good works . . . [However], for some years, instead of the honor and glory of God and the said saints only things to the contrary have been produced . . . .Derisions and insolent behavior like games of dice, blanques, quilles, cards, and banquets . . . [lead to] such blasphemy. . . and excessive expenses that God is greatly offended . . .[16]

Dijon's chief police official went on to rail against the artisans who, on their festival days, dressed up in fools' costumes, with bells on their toes and tambourines in hand, and made all sorts of racket at the doors of the churches and even came into the churches with their bells and baubles "disturbing and interrupting the service of God." In the eyes of the authorities, such "willful disorder of the people" could only provoke the wrath of God and lead to disorder in the streets.

The Reformation

Martin Luther wrote in the sixteenth century that confraternities should be "snuffed out and brought to an end." In kingdoms and cities where Protestantism took hold and devotion was generally centered in the home and the parish church, confraternities were indeed disbanded. With them went the festive celebration of saints' days and the attendant processions, and if the cycle of religious festivals was not entirely eliminated, it was certainly reduced. What this meant was that community spirit was shifted on to other ground.

In Protestant lands guilds either absorbed the functions of the pre-Reformation confraternities (charity may no longer have been inspired

---

[16] Farr, p. 247.

by the doctrine of good works, but aid to disadvantaged brothers and their dependents continued to be embraced by guilds), or secularized clubs emerged with similar social welfare functions. Such clubs increased in popularity in the Dutch Republic and in Restoration England, especially after 1700. Benefit or "box" clubs were quite common among craftsmen in these Protestant countries. The woolcombers of Coggeshall, for example, established one in the 1680s "for the help of such as may be sickness, lameness, or the want of work," while their brethren in Wellington and Tiverton had set one up by the mid-eighteenth century for "the support [of] decayed brethern of the trade."[17] Entrance fees and dues to these "voluntary" societies were kept high enough to restrict membership and by excluding the poorer sort. Monthly meetings were often convened in the nearby alehouse, which also often had special clubrooms.

Such clubs were not just for the care of the sick, as the Norwich poem called "The Weaver," which was popular around 1720, testifies: "Twas then I could to jovial clubs repair,/ and pass my evenings pleasurably there/with boon companions talk of mutual trade/and spend the wagers we before had laid."[18] In eighteenth-century Birmingham hundreds of artisan clubs existed, and nor were they all just for care of the sick. Many were also lottery clubs where dues were paid into a common purse, and when the accumulated capital reached a certain amount, a drawing was held and a sum was paid out to a winner to build a house, or to use in his business.

Where Catholic theology taught that through certain ceremonies (notably the mass) one became a part of the mystical body of Christ, in practice the sense of earthly belonging was most visibly expressed in membership and practices of various religious sodalities and processions. For Protestants, the options were different, but many nonetheless answered the call and flocked to the various standards of the Reformed religions forming a select community of "saints." As many historians have demonstrated, the ranks of the new faithful were especially crowded with artisans. In French cities like Montpellier, Toulouse, Rouen, Dijon, Lyons, and Lille, as well as in the cities of Germany, historians have documented that artisans were attracted to Protestantism in numbers disproportionate to their representation in the population as a whole.

There is less agreement about the reasons for the attraction. Historians of northern French towns like Amiens or Lille make a convincing case that a correlation exists between proletarianization and impoverishment

[17] Peter Clark, *The English Alehouse: A Social History, 1200–1830* (London, 1983), p. 234.
[18] Ibid., p. 235.

and the willingness to embrace the new faith as a form of protest. Between the 1540s and the 1560s not all types of artisans in these towns were drawn to the Protestant faith. The craftsmen most attracted to it were weavers of light cloth and woolcombers, trades that counted many wage-workers in their ranks who were suffering a deterioration of their economic status.

The proletarianization thesis does not apply everywhere, however. In fact, elsewhere there is a strong correlation between Protestantism and relatively *high* levels of wealth, status, "art," and education (or at least literacy). The Evangelical, Lutheran, and Calvinist teachings of an unmediated relationship with God could and did appeal to many an artisan's cherished sense of independence. The sixteenth century saw a shift in the hierarchical structure of the city, and with the increasing vilification of manual labor and the dissociating of the nobility and elite urban dwellers from the artisanry, artisans were probably more receptive to a faith that granted them a sense of dignity and independence. It is certainly no accident that in most places the artisan trades most attracted to Protestantism – goldsmithing, printing, cabinet-making, to name the most notable – were also the ones artisans held to be the most "artful" and the least associated with the manual aspects of production.

The journeymen printers of Lyons studied by Natalie Davis illustrate these points exceptionally well. In a justly famous article she showed that these journeymen were attracted to the new faith, and grafted membership in its community on to a secular brotherhood that had previously been formed as an institution of opposition to the masters of their craft. Already formed in a solidary community, the company of Griffarins, these journeymen found appealing a faith that provided congregational participation. Moreover, a liturgy in the vernacular was especially accessible to this quite literate group. Thus a highly self-confident group of young men proud of their skills and arrayed in militant disobedience against the immediate authority of their world, the masters, found a faith that squared with their desires.

At least during the 1550s. In the 1560s, however, the informal religious movement that they had embraced became the formal Reformed Church of Lyons, and the increasing institutionalization and discipline that this entailed rubbed these journeymen the wrong way. Now they were denied an administrative role in the church, and found the Consistory disciplining them for the ceremonies and ritual practices which defined their sense of belonging in the company. Whereas during the 1550s the solidarity of the company and the experience of the new faith pulled in the same direction and reinforced one another, in the

1560s they came apart and worked against one another. Festive and excessive eating and drinking together secured the bonds of community, but they were also morally repugnant to the leaders of the Reformed Church. Initiation ceremonies "in which godfathers poured water and wine on the journeyman's head and gave him a new and usually coarse name, and the profane song in which the name of the Lord began and the name of the Holy Ghost ended each verse,"[19] were no less about bonding a community, but from the perspective of the godly they were sacrilegious and blasphemous. To make matters even worse, the Consistory inveighed against journeymen strikes, and held out the threat of excommunication and thus the denial of salvation to journeymen who dared square off against their masters in such a way. So, when forced to choose between communities, that of the Griffarins and that of the saints, what did the journeymen do? They opted for the Griffarins, and returned to the other religious community (which had said nothing of a connection between strikes and denial of salvation), the Catholic Church.

Historians have long focused their attention on France and Germany when discussing the appeal of Protestantism in the sixteenth century, but we find the patterns revealed there in more surprising locales. In the 1540s, for example, evangelical ideas were penetrating the artisan community of Venice, and as elsewhere, the largest numbers of those accused of heresy and brought before the Inquisition in the sixteenth century were craftsmen (292 of 676). Moreover, proportional to the general population, evangelical ideas found their most fertile ground among artisans in its elite trades, above all, as John Martin has demonstrated, among the silkweavers, the "traditional aristocrats" of the Venetian manufacturing world. These adherents to a new faith were also adhering to a new community, and were perceived by their neighbors according to these communal attributes. When a dozen or so evangelical artisans gathered for religious discussions now in one of their workshops, now in another, neighbors, who were fully aware of these not so secret meetings, tellingly referred to them as a sort of confraternity, a *scuole di lutherani*.

As in every city of Europe, the highly mobile world of the street and the workplace provided the conditions for spreading evangelical ideas, and this was certainly evident in Venice. Of the 327 persons whose origins we know that were accused of heresy by the Inquisition in the sixteenth century there, 78 percent came from beyond the lagoons. Perhaps surprisingly, heretical artisans were quite often tolerated, if not

[19] Natalie Z. Davis, "Strikes and salvation in Lyon," in *Society and Culture in Early Modern France* (Stanford, 1975), 14.

entirely liked by their Catholic fellows, at least until the late 1560s. This tolerance permitted the construction of cells of evangelical communities in Venice, shop and family based, which assembled for readings of the Gospels and prayers, and performed "counter-rituals" to the Catholic ones, even singing Protestant litanies behind closed doors in their shops while Catholic religious processions were staged just outside. To be sure, Venetian evangelists were sometimes ignored, sometimes reproved by fellow workers or neighbors, but they were seldom reported to the authorities. For example, in 1561 Nicolò da Cherso, a master ropemaker at the Arsenal, and his fellow workers were fed up with fellow worker Isepo Zanco preaching his heretical ideas to them, but they did not report him to the Inquisition. Instead, as Cherso said, "we kept him out of our docks, and even if he did come by once in a while, we wouldn't put up with him talking about [his religious] ideas."[20]

War, disease, and the counter-offensive of the post-Tridentine Catholic Reformation in the late 1560s and 1570s made Venice a much more dangerous place for evangelicals, and the official intolerance seems to have been matched by an increasingly less tolerant populace. Still, historians are just beginning to understand the complexity of religious belief and relative tolerance or intolerance, how faith in some situations can lead to murderous rage against others who believe differently, yet in other contexts men and women of rival faiths can peaceably co-exist, even intermarry. Recently historians have closely examined biconfessional communities and attempted to untangle lines of solidarity that run across and often against religious faith. For example, Peter Wallace has studied the Alsatian town of Colmar across a history that saw it move from being a Catholic imperial free city (but with many Protestants tolerated within its walls), and then in 1575 become officially Protestant (with many Catholics tolerated). After 1648 an official biconfessionalism confirmed by the Peace of Westphalia was in place, and remained there with Lutherans in the ascendancy until the French takeover in 1679. For most of this period, Protestants comprised a two-thirds majority of the populace, but regardless of which faith was politically ascendant, always all guilds and all neighborhoods were confessionally mixed, with membership in a particular religious community only one site of solidarity among many.[21]

---

[20] John Martin, *Venice's Hidden Enemies: Italian Heretics in a Renaissance City* (Berkeley, 1993), p. 65.

[21] Peter Wallace, *Communities and Conflict in Early Modern Colmar, 1575–1730* (Atlantic Highlands, 1994).

Neighborhood

Another site of community was neighborhood, and like guild, fraternity, or faith, brought together a consciousness of familiarity and a sense of belonging. Neighbors packed onto medieval and early modern streets. The neighborhood was defined by sight and sound, and extended as far as one could see or hear from the shop or house, including the street in front and the courtyard in back. Most streets were short and crooked, so the extent of the visible and audible was scarcely more than 50 yards in any direction. But within these confines dozens of peering eyes filled the windows and doorways, and multitudes of ears strained at walls to monitor the space. Artisans held a deep concern for the opinions of their neighbors, for neighborhoods no less than any other form of community was built upon inclusion and exclusion and awareness of informal and unspoken rules dictating acceptable behavior. Reputations were continually made and destroyed, and respectability had to be reestablished every day. An artisan's identity, both his self-image and the inseparable image others had of him, was closely tied to his neighborhood. Craftsmen established strong relationships with neighbors, both friendly and competitive. In this intensely public arena where interdependence and vulnerability were facts of life, individuals were extremely sensitive to neighborly judgment of their actions. The bonds between neighbors could be as tight as that of kin, faith, or craft, but there was also great potential for enmity in proximity.

Because neighbors were highly interdependent, they were continually vulnerable to one another. Disputes over any number of things could erupt, from conflict over common resources, to business partnerships (neighbors were often of the same craft and at times partners in business), to provision of credit and collection of debt. Indeed, it seems that much conflict between neighbors came from a violation of expected bonds of sociability. Recognizing the potential for and extent of conflict between neighbors is therefore important, but we must also appreciate how crucial the neighborhood was as an instrument for social control. Mutual obligations knit neighbors together and often prompted them to act collectively in defense of common interests. The loyalty, solidarity, and cohesiveness of artisan neighbors took very visible shapes, most notably in peacekeeping and providing aid in time of crisis.

Good neighborliness was valued everywhere. In Ghent as early as the thirteenth century we even find neighborhood associations called *gebuurten* (which were entirely independent of guilds or confraternities).[22] Members of these institutions usually came from just one street, or perhaps only a part of one and maybe some adjoining alleys. Whatever their size, their numbers grew, accelerating especially from the fifteenth century. By 1777 there were 211 of them in Ghent, each one averaging forty-five to fifty households, many of them artisanal. Through these organizations neighbors were called upon to fight fires, organize the night watch, and put on festivals and funerals. All adults were automatically members, paying dues to a common treasury, and meeting regularly in assemblies convened by a democratically elected dean. Neighbors here as everywhere, in good Christian fashion, were expected to live "in peace, love and friendship."

Peace between neighbors was a valued, and indeed Christian, ideal that artisans seem to have taken to heart. In France, when artisans sought admission to mastership the authorities inquired into the prospective master's *vie et mœurs* (way of life and values) often calling upon neighbors to give testimony. Depositions are full of accolades from neighbors about so and so being a "peaceable man." Of course, not all neighbors were peaceful, but when fights did occur in a neighborhood, neighbors were expected to "make peace" as soon as possible, and they responded in bunches when fights broke out. In 1643 in Dijon, for example, the son of a master plasterer named Léonard Guillaumot knocked down another master plasterer with a stone but was prevented from braining him "by all the neighbors running there." Indeed, neighbors often seem to be ready on the spot to prevent violence. In 1642 again in Dijon a journeyman tailor reported that a coppersmith's daughter was spared harm from a group of boys attacking her because "at the same instance her neighbors ran there" to intervene. A year later tailor Claude Lorrain, holding an ax in his hand, charged pastrycook François Jonas, but before he could land a blow, the weapon was ripped from his hand by another artisan neighbor.

Neighbors could unite for other reasons, too. In eighteenth-century Paris neighborhoods of artisans and others could come together against the authorities. In 1772, for example, the *jurés* lutemakers came into the Enclos Saint-Martin-des-Champs to seize some violins in the shop of a tailor who obviously had made them illicitly. Once the *jurés* were inside the courtyard, the neighbors closed the gate behind them, and having trapped them began to threaten them. The tumult that resulted led to the calling of the Parisian guard, three sections of which were needed to restore order.

Neighborhoods, clearly, could unite in defense of space or interest. It

22 Catharina Lis and Hugo Soly, *Disordered Lives: Eighteenth-Century Families and Their Unruly Relatives* (Cambridge, 1996).

is therefore surprising to find that such a unit could so effectively and readily mobilize when, if a couple of recent studies are indicative, most of its inhabitants had not lived there for very long. Even "permanent" residents did not stay put for long, reflecting the pronounced mobility of medieval and early modern urban populations. Take sixteenth- and seventeenth-century Dijon as an example. Half of the artisans living on the bustling rue du Bourg and on the Place du Morimont in 1556 were gone four years later, and by 1579 only 14 percent of the artisans of the rue du Bourg were still there, and only 3 percent of those of the Place du Morimont. Between 1630 and 1636 on the artisan hotbed of the rue des Forges, only 38 percent of the original inhabitants were still there in 1636, and by 1650 only 6 percent. In each of these cases artisan mobility was slightly more pronounced than that of the population as a whole.

A sample from eighteenth-century Paris confirms this pattern. Among 284 masons between 1750 and 1765, only 64 or 23 percent remained at the same address. Of course it would be hazardous and foolhardy to generalize from these examples, but they do seem to suggest a picture of substantial geographic turnover in artisan populations. Still, despite this mobility, neighborhoods remained cohesive units. Those who moved into a neighborhood and stayed a while shouldered the customary responsibilities and duties of neighbors. The data from Dijon suggest a core of residents who were more stable than a periphery of transients, but even so most neighbors could not have known their fellows on the street for very long. Perhaps it is for this reason that in an emergency those in trouble did not shout any particular name, but simply "neighbor!"

Of course, not all neighbors were artisans, and so bonds of neighborhood were forged between and among craftsmen and men and women of other walks of life. Still, the incidence of the overlap between artisan (often of the same trade), and neighbor was great. First, in most towns artisans constituted a sizable proportion of the population, usually from a quarter to a half, and habitation patterns reflect at once diffusion (artisans were spread all over town) and concentration (some trades concentrated in particular quarters). Strong correlation between space and occupation was especially marked in the medieval period, and though diffusion becomes more a characteristic of cities thereafter, we still find pockets of concentration even in the eighteenth century.

In late medieval Venice there is evidence of a correlation between workplace and residence in some trades, although certainly not all. Glassmakers, for instance, clustered on the island of Murano, and this probably encouraged trade solidarity. The same can be said of the tanners of the Giudecca. Both of these examples of concentration were probably dictated by health and safety concerns. Access to water also determined the location of some trades like fulling, dyeing, and again, tanning, as did noxious production odors or byproducts, like butchering, skinning, and again tanning. In 1248 King Ferdinand III of Castile decreed "that men of the same craft should be settled in specific areas and the streets where they resided should bear their names." In Seville, although the designated districts and streets generally continued to go by their assigned names, already in the 1300s craftsmen were setting up shop in areas not set aside for them by statute. By the sixteenth century only the skinners were still concentrated in their designated area, although members of the same trade still tended to cluster.[23]

Similar clustering patterns are evident in sixteenth-century Rome where over half of its master artisans concentrated in four of the city's fourteen *quartieri* – Ponte, Parione, Regola, and Campo Marzo. In sixteenth- and seventeenth-century Dijon the building craftsmen concentrated in Saint Nicolas and above all Saint Michel parish. The light clothweavers of seventeenth-century Lille were no different. They clustered in the parish of Saint Sauveur, where in 1686 about 40 percent of the men who lived there were *sayetteurs*. On some Lillois streets the density was even more pronounced. Of the eighty-nine men living on the rue du Croquet, fifty-four were *sayetteurs*. Textile craftsmen dominated certain sectors of the Spanish town of Lleida at about the same time, while in the parish of St. Giles Cripplegate just outside of London in the second half of the seventeenth century, we also find weavers concentrated. Here they were joined by a clustering of shoemakers, tailors, and glovers. These four trades far outnumbered the 211 other manufacturing occupations of the parish, counting 996, 583, 566, and 371 inhabitants respectively.

Even in such a cosmopolitan and diverse city as eighteenth-century Paris, we still find certain trades concentrated geographically (although not exclusively in these locales, of course): goldsmiths in the rue and quai de Gesvres and on the Ile de la Cité, the Place Dauphine, and the quai des Orfèvres; joiners to the north of Saint Eustache; cabinetmakers at the city end of the faubourg Saint Antoine; and butchers around the Vieille Place aux Veaux and in the Grande Boucherie at the end of the rue Saint Denis.

Probably the most marked geographical concentration of certain trades in early modern Europe were the shipbuilding trades of the Venetian Arsenal. This clustering emerged with dramatic suddenness

---

[23] Ruth Pike, *Aristocrats and Traders: Sevillian Society in the Sixteenth Century* (Ithaca, 1972), pp. 135–6.

with the expansion of the state shipbuilding yards in the late fifteenth and sixteenth centuries. There had been 6,000 shipbuilders in medieval Venice, but they did not live together in an occupational enclave, but rather scattered about the city. With the emergence of the Arsenal such an enclave appeared, the core of which was the *secco marina*. Here quite a few shipbuilders even owned their own homes, property in fact donated to them by the state as yet another means to secure a stable and disciplined workforce. The gang bosses or foremen as well as the managers clumped around the Campo dell'Arsenale, which was the ceremonial and religious center for the *arsenolotti* community. It was in the Beata Madonna dell'Arsenale church where arsenal foremen were invested with their offices, giving sacred legitimacy to a new hierarchical status. The rank and file *arsenalotti* clustered in four parishes, and were the dominant occupational group in each of them, ranging from about one in nine of the *popolani* households in San Ternità, to almost one in four in San Basio and San Martino, and nearly two of five in San Pietro.

Family and kin

In a world of high mobility like that of preindustrial urban populations, so typical throughout Europe, kin and immediate family played an important role. Most urban dwellers had recent rural roots, and they became beacons for relatives migrating from countryside to town. As a result, kin groups tended to cluster in particular neighborhoods, which meant, in turn, that the solidarity of family and neighborhood reinforced one another. Kin and neighbors were helpful to recent arrivals in a variety of ways – finding work, credit, raw materials, or customers, informing newcomers of voluntary associations they might join, making friends and contacts, perhaps even finding a marriage partner.

Indeed, marriage was the fundamental social institution for artisans, as it was for everyone, since it was at the heart of the value system centered on honor, respectability, and status no less than of the material system of production and reproduction. Indeed, marriage, honor, and business success went together. The symbolism of a civil ordinance in Augsburg in 1571 is pointed in this regard. It declared that craftsmen who went bankrupt had to suffer the indignity of sitting among the women at weddings, the ceremony that declared male economic independence as well as guild membership. We find the same kind of nexus between respectability and business success in eighteenth-century Paris, with business failure often coming on the heels of a lost reputation. This is precisely what befell the Parisian baker André Devaux who was driven out of business and shamed into leaving the faubourg Saint Marcel because the neighborhood had judged him and his wife to be disreputable. All bakers, indeed, all artisans feared this fate which usually was a result of accumulated charges repeatedly hurled as verbal insults in public, slanders which almost invariably centered on the man's dishonesty in business and his wife's sexual promiscuity.

Marriage and mastership coincided in most places. Guild regulations often required it, as did the practical imperatives of running an enterprise, for dowries often brought the essential capital for setting up shop or for buying tools, and wives often played indispensable commercial roles. Marriage was inseparably a working and sexual relationship, and as such it secured the most lasting and the least soluble social bonds that artisans forged. Marriage was at the center of economic, moral, and social ordering. Marriage and the wedding that celebrated it marked a rite of passage from one status to another. Marriage generally marked the difference between master guildsmen (who in many towns had to have a wife) and journeymen (who in many places were prohibited or at least discouraged from marrying), and thus the difference between authority and subordination. For any craftsman to sever the connection between mastership and marriage, for example, violated a cherished moral principle, and met with condemnation by fellow artisans. Thus, when the unmarried Georg Roll of Augsburg tried to set himself up as a master watchmaker in 1562, his fellow guildsmen reacted with violence, raining blows upon him for his violation of the moral norms of the community.

Marriage was not only the linchpin of the moral system at the heart of the well-ordered polity, but it also was the fundamental institution of reproduction, which in turn was central to the maintenance and devolution of property. Artisans no less than any other propertyholders in early modern cities were deeply concerned about their patrimonies, and as for everyone, marital formation was the most important decision in this regard that artisans (and their children) could make. Many historians have examined the marriage patterns of varieties of occupational groups, and if the research on artisans is not as extensive as one might hope, nonetheless one can venture a perhaps surprising generalization: the children of the great majority of guildsmen did not marry spouses who were, or whose fathers were, in the same guild as themselves or their fathers. That is, guild endogamy was far from the norm. For example, in Venice between 1309 and 1419 guild endogamy was very low (only 5.5 percent). The same could be said of many trades in sixteenth-century Aix-en-Provence. There the great majority of leather-workers, shoemakers, carders, and especially tailors married outside the guild. Indeed, of the twenty-seven tailors that Claire Dolan found in her sampling of marriage contracts there, not one married the daughter of another tailor.[24]

In sixteenth-century Lyons only one in four of the daughters of master artisans married men in the same occupation as their fathers, while in seventeenth-century Nördlingen guild endogamy among masters ran below one-third. In Dijon from 1551 to 1650, it was only about one-fifth. The artisans of Lleida between 1680 and 1808 show a rate of guild endogamy of one-third, although the figure inched up toward 40 percent over the last forty years of that period. Eighteenth-century Parisian bakers were more endogamous within their guild than most other early modern artisans, but even among them the rate is still less than half (46 percent), and if we count just masters and their children the rate drops to 42 percent.

Of course, part of the explanation for a minority of guild endogamous marriages is the relative availability of eligible brides (in many towns at different times demographics must have conspired to provide little to choose from), but more voluntarist explanations also must be considered. Unfortunately, most historians who have measured guild endogamy have not followed up the results with this question: if artisans were not marrying fellow guildsmen or their daughters, who were they marrying? No doubt some married up the social ladder (catching a merchant or a lawyer or his daughter), but in most places upward social mobility slowed dramatically in the late sixteenth and seventeenth centuries. So who were they marrying? The unfortunate answer is, we do not know, at least not enough to make any generalizations. Were fourteenth-century Venice or sixteenth- and seventeenth-century Dijon typical? There we find *guild* endogamy low, but *artisanal* endogamy high. That is, artisans were *avoiding* marriage with other families of their guild while *seeking* matches with artisan families outside their guild. In sixteenth- and seventeenth-century Dijon we find that endogamous marriages were relatively infrequent, but when we note that the rate of marriages within the artisanry but outside the guild ran at 75 to 80 percent, we get a picture where craftsmen were deliberately marrying across guilds and within the artisanry. Of course, in other towns there were exceptions to this generalization (a majority of plasterers and weavers in sixteenth-century Aix married within their guilds), but the Dijon–Venice picture is repeated in eighteenth-century Turin and Brittany. Here masters deliberately wed their sons outside the guild. It was the broader social world beyond the guild but within the artisanry that

<hr>

[24] Clare Dolan, "The artisans of Aix-en-Provence in the sixteenth century: a microanalysis of social relationships," in Philip Benedict, ed., *Cities and Social Change in Early Modern France* (London, 1989), pp. 174–94.

mattered most. Artisans needed, as Simona Cerutti has noted, to knit family ties that spanned different crafts and economic interests, such a network providing business connections, sources of credit, and destinations for children as apprentices or spouses.

Among the eighteenth-century Breton building trades we also find a correlation between guild exogamy and artisanal endogamy, where craftsmen married to cross-match skills and business contacts. In 1723, for instance, Louis Bossard, a master glazier of Rennes, married Janne Jubin, the daughter of a roofer who also was a general contractor. In addition to bringing a dowry to the union, Janne brought management expertise she had learned from her father about building contracting and, just as importantly, business contacts through him as well.

The current state of research on artisanal occupational considerations in marriage is tantalizingly incomplete, sadly a conclusion we must also draw about the intersection of geographic and occupational endogamy. Only flashes of light illuminating the Venetian *arsenalotti*, eighteenth-century Parisian bakers, and the Dijonnais craftsmen of the sixteenth and seventeenth centuries can be glimpsed in an otherwise dark landscape. Sixty-five percent of the *arsenalotti* of San Pietro married within the arsenal shipbuilding community of that parish, while 46 percent of those living in San Martino parish did. And among those marriages of San Martino, one-third brought together men and women of the same street or *campo*. In eighteenth-century Paris 40 percent of the Parisian bakers married a girl from the same quartier, and one in six of them married one from their own street (these latter marriages were also the ones that produced the greatest fortunes). In Dijon 45 percent of the daughters of artisans living in Dijon married native artisans, while one-third of the daughters of masters married native masters.

Marriage was one important way to preserve the patrimony; passing down masterships from father to son appears at first glance to be another. In the eighteenth century critics of the guilds like the abbé Coyer, Bigot de Sainte-Croix and above all Clicquot de Blervache excoriated guilds as closed reproduction systems. Rétif de la Bretonne echoed these conclusions when referring to printers when he wrote that "a worker never becomes a master; the masters reproduce among themselves (*engendrent des maîtres*), and journeymen more journeymen from generation to generation."[25]

Were the routes to mastership as narrow as these observations suggest? Did masters actively aspire or even conspire to restrict access to mastership? The answer to the first question seems to be a qualified no,

[25] Quoted in Materné, p. 54.

but, paradoxically, to the second, yes. That is, from the sporadic evidence that we are able to assemble it seems that trades were more open than many a master might have wished and that many a historian has imagined. Demographic pressures and the fiscal attractions (higher fees were charged of non-kin) certainly could, and did, counter any aspirations masters may have had to restrict membership in guilds.

Let us look at some figures. In York from 1397 to 1534 sons followed in their father's craft 51 percent of the time, but this general figure hides enormous differences between trades. The pewterers, locksmiths, and goldsmiths were effectively closed to nonfamily members, with 83 percent of the sons of the first two becoming masters in their fathers' guilds and 78 percent of the sons of master goldsmiths doing so. At the other extreme were the masons (16 percent) and the carpenters (26 percent), with the leather trades (43 percent), clothing trades (42 percent), bakers (53 percent) and butchers (65 percent) ranged everywhere in between.

York provides a microcosm of the European experience from the late Middle Ages to the eighteenth century in that we can find examples of extreme openness as well as relative closure. Sometimes over time we can even find within the same guild a sharp trend from one state to the other, as was the case with the barrelmakers of Bruges. Here we discover over roughly the same period as the York sample (1375–1500) the percentage of sons of barrelmakers following in their fathers' guild plummeting from 50 percent to almost 0, or a state of complete openness.

Examples of relatively closed systems would be the guilds of Augsburg in the second half of the sixteenth century, where increasingly mastership became a family affair. Among the smiths there in the 1560s, for example, 87 percent of new masters had a father or father-in-law in the guild. The butchers of seventeenth-century Delft were also relatively closed (true of butchers almost everywhere), possibly because the number of masterships had been limited to thirty-two "since time immemorial." In seventeenth-century Nördlingen 60 percent of the sons of masters followed in their fathers' occupation, while the tailors of Reval (Tallinn in present-day Estonia) required that the only way to enter the guild was by birth as the son of a master or by marriage to the daughter or widow of one.

On the other side of the ledger are data that show openness, and on balance, especially as we move into the seventeenth and eighteenth centuries, this seems to be the rule more than the exception. The examples of the corsetmakers and joiners of Vienna or the painters of Delft appear to be typical. In Vienna during the Thirty Years' War among the corsetmakers and joiners 10 percent of the masters were sons of masters, while among the painters of Delft from the late sixteenth century to 1659 only 21 of 177 (12 percent) sons of master painters followed in their father's trade. In the eighteenth century the trend toward openness continued. In Bordeaux immigrants were needed to fill the ranks of mastership, and although masters' sons had priority, only a small minority of masters were the sons of one. Among the 250 tailors who became masters between 1757 and 1783, for example, only 16 were sons of masters and 44 their sons-in-law. The proportion among wigmakers was even lower, under 20 percent. In contemporary Vienna small, rich guilds like the sword-cutlers and goldsmiths seem to have been able to privilege sons of masters better than large, poor, and rapidly expanding crafts like tailors, shoemakers, and cabinet-makers, at least judging from the percentage of immigrants (and therefore not indigenous masters' sons) who became masters. Where 30 percent and 52 percent of the master cutlers and goldsmiths were not born in Vienna, 85–90 percent of the tailors, shoemakers, and cabinet-makers were not.

A trend to openness might appear surprising if we were to conclude from one body of evidence that shows that guildsmen in many cities at just this time were lowering or eliminating altogether the admission fees for sons and sons-in-law of masters and raising those for others. This was occurring in such diverse locales as seventeenth-century Barcelona, the German "home towns" between 1650 and 1800, and eighteenth-century Lyons, Dijon, and Paris. Yet despite these favorable conditions for sons of masters to become masters themselves in the same guild, openness to outsiders became the norm. The shoemakers of Barcelona, for example, even exempted a candidate from fees if the new master were the son of one and married the daughter of another master in the guild, but only one-fifth of the 232 shoemakers there received into mastership between 1599 and 1630 were sons of masters from Barcelona.

Similar figures can easily be gathered for other guilds in other cities. On the one hand, in Parisian guilds mastership fees for apprentices who were not sons or sons-in-law of masters ranged from twice to almost twenty times what sons or sons-in-law paid. The bakers stipulated in their revised statutes of 1719 that the *droits de maîtrise* for foreigners was 400 *livres*, but for sons of masters in the guild only 100 *livres*. The sons of master painters paid 160 *livres* while apprentices without the connection paid 300, while among the *peigniers-tabletiers* the rates were 22 *livres* and 400 *livres* respectively. Most trades ranged somewhere in between, like the tapestry-weavers (87 *livres* and 440 *livres*), the hatters (140 and 600 *livres*), and the goldsmiths (546 *livres* and 1,066 *livres*). On the other hand, these kinds of disincentives notwithstanding, we still find that among goldsmiths between 1720 and 1775 only about a third of the masters were sons or sons-in-law of masters (195 of 616, or 31.7 percent), the same rate we find among Parisian locksmiths between 1742 and 1776 (116 of 346, or 34 percent), and eighteenth-century shoemakers and bakers in Lyons. Dijon's rates between 1693 and 1790 were even lower, for under 20 percent of 7,861 mastership letters issued went to sons of masters in the same trade, and the rate was declining across the century from 30 percent at the beginning to 12 percent at the end.

So, were guilds ossifying into rigid, self-perpetuating oligarchies that became a drag on economic growth as their free-trade critics alleged and so many historians have assumed? Judging from the master artisans' aspirations to grease the wheels of their sons and sons-in-law advancement into their ranks and simultaneously raise the bar for other aspirants, one might think that the critics of guilds had a case. The statistics seem to say otherwise, however, pointing to increasing openness of the paths to mastership. Yet behind these figures there dwells another story, at least in York, Dijon, Paris, and the German "home towns," for here the guilds were not as open as they seem. It is true that sons of masters were not categorically staying in their father's trade, but many, and in some places most, new masters were sons of masters of *other* guilds within the same locality. That is, openness favored the sons of guildsmen in town, not the immigrant (Vienna seems an exception here) who tended to return to his native town or village to join the ranks of mastership there.

This colonizing across guilds, a pattern clearly visible in artisan marriages in towns like Dijon and Paris, could preserve the patrimony as effectively as succession within the same guild, and it held out the added advantage of forging lateral links in business. Where lateral links have been studied (and much more research needs to be done), it has been shown that artisans were keen on constructing these connections throughout their social relationships – through marriage and godparenthood, for example. A Parisian metal-polisher, for instance, in 1768 could count a brother and an uncle who were master shoemakers, and, on his wife's side, an uncle who was a master painter. Or take the framework knitter in 1771 whose close kin included a master goldsmith, an engraver, and a bookseller. Establishing spiritual kinship by godparenthood was another way to secure bonds across guilds. Between 1578 and 1646 in Dijon, for example, when a craftsman selected a godfather from the artisan ranks, over half chose a master from another guild. Journeymen show the same pattern. This is hardly surprising, since the key to weathering the vagaries of a precarious and fragile existence was to belong to multiple communities and shape them as best one could to be mutually reinforcing.

Journeymen brotherhoods

If life was precarious and uncertain for the relatively sedentary master craftsman, how much more so it was for the transient journeyman. For him, knowing and being known was of paramount importance because it was the only path to acquiring and preserving material security, respectability, and the social status all artisans of whatever rank craved. Journeymen brotherhoods have been studied mostly in Germany, England, and France, but wherever we find them we find the journeymen behaving in remarkably similar fashion for very similar purposes. As Michael Sonenscher crisply points out, "anonymity was the most dangerous condition that a journeyman could experience, because it was the surest route to exile from the trades and entry into the world of the hospitals and the poor."[26]

For journeymen, the community that provided the means of avoiding the dreaded anonymity was the brotherhood. Confraternities and their later incarnations provided the sense of belonging and the means for distinction in a world of fleeting encounters and ephemeral personal contacts. It is surely no accident that these brotherhoods were most prevalent among workers of stone, wood, leather, metal, and cloth, that is in trades where the pool of labor was large, the turnover high, and thus the demands for distinction most pressing. These were trades, as Sonenscher notes, where "a relatively small number of widely accessible materials were used to make a wide variety of different products," and journeymen placed a premium upon the ability to set oneself apart. Rituals were employed to accomplish this need for distinction. These brotherhoods were renowned, and are still remembered, for the distinct rituals of inclusion and exclusion they fashioned. These rituals made it possible to transform similarity into difference.

Many of the rituals employed by journeymen to construct and reinforce their brotherly communities were drawn from religious ceremony (which, of course, served the same purpose of defining membership in a community), with the aim not to mock the established religion (regardless of what the clergy thought), but to empower themselves and draw clear lines around their community. They sought to appropriate the force of Catholic ritual and to turn it to their own purposes. The

[26] Michael Sonenscher, *Work and Wages: Natural, Politics and the Eighteenth-Century French Trades* (Cambridge, 1989), p. 205.

parallels with Catholic ritual are indeed striking. For instance, ritual practices sanctioned the stages of a journeyman's life as the sacraments did those of the Christian. Initiation ceremonies of the brotherhoods were in fact baptisms, bringing the newcomer into the body of the community, and as part of this ceremony of incorporation, the newly baptized was rechristened with a new name. Journeymen appropriated rites of communion, too, for during these initiations the bonds of the community members were renewed by sharing bread and wine, and just as Christians did, performing a "secular communion" afterward by enjoying a feast in the brotherhood's favorite and regular tavern. These brotherhoods had their secret and sacred books, their sanctioned priest-like officials who presided over the ceremonies and through their special status in the brotherhood endowed the rituals with efficacy (the saddlers in France even dressed one of their members as a priest in real sacerdotal attire). They had a recognized hierarchy of officers – premiers, captains, lieutenants, treasurers, and so forth – who maintained discipline in the ranks. As in the Church, all of these trappings continually re-formed and reinforced the community securing its boundaries, defining its members.

In the eyes of the Church, naturally, all of these actions were sacrilegious, an illicit and unauthorized appropriation of the sacred as well as the authority of the priest. In 1655 the theology faculty of the Sorbonne in Paris condemned the ritual practices of the recently uncovered journeyman shoemaker brotherhood as "impious and sacrilegious," but authorities everywhere, as we have seen, also suspected the brotherhoods had more worldly, if no less illicit objectives. Already in 1383 the London master saddlers accused their "serving men" of organizing collectively "under false colour of sanctity" to press for wage increases.

Journeymen employed other rituals to stake out boundaries of community and to announce membership. For example, everywhere we find these brotherhoods we see emphasis on ritualized "welcomes" and "farewells." In early modern Germany ceremonies like strictly observed greeting formulas and gift-giving crisply distinguished insiders from outsiders, and regulated the passage of the latter into the former. By knowing the standard greeting (called the *Gruss*) and, after a two-week trial period, receiving before the assembled membership of the local chapter of the brotherhood the *Handwerksgeschenk* or gift, the newly arrived journeyman proved his right to belong. If the journeyman was not placed in a shop, he still received the gift, and continued on his way. After the assembly, which usually took place on Saint Monday, the journeymen collectively held a banquet in the tavern or inn favored by their craft.

Eighteenth-century Viennese journeymen had a similar system. The tramping stocking-knitter, for example, upon arriving in town went to the house of call or *Herberge* of the craft, there receiving "a half measure of wine and kreuzer-worth of bread." He was then joined by the two senior journeymen in town (the *Altgesellen*), exchanging "greetings and welcome" with the newcomer and then drinking a toast of another half-measure of wine with him. The newcomer was then escorted to the masters' shops in a strictly established order from oldest to youngest master, seeking openings for work. They then returned to the inn, drank another round, and if he found work, he would be escorted once again to his new shop. The following Sunday all of the journeymen stocking-knitters would convene in their inn to drink again, toasting the *Schenk*, or welcoming drink or round, to their new colleague. If no work were found, he would be sent on his way with some cash from the local treasury, which was stocked regularly by weekly dues of 1 *kreuzer* assessed each journeyman in town (a typical weekly wage was 16 *kreuzer* in cash and 7 *kreuzer* worth of "beer money"). This system of *Geschenk* and *Herberge* enabled migrant journeymen to survive, as they put it, in an "honorable way" by protecting them from having to find work outside their calling and below their rank. "For the journeymen of the early modern period," Josef Ehmer concludes, "and especially in the eighteenth century, ritual demonstrations of unity and solidarity were essential components of the process of accumulation and reproduction of the 'symbolic capital of honor.'"[27]

The printer journeymen had similar rituals marking membership. Like most of the brotherhoods, they generally obligated newcomers to become members of the local "chapel," as the chapters were called. Entrance to the sixteenth-century workplace of the Plantin press in Antwerp brought with it a payment called the *willecoem*, and over the next few centuries more elaborate initiation ceremonies evolved, complete with baptisms, oaths, communions, and so on. If one wished to work in the trade, one had to respect the demands of the community, or punishment would be meted out, as Benjamin Franklin discovered in an eighteenth-century London printing establishment. The abstemious Franklin never kept "Saint Monday," opting to work instead on that unofficial weekly holiday. He not only violated the proverbial dictate of "Sunday to God, Monday to friendship," but he also preached to his fellow workers against beer drinking. And when he refused to celebrate a "welcome" by not buying a round of drinks for his fellows, he was

---

[27] Josef Ehmer, "Words of mobility: migration patterns of Viennese artisans in the eighteenth century," in Geoffrey Crossick, ed., *The Artisan and the European Town, 1500–1900* (London, 1997), p. 191.

visited by "the chapel ghost" who punished deviants, this time by mixing Franklin's letters and transposing his lines.

It may seem an odd sort of brotherhood to have obligatory membership, but such requirements made it possible to clearly delimit the community, and by singling out deviants to define more sharply the rules of belonging. In 1643 the blacksmiths of France functioned in such a way, for in this year in Dijon the journeyman Nicolas Maillefert arrived and was greeted by a fellow journeyman blacksmith called Le Gascon. Calling Maillefert "comrade," Le Gascon told him that work could be found for him, but first he was taken to a shop where, as was customary for new arrivals, he was expected to demonstrate his capability in the craft. After that test, Maillefert was escorted by Le Gascon and three other journeymen to the inn of their *mère*, and there Maillefert shared food and drink with his new brothers. After the meal, Maillefert was taken to a room and there, again according to the "customs" of the brotherhood, he was expected to give up his doublet to the journeyman in town with the greatest seniority. He was also expected to pay the *escot*, or entry fee, to the brotherhood's local treasury. When Maillefert refused to surrender his doublet and his cash, he openly violated the customs of the community and paid for his actions by being roughed up so badly by the others that he fled to the police.

Violence was clearly a part of the ritualized actions of journeymen, and this no doubt had much to do with the importance of masculinity as a marker of community belonging. We have already seen that journeymen in Germany deemed it dishonorable to work in shops alongside women, and boycotts of shops where women were employed were common. In 1649 journeymen hatters in Frankfurt barred from their shops journeymen who had trained in the town of Fulda because the master hatters of Fulda were known to employ women in their shops as embroiderers. There was even a wave of riots and strikes that rolled across Germany in the 1720s when imperial authorities attempted to force journeymen to work in mixed gender shops. Some masters, like the saddlers of Linz, Austria, shared the journeymen's concerns about manhood, and made the same point about masculinity and community. These masters demanded that "all . . . masters shall take great pains to maintain proper male decorum among themselves, and to instruct their apprentices and journeymen in such male decorum."[28]

By the eighteenth century, the religious trappings of the brotherhoods' rituals and ceremonies received less emphasis, although oaths and baptisms are still central. Whether religious or secular, however,

[28] Quoted in Wiesner, "Guilds, male bonding, and women's work in early modern Germany," *Gender and History* 1 (1989), 128.

the ceremonies still mark rites of passage and entry into a new status and *corps*, *état*, or estate, to invoke the terms they specifically used to describe themselves. And by the eighteenth century the brotherhoods were there to stay, as the authorities simply had to recognize. One finds a strong sense of pride and self-confidence among journeymen brothers during this century. One journeyman in eighteenth-century Paris, when under interrogation by the police and asked his name, boasted that "he did not know his baptismal [i.e. Christian] name," and then defiantly added that "he had no need of registering [with the police as was required by law] or fear of police ordinances."[29] With the boast he proclaimed membership in a specific community, and announced a sense of autonomy and independence that, from the perspective of the authorities, was insolent and rank insubordination. The "registration" that so rankled this journeyman was no doubt the *livret*, which, as Kaplan has pointed out, evoked *la livrée*, or the livery worn by the lackey. To the journeymen this was a repugnant symbol of servitude that branded one a member of an inferior social category from which the journeymen were ever vigilantly intent upon distinguishing themselves.

How else to explain the journeymen hatters' response to a police ordinance in 1764 prohibiting them from wearing swords? Scores of these journeymen saw this as an insult to their status, an intolerable denial of their independence, and an affront to their manhood. So what did they do? They boldly and openly convened assemblies, which were illegal, and attended them resplendently attired in braided coats and lace-sleeved shirts, and sporting swords strapped prominently about their hips. They seem to have known that some of them would be arrested for such insubordination because they made a collection beforehand for a relief fund for any brothers who might land in jail. Six did.

Communities were held together by systems of interior discipline. Threats or the actual meting out of violence were a time-tested means to enforce the rules that defined the group and continued to be a part of journeymen behavior throughout the history of the brotherhoods. In the eighteenth century, however, we begin to see some emphasis upon regulating violent behavior. In this sense the brotherhoods were in step with a "civilizing process" that was sweeping through society at large. Sometimes we find brotherhoods regulating themselves against excessive drinking, fighting, or even cursing, although one wonders what the bacchanalian Ménétra would have thought about this. The journeymen

---

[29] Quoted in Kaplan, 294.

turners of Toulouse had a schedule of fines for spitting, for improper dress, and even for "breaking wind" during assemblies. For behavior which was deemed to weaken the bonds of brotherhood, fines could also be levied. Between June 1760 and January 1761 the locksmiths of Bordeaux fined each of the following the substantial sum of 2 *livres*: Claude Le Bourguignon (twice) and François l'Angevin for fighting with brothers, Jean-Baptiste Le Flammand for cursing, and François Le Languedoc, Jacques le Guépin, and Thomas Le Flammand for consorting or eating with "renegades," presumably journeymen who, for whatever reason, were no longer members of the brotherhood.

Ménétra, so much of whose remarkable *Journal of My Life* recounts his life on the road as a *compagnon*, illustrates in so many ways the varieties of the ritualized actions of the journeymen and the solidarity they were intended to secure. Perhaps Ménétra was able to recall in such vivid detail so many of his experiences (the memoirs were written near the end of his life) because those experiences were so steeped in ritual and ceremony, for rituals provide permanence to memories, especially pressing among a highly mobile population where personal, individual alliances were fleeting.

Ménétra's memoirs are full of celebrations of community, and the sense of belonging to a special group – the *compagnons du devoir* – fills much of the text. We read of violence (brawls with other groups, including the rival *compagnons de gavots*) and the man's sexual escapades (a demonstration of manhood, implied as a marker of belonging to the brotherhood), but above all we read of the actions of a man keen on celebrating brotherhood. In one fertile episode Ménétra tells us how, as first *compagnon* (or the one with a combination of seniority and recognition among the *confrères* of possessing leadership skills) in Lyons, he organized a huge celebration of Saint Luke's day. The bash was financed by contributions from journeymen (and even some employers) to a common fund, which was to be spent lavishly on food and drink, to be consumed in common. The festival was to last almost a week, and, as Ménétra was proud to emphasize, it was designed to bring all the *compagnons du devoir* together in one, big celebration of fraternal solidarity. Workers of all ages and whatever trade spent the week celebrating the values that journeymen, and Ménétra, prized so highly: generosity, the sharing of wealth. Celebrants were expected to buy drinks for one another, to feast together, even to share sexual partners. Such mutual sharing reveals the ethic of "gift-exchange" so evident in other journeymen rituals. Everywhere in this festival, and everywhere in brotherhood rituals, we can see the symbolism of solidarity, of giving and receiving, of belonging.

Bibliography

Entries marked with a * designate recommended readings for new students of the subject.

Boulton, J. *Neighborhood and Society: A London Suburb in the 17th Century.* Cambridge, 1987.

Brennan, Thomas. *Public Drinking and Popular Culture in 18th-Century Paris.* Princeton, 1988.

Clark, Peter. *The English Alehouse: A Social History, 1200–1830.* London, 1983.

Davis, Natalie Z. *Society and Culture in Early Modern France.* Stanford, 1975.

Deursen, A. T. van. *Plain Lives in the Golden Age.* Trans. Maarten Ultee. Cambridge, 1991.

*Farge, Arlette. *Fragile Lives: Violence, Power and Solidarity in Eighteenth-Century Paris.* Trans. Carol Shelton. London, 1993.

*Garrioch, David. *Neighborhood and Community in Paris, 1740–1790.* Cambridge, 1986.

Geremek, Bronislaw. "The world of work and the world of crime in late medieval Paris." Trans. Jean Birrell. In Bronislaw Geremek, *The Margins of Society in Late Medieval Paris.* Cambridge, 1987.

Lis, Catharina, and Hugo Soly. *Disordered Lives: Eighteenth-Century Families and Their Unruly Relatives.* Cambridge, 1996.

*Malcolmson, Robert W. *Popular Recreations in English Society, 1700–1850.* Cambridge, 1973.

Martin, John. *Venice's Hidden Enemies: Italian Heretics in a Renaissance City.* Berkeley, 1993.

Power, Michael J. "The East London working community in the 17th century." In Penelope J. Corfield and Derek Keene, eds., *Work in Towns, 850–1850.* Leicester, 1990, pp. 103–20.

Seaver, Paul S. *Wallington's World: A Puritan Artisan in Seventeenth-Century London.* Stanford, 1985.

Wallace, Peter. *Communities and Conflict in Early Modern Colmar, 1575–1730.* Atlantic Highlands, NJ, 1994.

7   Ceremonies, festivals, taverns, and games

Ceremonial and ritualized behavior was a common means of creating and reinforcing social bonds throughout society, but of course the forms varied from one social stratum to another, and even within them. This was certainly true within the artisanry. Francesco Sansovina, a late sixteenth-century Venetian guildsman, left a chronicle which tells us a great deal about guild festivity and ceremonial. He emphasizes diversity, saying that they took place "at different times, for different purposes and different occasions," and offers a typology of "'habits and customs,' 'welcomes for foreign princes,' and 'ducal processions.'"[1] Amid this diversity, however, we can isolate some common forms, among the more important being the procession and consumption (drinking and eating).

Processions

Artisans participated in many processions, each with its own specific purposes but with the general function of defining community (and often rank within it). Participants in processions became part of a larger body. The traditional idea of Christian brotherhood and sisterhood was deeply ingrained in public processions, and not surprisingly, confraternities employed the parade as a very important way to demonstrate membership and solidarity. Each guild had its own patron saint's day during which invariably the members of the guild marched about, sporting upon their persons, or even on floats, symbols of their craft. The lacemakers of seventeenth-century Lille, for example, paraded around town on their saint's day with a float bedecked with lace ribbons and upon which they had erected an enormous spindle. Indeed, processions were opportunities to demonstrate craftsmanship while they affirmed a claim to a particular social status. In Venice as early as 1268 the guilds marched in a huge procession for the new doge, and among

---

[1] Richard Mackenny, *Tradesmen and Traders: The World of the Guilds in Venice and Europe, 1250–1650* (Totowa, 1987), p. 136.

the craftsmen advertising themselves by their appearance were the furriers, who turned out appropriately clad in outfits trimmed with ermine, fox, and the skins of wild animals, while the weavers came attired in the fustians they had made. Doublet-makers marched in white jackets stitched with fleurs-de-lis and pearls, goldsmiths ostentatiously wore jewels, while glassmakers carried elaborate flagons.

In 1549 in Lyons artisans were no less taking the opportunity of procession to proclaim their skill and show their wares, the occasion this time being a royal visit. Hundreds of sumptuously dressed artisans participated in an enormous procession that paraded through town. In 1521 Albrecht Dürer recorded his impressions of a procession for the Feast of the Assumption in Antwerp, and specifically noted the sartorial splendor of the various guildsmen – goldsmiths, painters, weavers, masons, joiners, carpenters, butchers, bakers, and so on – as well as the emblem of each trade. In London the annual lord mayor's show provided a stage for guild display. In the sixteenth century the twelve great companies were joined by sixty smaller livery companies to put on the show, a festive occasion with a great deal of parading about that became increasingly opulent in the early seventeenth century. Artillery salutes, decorated barges, feasts, and of course elaborate costumes sorely taxed the treasuries of the participating guilds. Spain was no different. In sixteenth-century Seville artisans rendered visible their sense of community and advertised themselves by marching in processions, with guild officers dressed in brilliant uniforms and flying banners of the guild's insignia. In 1579 during a procession accompanying the transfer of the remains of King Ferdinand III of Castile from their place in the cathedral to a new chapel built for the purpose, two hundred tailors, hosiers, and doublet-makers marched as brothers of the confraternity of San Mateo, each wearing breeches trimmed in gold with matching hats. Fifteenth-century London guildsmen similarly decked their masters in liveries specific to the craft at all sorts of public events from feasts, to lord mayor's days, to processions honoring reigning monarchs.

Clearly processions were about community (and advertising); they were also about hierarchy. At Blois in 1666 an ordinance from the royal court of the bailliage ruled that during a general procession in which artisans were to participate, the "ranks of the trades" be clearly displayed by their marching order with the highest ranking ("les plus qualifiés," here, but certainly not everywhere, this meant goldsmiths, clockmakers, and drapers) closing the parade with the rest arranged from start to finish ascending the social hierarchy.[2] Fifteenth-century

---

[2] Abel Poitrineau, *Ils travaillent la France. Métiers et mentalités du XVIe au XIXe siècle* (Paris, 1992), p. 207.

Coventry showed the same concern for status in its regular communal processions which made visible a particular hierarchical ordering. The weavers' ordinance there stipulated that "In every procession and all other congregacions for worschip of the citte and . . . of the seyd crafte . . . every man shall goo and sytt in order as he hath byn put in Rule of the seyd crafte."[3]

Drinking and eating

One of the processions best known to historians is the parade of Mardi Gras, and equally well-known is the close association between this procession and the celebrations of food and drink. Indeed, it is during carnival when we can often see how different forms of festive behavior can reinforce the bonds of community. In Paris in 1739, for instance, the butchers celebrated their guild festival during carnival, and staged a *bœuf gras* procession in their neighborhood. Groups of people consuming food and drink collectively has long been recognized by anthropologists as a way to define and reinforce group solidarity. These ritualized practices are arranged on a spectrum of relative formality, ranging from the formal annual guild feasts that regularly dotted the calendar to casual gatherings of artisans in one another's houses, or in nearby taverns. The rules of hospitality, visiting, and commensality were yet another part of the mosaic of rules and norms governing artisan communities, articulating inclusion and exclusion.

Eating and drinking together implied trust, and groups that ritually shared food and drink were making a collective statement about themselves as a harmonious body. Festive eating and drinking was a hallmark of guild behavior everywhere. The craft fellowships of fifteenth-century Coventry met three times annually, and, among other ceremonial practices, gathered for a banquet. For the Lillois weaver Chavatte, like all craftsmen everywhere in Europe, craft banquets and *beuveries* or drinking bouts were of capital importance because of what they said and did about community. Admission of a new master to the ranks of a guild always involved a banquet (usually paid for by the new master), where the brotherhood was enlarged and renewed. Collective dining could also be an act of social reconciliation between guilds, as it was in late medieval Coventry where conflict between two fellowships was explicitly to be sealed by a meal consumed together.

Journeymen no less than masters availed themselves of food and drink to bond ceremoniously. With the increasing mobility of journeymen in

---

[3] Quoted in Charles Phythian-Adams, *Desolation of a City: Coventry and the Urban Crisis of the Late Middle Ages* (Cambridge, 1979), p. 112.

the late Middle Ages, taverns and inns become increasingly important, not just as "houses of call" or clearinghouses for employment, but more viscerally as surrogate hearths and homes for men without families. Coincident with this increased mobility is an explosion in the number of taverns and inns in European cities. On the left bank of Paris alone in the fourteenth century sixty could be found, joining at least 200 and probably many more that went unrecorded in the city as a whole. There were 87 taverns in Rouen in 1556, a number that swelled to 478 by 1742. In Lille in 1665 83 can be counted in the city, but many more dotted the suburbs and thereby escaped the city tax. In 1693 in the Sarladais there were 220, and about 100 years later there were 1,500 in France's second largest city, Lyons, and fully 4,300 in Paris.

Alehouses in England were the counterparts to *Trinkstuben* in Germany or *cabarets* and *guinguettes* in France, and were frequented by "the mechanick part of mankind," artisans. A London pamphleteer remarked in the 1620s that most of the beer consumed in "tippling" houses was drunk by "handicraftsmen, workmen of all sorts . . .," while William Hornby composed a poem in 1619 with the same sociological observation, but here marked by a hierarchical message: "Tis great impeachment to a generous mind/A base and paltry alehouse to frequent/It best befits a tinker in his kind/Than any man of virtues eminent."[4]

Given this testimony, it is hardly surprising that in the early seventeenth century gentlemen tended to gather at inns, a picture confirmed by a study of customers at an alehouse in Kent by Peter Clark. Between 1590 and 1610 this particular establishment counted among its clientele scarcely three in a hundred, while one in three were artisans. The rest were tramping laborers and domestic servants.

Tudor authorities saw the alehouse as a place of political subversion and moral debauchery, and a rival to the church as a center for communal and neighborhood activities. Sometimes clandestine marriages were celebrated there. Alehouses also became locales of many quasi-religious celebrations like mumming at New Year, and fiddling and dancing at Candlemas, activities that had once been performed in the church but with the onslaught of Puritanism had been driven out.

Indeed, alehouses served a variety of needs in the artisan community. They were places where one might find short-term credit for food, drink, and a room "on tick." They also doubled as places where a craftsman might market his wares, or fence stolen or smuggled products. And they were a prime site for working out and sealing business deals,

[4] Clark, *Alehouse*, pp. 123–4.

ratified with a drink. In 1672 a foreign visitor to an English alehouse noted that "no kind of business is transacted in England without the intervention of pints of beer."[5]

Because of its unsavory reputation as a haunt of the disorderly and dangerous classes, authorities in the early seventeenth century intensified a regulatory assault upon the alehouse, primarily through a licensing program. By 1700 the alehouse had been largely tamed, a development reflected in its changing clientele. The Hanoverian alehouse now catered to the more "established society," "persons of good fashion and credit." The late seventeenth and early eighteenth centuries were a time of a relative buoyancy in the economic fortunes (as wages went up and prices dropped), and many artisans thus had more disposable income to spend on the increasingly diversified alcoholic beverages served in the alehouse. Still relatively class specific, the alehouse nonetheless now no longer was the haunt of lesser craftsmen or the working and tramping poor who henceforth went elsewhere for drink and sociability. Dram and ginshops operated in cellars, backrooms, or sheds in alleys, exploded in number after 1700. In 1736 in the metropolitan districts of Middlesex 3,835 dramshops were counted, while William Maitland estimated that there were 8,659 brandy-shops in London in 1737, or one for every eleven houses. In Whitechapel and Southwark these kinds of shops were even more densely packed, with about one in eight buildings proffering cheap drink. Spirits became the poor man's drink, costing less than beer and ale in alehouses.

As we have seen, journeymen everywhere had their "own" taverns or alehouses and inns where they might even have their own "club room," as it was called in England. Ménétra again is the classic example of the journeyman, everywhere in his memoirs hailing fellows with drink and continuing the tradition of conviviality while securing community and brotherhood. This glazier and his fellows had their haunts on the *tour de France*, no less than the early seventeenth-century tailors did (the Fatted Capon being their place in Dijon) or the late eighteenth-century locksmiths (Le Gros Raison and La Ville de Rome in Paris.) Here they not only socialized, but found short-term credit (often in pawn, usually from the owner), lodging, advice, information about masters, and jobs. They often slept two or three to a bed, and idled away the hours playing cards, rolling dice, and drinking. They drank for a variety of reasons. Certainly drink was an analgesic for a painfully harsh existence; but beyond that it provided an alternative sociability that was not available to them elsewhere, for they were rootless and mobile, far from family

---

[5] Ibid., p. 232.

and home. The tavern supplied a hearth, complete with brothers and mother (the *mère*). Moreover, as the authorities and the master craftsmen well knew, in the tavern journeymen felt release from the demands of subordination. No doubt this is why taverns everywhere were roundly condemned by the police as dens of debauchery, thievery, and violence.

It was not just journeymen who frequented taverns; Chavatte, like so many master craftsmen everywhere, constantly haunted the neighborhood taverns as well as the more distant *guinguettes* where the wine was cheaper because duty free. Indeed, in his memoirs he mentions taverns and the fellowship he found there many more times than he does his home and family, about which he says almost nothing. Given the sources and the state of current research, it is difficult to say what the social clientele was in these drinking establishments, but we can be sure that artisans were among the best customers. By the eighteenth century when the kinds of sources that permit closer and more exact scrutiny exist, it also seems that a kind of social segregation was occurring (mirroring, no doubt, the "dissociation" occurring in society at large) where certain drinking establishments were no longer frequented by urban elites. In Paris, for example, police lieutenant Lenoir reported that wineshops were haunted by "soldiers, workers, coachmen, [and] lackeys." The only women he mentions are prostitutes, and so the tavern was clearly masculine space. Probably a third to a half of the clientele of wineshops were artisans, and the general pattern seems to be that artisans clustered together, often with their neighbors.

In eighteenth-century Parisian taverns Thomas Brennan has found infrequent associating between social or professional levels. Between 1691 and 1771 nearly seven of every ten master craftsmen who frequented a tavern shared table and drink only with other masters. Journeymen were even more homogeneous (73 percent and 75 percent, respectively). When artisans of different rank did mix in taverns, in about one in ten cases we find masters sharing a table with journeymen, fewer than one in twenty doing so with social superiors, and never with day-laborers. Journeymen, too, were self-conscious of their rank and with whom they would raise a drink or share a meal, for fewer than 7 percent of them lifted drinks with day-laborers, and never with anyone further up the social scale than their masters.

Journeyman and masters may have seldom shared a table, but they certainly nonetheless did rub shoulders in taverns. Imbibing can promote an easy familiarity and even a sense of equality, but the sociability of the tavern could be fragile. The authorities' concern that taverns were violent places was based in fact, for many a criminal dossier is full of assaults, batteries, and even murders that occurred in bars. More mundane, but no less indicative of the "disorder" that seemed so prevalent in taverns, is the insubordination of a journeyman wheelwright in a Dijon bar in 1642. The journeyman, Claude Boulangier, came to a wineshop that master barrel-cooper Claude Rebourg ran out of his cellar. Somehow Boulangier's flagon was knocked to the floor, where it shattered. Boulangier blamed the servingmaid, and she him. Rebourg, who had not seen the incident, demanded that Boulangier pay for the broken flagon. The journeyman indignantly refused, and rained dishonoring insults upon Rebourg, calling him, among other things, a cuckold using the *tu* form of address. Perhaps aware that he had crossed the boundary of acceptable behavior and therefore expecting retaliation from Rebourg, Boulangier then bolted for the door. While clambering up the stairs he suddenly hesitated, and then loudly farted, captioning his timely gesture with the words "That's for you [*toy*] and yours!" Boulangier had indeed crossed the boundary, for now Rebourg, deeply offended by the insults and now this egregious, scatological gesture of disrespect and insubordination, dashed after him, collared him, and dragged him to the police.

Games and violence

Loyalties overlapped and criss-crossed throughout artisan culture, shoring up some communities while simultaneously weakening others. As we have seen, communities were constituted by inclusion and exclusion, and defining boundaries and thereby members was an inevitable part of building and reinforcing social solidarity. Of course, the act of exclusion, of defining brothers against others, carried the threat of violence along with it. Ménétra, for example, toasted drinks with his fellows by degrading the integrity of their rivals and thereby effectively challenging them to a fight. Indeed, we need not look far in artisan culture to find violence, and its use is often related to the reinforcement of community. Of course, in the eyes of the authorities, violence is usually illicit, and so violence and criminality are frequently joined.

Brawling, of which Ménétra was so fond, was certainly a form of violent behavior, but it was also a kind of spectacle akin to physical games. Despite what the authorities and moralists thought, it was not lawless savagery, but part of a code of behavior that defined community and even identity. It provided the opportunity to demonstrate the masculine attributes of prowess, agility, and courage. Perhaps most important of all, the field of play could double as a field of honor. All of these characteristics were part of the extraordinary "wars of the fists" studied by Robert Davis in late medieval and early modern Venice.

From the late fifteenth through the seventeenth centuries, several times a year, crowds dominated by artisans would fight for the possession of a bridge. Called *battagliole sui ponti*, these ritualized combats occurred on bridges on the city's outskirts, and constituted a kind of popular counter-ritual to the state ceremonies staged in the city's center. Where the latter visualized the values of wealth, decorum, social status, patrician power, and the peace and unity that was at the heart of the myth of Venice as the "Most Serene Republic," the artisanal fistfights inverted this elite ceremonial, using violence to proclaim another community and a different value system. The *battagliole* were opportunities for artisans to stake a claim to honor and to assert public status of their own. As one of the combatants put it in the mid-seventeenth century: "The aim of our contests . . . is not to kill or tear each other apart but to win . . . glory and reputation in the presence of the city."[6]

In these ritualized combats, dominated by artisans, ordinary bridges became tournament fields while canals, balconies, and rooftops become grandstands where hundreds, even thousands of spectators gathered and formed a public opinion that bestowed or withheld honor to the combatants. Sometimes these "wars" were fought between individuals, champions of certain groups, other times they were fights between scores of young men (sticks giving way to fists in the early 1600s). Combatants marched two abreast to the fighting bridge, declaring their masculinity to all through their dress and warlike chanting. This was yet another kind of procession, and women and children came to doors and windows to cheer them on, and, as Davis writes, "to bear witness to this collective assertion of male distinctiveness."[7] Indeed, these staged events were a crucial part of boys becoming men, a rite of passage as they left the feminine space of the hearth for the masculine terrain of shop, tavern, and fighting bridge. Fights among the Venetian artisans, just as with Ménétra and his fellows, either in taverns or on the bridges, were almost always about honor, and honor was about claiming a place in society.

Although the single-minded pursuit of status and reputation by the combatants could be lethal (fifty combatants died in a battle in 1606), killing was not the purpose of these events; the garnering of reputation was. The chronicler who left us so much information about these battles intoned, "Oh, how much power has the [desire for] reputa-

---

[6] Robert C. Davis, *The War of the Fists: Popular Culture and Public Violence in Late Renaissance Venice* (New York, 1994), p. 91.

[7] Ibid., p. 109.

tion!"[8] Losers were deeply shamed by their loss, and given the importance of honor and reputation in the artisan world, the stakes of these battles were incredibly high. Victors and their supporters might celebrate for days, in their feasting, drinking, and dancing, renewing community bonds.

Venetians were fierce partisans of two large groups that sponsored these battles, the Nicolotti and the Castellani. Membership in these groups was determined by where one lived, and so loyalty to one's group often split trades and even workshops, sometimes with deadly results. In 1670, for example, reportedly

Twelve or sixteen cobblers . . . part masters and part journeymen . . . decided to go see the festival that the Muranesi usually hold in August when they rebuild their glass furnaces, and, being together at an inn, since they were not in agreement over their support of the factions [the Nicolotti and the Castellani], they got into the hottest dispute, to the extent that one of the most ardent among them (maybe also incited by the anger of Bacchus) punched a companion in the face. Another, seeing his friend offended, knocked [the attacker] off his bench onto the ground . . . [A]nother pulled out one of the wide knives [that] they carry, cutting in a blow two fingers off [that one's] left hand . . . until [finally] everyone had pulled out daggers, knives, cleavers, swords, boathooks, harpoons, and [even] skewers from the kitchen . . . thinking nothing of being knocked down, disemboweled, or killed."[9]

Three ultimately died in this brawl, and eleven were seriously injured.

The "wars of the fists" slowly disappeared in the late seventeenth century. Local patricians were the first to desert the audience. With their withdrawal went much of the financing needed to stage these events and to celebrate victory afterward and, equally important, the protection these local patrons provided against the state authorities who now began passing edicts outlawing the fights. Long wars against the Turks in the seventeenth century also played a part in sapping the fights of their interest as they drained the Castellani faction of many of their fighters. The *arsenalotti* constituted the core of this faction, and they were called upon as part of their service to the state to man the galleys that shipped out to fight the infidel. As a result, the Nicolotti overmatched the Castellani on the bridges, and the crowds lost interest. The last big *pugni* occurred in 1705, the "wars of the fists" no longer considered by spectators and thus by participants as a source of honor and public respect. They gave way to more "refined" means of demonstrating reputation. Growing hostility towards the "brutality" of popular recreation in Venice, as everywhere in Europe, is evident in the eighteenth century. In part related to the underlying concern for labor discipline,

[8] Quoted in ibid., p. 93.
[9] Quoted in ibid., pp. 37–8.

events like the "wars of the fists" were increasingly seen as wasteful of time, energy and money, and gradually evolved into the more rule-bound modern sport activities.

One should not overdraw the "lawlessness" or "brutality" of artisanal recreational activities, however. This behavior may have appeared dis-orderly or indisciplined to the authorities, but to the artisans it func-tioned according to very clear norms, even rules. This is especially clear when we look at another kind of recreation that artisans seem especially fond of, game-playing.

To be sure, game-playing was often associated by the authorities with criminal activity and violence. In the fifteenth century an insider turned police informant betrayed a gang to which he had belonged, and the subsequent police investigation tells us a remarkable story about the Coquillards, a Burgundian band of artisan criminals. These men used a secret vocabulary that only initiates of the group could understand, and they supplemented the group's income from thievery by running a clandestine gambling ring, apparently rigging the operations by using loaded dice.

Gambling among Coquillards was criminal, and often violent, but most men in the late medieval and early modern period were extraordi-narily fond of gambling. Indeed, game-playing in general seems ubiqui-tous among all social groups, and male artisans were no exception. References to craftsmen (though rarely women) playing nine-pins, *quilles*, bowls, tennis, or *boules* dot the historical record frequently and regularly. These games of skill were usually considered by the religious and political authorities to be at worst harmless diversions, and even legitimate and healthful. Not so games of chance, their widespread popularity notwithstanding. All social ranks since the Middle Ages (and no doubt before) seem attracted, even addicted to games of chance (including women of the upper classes, at least from the seventeenth century on), and the avalanche of municipal and royal legislation every-where condemning such activity attests to its popularity as well as the inability of the authorities to curb it.

Dice-throwing was an ancient game of chance, and certainly was being played in the Middle Ages. Card-playing, on the other hand, appears only in the late fourteenth century, becoming increasingly popular from the mid-fifteenth. In the current state of research it would be impossible to prove conclusively that any particular social rank was more or less given to games of chance in any particular century, although contemporaries of the seventeenth and especially the eighteenth century were convinced that they were witnessing an un-precedented gambling mania among all walks of life, from courtly society to the world of the artisan to that of the indigent beggar and criminal.

What historical record we do have leaves no doubt that craftsmen were given to games of chance; but what meaning and significance they attached to games, specifically the games of chance of dice-throwing and card-playing, has received very little attention. Certainly play no less than work played its part in defining artisan culture. Play occurred in spaces specifically for it, space that was relatively autonomous, and as such, much like the workshop or the street, it served as another site in which community and identity could be fashioned. Of course, games of chance were conflictual in certain contexts, and competition was an inherent characteristic of them wherever they were played. They could be, although not necessarily, destructive to community. Gambling could and did at times emphasize impersonal social exchange. In card-playing if not dice-throwing, the role individual skill played in success or failure tended to social atomization, to turn, in John Dewald's words, "social connectedness into hostile individualism."[10] Furthermore, some gambling dens were open to all classes, and the free-wheeling gains and losses, according to Dewald, had an egalitarian effect.

How many artisans were rubbing shoulders with aristocrats around gaming tables or the pits of cockfights is impossible to know. Samuel Pepys was struck in 1663 by the social mix at a cockfight: "But Lord! To see the strange variety of people, from Parliament men . . . to the poorest 'prentices, bakers, brewers, butchers, draymen, and what not; and all these fellows one with another cursing and betting."[11] The picture Rétif de la Bretonne sketched of a cardroom he happened upon a century later was more socially homogeneous. That this one was only populated by "workers of every trade, and a few small merchants"[12] is perhaps not so surprising, given the growing stratification and cultural segregation we know was occurring in early modern society.

As we ponder the importance of play in artisan culture, consider that play activity is distinct from "ordinary" life by its locality and duration, that it constitutes, as Johan Huizinga put it, "a stepping out of 'real' life into a temporary sphere of activity with a disposition all its own."[13] Also note that the site of play activity, the "play-ground," is kin to sacred space. It is sharply delineated, "hedged round," in his words, within

[10] Johnathan Dewald, *Aristocratic Experience and the Origins of Modern Culture, France, 1570–1715* (Berkeley, 1993), p. 165.
[11] Quoted in Peter Earle, *Middle Class*, p. 57.
[12] Nicolas-Edme Rétif de la Bretonne, *Les Nuits de Paris* (New York, 1964), p. 150.
[13] Johan Huizinga, *Homo Ludens: A Study of the Play-Element in Culture* (Boston, 1955; orig. edn. 1938), p. 8.

which specific and inviolable rules obtain.[14] Third, he observed that participants in play activity constitute, again in his words, a "play-community . . . mutually withdrawing from the rest of the world and rejecting the usual norms."[15] Such activity from this perspective can be interpreted as a form of resistance.

Many historians have explored the relationship between work and leisure, often in the context of the development of the disciplining of the workforce. As the work day became increasingly defined temporally, so too did the time available for nonwork activity, or leisure. The watershed in the transformation of the relationship between work and leisure, so this argument goes, has been thought to be industrialization, after which work became regulated by the clock rather than by the requirements of the task. There is some truth in this script, as we have seen, but we would be mistaken if we concluded that the concern for disciplining the worker was especially an industrial, or even narrowly an economic matter. Nor should we assume that time devoted to leisure, or more appropriately, play activity, was any less structured before industrialization. Philippe Ariès suggested that leisure only exists as a "function" of work, and that the game is suspect because it risks being more than a stoppage of work, but a competitive activity. In a sense, he is correct, but only partially. Play did compete with work, but play should not be thought of as its negative complement. Playing games, especially games of chance, were more than activities competing with work, but manifestations of an alternative aspect of social production. This alternative contested the normative production of the religious and political authorities, and, when engaged in by journeymen, at times contested that of the masters as well. As Eileen and Stephen Yeo have pointed out, leisure was "at the center of [social] . . . struggles. Far from being a neutral, free zone it was contested territory, with no party to the conflicts being in any danger of under-politicizing it . . . " Furthermore, they add, leisure activities were "manifestly about the production of meanings, ways of living and seeing . . . "[16]

If gaming activity can be usefully understood, then, in one sense, as resistance, what was being resisted? And where? And how? And why? Rather than posit work as the basis from which an analysis of play can be drawn, think of work and play as independent activities rendered meaningful by the place they occupy in the system of cultural production as a

---

[14] Ibid., p. 10.   [15] Ibid., p. 12.

[16] Eileen Yeo and Stephen Yeo, "Ways of seeing: control and leisure versus class and struggle," in Eileen Yeo and Stephen Yeo, eds., *Popular Culture and Class Conflict, 1590–1914: Explorations in the History of Labour and Leisure* (Atlantic Highlands, 1981), p. 150.

whole. In the early modern period, this system was, as we have seen, rigorously hierarchical, and its authoritative structure voiced everywhere in terms of discipline. Discipline in the workplace was a fundamental concern, and so was discipline outside of it. It was a transcendent value, an organizing principle of society that theoretically ordered the workplace, the street, the home, the state, the tavern, and the gambling den. Of course, its application was imperfect and incomplete in all of these spheres, variously embraced or resisted by the different ranks of society. Judging from the extraordinary volume of legislation proscribing games of chance, the places where they occurred, and the people involved, play activity of this type was construed by the authorities as especially indisciplined.

France appears typical of the rest of Europe in this regard, and is certainly the country best studied by historians. In the early eighteenth century Nicolas Delamare devoted an entire section to "Games" in his magisterial *Traité de la police*. He asserted that "Religion and the State" have a fundamental interest in "disciplining games," especially games of chance. These *jeux de hasard* he closely associated with the disorderly personal characteristics of "agitation, impetuosity, anger, violent passion, [and] fury, [traits] that are . . . appendages of these sorts of games." He continued, "from all the points of morality that are the object of police, there are few that have given occasion to so great a number of laws than games of chance."[17] Judging from the evidence from, to name just a few cities, Amiens, Strasbourg, Dijon, Paris, Toulouse, Lille (one could cite countless other cities from all across Europe) between the fifteenth and eighteenth centuries, one would find it difficult to disagree with Delamare's assertion. Among many laws Delamare himself cites, consider the following: in 1397 an ordinance from the provost of Paris reported that

many *gens de métiers* and other *petit peuple* leave their work and their families during workable days to go and play tennis, boules, dice, cards, and 9-pins and other games in . . . taverns and other public places; many among them, after having lost everything, are given to rob and to kill and to lead a very evil life . . . To prevent . . . [such] disorders, [the provost] prohibited persons of this rank to play during workable days under pain of prison and fine . . ."[18]

In this ordinance, games of chance and games of skill are lumped together and collectively proscribed. The multitude of examples that Delamare offers from subsequent centuries increasingly focuses on games of chance, supporting the perception held by Henri III in 1583 that the incidence of such games was increasing at an alarming rate.

[17] Nicolas Delamare, *Traité de la police* (Paris, 1729), book 3, section 4, pp. 481, 485.
[18] Ibid., p. 488.

Ariès is probably right that games of chance represent a fundamental counter-current to the moralizing of the seventeenth century.

In 1611 Louis XIII was concerned enough about the power of games of chance to divert good subjects "from the path of virtue" toward "dissipation," "license," and even bankruptcy, that he prohibited anyone from "assembling to play cards or dice." In 1643 the Queen-Regent wanted to support with her authority a discipline so important to the state that she prohibited *académies de jeu* (gambling dens), a position Louis XIV reiterated in 1666, associating these places with disorder.[19] The *parlementaires* of Toulouse were of the same opinion, condemning these gambling dens, the games of chance played in them, and the men "engaged in this disorder."[20] The cascade of legislation prohibiting games of chance does not end there, but pours over into the eighteenth century, recurring thirteen times between 1710 and 1781.

Of course, we cannot be sure that increased legislation signaled an increase in activity, but there seems little doubt that games of dice and cards were being increasingly organized and situated in specialized space, even at court – legislation notwithstanding – with king and minister at the table. Artisans were often singled out in the surviving evidence as especially eager to engage in these activities. They were frequent players of dice and card games in taverns at least since the fifteenth century, and in the *berlans* (dice dens), *académies de jeu*, and taverns in the seventeenth and eighteenth centuries.

The drive for discipline, of course, also had a religious face, and gaming was often proscribed for its supposed sacrilegious character. From another perspective, then, participation in games of chance also represents a resistance to the moral discipline that the religious and political authorities were attempting to impose during the early modern centuries, the attempt to bring "the cloister to the street."[21] Resistance to such discipline in the form of play, specifically of games of chance, was taken quite seriously by the authorities precisely because such play was so independent of it.

Like all play activity, playing games of chance can be interpreted as a "stepping out" into a temporary sphere with its own rules. Furthermore, as many anthropologists have suggested, play is very close to religion conceptually, and as a rival transcendental experience, can pose a challenge to religion. There are good reasons why religions often

---

[19] Ibid., pp. 490, 491, 495.

[20] *Arrest de la cour de Parlement de Toulouse*, Toulouse, 1681. Bibliothèque Nationale, Cabinet des Estampes.

[21] See James R. Farr, *Authority and Sexuality in Early Modern Burgundy, 1550–1730* (New York, 1995), chapter 2.

proscribe play activity, especially that which involves chance, fate, or divination. Both play and religion carve out a stable if fragile order from a universe without law, and legitimize it by forms of sacralization. In both chance (or fate) and God reside the terrible unknowable, both of which can bless or damn, inscrutably bestow bliss or misfortune. The sacred is ultimately inscrutable, ultimately uncontrollable, but that does not stop people from feeling a need to hedge it about, to contain it – in a church, in a tavern, in a tabernacle, on the *tapis vert* of the gaming table.

In some ways, games are also like festivals, and many historians have observed that festivals were ambiguous events. They were regulated by prescribed ceremonies but simultaneously preserved a flexibility that permitted invention and even retained the possibility that the tolerated license could escape the boundaries of the rules and lead to real disorder. Playing games of chance might be thought of as microcosms of festivals, or, perhaps more appropriately, as *fêtes quotidiennes*, for much the same reasons. Both occur in prescribed sites, both dictate their own flow of time, both allow invention and flexibility within prescribed rules, both can overflow into disorder. Both, above all, are expressions of, to recall Huizinga, "stepping out of 'real' life into a temporary sphere of activity with a disposition all its own . . . distinct from 'ordinary' life by its locality and duration." As autonomous and rival constructions of order, both festivals and games of chance can, moreover, represent challenges to the normative order.

Legislation makes it amply clear that municipal no less than royal authorities often singled out for discipline the "play space" of games of chance. The repeated card- and dice-playing in these locales equally demonstrates that the space was contested, that such discipline was resisted. Historians have often noted that taverns and churches were the opposite poles of social activity in early modern villages and urban parishes, with taverns, in a sense, being "anti-churches," and it certainly is no accident that the legislation prohibiting games of chance and the places where and the time when they were played are often cast in religious idiom. Moreover, at times the authors of these texts explicitly interpret this form of play as an affront to the sacred (as defined, of course, by the political and religious authorities). In 1745, for example, a royal ordinance condemned those individuals who "profaned" religious celebrations by playing games of chance in taverns or *académies de jeu* during them, "particularly cards and dice [which] are an assault against the sacred."[22] In 1583 Henri III had railed against the same

[22] Jean-Louis Calvet, *Les Jeux de la société* (Paris, 1978), p. 188.

behavior for the same reason. He lamented that the players of games of chance were playing "especially on [religious] festivals and Sundays instead of attending to the service of God."[23] His choice of "instead of" suggests that he viewed such activity as directly competitive with religious observation.

Municipal authorities spoke in the same voice. In 1600 the town council of Dijon, for example, proclaimed that

the confraternities of the *arts et métiers* [were] introduced to honor God and the patron saints . . . [However,] for some years, instead of the honor and glory of God and the said saints only things to the contrary have been produced . . . Derisions and insolences like games of dice and . . . cards . . . [lead to] such blasphemy . . . that God is greatly offended . . .

The Dijon magistrates reiterated the proclamation in 1604, 1607, twice in 1615, and again in 1635, 1645, and 1646 each time specifically singling out artisans for rolling dice or dealing cards during divine service and specifying that such activity took place in taverns and *berlans*.[24] In Lille in 1684, as Chavatte recounts, the town council similarly was concerned about artisans playing games of chance during saints' days, fearing that such a violation of sacred time would provoke the wrath of God against the entire city.

Religious legislation echoed political legislation, first directed at clerics in the Middle Ages, and then from the late fifteenth century on, against the laity. Synodal statutes condemned games of chance on the grounds that they were an affront to God and created conditions which led men to blasphemy, debauchery, and ultimately perdition, a stance endorsed by Saints Charles Borromeo and François de Sales. The Swiss theologian Lambert Daneau conceived of players of games of chance as "moquers et contempteurs de Dieu."[25] Condemnations of playing games of chance invariably are associated with blasphemy, as countless decrees, both royal and municipal, illustrate. In 1661 Louis XIV denounced "the cursing and blaspheming" that accompanied card-playing and dice-throwing, while Delamare catalogues similar decrees citing the "execrable blasphemies" uttered in gambling dens.[26] Popular preachers from the fifteenth to the seventeenth centuries never tired of asserting that the devil was behind games of chance, Daneau echoing this position in the late sixteenth century by asserting that

---

[23] *Declaration du Roy*, 22 May 1583, Bibliothèque Nationale, Cabinet des Estampes.

[24] James R. Farr, *Hands of Honor: Artisans and Their World in Dijon, 1550–1650* (Ithaca, 1988), pp. 247, 251.

[25] Lambert Daneau, *Nouveaux Traités très-utiles . . . Le Premier touchant les sorciers . . . Le Second contient une brève remonstrance sur les jeux de cartes et dez* (Paris, 1579), p. 133.

[26] *Declarations, Arrests, et édits royaux*, September, 1661. Delamare, p. 492 (ordonnance de Police, 6 April 1655); p. 492 (ordonnance de Police, 15 July 1667).

cards were invented by Satan. This Calvinist divine, by the way, bundled into one book his treatise on games of chance with his tome on witchcraft, the common thread linking the two being, of course, diabolism.

Of course, games of chance were not denounced solely on the grounds of religious morality – they also were seen as leading to the financial ruin of good families – but the religious idiom is hard to overlook. If we consider that the profane is only "profane" according to a specific, if dominant or normative, definition of the sacred, then understanding play activity as having "counter-sacred" characteristics, and thus being a form of resistance to the "moralizing effort," in Robert Sauzet's words, makes sense.

Play, especially games of chance, were a form of resistance to the normative, disciplining morality. It served other purposes in artisan culture, too, however. Play activity carves out autonomous space, orders it with rules, and becomes a peculiar and concentrated arena for social relations. Games, however, especially games of chance, can be both "disjunctive" and "conjunctive," to use the anthropologist Lévi-Strauss's terms. Police and moralists only saw their disjunctive effects, with gambling perceived as a threat to the social and moral fabric of society and the tavern or gambling den as the privileged site of this disorder. To be sure, artisans as well as men from many other social ranks were ruined at the game table, and "execrable blasphemies" flew from the mouths of the losers as freely as the money from their purses. But artisans also played games of chance for "conjunctive" reasons, as activity constitutive of cohesive social relations, as useful in the construction and maintenance of community and identity. As the sociologist Jeremy Boissevain has suggested, play can promote both a sense of togetherness and identity.[27]

In the fifteenth and sixteenth centuries, young artisans gathered in taverns to roll dice, often divided into teams, with the stakes not cash, or one's tools, but rather the next round of drinks. Loser buys. Cheaters were thought of as thieves, as *mauvais compagnons*, and refusal to play often met with violence. To play was to enter a circle of initiates, to join a community, and to refuse was to renounce the group.

In the eighteenth century games of chance played the same role among artisans. Ménétra haunted hundreds of taverns during his youth, and referred to the cohesiveness of card-playing when he casually observed at one point in his journal when he had been away from his friends on the *tour de France* that "the companions" missed him and

---

[27] Jeremy Boissevain, "Play and identity: ritual change in a Maltese village," in Jeremy Boissevain, ed., *Revitalizing European Rituals* (London, 1992), p. 151.

"wanted me to cut cards with them again."[28] The gambling by artisans in the taverns of Paris, like those of the gin palaces or inns of the cities of the Austrian Netherlands, was seldom ruinous – drinks or food for all the players, or perhaps a third or maybe a half of a day's wage. Similarly, the English craftsman John Smith rolled dice with a potter for tankards of beer at an alehouse in Wantage, ultimately setting himself back 10 shillings. Most losses probably were much smaller. Gambling like this, then, may be thought of as a form of reciprocity among the players, even a kind of investment in the cohesiveness of the group. Thus cheating, or keeping one's winnings, was a violation of sociability and an affront to the community. In eighteenth-century Paris a group of master artisans complained of a player who had joined their game and kept his winnings. The game had been played with the understanding that each would leave his winnings to cover the bill. The man who kept his was told to leave the group, and was further informed that he was not worthy of being in the company of respectable people. He had incurred a debt of honor, and had not canceled it with, in Brennan's words, "the appropriately symbolic exchange of shared consumption."[29]

Bibliography

Entries marked with a * designate recommended readings for new students of the subject.

Ariès, Philippe, and Jean-Claude Margolin, eds. *Les jeux à la Renaissance*. Paris, 1982.

Burke, Peter. *Popular Culture in Early Modern Europe*. London, 1978.

Davis, Robert C. *The War of the Fists: Popular Culture and Public Violence in Late Renaissance Venice*. New York, 1994.

*Huizinga, Johan. *Homo Ludens: A Study of the Play-Element in Culture*. Boston, 1955; orig. edn 1938.

Martin, John. "A journeymen's feast of fools." *Journal of Medieval and Renaissance Studies* 17:2 (1987), 149–74.

Muir, Edward. *Ritual in Early Modern Europe*. Cambridge, 1997.

*Thomas, Keith. "Work and leisure." *Past and Present* 29 (1964), 50–66.

Yeo, Eileen, and Stephen Yeo, "Ways of seeing: control and leisure versus class and struggle," in Eileen Yeo and Stephen Yeo, eds., *Popular Culture and Class Conflict, 1590–1914: Explorations in the History of Labour and Leisure*. Atlantic Highlands, 1981.

[28] Jacques-Louis Ménétra, *Journal of My Life*, trans. Arthur Goldhammer (New York, 1986), p. 66.

[29] Thomas Brennan, *Public Drinking and Popular Culture in 18th-Century Paris* (Princeton, 1988), pp. 253–4.

8   Epilogue: artisans in the era of industrial capitalism

Something happened during the late eighteenth and nineteenth centuries that fundamentally transformed the artisanry of Europe's cities. Of course, it is beyond the scope of this book to present this transformation in detail, but the long history of artisans and artisan culture would be incomplete without at least an overview, however cursory it inevitably will seem to specialists of the period, of some of the more significant developments that led to the eclipse of the traditional artisan. In fact, as is well known, multiple forces – legal, political, intellectual, demographic, and economic – converged during the era of industrialization, and one result was the destruction of the culture of the artisan and the transformation of his and her identity. Of course, it did not happen overnight (it took 150 years), but there can be little question that, *grosso modo*, Europe's cities in 1750 held hundreds of thousands of men and women who more or less conformed to the cultural profile that I have presented in this book, and that by 1900 very few did. These vestiges of the past were concentrated in certain places – Germany and southern Europe. Everywhere, regardless of the remnants of an earlier age, artisans gradually became something else – shopkeepers, mechanics, or waged workers – and thought of themselves as such.

In the world of ideas and discourse, over these two centuries, the eighteenth and the nineteenth, liberalism slowly displaced corporatism as the dominant idiom which informed social, political, legal, and economic organization and thought. Proponents of liberalism envisioned a natural economy that performed at peak efficiency only when governmental regulation was excluded, and a polity that in principle and in the name of freedom denied the place and influence of special privilege. The successful march of liberalism toward ideological dominance occurred at the same time that the the population soared and with it the number of new, urban, department-store-shopping consumers. And, of course, within the ascendant logic of industrial capitalism which liberalism helped to define, the economy was transformed according to principles of scale and conformed increasingly to a singular notion of *a* market economy. This defined out of existence (and obscured for future historians) the various kinds of markets (and market logics) that had existed during the old regime.

From corporatism to liberalism

We might think of liberalism, as we have with corporatism in chapter 1, as a cosmology, or as a rhetorical system for ordering the world and making sense of it. Though the historical varieties of corporatism and liberalism were great, in general it remains true that each articulated organizing principles which informed social, legal, political, and economic life. Where corporatism embraced the principles of paternalism, hierarchy, and discipline in the social and political realm, and the economic principle of containing competition and channeling production and distribution toward what was perceived as the public good, liberalism championed the principles of an unregulated or "free" economy based in what was thought to be "natural" market exchange (often called "liberty of commerce"), individual self-determination, and absolute private property.

As Steven Kaplan has recently pointed out, the organizing principles of both corporatism and liberalism – as all sweeping cosmological systems are – were imbedded historically in social taxonomies, which in turn were closely linked to the exercise of power. He cogently asserts that "the tools of distinction used to forge the classification system are tools of social and political control . . . This taxonomy must overcome and in some sense permanently disqualify rival systems . . ."[1] Kaplan thus encourages us, rightly, I think, to consider how social, political, and economic relations intermix to produce the social classification and the conditions for the appropriation by social actors of certain principles that inform these relations.

The rhetoric prescribing the corporate regime, as we have seen, was embodied in most polities of medieval and early modern Europe. As creations and creatures of political authority, guilds – the classic corporate institution – were simultaneously empowered and rendered vulnerable to political authority. As *choses du roi*, as they were called in France, their privileges may have been sanctioned by royal authority, but what would happen to those privileges, indeed, to the corporate system in general, if political authorities embraced a "rival classificatory system," to reinvoke Kaplan's phrase? In the eighteenth century the official

---

[1] Steven L. Kaplan, "Social classification and representation in the corporate world of 18th-century France: Turgot's carnival," in Steven L. Kaplan and Cynthia Koepp, eds., *Work in France* (Ithaca, 1986), p. 177.

system of classification, corporatism, was increasingly challenged by just such a "rival system," that came to be called liberalism; but the displacement of corporatism was hardly rapid or unconflicted. There was considerable ambivalence within the ranks of political authority, with cameralists, "Colbertists," and "liberals" of different stripes all vying for influence. Even within the ranks of "liberals" themselves there was little agreement. French "liberals" in the eighteenth century well reveal the ambiguity: while embracing the principle of "liberty," some were nonetheless reticent to dissolve corporate bonds for fear of unleashing the anarchy of social equality. As Catharina Lis and Hugo Soly have shown for the Austrian Low Countries, other "liberals" and entrepreneurial capitalists welcomed state intervention in the economy in certain situations where it protected new industries or seemed to encourage economic growth, while still others (who counted guildsmen in their ranks), as Gail Bossenga and Jean-Pierre Hirsch for Lille in northern France, Simona Cerutti for Turin in Northern Italy, Jaume Torras for Igualada in Catalonia, as well as Lis and Soly for the cities of Brabant and Flanders all show, wanted to preserve corporations because they were viewed as good bases from which to pursue individual interest and economic gain.[2]

French state policy, to cite the best-studied and most notorious case, reflects well this state of confusion. Despite the inroads the principles of liberalism had made among "enlightened" economists and philosophers, in a five-year span in the 1760s the crown again tried to universalize the corporate regime throughout the kingdom (recall the edicts of 1581 and 1673) yet permitted rural textile producers complete freedom from corporate regulation. Even more indicative of the confusion and contradictions within state policy and the varying hues of "liberalism" is the episode of Controller-General Turgot's attempt to abolish guilds in February 1776 and his abrupt dismissal in May. Turgot, a serious philosopher as well as a doctrinaire reformist government minister (he penned an entry in the *Encyclopédie* on epistemology and was an intimate of Gournay and the physiocrats), saw guilds as millstones around the neck of the French economy and so asserted that sweeping them away would liberate commercial and industrial activity. Turgot, however, was not thinking in simply narrow economic terms, nor were his opponents in the Parlement of Paris, those staunch

---

[2] Gail Bossenga, *The Politics of Privilege: Old Regime and Revolution in Lille* (Cambridge, 1991); Jean-Pierre Hirsch, *Les Deux Rêves de Commerce* (Paris, 1991); Catharina Lis and Hugo Soly, "Entrepreneurs, corporations et autorités publiques au Brabant et en Flandre à la fin de l'Ancien Régime," *Revue du Nord* 76 (1994), 725–44; Jaume Torras, "Corporations et liberté de fabrication en Espagne au XVIIIe siècle," *Revue du Nord* 76 (1994), 745–51.

defenders of corporatism. Both the minister and the judges were fundamentally concerned with preserving hierarchy and discipline, but equally fundamentally disagreed on how that best could be accomplished. Turgot sought to replace what he thought was the artificial and ineffective hierarchy of corporatism with a natural one, and so he shared no sympathy with his opponents who clamored that his edict would dissolve the bonds of subordination and was, therefore, a blueprint for anarchy. Turgot, however, did not equate liberty with equality, instead asserting that "entrepreneurs or masters" and "simple workers" converged naturally in the marketplace, the latter working for the former and thereby entering a relation which created a "distinction . . . which is based on the nature of things and does not depend at all on the institution of incorporated guilds."[3] The Parlement of Paris thought Turgot's natural hierarchy a dangerous illusion, and denounced the Controller-General's edict in the name of corporatism and the social order it supposedly guaranteed. These jurists proclaimed that the "principle of incorporation" embraced all of France in a "chain" whose links led directly to the "authority of the throne."[4] To sever one link was to destroy the chain, and ultimately the monarchy itself.

Turgot lost the battle, but liberalism eventually won the war. Conflicted as its history was, over the long run liberalism did prove corrosive to corporatism in general and to guilds in particular, as the cascade of liberal-inspired legislation in the late eighteenth and nineteenth centuries abolishing them all across Europe attests. The assault on corporations may have been largely economically inspired, but corporations were more than simply means to organizing work; rather, they were a fundamental unit of the entire system of social representation and social control. Their dissolution could only have widely felt cultural ramifications, most notably, for our purposes, in the world of the artisan.

During the eighteenth century, especially in England, we find the language of the law shifting from a defense of traditional collective rights to one of utility based on individual rights. Artisans had "since time immemorial" based their sense of status upon widely held notions of customary legitimacy. As the law shifted ground, however, the artisan's claim of traditional, collective rights lost its bite. As a result, craftsmen were confronted with a new legal world, and had to adapt to it. In France during the Revolution, the law changed more abruptly, and artisans promptly responded to it. A declaration by the National Assembly on August 11, 1789 simply called for the "reformation of the trades," but guilds were only officially abolished by the Allarde law

---

[3] Emile Coornaert, *Les Corporations en France avant 1789* (Paris, 1968).
[4] Kaplan, pp. 197–8.

enacted on March 17, 1791. This law legislated free contract to be the foundation of the new social order and abolished all bodies (notably corporations) and any regulation that hindered such relations. The Allarde law at first glance seems most detrimental to master artisans and seems to empower journeymen, for now no institutions, like guilds, legally existed to mediate labor relations as they had done in the past. Indeed, since 1789 journeymen and even apprentices had been claiming freedom from the constraints of guilds on the basis of individual rights, citing the *Declaration of the Rights of Man and Citizen*, the text of which was approved by the National Assembly on August 26. This is precisely what the apprentice wigmakers of Bordeaux claimed in late August 1789, the ink hardly yet dry on the *Declaration*. They asserted a right to be self-employed because, they inferred, guild regulations "were abolished by the Declaration."[5]

Given the history of relations between masters and journeymen and apprentices that was steeped in a deep concern among masters about labor indiscipline that during the eighteenth century virtually reached the point of terror, we might expect the masters to have steadfastly opposed the Allarde law. In fact, after the law was passed masters seem most concerned about their property investment in mastership licenses which, after the Allarde law, were technically worthless. The licenses were replaced by a new tax, the *patente*, which was assessed on all artisans running their own shops. In the wake of the Allarde law masters spent their energy suing in court for refunds on their Old Regime investment, but we do not hear the expected outcry against the law in terms of a breakdown of order prompted by labor insubordination. No doubt this was because another law more in their interest followed on the heels of the Allarde law. Three months after the Allarde law was passed, the Le Chapelier law was enacted, and here all forms of trade organizations or combinations were declared illegal. This meant journeymen brotherhoods, and so at a stroke the Le Chapelier law banned the basic institution upon which journeyman power had rested for centuries. With journeymen brotherhoods now outlawed, the masters' concern for labor indiscipline was considerably assuaged.

The gradual displacement of corporatism by liberalism affected more than labor relations, for by sweeping the guild from the historical stage, it deeply affected an artisan's sense of status and identity. Guilds, I have argued, served a fundamental purpose of placing members and non-members in the social and political firmament, offering a device for social distinction, differentiation, and rank. As we have seen, Old Regime

[5] Josette Pontet, "Craftsmen and revolution in Bordeaux," in Geoffrey Crossick, ed., *The Artisan and the European Town, 1500–1900* (Aldershot, 1997), p. 123.

society everywhere in Europe was, to recall what Harold Perkin said of England, "a finely graded hierarchy of great subtlety and discrimination, in which men [and women] were acutely aware of their exact relation to those immediately above and below them." To be sure, life was in part a struggle for access to material resources, but it was also, and perhaps more profoundly, a struggle over classification, a scramble to accede to or to preserve one's *état*, degree, or *Stand*. Definitions of property folded smoothly into this classificatory system. According to the legal definitions of property in the corporately organized old regime, alongside absolute private property which an owner could dispose of as he saw fit, there was property in public functions – venal offices, or, for master artisans, masterships. This last form of property was critically important because it carried legal privilege with it, and so conferred upon the holder his rank and public standing. It legally defined his place in society. Most of the varieties of property did not survive the French Revolution, the case nearly everywhere in Europe (parts of Germany seem the notable exception, where masterships still carried legal sanction and formed the basis of a *cursus honorum* within the trades well into the second half of the nineteenth century),[6] when liberal political and legal regimes were established. The drastic narrowing of the legal definition of property meant that privilege and property were now severed, and so no longer was property a possession which legally conferred rank and distinction. For a guild member of the early modern period, his rank had been represented by his mastership and guild membership, conferring a distinction which helped secure a living, but also which conferred a social identity.

Such a hierarchical system had been equally a power structure, and so distinction and difference were animated by a deeply felt concern for subordination and discipline of inferiors. Breach of discipline by journeymen or wage-workers reflected more than instability in the labor market, but also and more dramatically, a perceived threat to hierarchy and the principle of distinction. Masters were viscerally sensitive to insubordination by journeymen and wage-workers, and journeymen were keen, in turn, not only on contesting masters but also on maintaining the inferiority of wage-workers beneath them. Both masters and journeymen invoked hierarchy and distinction to fashion social identity. When this system of social and political classification was undermined in the eighteenth century and eventually displaced in the nineteenth, the guilds disappeared in most places and legally enshrined masterships

---

[6] See Heinz-Gerhard Haupt, "La Survivance des corporations au XIXe siècle. Une esquisse comparative," *Revue du Nord* 76 (1994), 806.

with them. This left masters and journeymen to their own devices to attempt to fashion a sense of place and a sense of self in a differently configured world.

The tidal wave of liberal legislation (especially its legal and economic aspects) inundated most of Europe in the nineteenth century. The Prussian *Stadtordenung* of 1808 followed France's lead in narrowing the definition of property by severing its links with privilege and thus formal rank. Henceforth possession of absolute private property (this did not include mastership in a guild) was the sole criterion for citizenship. Elsewhere as well the meaning of property was narrowed, and incorporated guilds were juridically attacked. During the Napoleonic occupation of Westphalia and the Rhineland guilds were abolished, but even in areas where they survived, corporate rights were increasingly limited, especially concerning regulation over admission to the guild. Indeed, all across Europe corporate regimes were redefined, disempowered, or dismantled, and guilds abolished. In Spain guilds met their demise in 1812, in Sweden in 1847, in Austria in 1859. Where guilds were closely tied to municipal governance, as in southern Germany, or where indemnities were to be paid master artisans for the proprietary loss of their masterships, as was the case in Prussia, they lasted longer, but over the course of the first seventy years of the century, despite intermittent periods where "reformism" lost influence in government (as in Prussia in the 1820s), a powerful incursion of liberalism is evident. Prussia legally embraced freedom of commerce in 1810 (striking a blow at the corporate privileges of monopoly), and in 1870–1 the unified *Reich* applied it everywhere. In England, even though the livery companies had lost any practical purchase on guild regulation or even economic importance in the eighteenth century but remained important as the avenue to municipal office, the companies lost their legal right to control the apprenticeship system with the repeal in 1814 of the Statute of Artificers of 1563.

Status, independence, and skill

By 1870 everywhere in Europe corporatism had been largely dismantled, displaced by liberalism. Certainly such a sweeping displacement could only have a thunderous impact on the lives of artisans, something of which historians have long been aware. Part of the artisan's response, as we will see, was a *de facto* continuation of collectivist expressions, even though they were deprived of any basis in law. In the face of these changes, what was to become of the much-valued sense of status and the sense of independence that was at the core of artisanal identity? In 1826 John Gast, an English shipwright and leading activist of the labor movement, wrote:

Let all the useful and *valuable* members of every trade who wish to appear *respectable*, unite with each other and be in friendship with all other trades, and you will render yourselves *worthy* members of society, at once *respectable* and *respected*.[7] [my emphasis]

In this call for worker unity Gast was addressing fellow artisans – masters and journeymen – and he strikes the chords of respect, respectability, worth, and value that he assumes will resonate in his audience's ears. These interlocking values spoke directly to an artisan's identity and his sense of status. German "home townsmen," perhaps the quintessence of the corporate-minded artisan, would have understood Gast's speech as an appeal to *Eigentum*, the guildsman's identity, which was couched in *Ehrbarkeit*, or honorable status, in Mack Walker's words, "something sensed and displayed and received within a community."[8] The sense of worth, respect, and respectability under the corporate regime only implicitly assumed a master's independence; rather, it was represented by the estate of mastership, a legal and social status dependent upon hierarchical distinction where masters in the nature of things were superior to journeymen who were superior to nonguild wage-workers.

As mastership lost its official place in the late eighteenth and nineteenth centuries, master artisans were forced to devise a new criterion of distinction, and they seized upon independence. In a sense, there is continuity to the corporate world, but independence emerged as a more clearly defined and increasingly urgent value in the nineteenth century. Masters, no longer distinguishable from their inferiors by corporate status, now separated themselves from the lower elements, the "ill-bred workmen," by a "respectability" overtly resting upon independence. But how independent were masters in the increasingly new scheme of things? The redefinition of status from mastership defined through corporatism to independence, in any case, hardly shifted artisans onto firmer ground.

Without a legally sanctioned mastership, how was independence to be represented? Freedom from penury (and from charity) or proletarianization was part of it, but once again we must guard against reducing the meaning of identity directly to economic factors. After all, for centuries

---

[7] John Breuilly, "Artisan economy, artisan politics, artisan ideology: the artisan contribution to the nineteenth-century European labour movement," in Clive Emsley and James Walvin, eds., *Artisans, Peasants, and Proletarians, 1760–1860* (London, 1985), p. 189.

[8] Mack Walker, *German Home Towns: Community, State, and General Estate, 1648–1871* (Ithaca, 1971), p. 101.

an artisan's sense of status was supported by a sense of custom and legitimacy. Earnings were vitally important – they always had been – but they were important precisely because they had to be sufficient to support a lifestyle proper to one's status. Money was traded, in effect, for forms of cultural capital through which one's status could be demonstrated, read, and socially secured. Independence from public charity was essential, and so money was needed for membership in "friendly" or mutual aid societies, clubs, and eventually trade unions. Money (and credit) was also the oil that greased the wheels of informal yet hardly trivial sociability, needed to buy a round of drinks for one's fellows at the local wineshop, alehouse, or pub (the modern form which clearly emerged in the 1830s).

Among the many meanings mastership carried in the old regime, one was competency in the craft to create products useful to the public. Competency, in turn, carried with it a tacit possession of what has come to be called, somewhat anachronistically, "skill." As we have seen in chapter 1, skill meant much more than manual facility, as the co-ordination of perceptual and motor activity. Rather it was a quality, and a possession. Apprentices and journeymen destined for mastership were invested with this quality through educational training, while the wage-worker, who may have been able to perform certain tasks adequately and even as well as some journeymen, was not in possession of the full know-how, the "mysteries" of the trade. Masters shared knowledge with a chosen few, thus keeping the labor force, to recall Sonenscher's term, "dis-integrated" and therefore, hoped the masters, more easily disci-plined. Masters knew well that knowledge and authority were con-nected. The quality and property of skill, therefore, for all of its importance in the fashioning of marketable products, was a critical indicator of status and was used to discipline the workforce. It was possessed by the master and the journeyman destined for mastership, and so created a core of "skilled" workers surrounded by a periphery of "unskilled," a division that articulated rank hierarchy and the distribu-tion of power within the workplace according to its possession.

John Rule confirms this picture for eighteenth- and early nineteenth-century English artisans by demonstrating that skill was a property and thus a "distinguishing mark separating the artisan from the common labourer." A technical aptitude in the fashioning of products, true, but skill gained its meaning as symbolic capital, the possession of which "entitled its holder to dignity and respect." It was conferred by a community and was protected as a "right" by tradition and custom.[9]

9 John Rule, "The property of skill in the period of manufacture," in Patrick Joyce, ed., *The Historical Meanings of Work* (Cambridge, 1987), p. 108.

Sonenscher similarly emphasizes that skill was invested with meaning in France by its place in a system of difference and distinction. Focusing on the world of journeymen, he points out that prowess to fashion an item well was certainly valued among these men, but such skill was valued for social reasons as much as economic ones. In a world where a vast pool of laborers worked in trades with a "relatively limited range of materials" and that saw few "rigid technical and occupational divisions," there was a wide dissemination of similar abilities. So when journeymen brotherhoods ritually demonstrated the feats of prowess of their members in competitions, they were securing their community and articulating its boundaries by transforming "similarity into difference in a world in which too many people could do the same thing."[10]

Recent research on women's work has deepened yet further our understanding of the meaning of skill. The "skill" of female artisans had been undergoing a process of devaluation for centuries before industrialization, a process which had nothing to do with technology, factories, or fixed capital. Instead, since the devaluation of female skills was inversely related to the definition of skill by men, such "deskilling" was a product of particular social and gender relations. Among the lessons we learn from this gloomy process is that it is not enough to define skill as manual facility, nor is it sufficient to define skill as knowledge of the properties of materials and how to assemble them into products, however necessary that is. As we have seen, seamstresses, after all, according to this definition, were skilled, yet they were construed by the men of their world to be "unskilled."

Equally "unskilled" in the eyes of male master artisans and journeymen were the "chamberers" or "roomworkers," those clandestine workers we met in chapter 3. Judging just from their technical aptitude, many of these workers would seem "skilled" to us, but judging from the avalanche of complaints by master guildsmen of the widespread existence of these clandestine workers and the legislation designed to regulate them, they were disparaged as "unskilled" and, as the French language of the time tellingly put it, sans état, or literally "without rank."

Skill, then, was as much a cultural construct delimiting boundaries of a community defined by status and a sense of difference as an indicator of the technical capacity of a worker. For masters skill, or the lack thereof, helped articulate a system that created a hierarchical slot (as well as a division of labor) for women, for apprentices, for journeymen,

---

[10] Michael Sonenscher, "Mythical work: workshop production and the compagnonnages of eighteenth-century France," in Patrick Joyce, ed., *The Historical Meanings of Work* (Cambridge, 1987), p. 56.

for "roomworkers," and, of course, for themselves. Hegel perceptively pointed out that the evidence of a master craftsman's "skill" was not his technical wizardry, but rather his membership in his guild community. Such membership conferred a collective status upon the guildsman via his mastership, and granted him a sense of possessing a "property in skill" which marked him off, in his mind, from others supposedly without it. Through mastership the property in skill was, in theory, legally secured. Skill so construed was imbedded in a male master artisan's identity which was rooted in the soil of rank and hierarchy.

In the eighteenth and nineteenth centuries we find the defense of skill and its association with status and dignity even more emphasized by artisans than it had been previously. This is because the status associated with a possession of skill and the knowledge and power it carried was being increasingly contested, threatening the degradation of the master artisan and the "skilled" journeyman alike. The property of skill was a frontier to be held against the unskilled (including many women), the numbers of whom were rising with the burgeoning population of the late eighteenth and nineteenth centuries. This was the real threat of technical innovation, mechanization, and factory production. These newcomers to the economic scene did not throw many people out of work, but they did rob them of their property in skill and so undermined their status. Artisan technique had been based on rule of thumb estimations, a way of knowing that was under attack in the late seventeenth and eighteenth centuries by scientists and engineers whose knowledge was based on a rational and analytical evaluation of procedures and materials. The largely organic artisanal language of thickness, weight, and height was challenged by the mechanistic language of physics, which, moreover, was embraced by the administrative elite in government who yoked such a way of knowing and thinking about production with the idea of progress. They tried, as Daniel Roche writes, "to place technical invention under the tutelage of scientific experts."[11] Thus in France during the 1780s under the administration of finance minister Jacques Necker, 1300 inventors were registered by a government bureau. Reflecting the artisan's ability to adapt to new conditions, note that two out of three of the inventors were urban artisans, two-thirds of them hailing from provincial cities, not the capital.

The invasion of a different way of knowing about physical work was joined by inexorable changes in the organization of production. Mass production and standardization further fragmented artisanal knowledge and recast relations of authority. Loss of independence and "deskilling"

---

[11] Daniel Roche, *Histoire des choses banales* (Paris, 1997), p. 65.

did not simply erode the skilled artisan's economic security, although it did that. More broadly, it further contributed to the replacement of the traditional template against which status was understood, and through which artisans knew who and what they were. This is one reason why English masters defended the apprenticeship system long after livery companies and guilds had any economic significance. It is also why masters struggled for the better part of the nineteenth century to resurrect corporatism, even if it had to be *sans la lettre*.

Collectivism

William Sewell, Bernard Moss, and Cynthia Truant have eloquently and persuasively written about nineteenth-century French journeymen drawing upon a collectivist tradition in their effort to staunch the erosion of their status which was ebbing as their property in skill was threatened. We now know that there existed clear connections between corporate craft traditions and early forms of socialism, and that there were remarkable continuities between the "rites of labor" that defined the journeymen brotherhoods of the old regime and those of the era of industrialization. Sewell has found that even in 1848 skilled workers were still thinking in terms of distinction determined by membership in *états*, evidence of a reconfiguration of corporatism, and that "unskilled" workers were so designated not because of a glaring lack of technical aptitude, but because they had no corporate traditions. This picture which portrays connections between worker collectivism and Old Regime corporate attitudes has been confirmed by scholars working on Italy, Spain, Britain, Germany, and elsewhere. Each of these accounts has been framed within the historiographical tradition of locating the origins of trade unions in particular and of the working-class movement in general.

Space does not permit recounting here the histories of trade unionism or of the working class movements in Europe during the era of industrialization, but it is worth briefly considering in two significant examples – Britain and Germany – the varieties of trajectories from an Old Regime artisanry that such formation could follow. In Britain, the "tramping system" preserved strong continuities with the old regime until the 1840s. A journeyman on the road could expect a friendly reception at his trade's house of call and a night's hospitality there. He could also expect that his brothers, as they had for centuries, would either find employment for him, or point him toward a town where work might be available. These networks could be extensive, and the numbers of tramping journeymen huge. For example, in 1800 20,000 journeymen tailors were organized in a network that spanned forty houses of call, and despite the masters' demand for action by the magistrates against the houses to "destroy communication" among the workers, in 1818 the network was still in place. So pervasive in so many trades were these tramping networks that R. A. Leeson has concluded that "the tramp helped build the [trade] union . . . Thanks to the tramping system, the unions were able to grow, defying both the employers and the law. As both a passive and active factor, 'tramping' brought the nineteenth-century trade unions into being." [12]

Tramping certainly played its part in the British worker movement, but we also must consider the role played by the "friendly societies." The Combination Acts of 1799 and 1800 outlawed worker combinations whose objective was to seek wage increases or to oppose cuts, to alter the length of the work day, and of course, to call a strike, but these laws left untouched the friendly societies. Almost immediately suspicions among lawmakers and employers arose about these organizations being "frequently made the cloak . . . [offering] commodious opportunities to foment sedition and form illegal combinations." And it was not long before a government official could pronounce that the Combination Acts had been "in general a dead letter upon those artisans upon whom it was intended to have effect."[13] To make matters worse for the authorities, these clandestine but widespread artisanal "societies" began to transcend trade boundaries as journeymen began to share the recognition that the problems facing individual trades were in fact universal. Between 1820 and 1826, for instance, steam-engine makers, smiths, papermakers, shipwrights, pottery-makers, and others organized into one trade society pitched toward mutual support in the form of financial solidarity during strikes.

The growth of labor unions and the economic slumps of the 1840s combined to signal the approaching end of the traditional British tramping system. The waves of industry-wide mass unemployment and the means of more rapid travel and better communication undermined the need and the effectiveness of finding employment by hitting the road. Workers in the industrializing sectors of the economy came to adjust themselves to the boom and bust cycles of early industrial capitalism, and increasing numbers of them opted to stay home during periods of unemployment and ride out the storm until the production cycle resumed. The workplace in these sectors was undergoing a steady

---

[12] Leeson, *Travelling Brothers: The Six Centuries Road from Craft Fellowship to Trade Unionism* (London, 1979), p. 156.
[13] Quoted in ibid., p. 113.

process of structural change, and some artisans were redefining their role within it. As Clive Behagg observes, many a journeyman/worker increasingly abandoned the language of customary rights to justify his relations with his master/employer while he increasingly adopted the language of the market. In 1869 a member of the Operative Gunmakers Society gave an address to the Birmingham Society of Artisans on the topic "Trades' unions: are they consistent with the laws of political economy?" a question he answered decidedly in the affirmative.

The trajectories toward working-class formation from craft traditions are varied in Germany, too. As in France and Britain, some historians have pointed to apparent connections between the traditional craft system and the rise of the labor movement, and likewise they have focused on the 1830s and 1840s as a pivotal time when collective worker organizations like friendly societies and workers' education clubs recruited their membership largely from journeymen tailors, shoemakers, carpenters, masons, and so on. The German labor movement was anti-corporate in its rhetoric, a clear difference from the French experience, but in many other ways they were similar. Other historians, however, have noted the continued legal existence of guilds throughout the first half of the nineteenth century (in contrast to Britain and France), and have concluded that the craft tradition (where the master was still very much the dominant figure in the system of labor discipline due to the survival of corporate rules) remained relatively independent of the worker movement which grew parallel to, and not out of, the craft tradition. In fact, these historiographical approaches are not as far apart as they may seem, although most historians today would tilt toward the first interpretation rather than the second. As Jürgen Kocka reminds us, clear evidence exists that in some places, like Hamburg, "local . . . unions grew directly out of previously existing journeymen organizations."[14] Moreover, Kocka insists, by the 1860s the free labor contract had been legally established everywhere and corporate laws had been rescinded. The tramping system of journeymen (Gesellen) had already buckled and begun to break apart as a result of the economic slumps and unemployment of the 1830s and 1840s, and the industrialization boom of the 1860s and 1870s largely finished them off. In this crucible of structural change, German journeymen/workers, like their British counterparts, adapted to the new circumstances, not only or even primarily reacting defensively against innovation and change, but proactively, fashioning the worker movement into a movement of

[14] Jürgen Kocka, "Craft traditions and the labour movement in nineteenth-century Germany," in Pat Thane, Geoffrey Crossick, and Roderick Floud, eds., *The Power of the Past* (Cambridge, 1984), p. 103.

emancipation and demanding a fair share of the rewards of the economic progress that liberals were forever crowing about.

Most of the historiography about the fate of artisans in the nineteenth century has, as we have now seen, been framed by questions about the origins of the workers' movement. What such a perspective invariably leaves out is the trajectory of the master craftsman. We can hardly find it unexpected that the master artisans of Germany (many of them "home townsmen") fought, vainly as it turned out, to roll back the liberal dismantling of corporatism at the Frankfurt Parliament in 1848 (although journeymen lobbied here for easier entry into guilds), a demand they resurrected in the 1860s. Less well known, however, is the resurgence of corporate ideology among master artisans in Napoleonic France. Demands for the institutional restoration of corporate structures in commerce and industry rested on the familiar argument that such structures would maintain social and economic stability, assure high quality products, and discipline labor. In 1806 a butcher's words would have made an eighteenth-century *parlementaire* proud: "masterships and guilds suit a monarchical state; they are one of the mainstays of this kind of government; they help it to police the secondary and lower classes of society."[15] Corporatism was not resurrected to become the law of the land once again, but technically illicit employer associations of master artisans nonetheless were formed in the first two decades of the nineteenth century. Membership *per force* was voluntary, and these groups never counted a majority of masters in their ranks, but it is telling that a syndicate of master shoemakers established in 1818 was dominated by the small masters, and their primary goal was to bring discipline to the labor market by controlling the employment agency of the trade. The resurgence of extra-legal corporatism found expression not only in working-class trade unionism, or even socialism, but also in the employer associations of tradesmen and shopkeepers that dotted the business landscape of the nineteenth century, and not just in France.

The collective spirit among masters as well as journeymen also found expression in the burgeoning of "friendly societies." In 1793 in London such mutual aid organizations (close descendants of Old Regime confraternities) enrolled at least 650,000 members, by 1803 704,000, and by 1815 925,000. These figures are undoubtedly underestimates because they are based on only those societies that registered with the authorities, and in 1800 probably only about half of them did. In that year 654 societies registered in Middlesex, 254 in the City of London

---

[15] Michael Sibalis, "Corporations after the corporations: the debate on restoring the guilds under Napoleon I and the Restoration," *French Historical Studies* 15 (1988), 721.

alone. These societies grew while the Combination Acts of 1799 and 1800 were on the books, no doubt because they were not covered by those Acts. We find similar developments in France. In Paris in 1820 there were 120 artisan mutual aid societies, while just two years later there were 143 involving sixty crafts and counting 13,000 members. Some of these societies were craft specific, many others were not, but whatever their occupational specificities, they continued to expand, so that by 1846 there were 262 in the capital alone.

Industrialization

For most of the twentieth century historians have debated, often heatedly, the processes of industrialization from the mid-eighteenth century well into the twentieth. Of course, the consensus for most of this time was that an Industrial Revolution occurred. In the past twenty years, however, many historians have opted for an evolutionary view instead. Whatever the pace of change, however, few disagree on its eventual magnitude. We have long known that industrialization had an impact on artisans and handicraft production, but only recently have they been the subject of close and systematic scrutiny. Among some of the focuses of these more recent studies have been the following, each of which was important to the status, identity, and experience of master and journeyman artisans: the reformulation of the role of the state in economic activities; the uneven pace and impact of capital accumulation and distribution through credit; the emerging integrated, capital-intensive economies of scale alongside continued undercapitalized handicraft and provisioning trades that remained dis-integrated or ancillary to the larger integrated enterprises; and changes in the organization of labor influenced as much by cultural factors as purely economic ones. Technological innovation, mechanization, and factory production, though not ignored by historians, no longer hold pride of place. Several historians of both England and France have demonstrated, in fact, that production was structurally transformed in various sectors of the economy by capitalism in the eighteenth and nineteenth centuries but without either mechanization or factories.

The appearance of industrial capitalism without mechanization or factories has prompted considerable rethinking about working-class formation, as has an appreciation of the cultural factors involved in such formation. Moreover, Christopher Johnson has observed that "a good deal of our work as historians of the industrial transition has concerned the ways in which that vast, amorphous, and ill-defined category of handworkers called 'artisans' experienced the profound legal and economic changes of the age."[16] Most of the literature on artisans has focused either on their radical politics or their proletarianization. There is truth in these scripts – some artisans were radical and some were proletarianized – but again it leaves out of account many sectors of the artisanry. Indeed, such a narrative omits many of those artisans that have been the focus of this book, notably the provisioning trades and the small commodity producers, most of whom were master artisans, and a vast number of whom all across Europe preserved their artisanal workshops until the 1860s, even the 1880s in some parts (like southern Europe). Moreover, scholars have discovered that the industrial transition did not immediately destroy small-scale production, but rather for a time (late into the nineteenth century) produced a whole new set of possibilities for small commodity producers. Only in the last quarter of the century, even later in some parts of Europe, did mechanized, factory production, in a quantum sense, overwhelm the master's shop. Still, prior to that masters everywhere were nonetheless affected by the gradual transition to industrial capitalism. Proletarianization was not the only means by which capital subordinated labor, and becoming a factory worker was only one of the trajectories an artisan might follow in the eighteenth and nineteenth centuries.

Although many masters retained their own shops, working the interstices of large-scale industry or mass marketing or directing their energies toward neighborhood provisioning, they nonetheless found their independence and security increasingly undermined by limited access to credit, raw materials, labor, and markets. In England, this process was well under way by the mid- to late eighteenth century. Coupled with the dismantling of corporatism, the assault of industrial capitalism prompted the ideal of independence to be thrown into relief, an independence that was increasingly illusory. In the eighteenth and nineteenth centuries the ambiguous world whereby the ideal of independence rested awkwardly against the dependency that resulted from liberalism, the extension of capitalism, and galloping population growth, and thus more consumers, can be seen in a variety of trades in England, France, Germany, Austria, and no doubt elsewhere. In mid-nineteenth-century England, capitalistic industries like sawmilling, ironmaking, and steelmaking generated an increase in work for the small workshop. Likewise steam-driven sawmills turned out wood that still had to be fashioned in the carpenters' and furniture-makers' shops, while the enormous furnaces of the Black Country provided large quantities of

[16] Christopher Johnson, "Artisans vs. fabricants: urban protoindustrialization and the evolution of work culture in Lodève and Bedarieux, 1740–1830," *Mélanges de l'école française de Rome* 99:2 (1987), 1047.

material to thousands of local smiths toiling in their own shops. The cutlers of Sheffield similarly worked the metal rolling out of the local steelmills. These shops were organized in the traditional manner, with masters taking on or laying off workers and journeymen (labor was abundant due to population growth) as industrial output and the pace of demand dictated.

Yet beneath the similarities with the old regime there lurked a difference, for the seeming independence was built increasingly on a foundation of dependency. No longer did masters, or shopkeepers, for that matter, have much control over the access to their materials, now provided by merchant industrialists, factors, and wholesalers. Moreover, masters came to rely on a steady flow of orders, often from only a few middlemen or owners of factories. The same can be said of access to credit and to markets which was increasingly controlled by merchant operations. Of course, even in the old regime masters were not entirely independent either, especially in emerging economies of scale and those like textiles organized on the putting-out system. But the urban master tailor, shoemaker, cabinet-maker, cutler, butcher, or baker was not as encumbered by these dependencies as his descendants experiencing the transition to industrialism would be.

Population growth across Europe in the late eighteenth and nine-teenth centuries triggered overcrowding and underemployment in most trades, and the market for consumer goods which moved more regularly by developments in the transport system, expanded dramatically and became increasingly well integrated. Joined by the deregulation of prices, craft entry, production levels, and the labor force which the credo of "liberty of commerce" so dear to liberal regimes would bring in its train, these forces structurally altered most trades in the towns of Europe well before mechanization and factory production became the norm. This is especially true for the garment trades, where the trajec-tories toward proletarianization or dependency are quite evident. In Paris between 1800 and 1850, for example, tailors had to contend with an influx of migrants from the provinces at the same time that confection (the production of ready-made clothing) was taking hold. Confection was based on cheap materials, volume production, mass marketing increasingly through department stores, and sweated, cheap labor (outwork rather than work done in the master's shop), performed increasingly by women. By 1850 real wages had plummeted as sweated labor represented a shocking 83 percent of the workforce. This is proletarianization by most any measure, but what happened to the master tailors? Some, of course, sold higher quality clothing to consu-mers dissatisfied with off-the-rack apparel, but many others were driven to confection. Overcrowding in the trade and the competition of out-working increasingly brought master tailors into a dependency upon the merchants who provided the raw materials, the credit, and the outlet to markets.

The nineteenth-century Parisian tailors epitomize the processes of proletarianization and dependency without the factory, and it is a tale that can be told of other consumer-oriented trades, and not just in France. Indeed France, which experienced population growth but relatively slower than that felt in Germany and England, seems to have suffered relatively less from proletarianization. In Germany, laws permitting free migration and unrestricted entry into crafts led to over-crowding and underemployment, and in trades like the garment crafts this drove many journeymen and poorer masters toward proletarianization (87 percent of craftsmen in these trades in 1890 were solitary outworkers working for piecerates or wages).

But proletarianization was not the universal fate of the provisioning tradesman or the small commodity producer in general. Small produ-cers able to maintain their shops and the appearance of independence remained numerous. In 1803 England and Wales counted 25,000 shop-owning artisan families and another 74,500 shopkeeping households. The description of Britain as the "workshop of the world" was apt. In London in 1841 a census listed 840 separate craft occupations, re-flecting the traditional response to increased demand which was the continual subdivision of the steps of production within "crafts" and the reduction of production to a series of separate component tasks. In London a decade later a census reveals that three-quarters of London's firms still employed fewer than five men, and 86 percent fewer than ten. And this probably underestimates the actual number of firms, especially the small ones, for we find listed in the 1853 *Watkins' London Directory* 2,555 shoemakers and 3,207 master tailors where the census of 1851 listed only 1,841 and 1,782 respectively. Still, just going by the census, one is struck by the numerical preponderance of small-scale enterprises: 97 percent of the bakers employed four or fewer workers, while the same can be said of 79 percent of the carpenters, 72 percent of the cabinet-makers, 71 percent of the shoemakers, and 70 percent of the tailors. We can find only eighty enterprises employing more than a hundred workers, and just twelve over 300. Such a profile looks remarkably like the bipolar, core–periphery structure of the old regime, especially when we observe that many of the smallest firms in fact were outworkers employed off site by the larger ones that, increasingly engaged in production of scale and having the means for high and sustained capital investment, clearly had a competitive edge over the smaller ones.

In Germany in 1875 40 percent of all persons active in the industries of factories, craft, mining, and building were self-employed, running enterprises with fewer than five employees. Likewise nineteenth-century Paris has been called "the city of the small workshop" par excellence, responding to mounting demand as the craft economy always had, by an increased division of labor. Indeed, even with technical innovations we associate with industrialization and factories – the steam engine, the gas and electric motor – we find right to the end of the century many of these small shops using the new machinery on a small scale. In 1906 we still find that half of the French workforce was employed in firms hiring five or fewer workers. This has led many historians to conclude that industrial production (in France especially) seems not to have grown by following the path of factories or capital-intensive technology, but rather through the proliferation of wide varieties of dispersed production.

But, of course, large industrial production *did* come to dominate the economy – no historian disputes that – but more gradually and certainly later than has often been suggested. Much current research points toward the last quarter of the nineteenth century in some parts of Europe (Britain, Germany, the Low Countries, to a lesser extent, France), the early twentieth century in other parts (southern Europe) when we see a quantum transformation in production, processing, and retailing. This transformation was enabled by regularization of demand smoothed by the dramatic changes in transport and communication, price elasticity, capital- intensive, and increasingly standardized production culminating in the assembly line, and, ultimately, the scientific management principles of "Taylorism" and "Fordism." Amid such changes, artisans did not suddenly disappear, but they did become something altogether different, gradually but ineluctably more integrated into production and distribution networks that were controlled by large capital. Intensive subdivision of tasks and subcontracting continued apace, and as independence became increasingly a chimera, artisans gradually evolved into mechanics, shopkeeprs, or waged workers. In Germany, where industrialization after 1870 was rooted in large-scale finance and centered on capital goods production, small commodity workshop production declined noticeably. In 1882 60 percent of German industrial-manufacturing enterprises still had five or fewer employees, but by 1907 only 31 percent did. In France in 1906 10 percent of the workforce was employed in large factories of more than 500 employees.

What these figures suggest, and current research continues to affirm, is the existence from mid-century of a dual economic structure which had an artisanal and an industrial face, but one that saw the balances tilting decidedly away from artisanal favor. The situation in Groningen illustrates this well. During the last quarter of the nineteenth century artisans accounted for about three-quarters of the labor force there, a total labor force which had grown between 1889 and 1910 by one-half. These were no halcyon days for artisans, however, for upon closer inspection we can see that Groningen's manufacturing economy was bifurcated, made up of large and small mechanized firms on the one hand, and large and small craft enterprises on the other. Thus we find a dualism in the industrial economy at large and in the labor market in particular, with nonmechanized artisanal enterprises increasingly incapable of competing with the firms that used the new gas and electric motors in their enterprises geared toward mass production. Those artisans that were not eventually absorbed into the industrial workforce and workplace sank into a position of inferior status and relative penury.

From artisans to workers, mechanics, and shopkeepers

There was no legal restoration of corporatism in the nineteenth century, of course, and its gradual if relentless displacement by liberalism, capitalistic market culture, and, in many places, an intrusive state apparatus, ultimately recast the mold within which artisans fashioned their identity. Perhaps the fate of the German "home towns," those polities that in many ways expressed in rarefied form the essence of the European artisanry, can best illustrate this transformation. The artisan of "home town" society thrived in an environment that kept the imperial government out of local political and economic affairs, and in this "incubator," as Mack Walker called it, the artisan was keenly aware that "his personal identity was found in the web and walls of familiar community."[17] Dramatic political, administrative, and economic changes in the nineteenth century broke the incubator, especially after mid-century. State administrators, notably in Prussia but also in many other duchies and principalities, sat on communal councils as part of a general expansion of central government bureaucracy, with the result that the "state had replaced community as guardian of internal stability."[18] Converging with political changes were economic ones, as the growth of banking, credit, investment, integrated transport networks, and increasingly concentrated heavy industrial production showed that the economy was moving in regional and national directions and rested more and more on interdependence. These forces destroyed the basis of "home town" community, and the artisans within had to seek a different grounding for their identity.

[17] Walker, p. 406.   [18] Ibid., p. 408.

Corporate attitudes among craftsmen did not disappear at the same pace everywhere; they were largely gone from England by 1850, from France probably by 1890, while they lingered longer in Germany. In any case, by the turn of the twentieth century one would be hard pressed to find an artisan who self-consciously defined himself in terms that his forebears of a century or two earlier had. Instead, he was now a skilled worker, a mechanic, a shopkeeper, and he thought of himself as such. Women, as we have seen, never had much claim to artisanal identity in the old regime, and the age of industrialization brought no change on that score. If anything, the incursions of the middle class ideal of domesticity and the assumption that the woman's place was in the home more and more took hold in the world of the mechanic and shopkeeper, if not yet the waged worker.

The nineteenth century also brought a crystallization of the processes that separated the artisanry into productive and retail segments that historians have traced to the eighteenth century in some trades but to the nineteenth in many more, and this no doubt is central to the story of the transformation of the artisan. The important point is that, however segmented the artisanry had been in the Old Regime, most artisans entered the nineteenth century with a corporate sense of themselves and exited it without one. In the interim, they had passed through a filter that dismantled the political, legal, and intellectual framework of corporatism, and, while suffering the unrestrained violence of the capitalistic market, left them to their own devices to fashion a new meaning to their existence, and a new sense of who they were. The traditional conceptual tools for making sense of the world gradually ceased to be adequate to reduce it to meaning and to place oneself satisfyingly within it. The template against which status was measured and identity was constituted was irrevocably transformed, rendering the question for historians – "what was an artisan?" – necessarily in the past tense.

Bibliography

Entries marked with a * designate recommended reading for new students of the subject.

Aldrich, Robert. "Late comer or early starter: new views on French economic history." *Journal of European Economic History* 16 (1987), 89–100.

Aminzade, Ronald. "Reinterpreting capitalist industrialization: a study of 19th-century France." In Steven L. Kaplan and Cynthia Koepp, eds., *Work in France*. Ithaca, 1986, pp. 393–417.

Behagg, Clive. "Custom, class, and change: the trade societies of Birmingham." *Social History* 4 (1979).

"Secrecy, ritual, and folk violence: the opacity of the workplace in the first half of the 19th century." In R. Storch, ed., *Popular Culture and Custom in 19th-Century England*. London, 1982, pp. 154–79.

"Masters and manufacturers: social values and the smaller unit of production in Birmingham, 1800–1850." In Geoffrey Crossick and Heinz-Gerhard Haupt, eds., *Shopkeepers and Master Artisans in 19th-Century Europe*. London, 1986, pp. 137–54.

Politics and Production in the Early Nineteenth Century. London, 1990.

*Berg, Maxine, and Pat Hudson. "Rehabilitating the Industrial Revolution." *Economic History Review* 45:1 (1992), 24–50.

*Berlanstein, Lenard R., ed. *The Industrial Revolution and Work in Nineteenth-Century Europe*. London, 1992.

Blackbourn, David. "Between resignation and volatility: the German petite bourgeoisie in the 19th century." In Geoffrey Crossick and Heinz-Gerhard Haupt, eds., *Shopkeepers and Master Artisans in Nineteenth-Century Europe*. London, 1986, pp. 35–61.

*Bossenga, Gail. *The Politics of Privilege: Old Regime and Revolution in Lille*. Cambridge, 1991.

*Breuilly, John. "Artisan economy, artisan politics, artisan ideology: the artisan contribution to the nineteenth-century European labour movement." In Clive Emsley and James Walvin, eds., *Artisans, Peasants, and Proletarians, 1760–1860*. London, 1985, pp. 187–225.

Crossick, Geoffrey. *An Artisan Elite in Victorian Society: Kentish London, 1840–1880*. London, 1978.

*Crossick, Geoffrey, and Heinz-Gerhard Haupt, eds. *Shopkeepers and Master Artisans in Nineteenth-Century Europe*. London, 1984.

Edgren, Lars. "Crafts in transformation? Masters, journeymen, and apprentices in a Swedish town, 1800–1850." *Continuity and Change* 1 (1986), 363–83.

Fores, Michael. "Technical change and the 'technology' myth." *The Scandinavian Economic History Review* 30:3 (1982), 167–88.

Freifeld, Mary. "Technological change and the 'self-acting' mule: a study of skill and the sexual division of labour." *Social History* 11 (1986), 319–43.

Gullickson, Gay. *The Spinners and Weavers of Auffray: Rural Industry and the Sexual Division of Labor in a French Village, 1750–1850*. 1986

Haupt, Heinz-Gerhard. "La Survivance des corporations au XIXe siècle. Une esquisse comparative." *Revue du Nord* 76 (1994), 806.

*Heywood, Colin. *The Development of the French Economy, 1750–1914*. Cambridge, 1992.

Hirsch, Jean-Pierre. *Les Deux Rêves de Commerce. Entreprise et institution dans la région, illoise, 1780–1860* Paris, 1991.

Hobsbawm, E. J., and Joan W. Scott. "Political shoemakers." *Past and Present* 89 (1980), 86–114.

*Johnson, Christopher H. "Economic change and artisan discontent: the tailors' history, 1800–1848." In Roger Price, ed., *Revolution and Reaction: 1848 and the Second French Republic*. London, 1975.

*"Artisans vs. fabricants: urban protoindustrialization and the evolution of work culture in Lodève and Bedarieux, 1740–1830." *Mélanges de l'école française de Rome* 99:2 (1987), 1047–84.

*Kocka, Jürgen. "Craft traditions and the labour movement in 19th-century Germany." In P. Thane, Geoffrey Crossick, and Roderick Floud, *The Power of the Past: Essays for Eric Hobsbawm*. Cambridge, 1984, p. 95–117.

Lis, Catharina, and Hugo Soly, "Entrepreneurs, corporations et autorités publiques au Brabant et en Flandre à la fin de l'Ancien Régime," *Revue du Nord* 76 (1994), 725–44.

*Martin, Benjamin. *The Agony of Modernization: Labor and Industrialization in Spain*. Ithaca, 1990.

*Mayer, Arno. "The lower middle class as historical problem." *Journal of Modern History* 47 (1975).

McBride, Theresa. "Women's work and industrialization." In Lenard Berlanstein, ed., *The Industrial Revolution and Work in 19th-Century Europe*. London, 1992, pp. 63–80.

McClelland, Keith. "Some thoughts on masculinity and the 'representative artisan' in Britain, 1850–1880." *Gender and History* 1:2 (1989), 164–77.

More, Charles. *Skill and the English Working Class, 1870–1914*. London, 1980.

*O'Brien, Patrick, and Caglar Keyder. *Economic Growth in Britain and France, 1780–1914*. London, 1978.

*Prothero, Iowerth. *Artisans and Politics in Early 19th-Century London: John Gast and his Times*. Folkestone, 1979.

Rabinbach, Anson. "The European science of work: the economy of the body at the end of the 19th century." In Steven L. Kaplan and Cynthia Koepp, eds., *Work in France*. Ithaca, 1986, pp. 475–513.

Reddy, William. *Money and Liberty in Modern Europe: A Critique of Historical Understanding*. Cambridge, 1987.

Rose, Sonya. "Proto-industry, women's work and the household economy in the transition to industrial capitalism." *Journal of Family History* 13 (1988), 181–93.

*Sabel, Charles, and Jonathan Zeitlin. "Historical alternatives to mass production: politics, markets, and technology in 19th-century industrialization." *Past and Present* 108 (1985), 133–74.

*Scott, Joan W. *The Glassworkers of Carmaux: French Craftsmen and Political Action in a Nineteenth-Century City*. Cambridge, Mass., 1974.

Sheehan, James J. *Germany History, 1770–1866*. Oxford, 1989.

Sibalis, Michael. "Shoemakers and fourierism in nineteenth-century Paris: the société laborieuse des cordonniers-bottiers." *Histoire sociale–Social History* 20:39 (1987), 29–49.

"Corporations after the corporations: the debate on restoring the guilds under Napoleon I and the Restoration." *French Historical Studies* 15 (1988), 718–30.

Sonenscher, Michael. "The sans culottes of the year II: rethinking the language of labour in revolutionary France." *Social History* 9:3 (1984), 301–28.

Torras, Jaume. "Corporations et liberté de fabrication en Espagne au XVIIIe siècle." *Revue du Nord* 76 (1994), pp. 745–51.

Vardi, Liana. "The abolition of the guilds during the French Revolution." *French Historical Studies* 15 (1988): 704–17.

Volkov, Shulamit. *The Rise of Popular Antimodernism in Germany: The Urban Master Artisans, 1873–1896*. Princeton, 1978.

Williams, Gwyn. *Artisans and Sans Culottes*. London, 1989, 2nd edn.

Index

NEW APPROACHES TO EUROPEAN HISTORY